P9-DNB-824

MONEY
MAKEOVERS

MONEY MAKEOVERS

How Women Can Control Their Financial Destiny

DR. CHRISTOPHER L. HAYES

AND

KATE KELLY

DOUBLEDAY

New York London Toronto Sydney Auckland

PUBLISHED BY DOUBLEDAY
a division of Bantam Doubleday Dell Publishing Group, Inc.
1540 Broadway, New York, New York 10036

DOUBLEDAY and the portrayal of an anchor with a dolphin are
trademarks of Doubleday, a division of Bantam Doubleday Dell
Publishing Group, Inc.

Text design by Stanley S. Drate/Folio Graphics Co. Inc.

Library of Congress Cataloging-in-Publication Data

Hayes, Christopher L.
    Money makeovers: how women can control their financial destiny /
Christopher L. Hayes and Kate Kelly.
        p.   cm.
    1. Women—Finance, Personal.   I. Kelly, Kate, 1950–
II. Title.
HG179.H349   1998
332.024'042—dc21   97-12517
CIP

ISBN 0-385-48540-9
Printed in the United States of America
January 1998
First Edition

10 9 8 7 6 5 4 3 2 1

To my wife, Diane,
who taught me the wisdom of patience, who has helped
me understand how a couple can "work as a financial team,"
and who has given me the freedom to pursue my life-long
passion to change the economic condition of future
generations of women.

—C.H.

To my middle daughter, Bibi,
whose early entrepreneurial skills and interest in investing
give me great pleasure for I know that she, and I hope others
of her generation, will be financially prepared for the future.

—K.K.

ACKNOWLEDGMENTS

Many individuals need to be recognized for their support and assistance in making this book a reality. First and foremost, I am indebted to the women who opened their financial lives and had the courage to tell their stories for the benefit of others. I would like to thank my National Center for Women and Retirement Research staff: Dr. Deborah Anderson, who spent many hours giving me input and feedback on the draft chapters; Dottie Clarke, who gave me many thoughts to ponder on how women address financial concerns; Charlene Cheshire, who helped me interview women; and Carol Anderson, who acted as coprincipal investigator on the Women Cents Study.

Our PREP (Pre-Retirement Education Planning for Women) Program representatives throughout the country play an invaluable role in helping to spread the word about the importance of financial planning for women. One specific PREP representative, Liz Davalos, CFP, of Everen Securities in Santa Clara, California, spent countless hours going over the financial information presented in Section III. Her "education first" philosophy has helped hundreds of women going through our seminars each year, and I appreciate her adding her wisdom to the book.

Financial corporations are beginning to see the importance of addressing the needs of women. In this regard, the Women Cents Study could not have gone forward without the support of our corporate sponsor, Prudential Securities. In particular, many thanks go to Steve Samuels of Prudential, who believed in this project from the beginning and gave of his time and energy to make Women Cents a reality. An in-depth version of the Women Cents Self-Test offered through Prudential can be found on their Web site (www.prusec. com). We are also extremely appreciative of the other corporate sponsors that have funded NCWRR studies in the past.

In addition, Lacie Venzara of Prudential Securities in Palm Beach, Florida, contributed to the chapter on financial advisors. Lacie was also kind enough to provide us with an excellent case study for Chapter 19 that demonstrates the invaluable role a financial advisor can play in helping women clients. I must also mention Angela Cox of Prudential's Investment Program for Women and Susan Atran, manager of public relations, for their assistance throughout this project.

I could not have written this book without the immense support provided by Long Island University's Southampton College, which continues to support the mission of NCWRR. In particular, I want to thank Dr. David Steinberg, president of Long Island University, and the Board of Trustees, who honored me with the 1996 Trustee's Award for Academic Research for the Women Cents Study upon which this book is based. The proceeds from this award are being used to set up a women's financial research scholarship fund at Southampton College.

I am eternally grateful for the support, guidance, and nurturing provided by my agent Martha Kaplan. Besides finding a wonderful writer for me to work with, she is a terrific human being who believed in this book from the beginning. A champion of women's issues, Martha always kept me focused on the task at hand—to produce the best book possible to help women address their financial future.

Agent Judith Riven was also an important member of this team. She provided vital input on all stages of the manuscript, and I am indebted to her for her careful reading and her efforts to see this book through to successful completion.

In writing a book, an editor can make a tremendous difference in the magic of translating complex thoughts and ideas. The magic of *Money Makeovers* has to be attributed to Judy Kern, our editor at Doubleday, who is a true artist at what she does. Since the first time we met, Judy has believed in the project and the importance of alerting women to the necessity of addressing financial fear. Judy, your efforts will make a true difference in the lives of many women, and for this, I will be eternally grateful.

Lastly, writing this book with Kate Kelly has made the project a wonderful, gratifying experience. I have always believed that the secret to addressing gender issues is for both sexes to work together for the common good. Our successful collaboration is a testament to the power of creating a "gender bridge." Throughout the months of work, Kate brought a richness to the material that I could not have accomplished working alone.

Dr. Christopher L. Hayes
Southampton, N.Y.

CONTENTS

ACKNOWLEDGMENTS   vii

INTRODUCTION   xv

SECTION

I

1   THE LAST FRONTIER FOR WOMEN: Money
     Management and the Accumulation of Wealth   3

2   WHEN IT COMES TO MONEY, WHO ARE YOU?
     The Women Cents Self-Test   15

3   PREADOLESCENCE: When You Were Captain of
     Your Own Ship   33

4   EDUCATION: Missed Starts for Too Many Girls   53

SECTION

II

5   DO YOU EVER TAKE A CHANCE? Understanding
     Your Level of Risk Tolerance   73

6   THE WAY THINGS ARE: Do You Like Change or
     the Status Quo?   97

7   CALLING THE SHOTS: Who Is in Control?   119

8   MARITAL MONEY DYNAMICS: Working Out
Control Issues with Your Partner   139

9   WHAT COMES FIRST—PRESENT-DAY OR
FUTURE PLANS? Your Outlook on the Future   157

10   DECIDING WITH YOUR HEAD OR YOUR HEART?
Financial Decision-Making   175

11   FINANCIAL TRUTHS: Doing Away with Myths
and Misperceptions About Money   189

12   "HEAD IN THE SAND" SYNDROME: Lack of
Knowledge About Planning and Investing   207

SECTION

III

13   YOU'VE COME A LONG WAY ALREADY   227

14   FINDING THOSE INVESTMENT DOLLARS   231

15   WHAT DO YOU WANT? WHAT DO YOU NEED?
Setting Realistic Financial Goals   251

16   PROTECTING WHAT YOU HAVE   263

17   LOOKING AHEAD: Life Planning for All Ages   281

18   NOT-SO-RISKY BUSINESS: Basic Investment
Strategies   311

19   ALL FIRED UP WITH NOBODY TO CALL?
Creating a Financial Support System   341

APPENDICES

APPENDIX A: Glossary of Investment Terms   369

APPENDIX B: Assessing Your Net Worth   379

APPENDIX C: Additional Resources   385

APPENDIX D: About the National Center for Women
and Retirement Research   395

APPENDIX E: About the NCWRR Research Studies   401

INDEX   407

MONEY
MAKEOVERS

INTRODUCTION

SOME ANSWERS TO WOMEN'S MOST FREQUENT CONCERNS ABOUT TAKING CHARGE OF THEIR MONEY

By buying this book, you have taken a positive step toward gaining control of your financial destiny, but if you're like most women, you still have very valid concerns and hesitations about what this step can—and should—mean to you.

In my work as founder of the National Center for Women and Retirement Research, I've heard from thousands of women across the country who have expressed concern about taking charge of their money. Many have spoken to me at financial seminars sponsored by the NCWRR; others have conveyed their worries when they've participated in one of our research studies.

I'd like to begin by sharing with you the doubts aired by these women as they confront the prospect of taking the next step forward (in column 2 you'll find my brief responses; the book itself provides the in-depth answers and reassurance):

"I don't have enough money to start a savings or investment program."	You probably do. Even a small amount is "enough," and if you're not saving now, we'll show you how to start.

"I'm so confused. I must have talked to a dozen different people about what to do with my money, and I've gotten at least a dozen answers!"	That's why you need to learn enough so that you can make the decisions yourself. By the way, there are no "right" answers; and the only "wrong" answer is inactivity.
"I know I should have started sooner."	It's never too late. Some planning is *always* better than no planning. Don't worry, just start.
"I'm juggling so many roles already! I don't have time to take on one more responsibility."	Countless women come to our seminars and tell me this. That's why I've developed a method of financial planning that doesn't require a major time investment. In fact, those who begin report that they enjoy it—they like the feeling of empowerment they gain by taking charge of their financial future. Many say they actually find the process quite interesting.
"When experts talk about money in 'financialese,' it makes my eyes glaze over!"	You're not alone. This book is written to be clear without being simplistic. You'll learn what you really need to know, and it won't make your eyes glaze over!
"My husband has had full responsibility for our finances. How can I get involved without making it look like I doubt him or without acting like I want to take over?"	Couples run into this all the time. In this book you'll find suggestions for opening a conversation so that you can start learning what you need to know and then begin to participate in the family's financial affairs.

"I'm doing some investing, but taking these risks makes me nervous."	Many people feel the same way. This book will change your perception of risk so you needn't feel so concerned about it.
"I'm totally ignorant, and I barely made it through math. How am I going to take charge of my money?"	Like anything else, taking control of your financial future involves skills that can be learned (and taking charge of your money has more to do with planning than it does with math). I guarantee that learning about personal finance won't be as difficult as you think.
"I'm scared of investing. What if I make a bad decision and lose it all?"	Many people worry about this. But if you diversify where you put your money and resist the urge to let someone "take care of it" for you, your risk can be greatly reduced.

And finally, a deep-seated fear I hear voiced again and again—from the minimum-wage worker right through to the well-to-do: "I'm afraid if I quit working or invest poorly, I'll have nothing . . . I'll be a bag lady."

And that's why I've written *Money Makeovers: How Women Can Control Their Financial Destiny.* The book is designed to guide women in managing their money and maximizing their investments.

What's more, studies conducted by my organization, the National Center for Women and Retirement Research, over the last ten years have revealed the real reason for the gulf that exists between the sexes in matters of investing interest and prowess. What makes the difference has nothing to do with *actual* ability; it is each gender's *perception* of its abilities that creates the disparity. NCWRR research indicates that what holds women back is self-esteem, and the problems with that can be traced all the way back to early educational and parental experiences. If there is any one central message to be found in this book, it is that women must believe in themselves if they are to topple the barriers that have prevented them from developing their full financial potential. If they do, their desire to build a secure financial future will quickly become a reality.

So Why Did I—A Man—Write This Book?

A financial book for women by a woman carries with it instant credibility. To the reader, the author is someone who has been there and knows what it's like.

Since I lack those credentials, I want to tell you a bit about why I wrote this book. In different ways, I've "been there," and perhaps more than most people, I "know what it's like." What's more, this book is no passing fancy. Because of my experiences, I have devoted my career to women's issues and financial planning. Let me tell you why.

Both my parents "lived for today" and invested no money. Now my mother, cannot afford to retire because they have inadequate financial resources. At Christmastime in 1995, my mother turned to me and said, "I just never thought about planning. If I had, I would have done things differently." Here is a bright, intelligent Ph.D. who, because of a lack of financial awareness, will probably have to work until she is eighty. Obviously, as her son, this is very painful to watch. It makes me even more committed to addressing ways in which women can plan financially.

But my awareness of the need for women to develop financial expertise began much earlier. I was the oldest of four children and was born with a "broom and mop in my hand." During my early childhood, my mother was committed to becoming a clinical psychologist and raising a family at the same time (obviously, an early "supermom"). She relied heavily on me to complete household chores and take care of my siblings so that she could attend school. My father fulfilled the traditional breadwinner role, but made no additional effort to help my mother live up to what she saw as her potential, and this made me realize, at a very young age, the difficulties women experience as they work toward having an identity beyond motherhood.

The plight of older women was brought home to me when, at the age of sixteen, I took a job working in a nursing home. I held this job for seven years while putting myself through college, and over and over again. I saw the same thing. The majority of patients were women who had ended up in an institution because of inadequate financial planning and limited family support. Many had nothing and were simply "waiting to die."

When I finished my graduate work and became a psychologist with a specialty in gerontology, my nursing home experience led me to start my own nonprofit organization dedicated to providing counseling to older adults. Again, I confronted a situation similar to what I had observed in the nursing home: In far greater numbers than men, women from all walks of life had failed to make any financial preparation for old age. When they came for counseling, they were shocked at their predicament, and their helplessness frequently resulted in depression. The "golden years" were hardly golden for these women. To this day, I can still hear their voices saying, "Dr. Hayes, I never planned to live this long." This was when it dawned on me that aging was truly a woman's issue. Because of their greater longevity, women can least afford to leave their future to chance.

After having witnessed so many women suffering through their retirement years, not because of ill health or loneliness, but because of being in poor financial straits, I told myself that if I ever got a chance to change this picture, I would.

My opportunity came when I received federal funding to develop a pre-retirement program (PREP—Pre-Retirement Education Planning for Women) to help younger and middle-aged women before they became impoverished. As I developed the program, I realized that women have rarely considered the likelihood that widowhood or divorce might leave them alone to cope with planning for and financing their later life. To further help these women, I eventually obtained funding to start the National Center for Women and Retirement Research, a nonprofit organization based at Long Island University–Southampton College that is committed to educating women on how to live independent, financially secure, satisfying lives. The NCWRR has pioneered numerous landmark studies on women and money. It was the first to study the financial needs of midlife women. It was the first to study the effects of divorce on women over forty emerging from long-term marriages, and it has done extensive studies of the development of self-esteem in women and men. The organization has established a name for itself as an

innovative research, education, and training center, and it continues to be the only university-based entity of its kind.

Over the last ten years, I've encountered obstacles in my work,
but these have only served to fuel my desire to dedicate myself to
helping women plan for their financial futures. First, I was very
naive to think that the world was ready for a man to advocate for
the needs of women. In 1988, after our financial planning materials
were developed, I was able to gain some additional federal funds to
conduct a national public awareness program on the importance of
early financial planning for women. As the word got out regarding
the NCWRR and its materials, I began to receive many calls from
women in advocacy organizations who were outraged at the fact
that a man was running a women's center. Many believed that a
man could never understand women.

I even received hate mail, letters that initially tore me up inside.
After much reflection, I grew to understand what gender bias and
discrimination meant. Many were judging me not by the quality of
my work or passion for the cause, but by my gender. This made me
more committed than ever to advocate for women, in the belief that
someday we will live in a society in which women can advocate for
men and men can advocate for women.

Another experience that shaped my perspective on women and
money was my initial effort to convince financial corporations that
there was a woman's market for their services. I wanted these corporations to sponsor financial seminars, develop financial self-help
materials for women, and conduct new research on the financial
planning needs of women. During 1988–90, I met with over eighteen heads of major corporations (all men) who kept giving me the
same message over and over:

- Women don't have the desire to invest money.
- Women don't have the money to invest.
- Women are not in a position to make investment decisions
  within a family.
- Women are too conservative to be interested in investing.

Despite all my research proving these assumptions to be untrue,
I began to realize that the reason women weren't being adequately
addressed by financial planners is that men (usually over the age
of fifty) headed these corporations and had stereotypical views of
women's approach to money.

My desire to learn everything I could about financial planning was a direct response to my inability to get anyone in these corporations to listen. For a solid year, I devoured anything and everything I could get my hands on concerning financial planning, with the intent of translating it into self-help materials and programs for women. During this phase of my career, I was outraged over the financial community's lack of insight into and sensitivity toward women. I decided that if these institutions weren't going to meet the need, we were!

Now, eleven years later, much is changing. Currently, I split my life between overseeing the work of the National Center for Women and Retirement Research and my teaching responsibilities at Long Island University, where I am a professor of psychology and chairman of the graduate program in gerontology at LIU's Southampton College.

To my great satisfaction, the NCWRR now boasts a broad network of financial planners who conduct seminars nationwide. The NCWRR self-help financial materials have reached several hundred thousand women, and—as indication that the corporate world is now taking a serious look at the women's market for financial products—we've been funded to conduct numerous studies on women's attitudes toward financial planning.

The NCWRR has undertaken eight separate intensive research inquiries over a period of seven years on various aspects of women's financial planning needs. We've talked to almost 65,000 women to learn more about their attitudes toward money; men have also been included in these studies because we wanted to learn how men differ from women in their approach to finance. The results provide an unprecedented look at the financial needs of women.

One question we always encounter—and one that has been influential in the writing of this book—is, Do men and women really have different financial planning needs? Our research has verified what we've suspected: Yes, very much so.

For many years institutions misguidedly believed that both genders approach financial decision-making the same way and that their needs are similar. Our research proved that women have very different financial needs: Early socialization creates a different mind-set for dealing with money (it's difficult for women, raised to be caregivers, to become comfortable putting their own needs first), and gender discrimination (it still exists) has kept women from better-paying jobs, where they could amass more money and gain some advantage from company savings and benefits programs. Add to that the fact that women live longer than men, mix in the well-documented negative effects of divorce and widowhood on women's finances, and it makes for very different financial circumstances for women; you'll read more about this in Chapter 1.

The media have referred to me as the nation's foremost expert on women and money, and I suspect that, between my direct experience in conducting seminars and the knowledge I constantly accumulate through the studies we're doing, there is justification for that view.

Certainly, I understand what kind of financial information women need. Like others who have gone before me, when I first started offering financial seminars I believed that providing financial information was key. But after doing follow-up work with seminar attendees and taking into account the results of our extensive research, I began to realize that this was just one part of the picture. Knowledge about finances alone was not enough—I began to see that women's identity development and personality traits play a vital role in whether they are able to utilize the information and move forward financially.

Most books on women and money fall into the trap of offering financial advice only. They assume that definitions of financial terms and a clear "how-to" approach will send women to the nearest stockbroker, mutual fund, or financial planner with a new lease on their financial lives. From my research and years of experience, I know this will not happen until women understand how their experiences, past and present, have shaped their financial personalities and behaviors. Only through becoming aware of the messages they absorbed as girls will women begin to understand their own "money personality" and how it either hinders or enhances their financial well-being.

To help women come to terms with this "piece of the developmental pie," I have created a psychological self-test that provides them with a profile of their attitudes toward money and investing (see Chapter 2). This self-test has been used extensively in our financial seminars, and armed with new self-knowledge *as well as* information on the world of finance, the women who attend our seminars have become better investors and have been able to take control of their financial destiny.

As more and more seminar attendees proved capable of mastering their finances, the next logical step was to put the information in book form so that as many women as possible could benefit from what we had learned through the study. I hope for readers that this book will prove to be the key to broadening their possibilities for a bright financial future.

How to Use This Book

This book is for you. Whether you're married or single, in your twenties or sixties, it provides you with the knowledge and confidence you need to create a clear plan for becoming an active participant in your financial planning.

Money Makeovers turns a beacon on emotional issues and will help you:

- Conquer your fear of risk-taking
- Negotiate control issues with a spouse
- Understand which of your personal beliefs have come about because of family myths about money
- Identify those aspects of your personality that are assets and those that are potential liabilities to being an informed investor
- Learn to make well-reasoned decisions about money
- Be careful consumers of financial products
- Feel comfortable with and create time for overseeing your finances
- Believe in your own talents to make your money grow

In addition, this book will show you how to reconcile the conflict that arises from knowing how important it is to plan for the future while still feeling challenged and fearful at the prospect of risking what you've struggled to attain.

Throughout the book, you'll find case histories of women of all ages who have encountered—and overcome—obstacles on their way to taking charge of their finances. The women you will meet represent role models from all walks of life: women who are married or divorced, women of color, and women who are working with very little money as well as some whose resources are greater. I am proud to say that these are ordinary women who have made extraordinary strides to develop their own financial identity. If there is one quality they all have in common, it is that all of them now consider themselves to be "investors" in their own future. By letting them tell their own stories—what happened that put them at a financial disadvantage and how they went about learning to invest their money—I think you'll better understand what's right for you.

You will benefit most from this book if you consider it a reference tool—something you will return to again and again. Some of the personality traits can take time to alter; a lot of the financial information takes reviewing to absorb. Be patient with yourself, and don't expect to master everything all at once. Just reread what you need to when you're feeling uncertain.

Here's what will be helpful to know about the book's contents:

Chapter 1 offers helpful background and will lead you directly to the Self-Test in Chapter 2, an interesting way to learn more about your own attitudes toward money. The test should take you only fifteen to twenty minutes, and in addition to being fun, you'll find it enlightening.

After taking the Self-Test in Chapter 2 and referring to the analyses, you'll want to proceed directly to Chapters 3 and 4; these chapters will provide you with background on female development. In Chapter 3, we'll look at societal and family influences that keep girls from maintaining an independent spirit and a "can do" outlook. Chapter 4 examines what happens at school. By understanding the subtle (and not so subtle) messages delivered by our society, you'll find it easier to put the past behind you and take charge of your life and your money. (I guarantee that if you begin feeling more comfortable in one area of your life, there will be positive spillover to everything that you're doing!)

Next, check the table of contents for the different personality traits covered in Section II of the book. (The Self-Test will identify the areas where change would benefit you most.) You may want to read about them all, but you might like to start with the obstacle (fear of taking risks? dislike of change?) with which you most strongly identify.

Section III provides a blueprint for taking charge of your financial destiny. Keep in mind that Section III must be digested over time. Read about and act on what interests you now; come back to it in a few weeks or a couple of months and decide what to do next.

Throughout, there are quizzes and worksheets. You might like to make photocopies of these pages to make them easier to use.

MY CONTRACT WITH READERS

I agree to provide you with the means to create a solid financial future for yourself. At the same time, you agree to work on those aspects of your personality and development that have prevented you from feeling financially independent. You hold up your part of the bargain, and I'll hold up mine.

Remember that becoming involved in managing your money is the best thing you can do for yourself. Women, as you will learn, are uniquely qualified to do an extraordinarily good job of it.

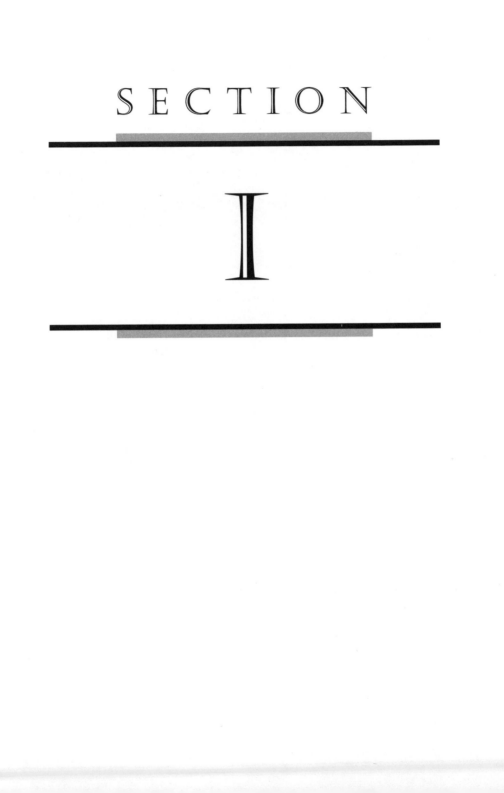

SECTION

I

1

THE LAST FRONTIER
FOR WOMEN
Money Management and the
Accumulation of Wealth

*"For the first time in my life I've taken charge of my
own money, and I'm having a great time!"*

I magine having the confidence to take the money you've worked
so hard to save and invest it in financial products that you know
will pay off for you—and doing this with enough surety that you
actually enjoy it.

An impossible dream? Not at all.

As more and more women overcome gender barriers in the workplace, they find themselves in a new position: They have money of
their own. Like other wage earners, they are spending much of their
income on basic necessities, but women are beginning to realize that
they are at an important crossroad: They can continue as they have
been doing, living day-to-day, or they can take charge of their
money and start asking long-term questions:

- What are my needs concerning money and security?
- How can I ensure a secure financial future?
- Will I ever be able to save enough to make a difference?

3

4   MONEY MAKEOVERS

Ten years ago, the National Center for Women and Retirement Research was created (and funded through government grant money) to help women answer questions like these. As executive director, I have had the pleasure of watching the Center grow as more and more women have come to take our financial seminars or called for our workbooks and resource materials.

I have conducted financial seminars for over ten years now, and I continue to be struck by the fact that, although they come from diverse backgrounds and represent all ages and socioeconomic groups, the participants share one feeling in common: relief. Simply having come to the seminar represents a positive step in taking charge of their financial future, and for them, the experience is a significant event. They are nervous about the responsibility, but they are eager to learn, and they are incredibly relieved to hear that it's okay to finally say, "But what about me?"

As each seminar progresses and these women learn about what has kept them from taking charge of their money and what they can do about it, we see the weight of socialization drop from their shoulders as they realize, "Even if I haven't paid attention before," or "Even if I wasn't good at math," or "Even if I used to think invest-ments were boring, I can still learn to be good at this!"

A few years ago, a woman in her forties came up to me at the end of the seminar, overwhelmed with emotion. Although many people had questions I needed to address, she waited patiently until every-one had finished, and then she approached me and grabbed my hand tightly, saying, "You will never know how important this night was for me. You made me understand that I can *believe* in myself."

In understanding that, this woman had grasped an important aspect of personal finance: belief in yourself. The NCWRR has con-ducted numerous studies showing that women are perfectly capable of becoming expert investors, although they may have to make some changes in order to do so. In *Money Makeovers* you will find information that challenges you to alter certain approaches to life (such as learning to take financial risks), and if you're married, cer-tain suggestions may have an impact on your relationship with your spouse. In addition, you'll be presented with a great deal of informa-tion about investments and money management. Throughout, I hope you will hear—and hear again—the essence of what that woman said: "I can believe in myself." You can do it—and for the sake of your own future, it's vital that you do.

Financial Information: Only Part of the Picture

As I observed the participants who came to the NCWRR seminars during our first years, I was gratified to watch many succeed in taking hold of their financial future, but puzzled and troubled by those who, although desperate for information, revealed in follow-up calls that they had done little or nothing to change their situation.

Many of these women came to the NCWRR after attending as many as ten financial seminars prior to ours. It was quite a puzzle; they were obviously still interested in acquiring financial knowledge, but, as we learned from them in the seminars, few had taken the plunge and started changing the way they managed their money. Why weren't more of them moving ahead with their newly acquired knowledge? Obviously, a key element was missing.

As a psychologist, I suspected that, although they were processing the financial information, they must have been encountering emotional barriers. I devised a questionnaire that would help me to understand what those barriers were so that we might find a way to overcome them. The questionnaire for the initial study (there have been subsequent ones as well disseminated by Prudential Securities) was designed to reveal:

- How women feel about money
- What prevents many women from investing their money wisely
- What helps them make smart choices
- What happens when the women go home with their newly gained knowledge

This study, the Women Cents Study, conducted with the cooperation of *Working Woman* magazine and Prudential Securities (which was also the corporate sponsor), soon gave me the answers.

The 1,100 respondents indicated quite clearly that a woman's personality—how she takes charge of her life, copes with change, handles risk, makes decisions, and views her destiny—largely determines how well she manages her money. The study also made clear that **how she feels about money, more than anything else, dic-**

tates whether or not she will succeed in managing her money and accumulating enough to live comfortably now and in her retirement years. Even though more and more women are adopting healthy, realistic attitudes about money and placing a priority on financial planning, many are unable to fulfill their perceived goals because they have not reckoned with the personal psychological barriers they have concerning money.

I want to share with you some of the key findings, as you may identify with some of them:

1. **A woman's individual personality plays a critical role in her financial decisions—far more so than her income, age, or marital or career status.** Your personality traits affect how you handle your financial affairs. This means that the better you understand your own personality and motivations, the better you'll understand—and be able to manage and invest—your money.

2. **Assertiveness, openness to change, an adventurous spirit, and an optimistic outlook are the qualities that tend to lead to smart money choices.** Women who are optimistic about moving ahead with their lives are more likely to set specific financial goals, to save and invest regularly, to make retirement planning a priority, and to educate themselves about money management.

3. **Fear of failure and fear of the unknown are the greatest obstacles to a woman's financial success.** Seventy-four percent of all respondents reported that a lack of knowledge about how to select the best stocks, bonds, and mutual funds for their needs is a major obstacle to their becoming more active investors. More than half postponed financial decision-making out of fear of making a mistake.

4. **Women's attitudes about money and investing are evolving significantly for the better, but a sizable percentage of women are not investing in the kind of instruments that will provide substantial income for their retirement years.** For the first time, women are acknowledging the importance of actively investing in stocks and mutual funds, and those who report they are happiest when they save and invest (44 percent) exceed those who prefer to spend (15 percent). But only one in four actually makes saving a top priority. And when they do put money away, 72 percent are selecting go-nowhere investments such as money market accounts and CDs.

These findings were a tremendous relief to me, because I knew that we now had the key to helping women succeed. As a psychologist, I know that the traits that lead to financial prowess can be developed and nurtured, and I know that doing so can have a positive effect on a woman's self-esteem, a quality that is both helpful in life and vital to confident investing.

These results also finally clarified for me why taking charge of one's money has been the "last frontier" for women. Though women have made progress in the workforce and can now be found on almost every rung of the corporate ladder, they often leave their own financial situation on the back burner.

During childhood, subliminal messages constantly reinforce the idea that girls aren't supposed to worry about money, and as a result, they are often not exposed to the basic elements of personal finance. Is it any wonder, then, that as adults, women tend to adhere to the role that has been set for them?

Yet with these new findings, we've been observing that if women become aware of the developmental issues and gender biases that have led to their passive approach to handling money, they are able to develop a new level of confidence in dealing with investments and with life. One can't wrestle with traits such as risk aversion or fear of the future without emerging with a new understanding about everything from family to finance.

You should also be aware that these study results have shown that cultivating a new "money personality" is a process that takes time, patience, and a willingness to make some occasional mistakes. However, the results are worth it. It is perfectly possible—and not all that difficult—to become an active, confident, and accomplished manager and investor.

Fear as the Great Motivator

If your motivation should flag during any part of this book, reread the following statistics. They will keep you going.

Currently, women face a crisis: Regardless of their present earning power, between one- and two-thirds of women thirty-five to fifty-five years old will be impoverished after age sixty-five if they do not immediately start to prepare financially for their later years.

According to NCWRR research, our society is well on its way to creating another generation of impoverished older women.

Many external forces have put women at a disadvantage when it comes to the accumulation of wealth:

WAGE GAP

Women still earn less than men, despite the oft-trumpeted gains they have made toward achieving equality in the workplace. The average woman currently earns 74 cents for every dollar a man earns. This puts women at a serious disadvantage when it comes to savings plans and retirement benefits.

INTERMITTENT WORK CAREERS

Women still work more intermittently than men, averaging 11.5 years out of the workforce compared to 1.3 years for men. Women have typically been the ones to rear children, be supportive of husbands' careers, and care for family members, all of which has been enormously costly to them. Reduced opportunity for job income means reduced opportunity for savings and benefits. Although younger women are experiencing fewer career interruptions than their older counterparts, the midlife women in the workforce today will still "pay" for their time out of the workforce.

GENDER BIAS IN PRIVATE PENSION PROGRAMS

Fifty percent of working women currently have no pension program, and those who do will generally have a smaller payout because of lower salaries and interrupted work histories. Today, twice as many men than women receive pension incomes (46 vs. 23.5 percent and in the case of private pensions 32 vs. 13.6 percent). Divorced and separated women have the lowest rate of pension protection. While statistics will shift as more women stay in the workforce longer, the change will be slow because women remain clustered in lower-paying occupations, and their work histories are still subject to interruption. In addition, some innovations such as job sharing and steady part-time employment—which attract more women than men—generally offer no pension benefit.

GENDER BIAS IN SOCIAL SECURITY AND OTHER RETIREMENT PLANS

Though there has been some effort at reform, the Social Security system still favors the single breadwinner. If her payout will be greater by claiming spousal benefits, a working woman must forgo her own benefits. However, the need for retirement equity is apparent and some policies have been adopted to counteract this. The Retirement Equity Act of 1984 has helped by reducing the age at which pension plans begin counting service; by allowing employees to take five years off work without losing pension credit; and by making survivors' benefits automatic.

LACK OF FEMALE REPRESENTATION IN THE FINANCIAL INDUSTRY

Within the banking and securities industry, female employees are overwhelmingly clustered in clerical positions. According to recent statistics, only about 15 percent of the roughly 101,500 brokers nationwide are women, and out of twenty-five directors on the New York Stock Exchange, only one is a woman. These statistics reduce the likelihood of women learning to trust a financial advisor through woman-to-woman networking or casual acquaintance.

LACK OF RECOGNITION OF A FEMALE MARKET IN FINANCIAL PRODUCTS

Until the NCWRR began its studies, the financial industry had felt there was no need to market to women. Women were not viewed as a viable customer base, nor were their needs seen as being different from men's. The results of the 1988 NCWRR Survey on Women's Financial Literacy (published in *McCall's*) documented the need to present information that addressed a woman's extended life span and her greater need for financial preparedness, but only recently has the impact of addressing women as a separate market begun to be felt.

MARITAL STATUS

Widowhood and divorce place large numbers of women in serious financial jeopardy. The average age for widowhood among women in the United States is fifty-six. One out of two current marriages will end in divorce. The number of women divorced in midlife tripled between 1982 and 1996, and studies show that one year following a divorce, the average annual income of divorced midlife women is only $11,000.

The cumulative effect of these circumstances becomes almost unbearable in a woman's later years:

- The median monthly Social Security check for women in 1995 was $588.
- Only 20 percent of women receive any benefits at all from private pension plans.
- Of the elderly poor, nearly 75 percent are women.
- Women outnumber men two to one in the over-seventy-five group, for whom health care costs are highest.

This current national crisis is real. Though social reform is desperately needed, it will come too late to help the poor elderly women of today. That's why every woman must come to grips with what she needs to know about money and take charge of her financial future.

But there's more to it than simply learning about money. We must also chip away at the psychological mind-set that has been created by a society that has assumed women needn't trouble themselves with personal finance. **When it comes to taking charge of their money, women can't afford to stay on the sidelines.**

Why Women Are Prepared to Succeed

If women have traditionally been considered society's nurturers, then money management will be something at which they excel, for in truth, financial planning is one of the most loving steps you can take to care for both yourself and others. By planning ahead, you assure that there will be enough money for:

- Day-to-day living
- Caring for elderly or ailing parents
- Surviving the death of a spouse
- Short-term savings for items such as summer vacations
- Long-term savings for the children (college tuition)

- Long-term savings to provide a comfortable retirement for yourself and your spouse

You can give your family all the love in the world, but if there are day-to-day worries or long-term concerns about money, everyone in the family suffers.

The Women Cents Study and other studies conducted by the NCWRR have shown that **women have the potential to be better investors than men if they allow themselves to get beyond years of negative socialization.** For example, some 88 percent of the women who responded to the Women Cents Study profess to be open to new investment opportunities; 80 percent characterize themselves as optimistic; and 58 percent believe they have enough control over the direction of their lives. These attitudes are indicative of people who are capable of planning wisely.

When you consider your own abilities to take charge of your finances, remember that over the course of your lifetime, you've been honing the necessary skills. Don't be put off just because the subject is money! Consider:

1. **Women are more analytical and are willing to say no if they are dissatisfied with the results.** Women have long been excellent consumers. Whether bargain hunting for groceries or returning a product because the quality is substandard, women know how to get value for their money. Studies of the ways women make financial decisions reveal that some 82 percent are typically slow and methodical when making investment decisions, and 80 percent do considerable research before taking the plunge.

2. **Women use their "networks."** Women have always been comfortable relying on their female friends for support. According to the Scudder Baby Boom Generation Retirement Preparation Survey, women are three times more likely than men to consult family and friends about investment choices and financial planning resources. As more and more women take an interest in investing, this networking will provide them with information about everything: from which financial planner comes highly recommended to what stock has good potential. Networking at its finest is exemplified by the all-female investment clubs that have been created,

and the numbers prove their success: All-female clubs have outperformed all-male clubs between 1992 and 1996.

3. **Women have a tendency to be more "honest" about what they know and what they don't know.** Men have a much greater ego need to be perceived as financially literate, and they have a tendency to bluff about their financial prowess. On the other hand, women are more reality-based about their lack of financial expertise and are more willing to seek out information and education. This is why women are three times more likely than men to take a financial seminar.

4. **Women have been socialized to nurture.** As women begin to understand that money management is the height of nurturing—and they become more comfortable with the concept of self-nurturing—they will step in and take control.

5. **Women are "nesters."** Women put a great deal of energy into their home setting. To establish a solid financial future, you have to "build" a set of investments that reflects your tastes. Women can utilize their nesting instinct in the financial arena by selecting investments that create a solid financial foundation and then building on top of this base.

6. **Women can juggle multiple roles.** A woman would think it odd if all she had to worry about were her job. On any given day, a woman is routinely balancing many things in her life—work, planning a child's birthday party, picking up something for dinner, stopping at the dry cleaners, and checking on an aging relative might all be a normal part of her day. This ability to diversify one's energies is an important aspect of investing. A good portfolio is going to consist of several elements, not just one, and a good investor will be able to keep track of them all.

7. **Women have a sixth sense when sizing up people and things**, and this can be a powerful tool. When it comes to money and investing, this quality can help with everything from selecting a broker or financial advisor to listening to a "gut feeling" about whether or not to buy a stock.

8. **Women are good at setting and reaching goals.** Whether it's selecting a pediatrician or planning a major presentation at work, they know how to get things done. Women have proved to be excellent at establishing financial goals once

they come to terms with the importance of planning for their financial future.

9. **Women can be good savers.** Because women are very security conscious, they tend to be savings-oriented, but they have rarely received realistic guidance about what to do with their money. Those who have kept it in savings accounts will benefit by shifting their money to more profitable investments.

10. **Women are patient.** Money management requires patience—patience to explore various financial avenues, and patience to let the money grow. Because women are less likely than men to act impulsively, their money will increase over time.

There's no doubt that women have what it takes to become good money managers. While it is distressing that societal forces have made money management the "last frontier," understanding what has happened—and that you have the skills and ability to learn about investing and money management—is your first step toward taking charge of your finances.

Now you're ready to take the next step. Set aside the next twenty minutes to begin exploring your own personality and attitudes toward money by taking the Women Cents Self-Test.

2

WHEN IT COMES TO MONEY, WHO ARE YOU?
The Women Cents Self-Test

"I found this test interesting and nonthreatening. When you sit down with a financial advisor who asks you questions about your income and expenses, it can be very intimidating. With this test, you get the same profile, but it's friendlier."

Have you ever considered that the way you manage your money mirrors the way you manage your life?

Landmark studies conducted by the NCWRR prove that personality plays a critical role in how well you manage your finances. Consider gaining insights into issues such as these:

- What are the traits that make it difficult for you to save enough for important goals such as a financially secure retirement?
- Which personal characteristics make you a more successful investor, and which ones hinder you?
- How does your decision-making style affect your management of money?
- How financially knowledgeable are you?

The answers to these and other questions will help you to understand your financial profile and determine what you can do to make the most of your money.

The quiz that follows will take only about fifteen to twenty minutes. It is designed to identify those aspects of your personality that prevent you from making smart money decisions as well as to validate your strengths. It will help you to evaluate how you handle risk, cope with change, make decisions, and view the future. The score analysis will explain how these traits affect the way you control your finances and what steps you can take to become a wiser investor.

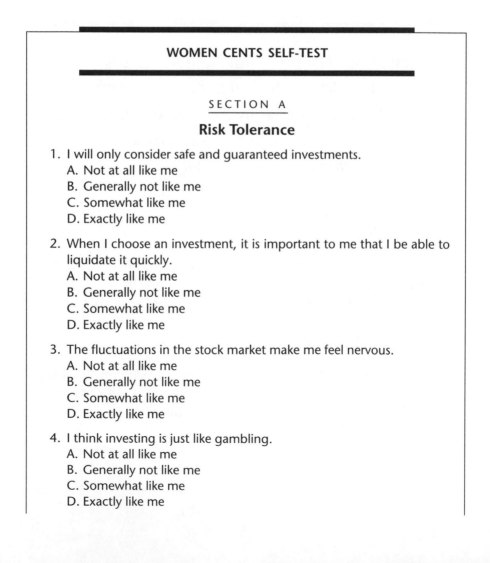

WOMEN CENTS SELF-TEST

SECTION A

Risk Tolerance

1. I will only consider safe and guaranteed investments.
   A. Not at all like me
   B. Generally not like me
   C. Somewhat like me
   D. Exactly like me

2. When I choose an investment, it is important to me that I be able to liquidate it quickly.
   A. Not at all like me
   B. Generally not like me
   C. Somewhat like me
   D. Exactly like me

3. The fluctuations in the stock market make me feel nervous.
   A. Not at all like me
   B. Generally not like me
   C. Somewhat like me
   D. Exactly like me

4. I think investing is just like gambling.
   A. Not at all like me
   B. Generally not like me
   C. Somewhat like me
   D. Exactly like me

5. I realize that I cannot expect substantial financial returns unless I am willing to accept some financial risk.
   A. Not at all like me
   B. Generally not like me
   C. Somewhat like me
   D. Exactly like me

SECTION B

Perspective on Change and the Future

6. I generally prefer to stay in a known situation, rather than take a chance on a new situation.
   A. Not at all like me
   B. Generally not like me
   C. Somewhat like me
   D. Exactly like me

7. I believe that change adds zest to life.
   A. Not at all like me
   B. Generally not like me
   C. Somewhat like me
   D. Exactly like me

8. I am open to considering new investment opportunities and strategies.
   A. Not at all like me
   B. Generally not like me
   C. Somewhat like me
   D. Exactly like me

9. I don't mind adjusting my savings/investment strategy to fit my changing circumstances.
   A. Not at all like me
   B. Generally not like me
   C. Somewhat like me
   D. Exactly like me

10. I am optimistic about the future.
    A. Not at all like me
    B. Generally not like me
    C. Somewhat like me
    D. Exactly like me

Center of Control

11. I often feel that I don't have enough control over the direction my life is taking.
    A. Not at all like me
    B. Generally not like me
    C. Somewhat like me
    D. Exactly like me

12. I will rarely make a customer complaint even when I am quite dissatisfied with a product or service.
    A. Not at all like me
    B. Generally not like me
    C. Somewhat like me
    D. Exactly like me

13. I am usually the one to concede if my plans conflict with the plans of those close to me.
    A. Not at all like me
    B. Generally not like me
    C. Somewhat like me
    D. Exactly like me

14. An obstacle to my participating in financial planning activities is that my spouse/partner doesn't really want me involved.
    A. Not at all like me
    B. Generally not like me
    C. Somewhat like me
    D. Exactly like me

15. A sense of personal accomplishment motivates me to be involved in financial planning/investment activities.
    A. Not at all like me
    B. Generally not like me
    C. Somewhat like me
    D. Exactly like me

Attitudes Toward Money and Investing

16. I think saving and investing are pointless unless you have a lot of money to work with.
    A. Not at all like me
    B. Generally not like me

C. Somewhat like me

D. Exactly like me

17. In general, I think people with lots of money have more options and opportunities in life.
A. Not at all like me
B. Generally not like me
C. Somewhat like me
D. Exactly like me

18. Conversations about money and investing are boring to me.
A. Not at all like me
B. Generally not like me
C. Somewhat like me
D. Exactly like me

19. I wish women didn't have to be concerned about financial matters.
A. Not at all like me
B. Generally not like me
C. Somewhat like me
D. Exactly like me

20. I think it is very important to become an active and accomplished investor.
A. Not at all like me
B. Generally not like me
C. Somewhat like me
D. Exactly like me

SECTION E

Financial Planning and Investment Knowledge

21. Financial investment lingo intimidates me.
A. Not at all like me
B. Generally not like me
C. Somewhat like me
D. Exactly like me

22. Not knowing enough about investments is a big obstacle to my involvement in financial planning activities.
A. Not at all like me
B. Generally not like me
C. Somewhat like me
D. Exactly like me

23. Within the next year, I plan to take steps to become more knowledge-able about investment types and financial planning principles.

A. Not at all like me
B. Generally not like me
C. Somewhat like me
D. Exactly like me

24. I rate my level of understanding of investment types and financial planning principles as
    A. Expert
    B. Advanced
    C. Know the basics
    D. Little or nothing

25. During the past year, I sought financial information from one or more of the following resources: radio or television programs, classes or seminars, newspapers, magazines, or books.
    A. Yes, often
    B. Yes, occasionally
    C. Yes, but hardly ever
    D. No, never

SECTION F

Decision-Making Style

26. On most decisions, I tend to "lead with my heart."
    A. Not at all like me
    B. Generally not like me
    C. Somewhat like me
    D. Exactly like me

27. After making a big decision about money, I tend to worry a lot about my decision.
    A. Not at all like me
    B. Generally not like me
    C. Somewhat like me
    D. Exactly like me

28. I am likely to make an investment decision on the basis of a "hot tip."
    A. Not at all like me
    B. Generally not like me
    C. Somewhat like me
    D. Exactly like me

29. I often put off making financial decisions because I'm afraid of making a mistake.
    A. Not at all like me
    B. Generally not like me
    C. Somewhat like me
    D. Exactly like me

30. I do a lot of research and planning prior to making an investment.
    A. Not at all like me
    B. Generally not like me
    C. Somewhat like me
    D. Exactly like me

SECTION G

Financial Planning and Investment Activities

31. I have established a specific dollar amount as a savings/investment goal.
    A. Not at all like me
    B. Generally not like me
    C. Somewhat like me
    D. Exactly like me

32. I save and invest in order to reach my financial goals.
    A. Not at all like me
    B. Generally not like me
    C. Somewhat like me
    D. Exactly like me

33. Within the next year, I plan to start or add to my investment portfolio.
    A. Not at all like me
    B. Generally not like me
    C. Somewhat like me
    D. Exactly like me

34. During the past year, I consulted with a financial planner, broker, or investment representative concerning my financial planning needs.
    A. Not at all like me
    B. Generally not like me
    C. Somewhat like me
    D. Exactly like me

35. Over the past three years, I have been very satisfied with the rate of return on my investments.
    A. Not at all like me
    B. Generally not like me
    C. Somewhat like me
    D. Exactly like me

SCORING

SECTION	POINTS	YOUR SCORE
Section A: Risk Tolerance	1. A-4; B-3; C-2; D-1	_____
	2. A-4; B-3; C-2; D-1	_____
	3. A-4; B-3; C-2; D-1	_____
	4. A-4; B-3; C-2; D-1	_____
	5. A-1; B-2; C-3; D-4	_____
Section B: Perspective on Change and the Future	6. A-4; B-3; C-2; D-1	_____
	7. A-1; B-2; C-3; D-4	_____
	8. A-1; B-2; C-3; D-4	_____
	9. A-1; B-2; C-3; D-4	_____
	10. A-1; B-2; C-3; D-4	_____
Section C: Center of Control	11. A-4; B-3; C-2; D-1	_____
	12. A-4; B-3; C-2; D-1	_____
	13. A-4; B-3; C-2; D-1	_____
	14. A-4; B-3; C-2; D-1	_____
	15. A-1; B-2; C-3; D-4	_____
Section D: Attitudes Toward Money and Investing	16. A-4; B-3; C-2; D-1	_____
	17. A-1; B-2; C-3; D-4	_____
	18. A-4; B-3; C-2; D-1	_____
	19. A-4; B-3; C-2; D-1	_____
	20. A-1; B-2; C-3; D-4	_____
Section E: Financial Planning and Investment Knowledge	21. A-4; B-3; C-2; D-1	_____
	22. A-4; B-3; C-2; D-1	_____
	23. A-1; B-2; C-3; D-4	_____
	24. A-4; B-3; C-2; D-1	_____
	25. A-4; B-3; C-2; D-1	_____
Section F: Decision-Making Style	26. A-4; B-3; C-2; D-1	_____
	27. A-4; B-3; C-2; D-1	_____
	28. A-4; B-3; C-2; D-1	_____
	29. A-4; B-3; C-2; D-1	_____
	30. A-1; B-2; C-3; D-4	_____
Section G: Financial Planning and Investment Activities	31. A-1; B-2; C-3; D-4	_____
	32. A-4; B-3; C-2; D-1	_____
	33. A-1; B-2; C-3; D-4	_____
	34. A-4; B-3; C-2; D-1	_____
	35. A-1; B-2; C-3; D-4	_____

Totals.
Section A   _____
Section B   _____
Section C   _____
Section D   _____
Section E   _____
Section F   _____
Section G   _____
  GRAND TOTAL _____

Point range for each section: 5–20
Point range for total score: 35–140

You now have two different scores: your *section* scores, which explain how your personality traits affect your aptitude for financial management; and your *overall* score, determined by adding up your points for each section, which reveals how you're doing at managing your money and what you need to do next.

HOW TO INTERPRET YOUR OVERALL SCORE

35–61 Points: The Danger Zone

If your score is in the Danger Zone, you may often feel that you're not in control of your life—a feeling that usually extends to financial matters. You probably don't know much about investing or the basics of financial planning, and you are likely to be intimidated by financial terminology. Because you feel ignorant, you may defer decisions about money matters to others.

Your choices about where to put your money often reflect a strong preference for the familiar over the unknown, an aversion to risk, and difficulty in coping with change. For example, even as your income rises, you're likely to put your savings into money market accounts, certificates of deposit, and other familiar vehicles that promise not to lose any money. The trouble is, they won't *make* very much money either—a fact that is likely to haunt you as you grow older and find yourself still struggling to achieve financial security. In an attempt to avoid risk, you've actually placed yourself at greater risk.

What to do: Don't despair, but don't delay in moving forward either. One of the biggest obstacles to taking charge of your financial life is also the easiest to overcome: lack of knowledge. Reading *Money Makeovers* and learning more about how to manage your money will help you to gain a sense of control over the direction your life is taking and increase your confidence in making financial decisions.

62–88 Points: The Caution Zone

The ups and downs of daily living preoccupy your thinking if you're in the Caution Zone. You believe you can't do much to shape the future, so you focus on the here and now rather than on long-term needs. When prioritizing financial matters, for example, you may be motivated to save for a new car but not inspired to put aside money for retirement and other faraway goals. You listen to your heart on most decisions, so when it comes to money and investing, you often make choices based more on feelings than on facts.

You are likely to perceive financial planning as pointless unless you have a lot of money to work with, and to reject as too risky any investment that is not guaranteed to protect your principal. Like Danger Zone women, you prefer the familiar, which keeps you from exploring investments that offer higher returns than CDs and savings accounts.

What to do: Your biggest challenge is letting go of preconceived notions about money and investing. Increasing your knowledge of the fundamentals of financial planning should help you to change your attitude toward money and teach you better ways to make financial decisions by using *both* fact and feeling. To overcome your resistance to planning for the future, begin thinking about your wants and needs over the long term, and refer to Chapter 15, where goal-setting is fully explained.

89–114 Points: The Comfort Zone

If you're in the Comfort Zone, you usually feel in control of your life. You're likely to be optimistic about the future and to realize the importance of taking responsibility for your finances. In addition, you feel capable of understanding money and investing and have learned the basics about the kinds of investments that are available to you and the principles of financial planning.

Your problem is that sometimes you feel too comfortable. You may realize that you ought to take a more active role in managing your investments, but because there's no urgency, you never get around to doing it. It's easy to put off making financial decisions or investigating new investment options, largely because the subject doesn't really interest you. In fact, you are usually bored by conversations about money and investments.

What to do: Regardless of your current circumstances, it is still important to move ahead. Besides, you're actually way ahead of many other women, and you ought to capitalize on the strides you've made. In addition, if you begin thinking of yourself as someone who has mastered some of the skills and knowledge that are required for successful financial planning, you may find you actually enjoy it more.

You're going to need to make financial planning a top priority to make sure complacency doesn't keep you from achieving financial security. Set aside at least an hour or two each month to review money matters (research a new mutual fund or check to see whether you need to make any changes in your portfolio). Mark the time down on your calendar as you would any other appointment, and set deadlines for any decisions that need to be made. You may also benefit from joining an investment club. Working with other people to select investments makes the process more interesting and more enjoyable, and committing to monthly meetings makes it happen.

115–140 Points: The Action Zone

There's little to prevent you from becoming an accomplished investor. You are open to a wide range of investment opportunities and understand that you must put some money in riskier, growth investments like stocks in order to earn higher returns. You aren't easily intimidated by financial lingo, and you'll ask questions until you are sure you understand. What's more, because you're generally assertive about your rights, you will challenge any financial professional who gives you poor service or questionable advice. Though you value your ability to enjoy the present, you want to be in control of your financial future, and you regard planning as essential to meeting that goal.

What to do: Congratulations! You are an active and accomplished investor or on your way to becoming one. If for some reason (procrastination? lack of confidence?) you haven't quite taken the plunge, do so now because you're ready. Section Three will provide you with the information you need to start building for a financially healthy future.

WHAT YOUR PERSONALITY TRAITS REVEAL

The Self-Test was designed to provide not only a measure of your financial awareness but also a way to identify and evaluate the seven personality traits that define your money personality and influence your progress toward reaching your financial goals. Refer back to your subtotals and note how you ranked for the following traits.

PERSONALITY TRAIT	YOUR SCORE
Attitude toward risk (Section A)	_____
Feelings about change and the future (Section B)	_____
Feelings about control (Section C)	_____
Attitude toward money (Section D)	_____
Understanding of money (Section E)	_____
Decision-making style (Section F)	_____
Current financial activities (Section G)	_____

To better interpret your scores within each section, read the following analyses with this breakdown in mind:

Danger Zone: 5–8
Caution Zone: 9–12
Comfort Zone: 13–16
Action Zone: 17–20

Your Attitude Toward Risk

Risk refers to the chance of experiencing a loss. In life, there are physical risks (going skiing for the first time), career risks (leaving your old job for a new one), emotional risks (committing to a new relationship), and financial risks (placing your money in an investment that is not guaranteed). Risk-taking often leads to the best experiences of our lives; the challenge is to become knowledgeable enough about risk-taking that it doesn't lead to the *worst* experience in our lives.

The Women Cents Study confirmed the findings of previous research that indicated women tend to be conservative, risk-averse investors. What people fail to realize is that conservative investments, while likely to be guaranteed, pose an even greater risk to financial security by not keeping up with inflation. Therefore, women investors should not avoid risk, but learn how to manage it. You will become more risk tolerant as you develop a better understanding of the relationship between risk and reward, and learn how to balance the risks you take on.

What to do: If you are uncomfortable with risk, your goal should be to become a *calculated* risk taker; one who gives her investments serious thought and then makes a decision by evaluating the chance of experiencing a gain against the chance of experiencing a loss. Always remember that there is no perfect investment—each has advantages and disadvantages that affect the risk and reward. Financial decision-making that includes evaluation of trade-offs between anticipated costs (actual or perceived) and anticipated benefits will help you to choose investments that better fit your financial goals.

Later on, you'll learn how to match short-term income-producing investments to short-term financial goals, and long-term growth-producing investments to long-term financial goals.

Another important principle is to diversify by placing your money in several instruments, not just one. Also known as asset allocation, diversification is a strategy for setting up an acceptable level of risk within a portfolio by placing your investment dollars in several different types of financial products. In this way, you will be assured of experiencing gains to offset any possible losses, and of having some money invested in instruments that will at least keep pace with inflation.

Understanding risk and how to become more risk savvy will be discussed in Chapter 5.

Your Feelings About Change

The Women Cents Study revealed that a woman's openness to change can influence her financial planning activities.

If your score for "Feelings About Change" was in the Comfort Zone or the Action Zone, you tend to be open and flexible about change and considering new opportunities, and to recognize the value of saving and investing.

If your score is in the Danger or Caution Zone, you are uncomfortable with and resistant to change, preferring what is known, routine, and predictable. Because focusing on the distant future (certain
to be filled with change) is frightening, your planning style is based
on the short term and emphasizes maintaining the status quo. Because women who dislike change prefer the familiar, they tend to
be intimidated by financial terminology and are not very open to
considering new investment opportunities and strategies.

What to do: To develop a more open and flexible orientation to
financial planning, first examine your daily activities and your overall attitude to life. (Specific strategies will be discussed in Chapter 6.)
Any small changes in your daily routine will encourage you to be
more flexible about your financial life as well. To feel less threatened
by learning more about finance, take it one step at a time—but keep
moving!

Your Feelings About Control

A woman's ongoing perception of who is "in control" of her life
(is she in charge, or is she constantly answering to others?) has a
profound effect on her self-esteem, confidence, and motivation.

Women are particularly prone to feeling out of control because
of the many demands placed on their time. But there are strategies
that can help even the most demand-torn woman!

The results of the Women Cents Study indicated that women
who feel they are in control of their lives (in the Comfort or Action
Zone) are more assertive in voicing their opinions and in following
through with their own plans, even when they don't match the
plans of others around them. A sense of personal accomplishment
and a desire for financial independence are big motivators to becoming knowledgeable about investing and being involved in financial
planning activities.

On the other hand, women who feel they don't have control
over their lives (in the Caution or Danger Zone) often acquiesce to
the opinions and plans of others. They are less likely to feel they can
control future events and so are not motivated to engage in planning and preparation. In addition, these women commonly feel that
anyone else's financial decisions are better than their own.

What to do: If you want to increase your sense of control in your
financial life, try taking more control in your daily life. Whenever

you have the opportunity to make a decision, make it! This will increase your confidence in your decision-making ability. As a consumer, if you are dissatisfied with a product or service, make a complaint. As you develop a sense of control, you will naturally want to have more control over your finances as well. Fear of making a mistake will likely discourage you at first, but persevere. The fear will quickly diminish as your sense of control increases.

Chapter 7 will provide you with ideas for gaining more control over your finances, and Chapter 8 will discuss financial control issues within a marriage and suggest strategies for involving both partners.

Your Feelings About Change and the Future

Some people are so caught up in day-to-day life that it's difficult for them to think about tomorrow; others have mastered the art of living for today while still keeping an eye on the future.

Women who are preoccupied with the present (those in the Caution or Danger Zone) are unlikely to prepare financially for their future needs. Their investment choices tend to be conservative, and they will resist making long-term investments for fear of not having the money available for a more present need or want.

On the other hand, women who look toward the future (those in the Comfort or Action Zone) are likely to spend time preparing for it. They are optimistic about what lies ahead and tend to feel that they have adequate control over future events. They learn to balance "living for today" with "planning for tomorrow," which sometimes means delaying gratification now to save for future needs and wants. They are more risk tolerant in their investment choices, focusing more on future growth and total return than on current liquidity and safety of principal.

What to do: To develop a proper balance, start by developing positive thinking about your future. When it comes to financial planning, this can be as simple as promising yourself that once a month you'll do one thing (undertake an additional recommendation in this book, enroll in a seminar) to prepare for the future.

You'll find additional suggestions in Chapter 9, and Section Three will help you develop a financial plan that accommodates both short- and long-term needs.

Your Attitude Toward Money

When attitudes about money are based on myth, negative responses can occur. For example, many women believe that it is pointless to save and invest unless they have a lot of money, and for this reason, they fail to set financial goals. Others avoid financial planning because they feel incapable of understanding money and investing, or because they believe that financial matters are boring and/or unimportant.

However, when attitudes about money are based on reality, a more balanced perspective is achieved. Keep in mind that nearly 85 percent of all women will spend some part of their retirement years living alone. Therefore, it is prudent that every woman prepare for her later years by developing financial awareness and a positive attitude toward money and investing. Single or married, it is equally important to become involved. If you're single, you need to take appropriate steps to plan for your future; if you're married, you should be talking to your spouse and his financial advisors to be certain that you agree with the plans they are making.

What to do: Women who hold reality-based attitudes toward money and investing believe it is important to become active and accomplished investors. If you are in the Danger or Caution Zone, you should become aware of your negative and positive feelings toward money and how these affect your behavior. (For example, do you sometimes buy things you don't really need, forgetting there are other things you could do with the money?) Becoming more knowledgeable about financial planning in general and your situation in particular will help you to develop a more positive attitude. Also read Chapter 11 for more suggestions on overcoming the attitudes you've learned over the years.

Your Understanding of Money

In the Women Cents Study, nearly one-half the respondents indicated that not knowing enough about investments was an obstacle to their involvement in financial planning activities. In contrast, the study also revealed that women who had a better understanding of investment possibilities and financial planning principles were more likely to have realistic attitudes toward money, were considerably more risk tolerant, and were far more confident about their financial decisions.

What to do: No matter how well you scored, there is still more to learn about financial planning and investing. Refer to Chapter 12 for suggestions about how to make financial education part of your everyday life, and read Section III for additional background material.

Your Decision-Making Style

Financial decision-making can be described as either emotional or cognitive in style. Emotional decision-makers are said to follow their hearts—they base their decisions on feelings and attitudes. Cognitive decision-makers use their heads, using facts to make their decisions.

Many emotional decision-makers are quick and impulsive because they don't like to devote much time to the decision-making process. However, other emotional decision-makers can be characterized as procrastinators, a decidedly negative form of emotional decision-making.

In contrast, cognitive decision-makers worry less about financial choices both before and after they are made, simply because their decisions are well thought out and supported by research and planning.

Ironically, neither type of decision-making style is "correct." Good decision-makers use *both* styles, depending on the circumstances. Some of the best decisions are made using both head and heart, reminding us again that women, who are generally more in tune with their feelings, are quite capable of making excellent financial decisions.

What to do: It is important to think of financial decision-making as a three-step process:

1. Recognize that a decision needs to be made.
2. Evaluate the alternatives.
3. Make a choice from among the alternatives.

If your score in "Decision-Making Style" indicates a need for improvement, take time to analyze which of these three steps is giving you the most trouble, and refer to Chapter 10. In addition, the information in Section III will provide you with a stronger fact base for decision-making.

Your Current Financial Activities

In many ways, financial planning is very much like planning an extended car trip. To get to your destination, you need to identify the route you want to take, which in turn will be dependent on what type of trip you will be taking. Do you need to get there quickly, or do you have time to sightsee along the way? You may even call a travel consultant for some help in making the appropriate plans. However, as you become more experienced at trip-planning (and know this route better), you'll soon find that your own instincts can be depended upon to get you where you want to go, though you may still ask for advice now and then.

If you're already taking some positive steps with your money and if you scored in the Action Zone in this "financial activities" section, then you're acquiring the experience you need to manage and invest your money. However, if you scored low in this area, you need to establish some financial goals and monitor the results.

What to do: Consider implementing the following strategies. (These steps will all be fully discussed later in the book.)

1. Establish a specific dollar amount for specific goals, such as your retirement or funding your children's education. (Set realistic goals. You have to succeed at this step in order to implement the others.)
2. Develop a realistic savings budget that requires you to "pay yourself first" each month.
3. Talk to a financial advisor to select investments that will meet your goals.
4. Faithfully monitor your investments/savings and how well you are doing at accomplishing the goals you have set.

Now that you've completed the Self-Test, read the next two chapters to discover how cultural, familial, and educational messages (which are often subliminal) have created an environment that makes it difficult for women to take charge of their money. Some of what you read will certainly surprise you!

3

PREADOLESCENCE
When You Were Captain of Your Own Ship

"Starting when I was about nine years old, my father developed a ritual we followed for years. When he came home, one of the first questions he would ask me was, 'What did the market do today?' and I was to tell him if the stock market was up or down and by how many points—information I would get for him by listening to the radio each evening. I guess it's pretty obvious why I work in finance."

You cannot separate the issues related to women and money from the issues surrounding female development. Many of the personality traits required for feeling comfortable with money management (risk tolerance, flexibility, optimism for the future, sense of control) are common to preadolescent girls. But the teen years bring about a change.

As author Mary Pipher notes in *Reviving Ophelia*, her landmark book about adolescent girls and their loss of self, studies show that girls' IQ scores dip and their math and science scores plummet shortly after they enter adolescence. Adolescent girls tend to lose their assertive, energetic ways and become more deferential, self-critical, and depressed as they conform to society's "script" for being female. This loss of assertiveness and self-confidence does not bode well for women's ability to take control of their financial future.

Writing this chapter, I am reminded of Amy, a young girl from our old neighborhood. When my son was two and Amy was about ten, she used to stop by often to play with him. Over a period of two years, I got to know Amy well. At that time, she saw the world as filled with endless possibilities and adventures. She bubbled over with excitement and had an endless stream of questions. Amy also told me that she wanted to become a doctor because she loved babies. When we moved two towns away, I missed our frequent chats, and over the next few years, we lost touch with Amy and her family.

Last year I was sitting in a pizza parlor near the college, having a bite to eat between classes, when I heard a familiar voice. It was Amy, sitting in a booth next to mine. As I was eating, I eavesdropped on the conversation she was having with friends. Their typical teenage talk was all about makeup, boys, and who was "hot" in school. As I greeted her later, it became clear to me that she had changed. I couldn't find the Amy I had known several years ago. A few weeks later I ran into Amy's mother, who, when I asked, admitted that Amy no longer talked of being a doctor.

What had happened to Amy and her aspirations? This chapter will discuss how girls change during adolescence, and how it affects their ability to take charge of their money.

If adult women are to manage their lives and thrive during their later years, making secure decisions that will affect their future finances, they need to draw on or develop the strengths that are never snuffed out in young boys.

How Family Background Affects a Woman's Development

Not surprisingly, a woman's family upbringing plays an important role in providing specific gender messages regarding the importance of earning money and the nature of "success." If the family messages are positive, a daughter receives permission to reach for her dreams and goals; if the messages are negative, the daughter's progress is limited.

The NCWRR Gender, Identity, and Self-Esteem Study found that

68 percent of women perceived that their mothers and fathers had been and continued to be a strong influence on how they managed their adult lives.

The family "story" lays the groundwork for a daughter's sense of self. It helps define how she is supposed to behave and illustrates for her what values are to be upheld (such as honesty, individualism, education, hard work). During these early years, girls also gain a sense of how money will fit into their lives; if money issues are treated secretively, as they are in so many families, a young girl is prevented from coming to terms with what it means to manage money.

PARENTS AS ROLE MODELS

Children grow up acting as receptive, although often unconscious, observers of how parents negotiate between themselves such issues as mutual respect, equality of gender roles, power, control, and self-worth. The lightning rod that often focuses these negotiations is money, which can be a polarizing force or a force that contributes to respect and understanding between the parents.

Power struggles over money often reflect how men and women view their gender roles, and how they view, value, and perceive their children. For example, a family in which all financial decisions are made by the husband makes a powerful statement to the children in that household; the family that purchases a car for the son but not for the daughter (so the son can get to a job during his teen years) is sending a very clear message about money and power. And one woman who came to the NCWRR Center described what it was like to have a father who mismanaged everything:

"I remember my father borrowing money from me when I was a little girl and not repaying it. Money seemed to burn a hole in his pocket," says Frieda R. *"As I got a little older, I realized he was pretty irresponsible with money, which meant my mother handled most of our family finances. As a result, I learned early on that women had to know how to handle money."*

The Gender, Identity, and Self-Esteem Study found that 72 percent of women believed that their parents' feelings of self-worth contributed to their own sense of self-esteem, which, in turn, affected their confidence in handling finances. If either parent had a strong self-identity, it had a positive effect on the children. Mothers and fathers, by virtue of their own confidence with regard to money management, can encourage and convey certain messages to their children.

Cynthia R. was a young woman whose family background instilled in her a strong spirit and a self-reliant approach to life. When Cynthia was ten years old, she and her family left their Caribbean home and relocated to the United States. She remembers both her parents working at paid jobs:

"My parents worked very hard and instilled in us a strong work ethic. We were always told that you had to work if you wanted to achieve anything in life—only bums didn't work.

"At one point in my adult life, I was working as an assistant manager for a large pharmacy chain. I found myself working seven days a week and not thinking much of it. I realized that this was my parents' influence."

Cynthia recalls that her family motto was "pay your bills first and then you can enjoy yourself." She has lived by this motto and put it to good use in her adult life. Cynthia was fortunate to have been exposed to such a positive influence early on, and as a result, she is well prepared to take care of herself all her life.

Angela P. also benefited from positive role models at home. Even though her mother was a traditional homemaker, her father respected Angela's mother, and they shared financial responsibilities. *"My mother could really squeeze a penny!"* recalls Angela. *"That's why he deferred to her a lot—she was an excellent money manager. Finances were discussed openly, and there was no mystery attached to how much we did or didn't have. Although my mother often had the final word in what she considered was best for the family, my father won his share of arguments too."*

Angela's early observations of her parents' mutual respect and openness about money left her with the belief that a good marriage involved sharing and respect, and that women were perfectly capable of managing family money.

Angela went on to marry a man with a very different approach to money: *"The men in his family worked hard and expected to be able to spend the money they earned. Over time, he and I were able to work out a compromise so that we saved enough for me to feel comfortable, but we spend some too. If I hadn't observed my mother's methods for so many years, I don't know that I would have resisted what my husband originally presented us 'the way to do things.'"*

Unfortunately, not all marital relationships are based on such respect and shared responsibilities. Often, daughters are left with images of relationships that are based on disrespect, condescension, and stereotypical gender roles. Edith G.'s parents reversed roles (her mother worked while her father took care of Edith and managed a home-based business on the side). Unfortunately, the strong image of a mother providing financial support for the family was undermined by a domineering, controlling father who belittled his wife's abilities: *"My mother made the money and my father paid the bills and made all the decisions. When I say he made all the decisions, that's exactly what I mean,"* explains Edith. *"He gave the impression that my mother was not too bright and that he always knew better about everything.*

"Even though she could have supported herself, he made her live with her parents when he went into the army; he felt women shouldn't live alone. In view of the fact that my mother had a successful career and had been out in the world, it would seem odd to an observer that she would accept that treatment. But she had been raised by a controlling mother and then my father took over that role. I guess it seemed natural to her."

Unfortunately, it became all too natural for Edith too, who grew up with little confidence in herself. For part of her adult life, she was dependent financially on her father and felt powerless at that time to change her behavior. Edith duplicated her mother's experience. She became pregnant at an early age, and because it was the early 1960s, she felt her options were limited. When she decided not to marry the baby's father, she moved back home, where her mother, who was then retired, took care of the baby so that Edith could continue working. Throughout, Edith was subjected to verbal abuse by her father, who continually harangued her, not with demands that she marry someone to take care of her, but with insults about how the money she was making was "peanuts." Ultimately, Edith obtained a job as an administrative assistant, and she held that position while attending night school to become a medical technician. Later on, she got her own apartment, and though she found single parenting to be difficult, she relished the fact that she was on her own. After counseling, Edith finally confronted her father and told him that she could no longer handle the disrespectful way he treated her, and to this day, she and her father have a distant relationship.

Stella R.'s impressions of marital money negotiations grew from her experience in a "traditional" family. Stella's mother was a homemaker who had been educated to be a teacher but gave it up when she married. Her mother played such a weak role in the family that Stella was hard-pressed to see how women could ever be capable of taking charge. Stella states: *"My father was very traditional and would never have permitted my mother to work. He made all the major household decisions, including handling all the money. Because he made all the financial decisions on his own, money was never discussed, and we kids learned early that it was none of our business. My father had the last word, and we deferred to him."*

After observing this dominant-subordinate relationship in her parents' marriage, Stella emerged with the impression that women were inferior to men, should remain dependent, and were not good at handling money. Even though she wanted to be financially independent, she, like Edith, found herself pregnant and back home dependent on her father's help.

Stella eventually made important changes that put financial control back in her own hands. Unlike Edith, she immediately recognized that moving back home was the wrong choice. The financial assistance was not worth the psychological price she was paying for her father's support. She took an intensive night course in computer processing and with those skills moved out of the house and into her own apartment. According to Stella, *"I remember as if it were yesterday, receiving my first paycheck from my computer job. That paycheck was more than just money to help support me and my child, it represented the fact that I was in control, and I could do it. I realized from earning that money that I could make it!"*

When grown children must resort to depending on their parents for financial support, their self-esteem suffers. In my research, I've found that women (even more so than men) are fighting to avoid financial dependency on their parents. Today's woman wants to be perceived as independent both emotionally and financially. However, because of increasing divorce rates, women are often left to raise children on their own, which makes it very difficult for them to avoid asking for help.

The positive images provided by Cynthia's and Angela's parents instilled in them the idea that women and men can respect each other and are capable of sharing family, household, and financial responsibilities.

Unfortunately, Edith and Stella were witnesses to men who did not respect women as equals, who were controlling and often intimidating in their relationships. These women's early view of women's place in the world left them with the idea that they were incapable of managing their own lives.

MOTHERS AND DAUGHTERS

If you have a daughter, you know how very difficult it is to raise a strong and independent female. A mother's knowledge about what society expects of women distorts many of the messages of "self"-preservation she intends to send to her daughter. A mother walks a difficult tightrope, trying to instill autonomy while at the same time trying to prepare her daughter to fit into our culture. Your own mother faced the same predicament, coupled with societal messages about female submissiveness that, until very recently, were even more resounding.

And if a mother has both a son and a daughter, she conveys two separate messages: The son is still raised to be primarily a worker (though there is a new emphasis on training sons to handle many household tasks, if not necessarily to be responsible for them), yet the daughter is now raised to juggle the roles of worker, wife, and mother—and to take full responsibility for them all.

What often happens is that daughters are raised with a set of mixed messages about how to fulfill these multiple roles:

- Be a good student—but watch out for being too smart.
- Speak up—but not too loudly.
- Be independent—but not too independent.
- Be honest and forthright—but "feminine wiles" (coyness and mild deception) can be useful, too.
- Plan for a career—but be careful not to achieve too much.
- Be your own person—but allow yourself to be dependent.
- Be assertive—but hide it behind femininity.

Women have traditionally been raised to be responsible for the emotional well-being of all family members and to protect them from the psychic dangers of the outside world. But status and worth are still built on economic achievement—the arena for which sons are groomed. What's more, women are still severely penalized for looking out for their economic well-being. At a recent financial seminar, a woman in her late thirties told me that it had taken her two years to build up the necessary internal resources to come to the seminar. A mother of two children, she felt overwhelmingly guilty about two specific things: taking courses that would give her a well-paying job, and the ability to take her own financial needs seriously. She said, *"It is so difficult for women my age to break free from all of these messages that surround us about being a 'good mother' but make sure you also bring home the bacon. If I drop either ball, I'm not perceived as successful."*

A mother who values her own abilities, who has a strong voice, and who makes her voice known can pass on that legacy to her daughter. In contrast, a troubled mother-daughter relationship can produce behavior patterns that may prevent a woman from achieving her full potential, from experimenting, and from taking healthy risks. Because she is not given guidance in shouldering the multiple-role burden allotted to women, she may be fearful of independence and lack confidence in her abilities—traits that may jeopardize career and financial goals. Or if she reaches her goals, she may not be gratified or feel the achievement was deserved.

"My mother always favored my younger sister, who was cuter and more adorable than I was," says one woman. *"I idolized my father, but only in the last twenty years has it been acceptable to follow in his footsteps. I can't tell you how it pained me to feel that I was unacceptable to my mother yet shouldn't be wanting to do what my father did."*

Our Gender, Identity, and Self-Esteem Study found that more than 40 percent of women still feel the strong influence of their mothers on their adult lives, so the messages that communicate from mother to daughter are vital to helping women succeed with their money.

In her book *Altered Loves,* author Terri Apter found that as girls reach adolescence they become very interested in their mother's gender strategies, how the domestic roles are divided, how the roles are negotiated, who makes the major decisions, including financial decisions, and what compromises are reached.

According to Apter, closeness between a mother and daughter is

not by itself an accurate measurement of a girl's developing inde
pendence. What seems to serve as a sign of maturity and firmness of
identity (which eventually translates into financial surety) is how a
mother treats a daughter and, most important, how her daughter's
ideas and beliefs are handled and valued. This is clearly revealed
by the stories many women told about their relationships to their
mothers.

Grace F. grew up in a blue-collar, lower-middle-class family in
the suburb of a large city. Her father was a bartender and her mother
a waitress. Though her mother was not highly educated, she was a
strong and good influence on Grace: *"Mom was a tough nut, like her
mother before her, and she ran the family. She handled all the finances
and was the authority figure in our house. In fact, we used to joke and
say, 'Poor Daddy, he has to put up with Mom,' but as we got older we saw
how difficult it was for her and how much responsibility she carried. I
remember my father saying that we could just as easily marry a rich man
as a poor one, and my mother scolding him, saying, 'If you pay your own
way, you never answer to anybody.' I guess this was the beginning of my
personal philosophy about finances. I know money was never a factor in
determining whether I would date a particular man or not."*

When Grace graduated from high school and started working,
she became a saver, opening savings and checking accounts and participating in her company's 401(k) plan. As a young adult she had a
head start on gaining control of her financial life. It never crossed
her mind that she would marry in order to have a man take care of
her.

A strong mother and two strong grandmothers were the women
who influenced Marian T. Marian's mother taught part-time in a
child care center and later took a full-time job with a government
agency. Because Marian's father found it impossible to save, the family couldn't afford their own home until her mother inherited a
small amount of money that served as a down payment.

Says Marian, *"My mother was always very open with me about
money, and I was allowed to make my own decisions. Her recurring message was, 'You need to do something to support yourself.' My grandmothers, both of whom had gone to college at a time when few women had
that opportunity, were also an influence. They were very strong women
whom I admired and wished to emulate.*

"My paternal grandfather was like my father, inept with money,

prompting my grandmother to become a real penny-pincher. In fact, she often hid money in the house, and when she died, they found $300 hidden in a hot-water bottle!"

Marian's mother tried to make it appear that Dad was in charge. Marian, however, saw through the facade and credits her mother for acquiring the money necessary for her to attend college. *"My mother taught me to take care of myself financially, and I really admire her. She never spoke ill of my father, but she always emphasized to me the importance of self-reliance."*

What is interesting in this story and in our findings is that, on a conscious or unconscious level, women who are independent and capable with money often have a vested interest in maintaining the illusion that the man of the house holds the financial power. Because of the schizophrenic nature of money relations, they can't outwardly display their competence.

Marian's grandmother had to go to great lengths to hide money because she couldn't control the financial situation. In the new Dreyfus Gender Investment Comparison Survey conducted by the NCWRR, 33 percent of women admitted they had to "hide" money from their spouses to pay bills. I would suspect that younger women today have to make one of two distinct choices about money: either following the lead of their mothers and grandmothers or developing a more realistic, honest, equality-oriented perspective on handling money within the marriage.

FATHERS AND DAUGHTERS

Historically, our society has not prepared men to be involved with their children, yet fathers know that it is their job to help sons fit into a society that encompasses work, power, and moneymaking. Unfortunately, they are only beginning to realize that they need to encourage their daughters in the same way.

Fathers have the power to do either great harm or great good for their daughters. If they act as agents for a gender-biased society, they can crush a girl's developing sense of self. Rigid fathers may sour a girl's dreams and dampen her self-esteem; sexist fathers undervalue their daughters' intelligence and encourage them to abdicate power and control to the men in their lives.

Positive fathers can instill in their daughters a healthy rebellion and willingness to take risks. They can encourage girls to look out for their own best interests, to protect themselves, and to fight back when they have been treated unfairly. Fathers can encourage life-building skills like earning and investing money, changing tires, building a deck, or meeting the challenge of taking a tough math course. The ideal message passed from father to daughter should be that "it's okay to be smart, bold, and independent."

In the Dreyfus Gender Investment Comparison Survey, 61 percent of adult women indicated that their mothers did an excellent job handling money. In fact, however, they were reacting to their mothers' ability to *manage* money, not to invest it. They were more likely to observe their *fathers* displaying the traits associated with investment—risk-taking, control, future-thinking, and a healthy dose of decisiveness.

Mary Pipher's research on father-daughter relationships (1994) found that the physical presence of the father had little to do with the quality of the relationship; rather, it was the emotional availability that counted. Her studies uncovered three types of father-daughter relationships, and I've adapted this information as it would apply to the father's influence on his daughter's attitude toward money:

Supportive. These fathers are nurturing and interested in their daughters' well-being and have found ways to create an ongoing relationship. As a result, they have daughters with high self-esteem, who feel confident and are very optimistic about their futures. These men are inclined to work as hard with their daughters as they do with their sons in building confidence, self-esteem, and risk-taking in relation to money. They help their daughters understand how the world operates with relation to money and encourage what I refer to as "money duality"—they can use money to help others, but they also must learn to help themselves by becoming more financially secure.

Distant. This was the largest category. These fathers do not possess the skills to create a close relationship with their daughters. They are generally unwilling or inept listeners and are lacking in empathy, flexibility, and patience. For the most part, they function as rule-enforcers and breadwinners. The only thing that daughters appreciate about them is their income. Distant fathers do little to help their daughters see themselves as unique, special, and powerful. Instead of encouraging their daughters to take a paper route or learn about "how the world operates," they don't get involved. Distant fathers tend not to be able to encourage or support the traits and qualities their daughters need to be good investors later on.

Abusive. These fathers hurt their daughters physically and emotionally through name-calling, ridicule, shame, and even physical attacks. As a result, the daughters are generally insecure and incapable of taking charge of their lives. Abusive fathers severely undermine their daughters' financial future by failing to provide them with even the most basic foundation for self-esteem.

According to our Life-Ties Study, almost 40 percent of women feel their fathers continue to be a strong influence—both positive and negative—on their adult lives. Today's fathers can help their daughters with money by encouraging a belief in self; by discouraging stereotypical roles; by demonstrating equality of the sexes; by encouraging risk-taking; and by recognizing that security can be achieved in many different ways—not only by nurturing others.

The following stories provide examples of how both positive and negative messages from fathers can influence a daughter's ability to navigate through her adult years.

Money, Money

Ann W. is an independent, direct woman with strong and definite opinions who recently sold her successful restaurant/catering business and is in search of a new business venture. Her business spun off good money for many years, and she invested her profits in real estate—a New York apartment in which she lives and several rental properties in a popular tourist community.

Ann grew up in a close-knit Italian family in Brooklyn, New York, where her family owned the building they lived in. Her father ran a candy store and owned four apartments. *"I worked with my father in the store from the time I was eight years old. When I wanted to start a concession selling ices and candy through a window to the street, he supported me. It was my operation and I got a cut of the profits. You could say I started my first business at age eight."*

The fact that Ann's father valued her and exposed her to the world of business gave her a jump start on becoming independent and confident in dealing with money. She also learned another difficult lesson when her father became terminally ill and died when she was eleven years old.

Because Ann's dad had prepared the whole family to manage their financial lives, her mother was able to take over the financial reins without much difficulty. However, his death made a very big impression on Ann. *"I loved him so much—his death was devastating to me. I remember thinking you can't count on anyone—you have to be able to take care of yourself. I began to believe that life is tentative and nothing is permanent. My attitudes toward my future were definitely based on those early lessons. I fully understood from that time on that I am responsible for myself."*

Janice Q.'s mother died when Janice was thirteen, but she had the encouraging support of a father and four brothers who respected her. Her ability to meet new challenges in the face of adversity and to manage her professional and financial life independently reflects the important role her father played in her early development.

"I grew up in a large city and had a loving but painful childhood. It was very frightening losing my mother when I was just reaching womanhood myself. But I was lucky to have a wonderful father and four brothers who always treated me with great respect. My father had great admiration for women and always said that a man was as successful as the woman he was married to. He always told me a woman should put herself on a pedestal and stay there! I guess that's why in every relationship I had, if I wasn't treated with respect, I was out of there.

"My father was an accountant and balanced the books for the New York City transit system. Even as a young girl I liked to sit with him as he went over the accounts. I enjoyed numbers, found them a challenge, and liked making everything balance out."

Having a father who valued her early in life helped Janice create the necessary resilience to manage the challenges she later had to face alone. When she was thirty-nine, her husband died, leaving her with six small children and a business to run.

"When my husband died, I was frightened but knew I had to take care of the children. I guess it helped that I had experienced my father's determination to raise a family without his spouse. I always remember him saying, 'You're the only one who thinks you can't make it.' "

Janice believes that her success, especially her financial success, comes from a combination of many things, but high on the list is her early upbringing and her father's constant encouragement.

Negative "father" messages, on the other hand, can foster financial dependency and self-doubt. Betty D. suffered from being raised in a family whose members were defined by strict gender roles. *"My father handled the finances and my mother knew nothing about it. My mother lived a sort of Doris Day existence; she never worked outside the home. In her thinking, if women went to college it was to find a man."*

Betty was a teacher but quit working to raise three children. She had expected that her husband would take care of all their economic needs and was brought up short when he walked out, leaving her in a financial bind. *"I thought that finding the right man would save me. Everyone I knew thought the same way, marriage was your goal, what you strived for; we certainly didn't think about careers."* There were few occupations that were acceptable for women: *" 'Just in case' jobs such as secretary, teacher, or nurse. The idea of getting an education in order to satisfy career goals and plan for an independent future never entered my mind. I certainly didn't think about money—that was a 'man's thing,' or so I thought."*

Even though her father was a "benign presence," his indirect message to Betty was that "women take care of the home front and men take care of the money front." Her value and survival rested solely on attracting a husband who would take care of her, and so she repeated the family pattern by marrying a man who took charge of their money.

After the divorce, Betty had to play financial catch-up. She is making progress and trying to put money away for her future, but she realizes that those early "family snapshots" of her father handling all the money while women weren't supposed to worry their pretty little heads about such things have hindered her achieving financial independence. To her credit, since Betty was brought to full financial alert, she has managed to get her financial house in order and is prepared for the future.

Joanne P. was another woman who left the financial starting gate late, largely because of early family socialization—in particular, her father's controlling behavior. *"My father was raised to believe that men handled the money in the family. He always handled the finances—the paying of bills, making decisions, etc. Except once, he allowed my mother to do it. I'm not sure what happened exactly, but I remember him saying 'never again.' Even when my mother did work, her income was considered only supplemental and went toward savings for our schooling. My dad also thought women couldn't handle mechanical things   repairs or any-thing to do with the car."*

Joanne's family was poor, and she grew up fearful of not having enough money. Her clothes were hand-me-downs, and there was never money for anything beyond the essentials. As a result, Joanne grew up an obsessive saver, although not necessarily a wise decision-maker. It was only much later, when she could relax a little about her finances, that she began educating herself about money and became more interested in ways to make it grow.

Adolescence—a Time of Clipped Wings

During childhood, girls are molded mainly by their parents and are not yet required to conform to all of society's gender roles. Society still sanctions androgynous qualities in little ones. Both film and television pay homage to courageous kids of both sexes who act with authority and speak up for themselves (while still performing daring rescues, of course).

At this stage, a little girl can have boundless ambition; she can be competitive, athletic, achieving, competent, fearless, and questioning. If she so desires, she can run faster than anyone, climb trees higher than anyone, and sing as loudly as she pleases (preferably outside). Her body moves in sync with her mind and emotions, and she thinks, she plans, and she knows she is capable of anything. One day she decides to be a lawyer, another day it's a veterinarian or a great artist, and in her spare time she'll teach dance.

Rebecca E., forty-eight, first came to the NCWRR seminars shortly after her divorce, when she was wrestling with what to do with her settlement money. Though Rebecca works as an administrative assistant to a senior executive with a public utility company, she knew the divorce settlement was vital to her future security, and she found herself unable to decide how to manage it: *"I know I should move the money out of my money market account, but I'm afraid of losing the money by investing poorly, and I feel so dumb about everything that I don't even know how to go about asking advice."*

While growing up in a Long Island suburb, Rebecca started out with all the "right stuff." She says, *"I was always taking on dares that I could beat friends (both boys and girls) in swimming races or roller-skating. I loved adventure and had no fear of exploring parts of the woods behind our house where I'd been forbidden to go. My knees and elbows were always scraped because I didn't worry about anything; I believed I could do anything and handle anything that came my way."*

Rebecca was also an early entrepreneur: *"When I was ten and eleven, I sold Kool-Aid and cookies at a neighborhood stand during the summer. I loved to collect all those nickels and dimes and quarters. I remember how they clinked together as I put them in a brown paper bag.*

"At school I thought I had all the answers, and if I didn't I just asked until I understood. Many a summer night was spent lying in the hammock, dreaming of becoming a reporter and traveling to exotic places like Istanbul, Paris, Buenos Aires—being a free spirit that made a lot of money."

Rebecca, sassy and scrappy as a girl, wasn't afraid to take risks. She looked happily toward the future, was flexible in her approach to change, and had a strong sense of control over her life. Many adult women who take the time to reflect back on their preteen years might see the same qualities in themselves—qualities that can help women take charge of both their personal and financial lives.

However, when Rebecca entered her teen years, her once-strong voice was drowned out by newly cautious parental and societal messages. *"Those were confusing years. My father spent most of his time with my brother and distanced himself from me. They had long, serious talks, and all I heard about was curfews. My mother was full of 'shoulds' and 'don'ts.' She was on a crusade to keep me 'safe' and nagged constantly: 'Don't risk your reputation by hanging out with that group of kids,' or 'I don't want you getting too serious about that boy, or you'll risk getting pregnant,' or 'Don't go driving with those kids, you might be in an accident.' I felt like my whole being was 'at risk.' I became fearful when I never used to be.*

"At the same time, I was struggling to fit in with my friends. My old self wasn't what people wanted. I became obsessed with my looks. My grades dropped because I was so focused on being accepted by the 'right' crowd, and I began to feel stupid. I became a nonperson. I worked summers, but quickly spent the money on clothes, makeup, and junk. There no longer was a brown bag full of clinking quarters, only a closet full of stuff that I thought would make me popular, beautiful, and happy, but it never did."

The girl in the hammock who dreamed of her future as a free-spirited reporter was replaced by a girl who could not think beyond her next Saturday night date.

Rebecca grew up but never recaptured that confident younger voice. She entered adulthood, as she described it, "feeling like I had just been airdropped over a foreign country."

She continues: *"On the outside I seemed like an adult. I got a secretarial job and shared an apartment with two other girls and continued spending my paycheck as fast as I got it. The women's movement was in full swing and I thought of myself as a liberated woman. What a joke. I was clueless as to what being independent meant. I was still listening unquestioningly to everybody, including the women in the women's movement. I was incapable of making hard decisions about where my life, money, and future were going.*

"Then Ted came along and offered me marriage and a 'future.' I listened to him, and we got married. He handled all the money and made all the decisions affecting our household and financial lives. I worked and took care of the house and the kids. I thought I was an independent working mom. I was in charge of buying things for the kids and the house, but I never went beyond that. Planning for my own financial future never even entered my head.

"Divorce put a different spin on my life. I found myself alone facing some hard choices. Right now I'm getting along day-to-day. The kids have finished college and are independent for now, but the future scares me. I have my settlement money, but until I get over this financial paralysis, I'm stuck."

Rebecca has hit a wall, and she can't move forward with her life or her money. Though financial seminars will provide her with the framework she needs to build her financial future, Rebecca's true gains will come when she looks at *why* she isn't able to focus on taking care of herself. If she overcomes the negative messages that beset her in adolescence, she will realize that women should—and must—start taking charge of themselves. In turn, this should release Rebecca from her paralysis, and she'll be better prepared to become financially independent.

Young girls who have been the recipients of a positive family upbringing are not afraid of taking risks; their voices and inner sense of control are strong. Their unlimited dreams make them very future-oriented. They are open to change, and their positive self-image makes many of them forthright decision-makers. All the qualities that the Women Cents Study found to be positive personality traits in adulthood are generally found in abundance, undiluted by society, in preadolescent girls.

Then, on the eve of adolescence, the challenge (and inherent insecurity) of going from girl to teen to woman silences that once-strong voice. Even in this age of women's liberation, adolescent girls are encouraged to conform and develop more "feminine" traits. Their skills, strong voices, and "can do" attitudes are undermined by society's messages: Be popular, be attractive to boys, be thin, quiet, and nice. If she was a tomboy or daredevil in elementary school, the adolescent's actions are now labeled unfeminine. Her sense of adventure and risk-taking is now dampened by concerns for safety and acting well behaved and polite. She has difficulty projecting herself into the future and sees only a string of todays.

While adolescent boys are being told they will have unlimited opportunities in life, a girl's world is contracting. In spite of women's progress, the world's hypnotic chant to teen girls is full of gender stereotypes, distorted images of femininity, and sexual objectification. When a girl stops listening to her authentic voice and vacates her inner self, the only validation left is from external sources. If these outside sources disapprove or reject her, she is left devastated and vulnerable.

Family Self-Test

The goal of this exercise is to begin to understand how your early parental relationships could have helped you leave your financial "starting gate" quickly and well prepared, or how these relationships could have delayed your journey to financial independence. Check off "yes" or "no," as appropriate.

	YES	NO
1. Did your parents openly discuss financial matters with you?	☐	☐
2. Did your parents share family financial decision-making?	☐	☐
3. Do you feel that your parents adequately prepared you to become an independent adult?	☐	☐

YES   NO

4. As a child, did your parents encourage you to work and save your money? ☐ ☐

5. Did you feel valued by your father? ☐ ☐

6. Did you feel valued by your mother? ☐ ☐

7. Do you draw upon positive lessons you learned about money from your parents? ☐ ☐

8. Did your parents praise your achievements and abilities? ☐ ☐

9. As a child, were you encouraged to make decisions? ☐ ☐

10. Did your parents encourage your future dreams and goals? ☐ ☐

SCORING AND ANALYSIS

Add up your "yes" responses and your "no" responses.

More "yeses" than "nos" means that your childhood provided good preparation for becoming independent and confident. A high number of "nos" indicates you had a delayed start.

If you had a high "yes" score, you can give your parents some thanks for having helped to foster your independence and for valuing you as a special person who could take care of herself. If you didn't have a high "yes" score, don't despair or give up and think that just because you didn't have the greatest encouragement as a child, you are doomed to be a financial disaster. There are other ways a woman can pick up speed and become independent and a good financial decision-maker.

If your parents failed to be good role models:

- Use the women in this book as role models. The characteristics and traits that are necessary to control your financial future are depicted in many of these anecdotes.
- Recognize that regardless of the messages you received concerning money and your competence to handle it, you can get support and guidance from other women. A good way is to join an investment club. It is never too late to regain lost financial ground.
- Although it is popular these days to blame others (particularly our parents) for our problems, the most important aspect of

being able to move forward is to put the past in perspective and learn from it.

We'll add into this mix the influence of education before moving on to explore what you *must* do to break the hammerlock of financial helplessness.

4

EDUCATION
Missed Starts for Too Many Girls

---

*"I remember in elementary school feeling embarrassed
in math class if I didn't have the right answer the
first time around. Boys got answers wrong sometimes,
but for some reason it didn't seem to bother
them as much."*

Over the years, I have been continually struck by women's lack of comfort with the topic of personal finance. I have attempted to explore why more men don't reflect the same degree of anxiety. I sometimes facetiously wonder if there is a "gender gene" that dictates interest in financial planning. Why has it been so difficult for me—and others in the world of finance—to motivate millions of women to invest their dollars for the future?

As an educator, I am now more convinced than ever that the traits that make a good, proactive investor (risk-taking, flexibility, control, and so on) could be cultivated and nurtured in early educational experiences, but unfortunately, even today they generally are not. I now believe that the reason why some women embrace financial planning and others have difficulty coming to grips with the subject can be directly traced to gender differences in classroom treatment and the family's support (or lack of support) of education.

To date, much of the focus on gender discrimination in education has been on the fact that girls are not encouraged to do well
in math and the sciences, and recent groundbreaking NCWRR
studies show that there is a circular relationship between math,
science, gender, and self-esteem. Previous studies have indicated
that girls are not encouraged in math and the sciences; the recent
Dreyfus Gender Investment Comparison Survey we conducted is
the first to explore the impact this discrimination has on women
in their later years.

What we found is that proactive investment behavior can be
clearly traced to self-confidence and math abilities. Unfortunately,
our study also showed that this self-confidence among girls declines
with age. During elementary school, girls' self-confidence concerning math was much higher than after high school. The survey,
which involved both men and women, showed a tremendous post–
high school gender gap concerning math abilities and confidence.
The study also revealed that:

1. Women who were challenged by a mother, a father, or both
   to be highly competitive academically were more likely to feel
   more comfortable with math subjects in both elementary
   school and high school.
2. Women who indicated they had teachers who were supportive had high levels of confidence in their academic abilities
   while in school and were more likely as adults to consider
   themselves proactive investors. In fact, the research demonstrates a strong relationship between academic confidence
   and positive investment behavior during adulthood.
3. In contrast, women who felt unsupported either by parents
   or by teachers had a tendency to save less in midlife.
4. Women who were least comfortable with math during high
   school and had low self-esteem were three times more likely
   in midlife to fear not having enough money in old age. They
   also tended to prefer simple, guaranteed investments and
   were more likely to worry about their present financial security.
5. Women who were most comfortable with math during high
   school had a greater tendency to feel they had more control
   over their present finances.

6. Women who perceived themselves to have "very good" self-esteem throughout their elementary and high school years were three times more likely to see themselves as "experienced investors" and were less risk averse.

When everything works in tandem—the family believes strongly in education and the schools provide appropriate and gender-free support—women are better prepared to take advantage of the financial opportunities long available to men.

If women continue to think, or have been encouraged to think, that they are deficient in math or that they lack some sort of "math gene," they will persist in shying away from taking responsibility for managing their financial lives and keep turning this task over to others.

I don't believe women as a group lack interest in finance; I believe that in most cases they have not been given the opportunity to nurture their financial prowess. This chapter will show you how your educational experience may have played a role in hindering your financial self-confidence and how you can still benefit even though the system may have initially done you an injustice.

Just as we saw in the last chapter how positive parenting has a decided impact, a positive, gender-neutral educational experience can give a girl the resilience, confidence, and strength that are necessary for making sound decisions, thinking positively about the future, being willing to take risks, and maintaining flexibility in meeting life's challenges—all qualities that are necessary for developing strong financial skills.

However, the wonderful thing about education is that it is a lifelong endeavor—what is not obtained at one stage can be corrected at another. Later in the chapter you'll read some inspiring stories of women who found ways to make up for lost time by spearheading their own self-education.

Remembering Your Own Past

This exercise is to remind you of your own early educational experience and how it may have helped you leave the financial starting gate quickly and well prepared, or how it may have held you back.

EDUCATIONAL SELF-TEST

Answer yes or no to the following questions.

TEEN YEARS AND EDUCATION

	YES	NO
1. Did you have high hopes for a well-paying career?	☐	☐
2. Did your parents encourage you to go to college?	☐	☐
3. Were you academically confident in high school?	☐	☐
4. Were you confident about your math abilities?	☐	☐
5. Were you confident about your science abilities?	☐	☐
6. Did teachers or counselors encourage you to take courses that were academically demanding?	☐	☐
7. Were your academic abilities praised by teachers?	☐	☐
8. Were your academic abilities praised by parents?	☐	☐
9. Was your self-esteem high in high school?	☐	☐

ADULT YEARS

	YES	NO
10. As an adult, have you gone back to school to take any type of classes?	☐	☐
11. Do you feel confident about working with numbers and mathematical problems?	☐	☐
12. Do you feel confident handling your personal finances?	☐	☐
13. Would you seek to educate yourself on financial matters that you do not understand?	☐	☐
14. Do you feel you are as smart as anyone else about handling money?	☐	☐

SCORING AND ANALYSIS

Add up your "yes" responses and your "no" responses.

If you had a high number of "yeses," you left the starting gate early and were well prepared to start building an independent and financially secure life If you had too many "nos," you have gained awareness right now. It is important for you to realize you have to become proactive and begin learning to manage your own financial life now. Remember, there is no math gene. You can do it!

Women Are Educationally Disadvantaged

Unfortunately, the world is slow to change. Studies show that many schools still uphold and reinforce society's gender-stereotyped values. (Recent studies indicate a narrowing of the gender gap in testing, but there is still more progress to be made.)

To begin with, there's a problem with curriculum. All day, girls sit in classes and receive subliminal messages that women's lives count for less than men's. In textbooks, only one-seventh of all illustrations of children are of girls, and boys are twice as likely to be depicted as role models. Girls are also exposed to almost three times as many boy-centered stories as girl-centered stories. Boys are generally portrayed as clever, brave, creative, and resourceful, and girls are depicted as kind, dependent, and docile. Girls also read six times as many biographies of men as of women.

Historian Linda Kerber suggests a connection between falling self-esteem and this curricular omission and bias. According to Kerber, "Lowered self-esteem is a reasonable result if one has been subtly instructed that what people like oneself have done in the world has not been important and is not worth studying."

The American Association of University Women is an organization that has undertaken a broad range of studies relative to the impact of education on female self-esteem. According to one AAUW report, girls are not encouraged to take personal credit for their achievements: Girls are more likely to attribute their success to luck, while boys are given cause to attribute their success to ability. As a result, boys are more likely to feel mastery and control over academic challenges, while girls are more likely to feel powerless.

Other findings reported by the AAUW include the following.

- Teachers give girls less attention, less praise, less effective feedback, and less detailed instruction than they give boys.
- Too often teachers and counselors track girls away from courses of study that lead to high-paying, high-tech careers.

- As a result of the educational bias, girls' self-esteem begins to erode, taking away many of their dreams and aspirations. (Girls are much more likely to say they are not smart enough or good enough for their dream career.)

A case in point is the experience of forty-eight-year-old Jill S., who is an example of what happens when teachers and the educational system do not support and nurture a girl's abilities, goals, and confidence.

"I was an A student through my sophomore year in high school and had aspired to become a veterinarian. That was until my male guidance counselor informed me that as a woman, I probably wouldn't get into Cornell University and that I would only end up getting married. He also informed me that it was more important for boys to get an education because they would be the breadwinners. I can't tell you how dejected this made me feel. I felt very naive and somehow believed my parents hadn't told me the truth about how the world really worked. I never recovered from that episode and was a mediocre student for the rest of my high school career."

When she was a senior, Jill was accepted at the University of Maine, but chose to attend a local two-year teachers college. She had come to believe it was more important for her parents to be able to pay for her younger brother's education.

MATH AND SCIENCE: BAROMETERS FOR THE FUTURE

Thus far, the AAUW's studies have concentrated largely on math and science ability, areas traditionally stereotyped as "male." Their studies have documented what happens to girls when they enter this boy-oriented arena. In elementary school, math is just another subject that girls tend to like; as a matter of fact, the study reports that 81 percent of girls in elementary school like math, with 24 percent citing it as their favorite subject. By the time they reach high school, however, only 61 percent of girls like math at all, and only 12 percent mention it as their favorite subject, while 28 percent name it as their *least* favorite subject. Moreover, by high school, only one in seven girls say they are good at math.

Unfortunately, this math and science "wall" puts women at a great disadvantage:

- When girls "learn" that they are not good at these subjects, their self esteem and aspirations deteriorate.
- Students who like math and science are more likely to aspire to careers as professionals.
- Girls who like math hold on to their career dreams more stubbornly and are less likely to believe they will end up being something other than what they want to be.

The Dreyfus Gender Investment Comparison Survey showed that in elementary school there was less difference between boys' and girls' attitudes toward math, with men only twice as likely as women to report they felt comfortable with math. By high school, men were three times as likely as women to report they felt comfortable with math subjects.

When you examine the studies closely, what is important to note is that the drop in confidence *preceded* the decline in achievement. In other words, it is a girl's perception of ability or lack of ability that partially determines whether she will succeed or fail in these courses.

Mary Pipher, author of *Reviving Ophelia,* notes: "Girls have trouble with math because math requires exactly the qualities that many junior high school girls lack—confidence, trust in one's own judgment, and the ability to tolerate frustration without becoming overwhelmed. Anxiety interferes with problem-solving in math. A vicious circle develops—girls get anxious, which interferes with problem-solving, and so they fail and are even more anxious and prone to self-doubt the next time around."

If a "can do" approach helps, then boys have girls beat hands down. In the Dreyfus Gender Investment Comparison Survey, men were three times as likely to agree with the following statement: "During my high school years, if I experienced an academic problem or other type of failure, my reaction would be to try it again." When boys have trouble with a math problem, they are more likely to think the problem is hard but to stay with it. When girls have trouble, they think they are stupid and tend to give up.

This finding illustrates the point that boys are often more likely than girls to be *encouraged* to try again. Women have not been in an educational environment that cultivates this trait, and that explains the following finding from the Dreyfus Gender Investment Comparison Survey:

In responding to the statement "I am comfortable working with numbers and problems that require mathematical computations," over 58 percent of males and only 30 percent of females strongly agreed.

This speaks to women's *perception* of feeling less adequate in dealing with numbers. When we get women to participate in educational seminars or investment clubs, however, their *actual* math abilities prove to be quite solid. In other words, a woman's perception of her math ability is often inaccurate. Women are often quite good at math, but the educational system has led them to feel ill prepared.

Solving math problems and dealing with finance certainly require problem-solving skills and analytical abilities, but we don't do justice to nurturing intuition (a sixth sense) when it comes to finance. Later in this book we will explain how intuition can play an important role in making investment decisions. It is my guess that girls would end up being much more confident, savvy investors (and possibly more comfortable math students) if they were allowed to add intuitive thought to the process. I strongly believe that math classes are based on a "male model" of thought that doesn't take into consideration all the possibilities.

Some school systems have experimented with separating girls from boys in math class, and they've discovered a wonderful thing: The girls feel comfortable speaking out and showing support for each other in problem-solving exercises, and the success rate is showing the effectiveness of this method. We've found a similar situation with NCWRR female financial seminars and investment clubs. Because the environment is supportive and nonthreatening, women feel more comfortable.

Certain traits that are inherent in both boys and girls (for example, problem-solving and analytical abilities) are not reinforced in girls by the current educational system. However, these traits don't disappear—they lie dormant until reinforcement is provided. These all-female classrooms have provided an opportunity for girls to develop abilities that might well have been snuffed out in coed math classrooms where, certainly by high school, boys tend to dominate. Without this type of support, it is more difficult for women to feel comfortable developing investment skills.

How Your Parents Valued Education Made a Difference Too

Whether or not women do well in the area of finance is also heavily dependent on whether or not they received parental encouragement to excel in school.

Girls whose parents valued them and saw the necessity of a good education have likely grown up to be adults who are comfortable dealing with money.

The following women were lucky. Their parents taught them to value education and instilled them with a lust for learning. While reading about these women is inspiring, remember that it's never too late to learn. Whether you attend a financial seminar, join an investment club, or find a positive role model among your peers, there are still plenty of opportunities for educating yourself. And to put an even more positive spin on it, this time you know what you're looking for, so your search will be positive and directed.

Keisha R. is an example of a woman for whom everything "clicked." She is a soft-spoken, intelligent native Ethiopian who emigrated to the United States. Education was very important to her family, especially to her father. She and her sisters all went to private school; part of the arrangement involved the daughters' contributing to their own tuition.

"Growing up, I was close to my father. He was a civil engineer before he started his own business. I used to go to the office with him, and I always knew I wanted to be an engineer like him. I was never discouraged in my choice, but he hinted that accounting might be easier, because the mathematics required for engineering might be too difficult." Even this supportive father was not immune to societal messages about girls and math. He knew Keisha was good at numbers, but he felt that accounting was safer and would be less stressful for her.

However, because her family believed in her and believed in her ability to excel, Keisha viewed her father's doubt as a challenge. *"I wanted to prove him wrong. I studied hard and was an excellent student and graduated at the top of my class. I did this for myself but also to show I was more than able to handle the work."*

Keisha persevered and became an engineer with the California State Transportation System. *"I know my father is very proud of me and my success."*

Linda J. is a personable, assertive, and risk-tolerant woman who also defied society's strictures. *"Neither of my parents was college-educated, but they stressed education for their children. I was very good in math and science and was confident with those subjects. In fact, the reason I'm an economist is that my mother plainly stated to me that I was good in those subjects, and while I could be a teacher, I'd make a better living as an economist. She always pointed out that marriage was great, but she'd rather see a degree on the wall. She is very independent and instilled that in me too; I'm just as outspoken and driven.*

"Throughout school my teachers were also very encouraging. When I was in grade school, we moved from Illinois to Michigan and my teacher was concerned about my math skills. My mother simply bought some flash cards and worked with me night after night until I was up to speed with the rest of the class."

Linda marvels at how she missed negative messages such as "a girl doesn't have a head for math," which are still so much a part of school today: *"My fifth grader, a boy, came home recently and said, 'Girls aren't good at math.' I said, 'I'm good at math, aren't I, and Grandma's good at math too, and we're girls.' Because of my positive experiences in childhood, I sometimes forget that there is still this stereotyping going on. When he was in kindergarten, I visited my son's classroom and was quite perturbed when I saw a bulletin board showing 'Jobs Boys Like to Do' picturing doctors, construction workers, firemen, etc., and 'Jobs Girls Like to Do' picturing movie stars and fashion models. The teacher didn't even realize what subtle messages these kids were getting. I talked with the principal and the pictures were removed, but I think the point is that this is where stereotyping begins—as early as kindergarten, if not before."*

Linda's self-confidence, good education, and ease with all academic subjects put her on a positive life path. She was hired as an economist shortly after graduation, and all through her adult life she has been investing and carefully managing her money. She is comfortable and confident with the financial world.

"I personally don't work with a broker. I listen to advice but I consider myself very informed and if there's a mistake to be made, I want to make it myself. Initially, I started educating myself by reading trade magazines, looking at financial programs on television, researching at the library, and studying the Value Line. Now I do a lot of research over the Internet. As far as making decisions to buy or sell investments, the decision is 100 percent mine."

Early education and gender-free confidence building in math

and science, as well as encouragement to strive for a challenging career, put Linda in a position to be financially secure. She continues to educate herself on financial matters and is a woman who is in control and well informed, but she need not be unique. Financial seminars, investment clubs, advisors, and supportive friends can all act as surrogate teachers. No woman needs to suffer for the rest of her life because of what happened in the past.

It's Never Too Late: New Learning and Financial Independence in Adulthood

Early education may have a negative impact on the self-esteem of girls, but the NCWRR study on Gender, Identity, and Self-Esteem found that women who continue to educate themselves, both formally and informally, can enhance self-esteem and continue personal growth during adulthood. Sixty percent of the respondents had returned to school as adults, and 90 percent of the women surveyed felt this additional education had contributed to their positive self-esteem. And, as our studies have revealed, this positive self-esteem will eventually result in more positive investment practices.

When women are resourceful and open to change, they can gain the practical knowledge they need, and in the process they are able to create better lives for themselves. They must, however, overcome the first hurdle—understanding that it is *never* too late. Initially, self-doubt may hold them back. As they begin to gain confidence, however, women are among the best, brightest, and most eager learners I have seen.

Multiple NCWRR studies have shown that there are specific steps women can take to overcome their "late start":

- Women who join investment clubs and regularly participate for one year (a form of education) become more risk tolerant as their participation proceeds.
- Women who indicate they have a female financial mentor have higher savings rates than those who indicate they have no financial mentor.
- Women who continue to pursue educational goals beyond high school tend to have a more positive attitude toward money and are more financially prepared for retirement.

We have already heard from Betty D., who grew up in a family that lived by strict gender roles (the Doris Day syndrome, she called it). Her early upbringing repeated itself when she married and became a traditional homemaker like her mother, until divorce put an end to her old lifestyle and her financial security. Following this wake-up call, Betty went back to school to retool for a career.

"Since the teaching market had dried up in the eighties, and I had no other skills, I took a job in retail but found it cost more than I was making to maintain the large station wagon I was driving to work. It was such a blow to my ego after belonging to the country club and living an upper-middle-class lifestyle to have to grovel to twenty-three-year-old supervisors."

Betty enrolled in a new adult education program studying theology. Additionally, she went to night school to earn a master's degree. In 1984 a large church in Philadelphia was looking for someone interested in youth and women's industries. *"I convinced them to hire me and fortunately had a very supportive and creative mentor who worked with me to devise interesting programs."* As her self-esteem increased, Betty became more confident about speaking up for what she wanted to do, and with early successes, this confidence grew.

Having improved her job and her financial situation, Betty began saving money and realized she needed to educate herself about how to manage and invest for her future. *"I've always been a good saver. I now have about $10,000 in a savings account and own my own home, but I never learned how to make my money grow."*

Betty has made important changes in her life, but her marital crisis made her realize she had to do more to secure her future. *"It's frightening. You can't count on the government. You can't count on anything. That in itself has given me the impetus to learn more. I often ask myself why I wasn't paying attention before. But I know why. Because I let a man do it for me."*

Betty, and women like her, actually benefit by coming to the learning process at a later stage of development. They bring to their financial education a "commodity" that younger learners simply don't have—experience. As a result, they see the tremendous relevance of the material presented. It is much easier to convince a woman that she needs to evaluate her financial future when she is a divorced mother who is at least partially responsible for her children's college education.

Ellie M. had a rough start because her parents took the view that education was wasted on girls. Ellie might have lacked a formal education and had to waitress most of her life, but she had the good sense to keep a separate savings account in her own name because she couldn't trust her husband not to spend everything.

"I began to realize that our family suffered because of my husband's irresponsible money management. I always felt I picked up the slack. I made very good money waitressing and I didn't mind working, but our life was becoming a nightmare. At thirty, with one child, I left. I really thought I would get married again. I dated a charming man but found his possessive nature more than I could stand. After this last relationship it dawned on me that this was it. I had to start thinking about fending for myself because no one was going to take care of me. It was a very precarious position considering that I had never planned for the future, but at least I'm taking action now.

"I've really started to educate myself about financial planning and money. I'm still working at waitressing and catering, but I learned that all my jobs off the books aren't going to help me when it comes to my retirement benefits. I'm doing a lot of reading and looking into investment clubs, and I met with a financial planner recommended by a friend. This year I began contributing to an IRA; I feel like I'm making a good start."

Ellie has become a self-learner and has taken important steps toward educating herself and acquiring the knowledge that will allow her to build a secure financial life. What women like Ellie are demonstrating is an exciting new trend: viewing education as a life-long process that is not confined to the classroom.

CONTINUING ED

Keisha R., the engineer whose family supported her quest for education, found that even then she was lacking when it came to knowledge of personal finance: *"I had been working for four and a half years when one day some coworkers were talking about our company benefits. It made me really furious when I realized that I'd missed some elements from which I could have been benefiting. After some research, I enrolled in the retirement plan they'd been discussing, and at the same time realized that there was probably a lot more I needed to learn regarding my own personal finances. It just seemed unthinkable that I could be so successful in other areas of my professional and personal life and know nothing about taking care of myself financially.*

"As I began to research women and finances, I was left with a lot of questions. If men and women are paid equally, why does it appear to be women who are inadequately informed about finances? Mainly, my problem was in the area of understanding different types of investments and the basics of financial planning. I wrote to the NCWRR and got further information about seminars and educational materials. I took notes from the materials I read and made plans to attend a financial seminar."*

Unlike many women who suddenly get a wake-up call to start financial planning in their middle and older years, Keisha was in her twenties when she realized she needed to start taking action. By starting so young she will be way ahead of the game when it comes to making her future financially sound.

As she states: *"I feel it's very important for a woman to plan for herself. I know a lot of women I attended school with who wanted to get married for financial stability. I wanted to get married to have a family and share the responsibilities, not to have someone take care of me. I believe you should be equal in a partnership, and you cannot do that if you are less educated in certain areas."*

The word "education" keeps appearing in Keisha's narrative about her life experience. She is a woman who has been encouraged all her life to inform and educate herself. This is a path that will continue to make her a self-reliant, independent, and financially savvy woman.

Marian T., introduced earlier, had several strong female role models—a mother and two grandmothers—whom Marian wished to emulate, so when her husband deferred to her, Marian was prepared. Her mother had been the money manager in the family, and Marian went on to assume that role. *"Since my husband wasn't interested, it was decided that I would be the one to learn how to make our money grow. As he put it, 'I'll be a money pump and you learn to manage it.'"*

Marian had the confidence to gather the financial information that would secure her family's nest egg. *"The first thing I did was attend a financial seminar I had seen advertised in a flyer at work. I invited two friends and we found it to be very interesting. I did need to learn more, although I was a bit more sophisticated than some of the women who attended who had actually never even written a check or paid a bill.*

The woman presenting the seminar seemed genuinely interested in educat-ing women and encouraged us to participate in our own investing. The suggestion to join an investment club seemed a good one because not only could it be fun, but it would provide a structure with deadlines that needed to be met. It was a concrete framework from which to start and gave the direction that is so important when you are just beginning."

Marian also expanded her understanding of financial matters by outside reading: *"I started going to the library and reading* Value Line *in order to research stocks. I regularly read* Fortune *and* Money *magazines. I use an on-line service and the Internet to obtain company profiles. I didn't do any investing for six months, but allowed myself that time to gather information and observe. After about seven months I purchased several stocks and mutual funds on my own. Now my friends and I discuss stocks and the market all the time. I even got my husband interested, and he makes suggestions as well. While I'm doing all the investing with my own funds at present, eventually we will be investing together. I find it interest-ing that I now read the business section of the paper before anything else. I feel that I have managed my life well, and I can do that with my finances too."*

The strong role models provided by her grandmothers and mother had a favorable effect on Marian's ability to handle both her own money and the investments she is making jointly with her husband.

Being able to aspire to a professional career, manage money, and make investment decisions with confidence, skill, and authority de-pends in part on a woman's positive and early education. However, we have also learned that even when women lack that early support-ive environment, they can still obtain the life and financial skills that are necessary to build a more financially secure future. Educa-tion is a lifelong process, and adults who had a bad educational start can make up a lot of ground by going back to school to gain job skills and financial information.

A Look to the Future

I wish I could end this chapter by predicting that life for our daughters is looking better and better, but unfortunately, I can't. Girls today have it both easier and harder than their mothers did. Yes, there are more career opportunities open to women; they are earning more money; there is more legislation to help women fight discrimination; and many gender issues are being discussed, debated, and researched.

However, adolescent girls, like their mothers, are surrounded by a culture that still limits their full development and is responsible for stunting their emotional growth. Young girls grow up in a "junk culture" saturated with abuse, danger, and sexist messages in media, advertising, music, and films. Physical appearance and the desperate urge to be thin are still the main markers for many girls who look to their bodies and faces for self-esteem while hiding their academic achievements. Girls are bombarded by messages that provoke drastic and often harmful behavior—from eating disorders and depression to alcohol and drug abuse and sexual promiscuity—all of which impact on their ability to negotiate and prepare for a secure adult life.

College Women: Smart Enough to See What's Happened

Over the last five years, I have had the opportunity to discuss financial issues with my undergraduates at Southampton College. What I've learned about their level of knowledge in matters of money management and investing is very disturbing. One overriding conclusion is that younger females (eighteen to twenty-two) are ill equipped to deal with the financial realities that await them.

Education has placed little emphasis on helping students understand the importance of such basic skills as maintaining a checkbook, managing credit, or securing a pension. Although Generation X females realize that the world is not perfect, they are uncertain, angry, and frustrated over how to gain a foothold. Stephanie Trent, a twenty-two-year-old about to graduate, wrote to me, expressing the following:

> Throughout my four years of college I have learned a lot that discourages me. In my sociology courses I've learned that marriage is an uncertain bet. In my political science courses I found that it will be unlikely that Social Security or Medicare will be around when I get old.
>
> Now you, Professor Hayes, are telling all of us that we better plan for our financial future. Plan for what? As a group, we

have been exposed to problem after problem, but little has been said concerning what to do about it.

In two months I will be graduating with $18,000 worth of loans. I have sent out 125 résumés and haven't gotten any interest yet. All I can think about now is getting a job—the idea of worrying about a pension or starting a savings program is beyond me. If you want the honest truth, many of us are angry. We are questioning how we are going to make it financially. I know many of my friends will have to move back in with their parents because they can't find a job.

If there is one universal observation I can make about young adult women, it is that they want all the same things their mothers wanted (a caring spouse, a secure job, a house). What's fascinating is that neither their parents nor the educational system prepared them for the financial realities they face. One must question why more mothers who fought so hard to find an identity didn't communicate the need to secure a firm financial foothold in the world. Or why more fathers didn't stress to their daughters the importance of basic financial skills. The aftermath can be seen in the following example.

Lynn R. is a twenty-six-year-old single woman who just recently was able to move into an apartment of her own. For the last two years, she has been making $28,000 a year. She has been unable to find a permanent position in elementary education, so she has worked as a substitute to try to maintain contacts for the future. Since her subbing brings in only $10,000 a year, she works nights at a local Toys 'R' Us store. She is often exhausted and questions the value of her college degree.

"Last year I hit a real crisis," she explains. *"The only way I could make ends meet was to max out on my credit card. My balance was over $10,000 and I couldn't keep up with the payments. I didn't know what else to do but ask my father for help. He gave me the money to pay the balance down but made me feel like a real heel. He said he had put me through college and was angry that he was still responsible for me financially. I don't think he really understands how hard it is.*

"When I look back over my education, none of my teachers or professors talked about financial management. To this day, we don't talk about money in my own house unless we get into some kind of financial trouble.

Getting out of college and trying to make it financially was like hitting a brick wall at ninety miles an hour!

"To be honest, I don't like to think about the future. My head is directed toward right here—now."

Many, like Lynn, are adrift in a world they don't feel they can control. Instead of looking to the future with positive anticipation, all they see is uncertainty and too few answers.

Although young men also struggle with making ends meet after college, there is one significant difference that cannot be denied. Young men have a greater chance of acquiring jobs with higher salaries, which will help to free them of debt. Even though we are close to entering the next millennium, younger women are still disproportionately represented in professions such as teaching and social work, which do not command top dollar. At the same time, younger women still have too few female role models or mentors in the business sector to help guide them toward a brighter financial future.

It is, therefore, critical that educators, parents, and society recognize that we need to cultivate confidence in both males and females, and that we should start teaching them financial awareness at a very young age.

In the meantime, keep reading. The point of this book is to help you overcome all that has preceded this day.

SECTION

II

5

DO YOU EVER TAKE
A CHANCE?
Understanding Your Level
of Risk Tolerance

---

*"I'm employed as a money manager and deal with
huge sums of money every day, but when it comes to
my own investments, I'm very uncomfortable with
taking a risk. My parents raised us to be security-
conscious, and I just can't tolerate the thought that I
might make a mistake and lose principal."*

W hat does the phrase "financial freedom" mean to you?
When men are asked this question, most answer, "Independence." They are likely to add: "I want to be free from having to
work and to be able to do what I want when I want."

What does "financial freedom" mean to women? When asked,
they answer: "Security."

This very simple response speaks volumes about why women
have not been as aggressive at risk-taking as men.

Every day the women we see at NCWRR express their concern
about security—the thirty-one-year-old self-supporting single who
has come to the realization that she'd better start planning for her

financial future; the forty-year-old mother who knows just how far
the money has to stretch each month; the forty-five-year-old divorcée who came out of a marital separation with much less than she
expected; the fifty-two-year-old widow who was left with less money
than she expected because of the way her husband set up his estate;
and the sixty-five-year-old retiree who realizes how vital it is that
she learn to manage the money she has. All these women have one
major question on their minds: "Will I have enough money to take
care of myself (and my family)?"

Yet, when told that long-term financial security will require some
investing—putting their money somewhere other than a savings account—they are very uncomfortable at the thought of risking what
money they have. Typical of those who come to the Center is Jean
F., a forty-year-old married mother of two who works full-time. *"My
husband and I work hard for what we have. We're putting away a little
for our children's education and some for our retirement too. I guess the
bank doesn't offer that good a deal on my money, but I just don't like the
thought of possibly losing what I have. I don't want to go backward with
my money; I want to feel secure, and I want to feel that by working and
saving we're making progress with what we're putting away.*

*"Even if I did want to get into riskier investments with higher returns,
I just don't know enough. I'd probably lose it all."*

Unfortunately, Jean is doing the very thing she wanted to
avoid—going backward with her money—because, between taxes
and inflation, Jean's savings, if left in a savings account, are guaranteed to be worth less over time. If Jean can overcome her fear of risk-
taking, she will be comfortable moving her savings into instruments
that will do better for her over time.

Simply defined, risk-taking is a toleration of uncertainty. **To
reach for something more, one must be able to face the possibility of giving up what one already has.**

When it comes to financial risk, one difficulty is that of perception. Many women view financial risk right up there with activities
like skydiving or bungee jumping; and when they hear the term
"stock market," they imagine their money flying out the window.
Yet, realistically, a responsible financial advisor would never place
you in a high-risk investment unless you begged to be in it. Financial

risk-taking is nothing more than making well-planned investments that are subject to some price swings and the *chance* that returns will be less than expected.

Financial risk can be profitable and fun, and wise risk-taking doesn't have to be anything like bungee jumping. This chapter will talk about:

- How to change your perception of risk
- The value of risk-taking
- How your personality affects your risk tolerance level
- Why men are more aggressive about risk-taking (and how women can benefit)
- How to become a calculated risk taker and profit from the results

Remember that acquiring confidence in risk-taking is progressive. I constantly hear experts admonishing women to be better risk-takers. This is like telling someone who is fearful of public speaking to just "get up there and talk to the crowd." It's just not possible. But by proceeding one step at a time, you will become more and more risk tolerant. Start small and move on to more adventurous investments when you are ready.

Personality and Its Effect on Risk-Taking

One of the things we learned from the Women Cents Study is that women who have difficulty with financial risk-taking also have difficulty taking personal risks. For example, 59 percent of respondents preferred the known over the unknown (the safe vs. the unsafe), and 62 percent said they would only consider "safe" or "guaranteed" investments.

When I mention "personal risk," chances are you think of true-life adventures like going up in a hot-air balloon or riding the rapids of the Colorado. Far "riskier" are such decisions as getting married (there is no guarantee it will work out) or going back to school in your forties (who would have guessed you'd be a straight-A student this time round?). When you look back over your life, you could list the results of the risks you've taken under three column headings: "Successful," "Okay," "A Disaster."

Chances are you have a long list of risks that have worked out just fine (your two children? your last vacation? the job you took ten years ago that has resulted in your current career?). For most people, there are a good number of risks that were just okay, but relatively few that were outright disasters (though we've all had some!).

Typical of those who have participated in our studies is Emma G., a young woman who found that until she learned to take risks in life, taking risks with her money was unthinkable.

Emma was an only child, born to older parents who were both artists. Because her mother was the more financially successful of the two, her father ran the household and managed the money.

From a very early age, her father began grooming Emma for a career in art, and her life revolved around pleasing her father. As Emma herself says: *"I had very little confidence in myself. I really felt I couldn't displease him."*

When she was twenty-four, Emma's career as a photographer began to take off, and she finally moved to her own apartment. However, she continued to work from her parents' apartment, where her father ran the financial side of her photography business and critiqued and controlled her work. Her money was parceled out to her on an "as needed" basis.

A few years later, Emma's father died of cancer: *"I was twenty-seven, and it was time to learn to trust my own judgment and learn the financial side of my business.*

"For the first year after his death, I had to confront the fact that I was making some mistakes. One specific memory stands out: A major food company wanted a series of photographs for a new product. The director of advertising called me to submit a bid, and since I'd never done this before, every time I sat down at the computer, it was as if my father was looking over my shoulder. After a week of uncertainty, I put the bid together and sent it. I got the contract but learned later that I'd underbid the job by $3,000—practically doing it for nothing.

"During this time, I had another major revelation. I started bidding on photography jobs that we'd never competed for before because my father always told me they were for 'big-league photography shops.' I realized that my father had never reached his full potential because he was afraid of failure and avoided risks. I almost followed in his footsteps. But once I started taking risks, I found that while you're bound to have some

disappointments, there are successes too, as long as you're willing to take the chance.

"In the meantime, I took control over my finances and the business aspect of my career, and I started investing in the stock market. It gives me great satisfaction to know I'm in control of my life. I finally have the security of knowing I am in charge of my own destiny. I wish I could have learned that sooner."

Emma was able to move ahead after she evaluated her upbringing and started to take control of her financial future. This control allowed her to dictate the level of risk with which she was comfortable.

Risk-taking is often perceived as a static quality. In reality, however, one's tolerance for risk can fluctuate depending on one's circumstances, age, and worldview. For example, a woman could be a risk-taking, adventurous person, but if she experiences a sudden loss, she may feel temporarily insecure and this will decrease her risk tolerance. Your goal is to evaluate your financial needs and undertake investments that are in harmony with those needs at that time.

What Emma learned is that risk and security are not polar opposites. As it happens, taking calculated risks and periodically reevaluating your risk tolerance level are the keys to being secure.

Your Attitude Toward Risk in Life vs. Your Risk Behavior When It Comes to Money

Do you take risks in your personal life?

If so, you're ready to take some financial ones.

Look back at how you fared in the risk section (Section A) of the Self-Test in Chapter 2. If the results revealed that you're conservative in both areas, this chapter will show you how to become more risk tolerant, one step at a time. To learn more about how your personal and financial risk levels compare, take the following quiz.

DIRECTIONS

Below are statements that relate to how you perceive yourself versus what you actually do with your money. Answer each question as honestly as possible.

	YES	NO

1. **Personal life:** I am willing to take a trip with a spouse or good friend without knowing ahead of time what the ultimate destination will be.

2. **Financial life:** I am willing to invest a modest sum of money without being certain of the final rate of return.

3. **Personal life:** I am willing to loan a coworker $200 with the knowledge that it may take a while for me to be re-paid with interest.

4. **Financial life:** I am willing to invest $200 in a mutual fund and have the confidence that it will prove itself sometime in the future.

5. **Personal life:** Although it's emotionally painful, I am willing to terminate a long-term relationship that has gone sour.

6. **Financial life:** Although I initially believed an invest-ment was good, I am willing to "cut my losses" if it con-tinues to be unfruitful.

7. **Personal life:** I am willing to meet a stranger for lunch if he or she was highly recommended by a friend or busi-ness associate.

8. **Financial life:** In searching for a financial advisor, I am willing to meet him/her despite the fact that the only thing I know is what I've been told by others.

9. **Personal life:** I am willing to consider buying a dress marked 30 percent off, knowing that the initial price may have been inflated.

10. **Financial life:** I am willing to consider a stock that I'm told is undervalued, even though I don't yet know much about the industry.

11. **Personal life:** I am willing to chance flying in a storm, even though it may be a bumpy ride.

12. **Financial life:** I am willing to invest in the stock market, though I know it will go down as well as up.

ANALYSIS

If you find that the number of times you answered "yes" to the personal life questions is about equal to those in the financial area, you have developed a fine balance. However, if you had more "yes" responses in your personal life (reflecting a willingness to take personal risks) and were more conservative (more "no" answers) in the financial area, there are several things you can do. Evaluate what in your personal life makes you willing to take risks and consider how these qualities could help with financial risk-taking. For example, your willingness to terminate a relationship that has gone sour shows that you know when something is over; consider the criterion you might use for judging when it's time to sell a stock.

You can also slowly build your risk tolerance through education. The more you learn about something, the less frightening it is. After reading about investments in Section III, revisit your financial "no" statements and see whether you feel different now about your responses. If you do, recognize that, whenever you face a challenge, you can build risk tolerance by learning more about the subject.

Experts use a pyramid diagram to explain the various levels of risk in the financial world (see Chapter 18). The base of the pyramid (lowest level of risk) is your financial foundation—such as the equity you have in your home and your life and health insurance. The stronger your financial foundation, the easier it is to scale up the financial pyramid to higher-risk investments like mutual funds (scaled as moderate risk) or even the riskiest speculative stocks (which are at the top of the pyramid).

Personal risk works the same way. Women with a strong personal foundation find it easier to move up the "personal risk" pyramid. In the Women Cents Study, 79 percent of respondents indicated that they enjoyed new challenges (where risk is part of the package), and 61 percent described themselves as adventurous. These women have obviously found sound footing in their personal life; they just need to translate this risk tolerance to their financial life.

Where Do You Stand When It Comes to Financial Risk?

The Risk Tolerant vs. the Risk Averse

To further help you understand how you rank when it comes to risk tolerance, it might help you to know about the personality attributes defined in the Women Cents Study. Based on our survey, we found that various levels of risk-takers displayed different attributes. Read the following two profiles and see which sounds more like you.

PROFILE A

By nature, you are not an adventurer. You enjoy the predictable and you love being surrounded by friends and family. At work you particularly enjoy tasks you can control. When your boss drops something in your lap unexpectedly, it drives you crazy!

When it comes to money, you prefer safe, guaranteed investments. (You're not alone; 72 percent of our respondents did too.) To you, investing seems like gambling. Though you're beginning to worry about your future, financial planning seems pointless unless you have a lot of money to work with. As a result, setting aside money for savings just hasn't become a top priority.

Though you don't usually participate in financial discussions, when you do hear friends talking about market fluctuations, it makes you nervous just thinking about it! (Fifty-eight percent of the women surveyed agree with you.) You're happy just knowing that you have ready access to your money because it's right there in your savings account. (Fifty percent of women surveyed also prefer to keep their money where it is instantly available to them, a feature that isn't provided by some of the higher-interest investments.)

If this profile sounds like you, it probably comes as no surprise that you are *risk averse.* You have many qualities that are very natural and understandable, and by taking small steps toward slightly greater financial risks, you can retain your sense of security while still increasing the return on your investments.

PROFILE B

At heart, you have always believed that things will work out. While you're very deliberate in your decision-making, you are also someone who can "go with the flow." If a friend invites you for a spur-of-the-moment weekend in the country, you're likely to go. Sometimes you pay a price for your adventures. While it was fun to spend the weekend away, what are you going to do about the report you'd promised the boss you'd finish by Monday morning? Despite an occasional lapse, you enjoy your job, like to travel, and are always interested in meeting new people.

You have a planned savings program and are investing in order to reach certain financial goals, including a secure retirement. While you plan to learn more about investing, you've found that if you put your money in various savings instruments (long-term and short-term), you can do pretty well even though you don't have a huge amount to invest. Because you've kept some of your money accessible, you're willing to sock some money away in long-term investments. (Forty-eight percent of our survey respondents would agree with you.)

When you hear the stock report each evening on the news, you don't panic if the market is down. (Forty-two percent of our respondents say they can live with hearing about the ups and downs.) You have a basic trust that because you've spread your money around, any downward fluctuations won't be catastrophic. After all, you know that some risk is necessary to get ahead. (Ninety-four percent of women surveyed understood this, even though they weren't quite ready to put the belief into action.)

If you identify with this profile, you already know that you are *risk tolerant.* Though you may still want to do better, you've begun to master the art of taking measured risks. If you continue in this direction, you will become quite an investor.

If you identified with some of the qualities in each profile, that's normal too. If you related to the personality attributes of the risk tolerant but have not yet begun to take calculated risks with your money, take heart. You've already got the personal qualities you need. You're ready to start exploring how best to invest your money.

Why Men Are More Aggressive Risk-Takers

I do not believe that either men or women are born with a "risk gene." However, the nature of risk-taking has traditionally been perceived as a masculine characteristic.

In Chapters 3 and 4, you learned that upbringing has a tremendous effect on how you handle money. For that reason, it is interesting to examine why men, in general, become more risk tolerant than women. As you come to understand some of these basic gender differences, you may be able to make slight modifications in your approach to risk-taking that will make a world of difference.

In my own family, my father encouraged my brothers and me to earn money through outside jobs, and we were praised for being productive. My sister, however, received no such message.

Although there are dangers in generalizing, I have observed that men tend to be emotionally drawn to monetary risk, probably because of the way they've been raised. Men gain ego satisfaction from investing and seeing their money grow. As they accumulate more wealth, the process of investing becomes a game of identity enhancement. At the same time, if their investments lose money, men are more likely to see it as "just one of those things."

So, what motivates men to take financial risks? Here's just some of what they learn growing up:

1. **To get ahead, one must risk.** Although this is a simple statement, men often take it for granted that risk is a part of life. Men have many successful role models (e.g., Donald Trump) for whom risk-taking is second nature. In contrast, women have only recently had such role models. And although some women role models are beginning to become better known, there are few who are household names simply because of their business prowess. The women who have built great wealth tend to have become public figures for other reasons. For example, Oprah Winfrey has taken great risks with her career, and in the process she has built an extraordinarily successful financial empire. Jane Fonda turned exercise into a money machine, though the public had long known her as an actress and a member of a well-known family. Businesswomen like Muriel Siebert, the first woman to buy a seat on the New York Stock Exchange, and Katharine Graham, who took risks that let the *Washington Post* empire she had inherited thrive, are risk-takers and excellent role models but have never really reached the "household word" status achieved by some male empire builders.

2. **Financial risk-taking is part of an exhilarating adventure.** Many men are drawn to investing because accumulating wealth relates to power and status. Accumulating wealth is not perceived as a one-shot deal; it is perceived as a *process* of ups and downs. At an early age a boy will experience losing a baseball game, but his parents are there urging him on: "Atta boy, you'll get 'em the next time." Loss is seen as a temporary setback because there is always the next battle.

3. **Risk is equated with reward.** In my experience, men have no difficulty perceiving the benefits of risk-taking. Playing the stock market or investing in mutual funds is a means to an end. Whether the reward is a more comfortable lifestyle, a sports car, or having a

larger pool of funds to invest, men always have their eye on the prize.

4. To risk is to be like the "big boys." A recent issue of *Money* magazine had a banner headline telling investors that by acquiring certain insights they would be able to "Pick Stocks Like the Big Boys." The unstated message is that to get into the "big leagues" you need to understand that "big boys" take risks.

5. To join "the club," you must risk. For years, women have wondered what men talk about when they get together. The secret is now out—they love to talk about money and investments. Why? A man who can brag to his friends that he made a killing on a specific stock is given more status by his peers. Men are attracted to learning how he did it, what broker he used, and what stocks he's currently investigating. Even at social gatherings, men love to speculate on the outcome of a sporting event—competition and winning increase status within "the club."

6. Risk is a state of mind. I have known very few men who have seriously analyzed their investment risk tolerance level. In general, men have been socialized to make their best judgment about an investment and go for it. To them, it would seem odd to ponder it too long.

Women Are Raised for Responsibility, Not Risk

Throughout childhood, girls are taught that to be considered "good," they must be responsive to and responsible for others. They are also raised to take responsibility for relationships. If an extended family stays in touch, it is likely because of the efforts made by women. This sense of responsibility for others often overrides women's obligations to themselves (such as looking out for their financial future).

The qualities that are valued in women are contradictory to risk-taking, which always carries with it the possibility of loss. Because women feel responsible for those around them, they are extremely fearful of making a mistake. (Fifty-four percent of respondents to the Women Cents Study fear making investment decisions because of the possibility of making a mistake.) Listen to some of the fears we help women work through at the center:

"If I lose that money, we won't have any savings for my son's college education."

"If I lose the money I invest, my husband will never let me hear the end of it."

"We need the money. My mother is in a nursing home, and we pay for part of her support."

And while there are certainly caring and responsible men who would equally feel the guilt, outwardly most men would be much more dismissive—"Well, those things happen." Security is not at the top of their list of priorities.

Men and women view life through different lenses. Men take the narrow view, which permits them to screen out all distractions and focus intently on school or career or making money—whatever is the most important element of their lives at the time. Women, always mindful of being responsible for and responsive to others, see life through a wide-angle lens and have an understanding of the big picture—the ultimate goal.

One woman told me a story that clearly illustrates this difference in perspective: One year her husband offered to take care of the preparations for Thanksgiving dinner. "He did a wonderful job cooking the dinner," she commented. "But he'd never thought about straightening the house, getting out the good dishes and linen, ordering flowers, or setting the table. He'd focused on only one thing—the dinner. When women do something, they are expected to think of it all."

If a woman had the luxury of just cooking the turkey, she would be spared feeling that it was also her sole responsibility to make the holiday dinner a success.

Yet think of what's involved in balancing these multiple tasks. And think what women could do if they used these same skills for tracking a variety of investments!

A New Challenge for Women

So, how do you free yourself from some of the elements that are keeping you from investing your money more aggressively? Start by considering these changes:

1. Women need to resolve the conflict between addressing their own needs and being responsible for others' lives and feel-

ings. A perfect example of this is the conflict that arises when women choose to take time off from work to raise children. In doing so, a woman is placing her children's needs ahead of her own, because her time out of the workforce will dramatically affect her ability to save for retirement.

Women must also realize that in demonstrating a need to become financially independent, they are not abandoning their responsibility to others. On the contrary, they are proving to themselves and others that they will be an asset *because* they are financially savvy. The more you become knowledgeable about investing and reap the monetary benefits, the greater the likelihood that you will be in a position to help your children, grandchildren, spouse, and community—the ultimate in nurturing.

2. Find a way to balance the needs of others with your own. At this point, you probably have not had much opportunity to focus on your own financial needs. By starting with a specific task such as writing down your concerns about your financial situation, you will find that it becomes easier to focus on solutions. (Chapter 15 will show you how to change your needs into financial goals.)

3. It's okay to "be your own person." Don't invest your money a certain way because your spouse, your father, or your friend does. Learn enough so that you can adopt a savings/investment program that suits your own needs.

4. Review your prior investment behavior and evaluate what has been working for you in terms of comfort and return. Once you get started, the most important part of addressing risk is to learn from your mistakes. Be ever mindful of what risk level you're comfortable with. As you review, you will likely realize that not all your past investment decisions have worked out perfectly. That's okay. All investors make mistakes, and once you realize that these mistakes are just bumps in the road, it will help you to understand what's working for you and what makes you uncomfortable. One new investor found that if she selected a stock that dipped when she expected it to go up, she was able to view the potential loss as a learning experience. But when a stock her *broker* got her into underperformed, she felt upset and out of control. She explains: "When I first started, I sometimes invested on the broker's recommendation without doing my own homework, so when those stocks went down, I viewed those losses as empty experiences from which I learned nothing. However, if I'd done my homework, and the stock didn't do what I expected, at least I felt I might be smarter for the next time."

5. Expect your risk tolerance level to fluctuate—everyone's does. If your mother has been ill and you've been helping with her medical expenses, you may not be in the mood to try something new with any of your money. Or if you've just lost money in an investment, you may have to rebuild your confidence by taking smaller risks so that you'll realize some gains. Life is fluid, and your risk tolerance level will be as well.

While there may be times when unexpected expenses or the simple vicissitudes of life mean that you move more slowly with your investment program, you don't want to get totally sidetracked by external events. The best way to avoid this is to set up a system where you routinely put money into mutual funds or the stock market, perhaps on the first of the month when you pay your bills. By establishing a disciplined system for handling your money, you're less likely to be diverted by life's uncertainties.

6. You can have your cake (security) and eat it (risk) too. To reduce your risk anxiety, build up your emergency fund (three to six months income for unanticipated events such as losing your job or a health crisis). Once your security needs are met, you can focus on long-term goals like retirement and make investments where more risk may be involved.

7. Understanding what investments can do for you will alleviate your worst fears and satisfy your needs. Many times a lack of understanding contributes to risk aversion. Additional knowledge will help you see that a good financial plan isn't so risky after all. By balancing your portfolio (see Chapter 18), by keeping some money in cash and by purchasing appropriate mutual funds or stocks and bonds, you can take some steps to protect against long-term loss.

8. The worst mistake you can make is to do nothing. By failing to make a decision about an investment, you are actually placing yourself at greater financial risk. After proper research and analysis of a particular investment, establish a cutoff date and move forward.

What You Risk by Not Risking

If these steps don't get you moving, some financial facts may do the trick. **What you need to know is that by doing nothing—or** by leaving your money in a savings account you're actually **exposing yourself to much greater risk than you would be if you bought a blue chip stock or invested in a mutual fund.** You can actually *decrease* your risk by investing!

In general, investors must accept some risk to earn greater long-term returns. If your money is currently in passbook savings, bank certificates of deposit (CDs), and/or U.S. Treasury bills, you could be doing better. (A recent survey revealed that 70 percent of women keep their money in cash or CDs, while only 34 percent hold stocks and only 23 percent own bonds, the latter two of which have much better long-term rates of return.)

Women who are uncomfortable with financial risk usually consider only the most obvious kinds of risk, which are *market risk* (selling something for less than you paid) and *liquidity risk* (is your money "liquid"—can you have it when you need it?). As a result, those who are trying to avoid risk invest too conservatively and expose themselves to other financial risks.

Inflation risk, the loss of buying power, is equally insidious over time. (This risk is particularly dangerous for women, who statistically have a longer life expectancy than men.) What does this mean in real terms? If you have $100,000 today and inflation averages 4 percent over the next thirty years, your $100,000 will be barely worth $30,000 in buying power.

Those in conservative investments also expose themselves to other forms of risk: *interest-rate risk* (the risk that interest rates will rise, causing the value of conservative investments like bonds and bond mutual funds to fall); *reinvestment risk* (a risk that affects short-term investments when investors are not able to reinvest as favorably if interest rates have fallen when their bond or CD matures); *holding-period risk* (the risk that an investment may lack liquidity for a time or that an investor will have to sell an investment at a time when it is worth less than when it was purchased).

What does this mean in terms of real dollars? Because every investment is different, we need to look at trends.

Historically, stocks have outpaced bonds and "safe" investments like CDs, money market funds, and Treasury bills. From 1926 through 1995, stocks returned an average of 10.5 percent per year, compared with 5.2 percent from long-term government bonds and

3.7 percent from Treasury bills. Inflation over that same period averaged 3.1 percent a year—meaning that after taxes, only stocks have significantly enhanced purchasing power. (Note that these statistics include the stock market crash of '29, demonstrating that long-term trends can overcome serious setbacks.)

That's why it's vital that you take a serious look at how to better handle risk.

Becoming a Calculated Risk Taker

Just as no one would expect a new pilot to take a plane up during a thunderstorm, it is unreasonable to expect new investors to immediately become high rollers who follow the most risky of investments. Our goal here is simply to help you feel comfortable with risk through *carefully calculated* risk-taking. Remember, too, that no change happens overnight.

Calculated risk takers are successful money managers because they follow a personal financial plan. They don't avoid risk or seek risk, but they *manage* risk by dividing investment dollars among different types of financial products and in a variety of business sectors.

Calculated risk takers choose investments by evaluating the chance of experiencing a gain against the chance of experiencing a loss while placing their money in investments that best fit their financial goals.

Success in money management *can* be predicted if you have a plan and follow it. Contrary to popular belief, developing a plan does not involve endless hours of work. It is as simple as putting pen to paper and deciding what you want to do with your money. Here are the basic steps you need to take (these steps will be more fully explained in Section III):

1. **Set goals**—both for the dollar amount you intend to save and for what you want (or need) to do with it in the future. Whether it's saving for a vacation, putting away money for a child's education, or looking at your long-term retirement needs, the financial goals you set for yourself will guide you in all your decision-making. The key to any successful financial plan is knowing *what you want your money to do for you.*

2. **Pay attention to your risk tolerance level.** Invest only as much money as you feel comfortable with at the time.
3. **Educate yourself.** Learn as much as you can about the process, and talk to several sources.
4. **Give yourself a deadline.** Specify a date when you will ultimately make a decision.
5. **Diversify.** You'll be able to sleep better at night if you have a mix of conservative and more aggressive investments. By diversifying your investments, you are making sure your money grows, countering the forces of inflation, minimizing taxes when possible, and addressing your need for security and safety.
6. **Become disciplined.** Discipline is the most important aspect of developing a plan. It involves not making investments without knowledge, never investing on the basis of a "hot tip," and not investing money you are going to lose sleep over. (If you need the money to pay this month's bills, you shouldn't be investing it.)
7. **Conduct routine financial checkups.** If you are like many people, you fear having routine physical checkups. But you can reduce your fear of having a catastrophic illness by heeding the doctor's advice and getting a physical regularly. It's the same with money and investments. You need to practice preventive financial care to make sure your investments are doing what they are supposed to be doing. By conducting financial checkups once a month, every six months, or every year, you are reducing your financial risk by staying on top of your investments.
8. **A buy-and-hold philosophy may seem safe but can actually be quite risky.** Although many financial professionals adhere to this philosophy, sometimes investments may not remain appropriate for changing life circumstances. Don't become emotionally attached to your investments. (Though your father, who died last year, left you 100 shares of stock, he, too, would want you to sell them when the time was right—money is not something to be sentimental over!) If your investments do not satisfy your changing plans, find ones that can.

Identifying Your Risk Tolerance Level in Dollars

The following two exercises should identify the dollar amount you feel comfortable putting away in an investment each month.

1. Pretend that you are going to a store each month to buy something for yourself. You want to spend cash and will not use a credit card. Identify how much money you will spend each month without losing sleep over it or feeling that you overindulged. The amount you identify should be the amount you place each month in some type of investment account or program.

2. If you really feel that investing is just like gambling, try this exercise. Pretend that you are going to play a "one-armed bandit" each month. You play the machine with the idea that at some point it may or may not pay out. How much money are you willing to put into the slot machine each month? The dollar amount you come up with may be a good way to start quantifying your risk tolerance level.

Just for fun, try these exercises again when you've finished reading this book, and see if the results have changed.

Here's another way you might identify the money you're willing to risk:

Most people don't like to risk money they've worked hard to earn. Do you have any "gift" money, such as an annual bonus, or a check you receive at holiday time from your parents? Or do you ever win money at bridge? Earmark all or part of this money for your riskier investments. As you begin to see gains, you'll likely start looking for ways to increase the fund!

REMEMBER IT'S YOUR RISK; YOU BE THE JUDGE

Cheryl F., now retired, started investing when she was in her thirties, and unfortunately, she had to learn the hard way that the only person who should judge your own risk is you.

"I had a management job with the phone company and was earning good money. I decided to spend $2,000 to $3,000 to buy some stocks, and I didn't feel this was a tremendous risk—if I lost it, the world wouldn't end. I made $1,500 the first year. Because I was new to this and didn't really know what I was doing, I devised a plan of reading the New York Times *business section and buying stocks of interesting companies I read*

about. Then, when I made a profit, I sold them. If I had continued in this way, I think I would have done okay. The problem began when I departed from my formula of buy low and sell high.

"One day my brother called with an idea for an investment where I could 'make a fortune.' I should have known better. The person with whom we invested was a high roller when it came to money. I initially lost $5,000, but I blamed it on a fluke and being new to this. I kept thinking I had to try riskier and riskier investments to make up what I was starting to lose. I finally realized that my brother's influence was not good for me, since he seemed to have a gambling mentality, which was rubbing off on me.

"Not only did I ignore my own comfort level about risk, but I was willing to take advice from others instead of sticking with the habit I'd developed of researching each investment carefully. I have now started attending seminars, reading, and I've joined a women-only investment club. I went from taking some calculated risks in the stocks I purchased to actually gambling with my money. Now I'm simply trying to level out and be more comfortable with my more secure long-term investments."

Cheryl learned an unfortunate lesson about investing. Although it is tempting to pursue the promise of a monetary windfall, doing so often requires moving beyond one's already established risk comfort level. One of my cardinal rules is to approach each new investment with a focus on learning first, followed by intuition and cautious decision-making. You must also recognize that only you can take individual responsibility for your own money. Cheryl did not lose her brother's money; she lost her own.

Educate Yourself

Ninety-four percent of respondents to the Women Cents Study understood that they could not expect substantial financial returns unless they were willing to accept some financial risk. As women become more comfortable with risk, their more cautious nature actually prepares them to be excellent risk-takers. While a man may be perfectly happy plunging into an investment based on a stock tip from a friend, women are more apt to ask questions and to do some research before moving ahead. (Studies have shown that in school girls are praised for hard work; boys are praised for knowing the right answer. As a result, women are the more dogged of the two.) Eighty-two percent indicated that they tend to be slow and methodical when making a decision about a new investment, and 87 percent indicated they would not invest solely on the basis of a "hot tip."

This combination—the willingness to take a risk combined with the intelligence to look before you leap—puts women in a good position to mature into excellent risk-takers.

As you evaluate potential risks, remember that there is no perfect type of investment. Each one protects against certain types of risk but is vulnerable to others. Risk management involves making investment decisions based on a process of evaluating the trade-offs between these risks. This process will help a woman investor to become more risk tolerant and to choose the investments that best match her financial goals.

Set a Date for Making a Decision

The only danger to the research aspect of investing is that it can become an end unto itself. At the Center I sometimes see women who get so involved in researching "one more thing" that they fail to keep working toward the end result. The "process" gets in the way of the goal—that of investing for the future.

If taking action is difficult for you, set a date and note it on your calendar. You're more likely to actually accomplish your goal if you've established a written deadline. By that time you should have had an opportunity to explore the investment and make a sound decision.

Diversify

Diversification—not putting all your eggs in one basket—will be fully discussed in Section III, but suffice it to say now that everyone from Bill Gates to your neighbor needs to diversify. Anything can happen and you need to have your money in different kinds of investments so that bad news in one arena doesn't mean bad news everywhere.

When I think of diversification, I'll always hear the voice of one specific woman from the past. During my counseling days I met a sixty-two-year-old woman who was close to being a millionaire. She had inherited her fortune from her father, who had invested in IBM stock some thirty years before. After her father died and she inherited the stock, she lived off the dividends, never selling or touching the principal. When family members and friends told her that she should diversify her assets, her retort was always: "Big Blue [the nickname for IBM stock] will never go down," or "I don't know where else to place my money." To compound the problem, she refused to talk with a financial advisor because she didn't believe that any other investment could be as safe as Big Blue.

Over a seven-year period, her stock went from $172 per share to a low of $58. In a panic because the company had cut its dividend in half, and she was living off these checks, she finally sold most of her shares at $68. As a direct result of her unwillingness to diversify, her total net worth went down by 70 percent. Today she has little of the security she once enjoyed.

Another aspect of diversification that will be more fully explored in Section III is dollar cost averaging. Invest regularly in good times and bad, and it should increase your chances for investment success.

One Who Learned to Take Financial Risk

Ellen P. is a forty-two-year-old executive secretary with two children who has been divorced for two years. Before her divorce she and her husband had a comfortable lifestyle because both worked and brought in a combined income of $86,000. During her marriage her husband assisted her in making all decisions concerning her company 401(k) plan. Although they didn't have a great deal of money to invest, she allowed him to buy a few mutual funds and individual stocks.

After the divorce, Ellen received an $18,000 cash settlement. Although she realized that she needed to invest a portion of the settlement, the idea of losing any portion of the money was overwhelming, so she kept it all in a passbook account. "This is all I had from my marriage," she explained.

Three years later, after many arguments with her former spouse about child-support payments, Ellen realized that when it came time for her children to go to college, her husband was unlikely to contribute. This understanding caused her to revisit her financial situation.

Though extremely nervous about having her money anywhere but in a savings account, she felt a certain degree of pride in the number of financial hurdles she had overcome since her divorce: Her husband's child-support payments had been erratic, so she had developed ways to manage. These included negotiating a raise and selling the family home at a profit and buying a slightly smaller one (in a location her children actually liked better).

Using these personal successes as a foundation, Ellen took her banker's suggestion to move one-third of her money into a bank-sponsored money market account that paid a higher interest than her savings account. Although she was petrified that she might lose the money, she gave herself six months to see what would happen. Three months into the venture, she heard on the radio that the stock market had declined 146 points. Ellen panicked and rushed to the bank, where she found that her worst fears had not come true—her account had *more* money in it than when she started.

This experience taught Ellen some vital lessons about her risk tolerance and how to move forward. She realized that ignorance was her number-one enemy, and that she needed to educate herself about different investment options. By talking to friends and going to a financial seminar, she learned that mutual funds could provide her with a way to diversify her money without losing sleep. Again, Ellen started slow—she took $2,000 and her income generated by the money market account and placed it in a growth and income mutual fund. She selected the mutual fund by establishing three rules that she follows to this day: (1) Only risk what I am comfortable risking; (2) learn about what is being recommended to me; (3) set a deadline for making a decision.

Since the initial money market investment, Ellen has spread her money into two other mutual funds while still keeping some in the money market account.

When the Shoe Is on the Other Foot

Every now and then a woman comes to the Center with a different sort of problem regarding risk: She's highly risk tolerant and can't get her husband to understand the necessity of investing their money. Jennifer was one such woman.

Jennifer H. is a thirty-two-year-old executive assistant with a Fortune 500 company in New York City. By nature, Jennifer has always enjoyed learning about the stock market and investments. Over the last ten years, she has taken several investment seminars (starting with the basics and moving up to more advanced ones). As she puts it, "I just have a head for money and have always enjoyed the challenge of making my money grow."

Jennifer came to one of our seminars not so much to obtain the financial basics as to negotiate a problem she has been experiencing for the last four years—ever since she got married to her husband, Luke. *"Although everyone always says to discuss sex and money before getting married, I covered sex, but not money. It is painful to say, but my husband and I are financial mismatches. We love each other dearly, but we just don't see eye-to-eye when it comes to investing. I want to put some of our funds in aggressive-growth stocks and mutual funds, and he is satisfied with CDs. I can handle risk; he can't.*

"Although I have tried to encourage him to take a financial seminar or read a variety of books, he is not oriented toward taking on any type of risk unless his money is insured by the FDIC. I really don't know what to do."

Men can also fear risk, and if they don't understand investing, they, too, will be fearful of the unknown. For women like Jennifer, who are trying to work with risk-averse spouses, I recommend that you determine how involved your spouse wants to be in decisions regarding investments and then work with him (to the greatest extent possible) to understand that your combined future (especially retirement) could be jeopardized if you don't find a happy medium between two divergent risk patterns.

Initially, Jennifer and her husband agreed to invest a small portion of their assets in riskier growth stocks and to reassess their financial situation in one year's time. In addition, Jennifer keeps her husband apprised of how their investments are doing based on their monthly statement.

What Have I Gotten Myself Into; or, What If the Stock Market Crashes?

"Dow Drops" is a headline that can send investors scurrying for the nearest telephone or on-line service, and scare off potential investors as well. But next time you read such a headline, try this:

Choose three companies and check to see how their stock fared during the drop. Chances are that individual stocks only lost $2 or $3 per share. Now, if you own 100 shares or more, this isn't to be sneezed at, but it isn't as if the share price of your stock had dropped 100 points.

Investors often get caught up in the possibility of a market in free fall, despite the fact that a crash causing the Dow to drop 20 percent in a single day has taken place just twice in this century. Drops of 10 percent or so are also rare, having occurred only four times this century, and in each case prices rebounded.

In one of the largest drops in recent years—October 19, 1987—the stock market plunged more than 500 points. Many people followed their brokers' advice to get into money market accounts for safety. However, during the next six months stock prices rebounded, and their cash investments returned 1.4 percent, compared with 18 percent on stocks. (This return on stocks was actually above average; generally, stocks average about a 10 percent return annually.)

An easy way to think of a downward stock trend might be to compare it to a child with a fever: While a spiking fever (market dropping) is more dramatic and does cause worry, a low-grade fever that lingers for more than a week may actually be more dangerous.

Don't take action based on today's news. Watch for trends, and consider your long-term goals.

We'll go into all types of additional strategies in Section III.

6

THE WAY THINGS ARE
Do You Like Change or the Status Quo?

"We've always put money in a company savings plan, and the rest is in a savings account. Between working and raising a family, I just can't be bothered with having to worry about what else to do with my money."

Making a change in the way you handle your money is a lot like starting an exercise program: The old you is perfectly happy sleeping until seven, getting up, having breakfast, and getting yourself and your family out the door to school and work. But the old you has put on a little weight in the hips, and the new you realizes that the extra weight has got to go.

What to do? There are so many popular options today that you decided to consult your friends. One recommended jogging, but you'd done that and it bothered your knees. Another recommended power walking, but it was the middle of winter, and there was no good place to walk; a third swore by exercise videotapes, but you didn't think you really had the self-discipline for that. Finally, a fourth, a coworker, said, "Meet me at the health club near work at eight-fifteen. We'll go every morning before work."

97

Well, that sounded good, and you got off to a flying start, despite feeling inept as well as embarrassed when the health club instructor checked your fitness level. Yet, notwithstanding your good intentions, the old you—who loves morning sleep—kept reappearing, and during the second and third weeks your attendance was spotty.

The fourth week, your fitness-conscious friend called to see if you would meet her again. When you demurred, she shot back: "I don't know why you won't take better care of yourself. You're only thirty-eight, and you get winded going up only three flights of stairs. You can rationalize all you want, but there is a really simple solution to being more fit, and you just don't seem to be willing to take those steps.

"I hate to give up on you because you're my friend, but I can't be your keeper. The only one who can help you is you," she said, and hung up the phone.

Everything that applies to increasing your physical fitness pertains to improving financial fitness as well. Just as your body will become flabby from lack of exercise, your money is also going to lose "muscle tone" sitting in a low-return savings account. And just like exercising, taking charge of your money is *vital to your long-term health*. I fervently wish that I could speak to each one of you personally to express to you one important point: **If your money is sitting in a savings account somewhere, you've got to start doing something else with it.**

Do these changes come with guarantees? Yes, but only long-term ones. Regular exercise will ultimately give you a more fit body, but that doesn't mean you'll never pull a muscle and be waylaid for a few days. And, as is pointed out throughout this book, investing in something other than a savings account will stand you in good stead over time, though your investment may go down—as well as up. That's just part of the long-term experience of increasing physical and financial health.

But change is not about cleaning out your savings account to put your money into high-risk stocks, and it's not about moving money around daily; it's about taking small steps and finding a balance—sticking with the status quo (your savings account or preferably some other, higher-interest account such as a certificate of deposit) when it feels right, but also being open-minded about making smart money decisions as your goals and personal needs change.

If you have any concerns about your attitude toward change, this chapter will help you to understand why you prefer the familiar and will help you to develop a more flexible attitude about money. We'll discuss:

- What you can learn about yourself and your attitude toward change
- How your family background influenced your attitude
- How to take smart steps toward being more open to change
- How to bring about a financial change that's right for you

Are You Open to Change?

The Women Cents Self-Test gave you a general idea of how open you were to change. To gain a deeper understanding of whether your attitudes toward change are in harmony with your investment practices, you'll enjoy answering the following questions.

DIRECTIONS

In each case, check off the answer that best corresponds to your response to the hypothetical scenario. Often your first reaction is closest to the real you. Select only *one* response per question.

1. Your friend has just presented you with a birthday gift to vacation with her in the Caribbean. However, you have just agreed to chaperon the local high school senior trip. You would:
   - [ ] 1) go without question; the school can find another chaperon.
   - [ ] 2) have to think about it but would be inclined to go and would help the school find a replacement.
   - [ ] 3) have to think about it but would be inclined not to go; others are depending on you to chaperon this trip.
   - [ ] 4) tell her immediately that you can't go.

2. Your first child is seven years away from entering college, and most of your assets are in a savings account. You are thinking of:
   - [ ] 1) beginning to explore higher-return investment options.
   - [ ] 2) delaying making a decision on different investments.
   - [ ] 3) placing any additional money you save in your savings account.
   - [ ] 4) keeping the majority of the money in your savings account but taking a small amount out to invest at a higher rate of return.

3. Your boss wants you to take a new position in the company that will pay more, but you will be required to travel and will be away from home and family for five days a month. You would:

☐ 1) say yes without hesitation.

☐ 2) ask for twenty-four hours to decide, in order to get your family's response.

☐ 3) ask for more than twenty-four hours to think it over, explaining that you have a family to consider.

☐ 4) say thanks for the offer, but no.

4. You have owned a specific mutual fund for ten years and just realized that the rate of return is much lower than the industry standard for this type of investment. You're going to:

☐ 1) immediately look for a similar type of mutual fund that has a better rate of return.

☐ 2) call the company to see what's going on and then make a decision.

☐ 3) continue to invest in the fund since you are familiar with the company.

☐ 4) make no decision, figuring, "It's bound to turn around someday."

5. A close friend wants you to join her in going to a hair salon that has a new stylist whom you've already heard is supposed to be terrific. You haven't changed your hairstyle in ten years. You would:

☐ 1) go at the drop of a hat, eager for a new look.

☐ 2) go and have a few minor changes made to your regular cut.

☐ 3) probably think it over but ultimately decide not to go, because you don't want to change your hairstyle.

☐ 4) immediately respond, "I don't want to change my hairstyle."

6. Your best friend has received an 18 percent return on a variable-interest investment. She is recommending that you invest in it too. You would:

☐ 1) ask her where to send your money.

☐ 2) conduct your own research on the investment and then make a decision.

☐ 3) call for more information out of curiosity but not take the investment opportunity very seriously.

☐ 4) thank her for the tip but not check it out—investments like this are a fluke.

7. You are two months away from your class reunion and need a dress to wear. While visiting a clothes store you find a dress that is very expensive but makes you look five pounds thinner. You:

☐ 1) buy the dress on the spot.

☐ 2) wait to buy it only if it goes on sale.

☐ 3) fantasize about buying it but later decide not to.

☐ 4) immediately decide not to buy it.

8. Your financial counselor wants you to make a decision as to where you feel the most comfortable in placing a majority of your assets. You would:

☐ 1) select investments that are variable but have a greater rate of return.

☐ 2) select investments that give you a consistent rate of return.

    ☐ 3) place the funds in an insured FDIC account.
    ☐ 4) not make a decision; let the financial counselor decide.

9. A national coffee distributor indicates you have won a prize with three different options. Which one would you select?
    ☐ 1) receive ten pounds of different varieties.
    ☐ 2) request a brochure to examine the options.
    ☐ 3) receive ten pounds of one variety.
    ☐ 4) decline the offer, thinking there must be a gimmick.

10. You are driving home from work listening to the radio and learn that the market has dropped 123 points. The commentator indicates that many financial experts believe this is the beginning of a bear market. You:
    ☐ 1) call your broker and buy more stock.
    ☐ 2) call your broker for advice.
    ☐ 3) follow what your friend is doing.
    ☐ 4) sell everything.

11. It's Saturday night and you're lucky enough to have invitations to several different parties. You decide you and your partner will:
    ☐ 1) go to the party where you would meet the most new people.
    ☐ 2) go to the party with a mixture of new people and old friends.
    ☐ 3) go to the party where you will know everyone.
    ☐ 4) stay home and not go out at all.

12. You have just received an invitation in the mail from a local community college to attend an educational program on financial planning for women. You:
    ☐ 1) sign up to attend immediately, going alone.
    ☐ 2) call a friend to see if she's interested in attending with you.
    ☐ 3) put the invitation in a drawer for future reference.
    ☐ 4) decline the invitation.

13. For the last ten years you have been living with a skin disorder that sometimes creates slight discomfort. Your doctor is recommending that you take a new test that will determine whether this problem will eventually become more serious. You:
    ☐ 1) immediately take the test.
    ☐ 2) take the test after calling another specialist for an opinion.
    ☐ 3) get a second opinion but still decide to wait and see if the situation eventually becomes more serious.
    ☐ 4) do nothing, figuring you'll live with the discomfort.

14. Your deceased father willed you 10,000 shares of a stock that has consistently paid out high dividends. Recently, your accountant recommended that to protect yourself you should sell a portion of the stock to diversify your investment portfolio. You:
    ☐ 1) take his advice and sell.

☐ 2) get the opinions of other professionals and then act.
☐ 3) listen to his advice but wait.
☐ 4) keep all the shares because they were from your father and the divi-
         dend check arrives each month.

SCORING

Your score can be analyzed in several different ways. For each
analysis, you'll need to determine your *personal change index* and
your *money change index*. Here's how to determine each:

Beside each check you made is a number. Add the numbers for
questions 1, 3, 5, 7, 9, 11, and 13. The total of these numbers is your
personal change index.

Now add the numbers for questions 2, 4, 6, 8, 10, 12, and 14. The
total of these numbers is your money change index.

ANALYSIS 1

How Averse to Change Are You?

High scores (above 9) in both areas reflect a personality that is averse to
both personal and financial change. Here are some strategies that will get you
started right now without causing undue stress:

Consider investments that will not fluctuate too much. Your scores indicate
that you will not tolerate ambiguity. Don't browbeat yourself about it! Just recognize that before you undertake any change or transition, you must think
through whether you will be comfortable with the decision.

If you want to develop more adventuresome qualities, go slowly. Whether
in the personal or financial arena, take steps that will build on your need for
the familiar: Undertake an activity in your personal life that may result in an
unanticipated positive change. For example, going to an adult education class
by yourself may lead you to meet some interesting people. If this event turns
out positively, follow it up by making a small change in your finances. For example, you might shop for a higher rate of return on your certificate of deposit.
Keep in mind that to change, you must adopt a slow and patient approach.
Don't let anyone convince you to make immediate changes in your investments. You must want to do this at your own pace and only once you have
enough knowledge to make you feel comfortable.

ANALYSIS 2

How Your Personal Openness to Change Compares to
Your Financial Openness to Change

Compare your personal change index to your money change index and
determine the point difference between the two.

- 2–4 points difference: This degree of differential indicates that your personal and financial attitudes are in harmony. If you are change averse in both areas, you'll want to make changes slowly. You'll feel more comfortable if changes happen over a longer period of time.
- 5–8 points difference: This indicates a modest difference between personal and financial change attitudes. Identify which index was higher. If you are more open to change in your personal life, start to educate yourself about change and volatility in the financial arena. If your score reveals that you are more open to financial change than to personal change, pick one area of your personal life that could use improvement, and make small changes one at a time.
- 9+ points difference: Don't panic! Your score indicates you need to close the gap between tolerance of change in your personal and financial lives. Your task is to identify strategies to bring these indices closer together. Strategies to consider: (1) Develop long-term personal goals that reflect your tolerance for change and then seek out investments that match your goals. For example, you might want to move to a new community in a few years, so your investments should be made with this long-term goal in mind. (2) Anticipate the consequences of your personal and financial decisions. An important issue to examine is how many times you checked option 3 in the money change index questions. By delaying important money decisions, you may be risking more than you think.

You'll learn more about how to make these changes as the chapter continues.

ANALYSIS 3

Smart in Money but Change Averse in Life

If you have a relatively low score in your money index, and a high score in your lifestyle index, consider the following.

1. Your score clearly indicates that you are comfortable with change when it comes to money, but not in other areas of your life. Consider whether you will allow yourself to enjoy your money at some future time! You don't want to spend your life working to build a secure nest egg if you will never enjoy the fruits of your labor.
2. Based on this score, I really want you to answer an important question: Are there voices from the past or present (for example, a parent or spouse) telling you that it is wrong to enjoy yourself and have fun? If so, you might want to consider how adding adventure and change to your life might provide you with more satisfaction.
3. Consider whether you feel *guilty* about adding diversity or change to your life. Your upbringing may have given you some messages that mean change and taking care of yourself are tantamount to being

selfish. I have worked with many women who are smart when it comes to money but who never allow themselves the luxury of enjoying themselves.

4. Try to identify some activities that will allow you to feel the exhilaration of breaking out of a set routine. You don't have to go wild. Take a weekend and go to a resort (alone, with your family, or with a friend—whatever is most comfortable), and spend some money that will bring enjoyment to you and others. Remember, you only go around once in life!

Who Enjoys Change, Who Doesn't

When it comes to money, the Women Cents Study showed a strong relationship between certain personal and financial traits: The women who were more flexible in their orientation (open to new ideas, willing to change plans when necessary, adept at resetting goals as needed) were also interested in exploring new investment strategies, felt relatively confident about their ability to handle math, were not intimidated by financial lingo, and were open to adjusting their investments during the coming year based on their goals and circumstances. Their Self-Test scores put them in the Action Zone.

The women who preferred the status quo (those who feel most comfortable when their days follow a set routine and prefer having a limited number of alternatives to choose from) felt that way about money too. They were Danger Zone candidates: They didn't want to move their money around, were intimidated by financial terms, preferred to keep their investments simple, and had no particular plans to do anything different with their money in the next year.

One optimistic note regarding this personality trait: It's not so difficult to remedy. If you're among those who'll quickly admit to preferring the known to the unknown, think back over your life. Chances are you've already met and managed an amazing number of challenges—most women have. The world is changing so much that no one really continues to live without making some alterations. If you use a microwave, an answering machine or voice mail, and a computer at home or in the office, you've already demonstrated the necessary skills to adapt to change. These "skills of adaptation" can easily be translated into learning about money management and investing.

What's more, financial change is best accomplished by small steps, not great leaps, so if you'll just keep reading, you'll already find yourself looking more positively on the notion of change.

The Not-Ready-for-Change Conflict

Change triggers conflict in almost everyone: The known vs. the unknown. The safe vs. the untried. The acceptable vs. the possibility of the unsuitable.

It's hard for most of us to remember that change is also a summer vacation, an unexpected job opportunity, a surprise visit from a beloved friend, or an impromptu walk in the park.

Human nature dictates that for most people, the initial reaction to change—even positive change—is concern: What does this mean? How will it affect *me*? What can I do to be certain everything will be all right?

Remember, too, that there are two kinds of change, both of which require some type of response. The first type of change is that which happens *to* you (and over which you have little control): You get a new boss, the family gets transferred, new neighbors move in, and so forth. The second type of change is one *you* create, like getting married, visiting a new place, or deciding to invest your money.

Either type of change, by its very nature, requires accommodation. How we cope with this adjustment is deeply rooted in how our families managed change as we grew up. Your family may have relished the unexpected. Or perhaps you grew up in a family where life was filled with spur-of-the-moment, unplanned activities that didn't ever work out very well. Or perhaps your family was traditional: Nothing ever changed because it felt unsafe to do things differently; routine was the most comfortable way of life. How you manage change as an adult depends on how you've adjusted to the messages you received growing up.

When these issues pertain to money, you have a wide range of possibilities—from the gambler who plays the tables at Vegas (attracted to the risk of uncontrollable change because of early family experiences) to the very conservative who insists every dime must be kept in a savings account (resistant to any possibility of change).

Somewhere in the middle, there are people who have found financial balance. They have turned away from savings accounts but would never rely on blackjack to provide what they need for retirement. They've created a sensible plan for managing their money, and it's just right for them.

Getting from "here" (the savings account) to "there" (investing), however, is not an easy transition for women to make.

Although the Women Cents Study showed that women *perceive* themselves as adventurous and open to change (61 percent of respondents described themselves as personally adventurous and 92 percent agreed with the statement "Change adds zest to life"), the *reality* is that the research uncovered a sharp contradiction between women's willingness to take on personal change and their comfort with financial change. A full 59 percent of respondents indicated that they preferred the known to the unknown.

Resistance to change is particularly strong when it comes to the question of money. Only 42 percent of all respondents reported that they were "moderately" (34 percent) or "very" (8 percent) satisfied with the return on their investments; yet 72 percent reported that they would consider only "safe" or "guaranteed" investments.

Think about what these statistics mean: Only 8 percent of the women surveyed are truly pleased with what their money is doing for them—meaning that 92 percent are dissatisfied to some degree—and 58 percent are definitely displeased. Yet almost all of them prefer the status quo. If 92 percent of customers were dissatisfied with a supermarket, you know what would happen: Sales would drop, and the store would go out of business. Yet people will persist in leaving their money in savings accounts!

Part of the problem, I feel, is that women don't know where to turn for reliable advice. New investors are bombarded by so much information via television business news and magazines that it's difficult to know what to do. Too much information can easily put anyone into a tailspin, and soon an interested investor decides it's better to stay put. (Later in the book we'll discuss finding reliable advisors.)

One of the deep-rooted fears people sometimes harbor about change is that if they do something different, it will propel them into chaos—something over which they have no control. Yet financial change isn't like that; you make a series of choices, and at many steps along the way you have the opportunity to guide and predict what your next course of action will be. The following are typical financial circumstances. In each case, change is merited, but it doesn't take you by storm or require an instant decision.

When your bank or financial institution notifies you that your two-year certificate of deposit, which is earning only 5.3 percent, is about to expire, you have the perfect opportunity for change. If you do some research, you may discover a conservative-growth mutual fund that is averaging 10 percent for a five-year period. This is a smart change. Or suppose you've bought a stock that appears to be losing value because of a down market or because it's temporarily out of favor. You might think it's time to change, but you'd first analyze *why* the stock is heading downward: (1) Is it because the fundamentals (basic financial situation) of the company are bad? If so, you could sell the stock and place the money in a different investment. (2) If, however, the fundamentals of the company are good but the stock market, or a category of stock (such as technology), is going through an adjustment, you may want to do nothing. The stock should rebound, and if you're in it for the long term, you needn't worry day-to-day.

Here's another exercise. If you have money in a certificate of deposit, note the date at which it will mature and use this time to acquire your own financial "maturity." Start doing some financial research. For example, if you have six months before the bank notice comes, pretend that you have already received the money and select a particular stock or mutual fund. Track that particular investment for the next few months and see how it performs. If it performs well, look at its three- and five-year track record. After observing this long-term trend, you might want to put your CD money into this investment instead.

If that exercise doesn't appeal to you, try this one as an alternative. If you are worried about pulling out of the CD, go ahead and roll the money over. But this time, I want you to consider investing a portion of the interest that you earn from it in a growth and income mutual fund or a high-dividend blue chip stock (see Chapter 18). When you think about it, what do you have to lose? Using this technique, you have safeguarded your entire principal and you have the opportunity to experience going into the market with greatly reduced risk. I'll bet you that this approach to change will help you the next time the bank asks what you want to do with your CD.

COMMON EXCUSES TO AVOID CHANGE

At the NCWRR, we hear some common excuses that reflect a temporary unwillingness to change. If you've used any of these, consider yourself normal, but here's what you can tell yourself from now on:

NOT-READY-FOR-CHANGE EXCUSES	NEW REPLIES
"I don't have time."	"Well, I had time to read a book on the topic (or attend a seminar), and Dr. Hayes says it will take an average of an hour or two per month to monitor my investments." If you're a long-term investor, you need to stay on top of what is happening to your investments to be certain they are living up to your expectations, but that doesn't require a huge investment of time.
"There's too much to learn; I'll never catch on."	"I can catch on, because I need only learn a little at a time."
"I want to learn a little more, but whatever my husband decides is really fine with me."	"My husband may be making good decisions, but it's important that we begin to discuss them and make decisions together."
"I just can't decide what to do with my money."	"I *can* decide, because I'm going to decide what my goals are, develop a financial strategy, and diversify my investments. It's that simple!"

The Challenges of Change

While there are any number of reasons why people resist change, we at NCWRR have identified four predominant types of women who find it most difficult to be flexible with their money.

1. Those who have finally got their lives pulled together and don't want to do anything that rocks the boat

2. Those who are too overwhelmed and busy with day-to-day life to contemplate the possibility of change for the future
3. Those who worry about how change will affect others
4. Those who grew up unaccustomed to any sort of change

1. THE WOMAN WHO FINALLY PULLED HER LIFE TOGETHER

It took Miriam H. a full ten years to overcome the financial disaster of her divorce. Since there were no children, Miriam's final divorce settlement was less than $200 per month for only two years. She had to give up any right to her husband's pension plan as part of the settlement, and at the time of the separation, the job market was tight, so Miriam worked three part-time jobs just to make ends meet, experiencing firsthand what happens when you have no cash reserve.

Only recently has Miriam begun to save. Two years ago, her parents died and Miriam, an only child, inherited the family home, which she has chosen to live in for now.

"Having the house really helps with living expenses, and I have a better job now," says Miriam. *"People say I could do better with my money by selling the house, but I'm worried about change. I have no one else to depend on and no one but me to take care of me.*

"I know I'm going to have to find a way to do better with my money, and I'd eventually like to be able to sell the house, but I don't think I can right now.

"I've gone to a few financial seminars, but I'm still intimidated. I'd like to understand some of the terminology and types of investments better before I do anything."

Like many others, Miriam has finally reached a point where she is comfortable, and she's reluctant to make any changes. She has actually reached the first stage of change, though, simply because she's aware that it's necessary.

Miriam has come a long way since her understandably insecure days following her divorce, but her fixation with security and day-to-day living expenses will keep her paralyzed unless she changes some critical elements of her money personality. She needs to redefine "security" in a way that will allow her to plan for the future. (You'll learn more about this in Section III.) With help she ought to be able to move forward financially and begin to utilize the investment knowledge gained in the financial seminars she's attended.

2. TOO OVERWHELMED TO CONTEMPLATE CHANGE

Jill D. married a man who was doing well financially, and soon she took time off from her teaching job to have children. Even without Jill's income, they lived a very comfortable life for the next twelve years, until her husband lost his job.

"He was having so much difficulty finding work that I realized I needed to help out. The teaching market had dried up, so I decided the only thing open to me was secretarial work, and I enrolled in an adult education program for women returning to the workforce. But it was a blow to my ego—to go from the country club pool to the secretarial pool."

Since that time, Jill has moved into a nonprofit management job she enjoys, but because her husband has not found comparable work, their financial situation has not improved much.

"I work, I have three children, and my mother has been in and out of the hospital over the last couple of years," says Jill. *"I know we need to think about doing some financial planning, but the thought of it is overwhelming, and I just haven't had the inclination to do it."*

Jill remains in the Danger Zone because of her continuing view that everything around her is "too overwhelming." Although Jill made a positive step forward in taking a job to obtain additional income, she's correct in her statement that she ought to be doing some financial planning—a manageable task if she breaks it into pieces. Even without devoting time to planning, Jill would begin to feel more in control of her future if she took one single, simple step and put $50 a month in an IRA account.

Another excellent strategy to use when you're overwhelmed is to think of the old adage "Control what you can, and let the rest go." While no one has the power to make everything better all at once, you can still take small steps to improve what you can. For example, even though Jill is having a difficult time, she could commit to saving regularly—even a few dollars a week is a good start. Or, a woman who was concerned about her future might purchase a disability policy or join her company's investment program. From a psychological perspective, it is easier to adapt to change if you assess what is bothering you, decide what you have the power to control and what you don't, and then do what you can to improve your situation. You'll find that these steps will bring a degree of security that will help you ride through what you can't control, such as a spouse's employment situation.

3. WORRIED ABOUT HOW CHANGE WOULD AFFECT OTHERS

The sudden death of her husband put Maggie R.'s life on hold. She has responded by putting her finances on hold too.

Maggie's husband, a self-employed businessman, died two years ago, leaving her with two high school age children and an extremely inadequate insurance policy.

"I couldn't believe it," says Maggie. *"Not only have we had to cope with the emotional sadness of his loss, but we're left without enough money."*

Maggie also described herself as "paralyzed" by the thought of doing anything different with the money she currently has in the bank. *"It's all we have other than my salary, and if we lose that, I won't even be able to get them started in college."*

Unfortunately, Maggie represents millions of Danger Zone widows who were totally unprepared to deal with a major change in their marital status—the unexpected death of a spouse. Maggie's story sends a resounding message to all married women. You *must* accept the fact that life is full of change, some of it painful and unexpected, necessitating adjustments on both an emotional and a financial level.

If Maggie had taken an active interest in their financial affairs during her marriage, she could have evaluated their life insurance policy to make sure it would be adequate to cover her children's education.

As Maggie herself told me at a follow-up interview: *"I hope my story gives other married women the impetus to change how they handle their finances before a crisis occurs. The problem for me was that neither my husband nor I ever really thought or talked about what would happen if either of us died."*

4. UNACCUSTOMED TO CHANGE

"I grew up in a lower-middle-class family, and my father took care of all money matters. My mother's work was considered supplemental to

anything he earned, and we children were never included in money discussions," says Cathy P. *"By the time I was a teenager, the women's movement was well on its way to increasing options for women, but my upbringing had been so conservative that I guess I stayed safe in my job prospects and safe with my money too. My deep fear of being poor stayed with me well into adulthood."*

Cathy's first job was in the marketing department of a manufacturing firm, and as she rose in the company, so did her salary. *"Even when I started making good money, I still put away as much as I could. What made me change was my husband.*

"We met and married in our thirties, and he was my exact opposite financially. He was an impulse buyer—not a comparison shopper like I was. He bought things like cars and stereos without thinking about the price, and he just couldn't understand my need for security."

Though Cathy insisted they maintain separate checking and savings accounts, they did open a joint account for certain household expenses. Cathy reports that this account started out as something they always disagreed about: *"I wanted to save and budget for large items, but my husband simply felt we should spend. I found myself sacrificing in order to make up for the money he spent."*

A confluence of occurrences helped turn Cathy's story around. Her husband, who was twelve years her senior, attended a company-sponsored seminar about retirement. This experience made him begin thinking about his retirement and what money they might have, and he began to understand the point of saving and participating in his 401(k) plan.

"As he began to change, I began to relax. Some of my friends worked in financial planning, and I began to listen to some of what they said. I actually took the CDs I had started in my thirties and invested them in a higher-risk growth mutual fund. I was still very wary, but when I saw that I did well with that investment, it made me realize that if I learned more, it would be to my advantage and I could make more money."

Cathy is one who has come full circle and now ranks in the Action Zone, due in part to her positive response once her spouse began to see things differently. Like Miriam, Jill, and Maggie, she was resistant to change and preferred remaining in a structured, known financial situation that she considered safe. Her story also illustrates the fact that in certain cases both husband and wife need

to modify their perspective on saving and investing to make significant progress. (See Chapter 8.)

Positive Change

Several years ago, I had the opportunity to study what made older women (sixty-five to eighty years of age) feel happy and content in later life. I learned that these women shared common characteristics, and knowing what they are may help you in your pursuit of greater financial flexibility.

1. During their early years, they had embraced personal change and viewed it as an opportunity. Those who worked had broken down gender barriers and found ways to get the career they wanted, rather than taking jobs that were traditionally open to women. Those who were homemakers found creative ways to change their routine in order to keep it vibrant—by taking night classes, serving as troop leaders, or heading up major volunteer organizations.

2. Specific crises and problems in their personal lives were acknowledged, dealt with, and put into proper perspective. These women did not allow a painful event to paralyze them—their motto was, "By nature, life is filled with twists and turns, thus one must move on." Their secret was that they put change in its proper perspective.

3. Planning was a pivotal part of their natural routine. Although they didn't dwell on the fact that their husbands might die or become disabled, they *prepared* for these possibilities. They understood the need to take action in their younger years to attain security in the future.

4. Each took personal responsibility for her financial future. They worked alone or alongside a spouse, making investments and learning about financial planning.

Although you might feel that one has to be born with a personality that adapts easily to change, most of these women acknowledged that they had acquired these qualities by trial and error and from plain old experience.

I can tell you another thing about change. It's easier to change if you're part of a trend, and the latest statistics show that more Ameri-

cans than ever are saying they are likely to put money into a retirement or pension plan "in the next few months"—20 percent in
December 1995, up 9 percentage points in two years.

A major finding of the Scudder Baby Boom Generation Retirement Preparation Survey, developed and conducted by the NCWRR,
is that individuals who made even slight changes in the amount
of money they were placing in their company-sponsored pension
program reaped tremendous results in their attitude about change.
We found that as boomers directed more funds into a company pension plan, their tolerance to risk increased proportionately. In essence, changing the amount you save even slightly will make you
feel better about change, and the more you put in, the better you
will feel.

How You Approach Change

Making a change in your attitude toward money is just like making any other change. By looking at an example from life, we can
outline the steps that will lead to a positive attitude toward change.

Let's suppose your husband comes home with the news that he's
being transferred—there's little choice, the entire office is relocating.
What happens to you?

1. *Awareness of the change:* First, any news of change must be
   digested. Anger is a normal reaction to many types of
   changes, and in this example, even the most tolerant would
   feel anger at the disruption.
2. *Acceptance of the change:* As you accept the news, you begin to
   work through the resistance, contemplating why you don't
   want this to happen and listening to the inner voice that
   preaches the unfairness of it all.
3. *Problem-solving phase:* As the idea of change is absorbed, you
   begin editing out the destructive and doing what you can to
   make the new situation palatable, or even fun.
4. *Continuous management:* Often, adapting to change requires a
   continued effort to work at making the change a good one.
   This couple, having relocated because of a job change, will
   likely face a year of feeling "new," so there is long-term coping ahead.

Think back to a time when you had to manage a significant change. What was your reaction? Can you trace a pattern in your reaction to change? Perhaps you reacted poorly at the initial news, but once you accepted it, you moved ahead efficiently. If you can find a pattern, you'll be able to predict how you are likely to manage financial change. Perhaps it's difficult for you to acknowledge that it's time for change, but once you do, you don't look back. That's important to know as you contemplate changing the status quo.

To help you manage financial change, consider the following questions.

1. Do you need to make a change?
2. What needs to be changed? (You should never make sweeping changes all at once; identify something specific and start slowly.)
3. What scares you? By acknowledging what makes you nervous, you'll be better prepared to select the changes you decide to make.
4. How can you best manage the change?

Another way of looking at change is to determine what the consequences will be if you *don't* take small steps forward in the savings and investment arena. When I conduct a financial seminar for women, I always ask myself one question: Have I done everything possible to alert these women to the need to change their savings and investment practices? You can ask yourself the same question: Do I realize what is at stake if I have not saved or invested enough for the future?

Changing Old Tapes to New Tapes

In the following two exercises, read about the issues presented and contemplate the old you vs. the new.

EXERCISE 1

Issue: My 401(k) statement just arrived in the mail.

Old me: I ignore it, or I try to read it and find that I don't understand it.

New me: I review the statement with the in-house benefits counselor.

Change: Arrival of the statement is perceived as an opportunity to learn more about pension benefits.

Benefit: I can make better decisions about my pension benefits.

Issue: My spouse is meeting with our financial advisor.

Old me: Let him do it. He has a meeting with him alone and things are fine.

New me: Ask to come along.

Change: Accompanying him implies joint responsibility for family finances.

Benefit: I can assess whether I'm comfortable with this advisor and how he handles my questions.

Issue: My company has just been downsized and my position has been eliminated.

Old me: I am petrified about the prospects of finding a new job.

New me: I work to identify my talents, explore different options, and develop a game plan to find a better position or possibly start a home-based business.

Change: Although job loss is anxiety-producing, I perceive this as an opportunity to find a more fulfilling job and trust my talents.

Benefit: Through recognizing that I have talents and abilities, I may find a job that is more rewarding.

Issue: I have only a modest amount of money to invest for my future.

Old me: Since I don't have a lot of discretionary money each month, I don't perceive myself as an investor, so I do nothing.

New me: I have to start somewhere, so I will invest what I can each month.

Change: By recognizing that with any amount of money I *am* an "investor," I have taken the first, most critical step in preparing for my future.

Benefit: My investments will start to grow and I will have begun the habit of putting money away.

Issue: I bought this book and have tried to become more familiar with investing, but I still haven't bought any financial investment products.

Old me: I will accept the fact that this is just me—buying an investment product is not my cup of tea.

New me: I will start slowly. I will make a well-educated decision based on what I have learned about investments, and I will invest a small amount of money in a money market account.

Change: I have changed my mind-set to being proactive instead of allowing my fears to paralyze me.

Benefit: Research has shown that by doing something rather than nothing, I have a three times greater likelihood of succeeding.

EXERCISE 2

The dilemmas outlined below are those that women mention most often when we discuss financial planning and investing. The goal of this exercise is to have a conversation between the old you and the new you. Next to the old you write down how you would *normally* respond, and then write down how you *want* to respond based on your newly acquired perceptions concerning change.

Dilemma: You have been invited to go to a women's investment club meeting tonight but you are rushing like mad to get dinner prepared, arrange for the baby-sitter, and change your clothes.

The old me would say: _____.

The new me would say: _____.

Dilemma: You have just sent away for information on an investment product. However, you don't understand much of the terminology.

The old me would say: _____.

The new me would say: _____.

Dilemma: You want to apply for a line of credit from your bank. The bank officer gives you a packet of information on different loan programs you don't understand.

The old me would say: _____.

The new me would say: _____.

Look at the difference between your first reaction and the reaction of the new you. By changing your mind-set, you can develop new strategies for making the unfamiliar more comfortable.

Remember that change doesn't come easy, but over time you'll benefit: By reevaluating your financial practices, you'll actually achieve more control than you ever had before. Being willing to change means taking responsibility for your actions and doing what's right for you.

Next we'll take a look at control and why you simply have to take charge.

7

CALLING THE SHOTS
Who Is in Control?

"I've always worked and taken care of my money. I keep some in savings and some in checking, but now a friend is telling me that isn't enough. She says that I'm not really in control of my financial future unless I'm investing so that it will grow."

One night a young career woman had a nightmare. She dreamed she was her mother and spent her days taking care of the house, raising the children, and greeting her husband at the door. Throughout the dream, the woman constantly carried her pocketbook, stopping frequently to look inside—yet it was always empty. The dream caused great anxiety, and when she awoke, she was greatly relieved to realize she was still herself—a successful working woman who earned a good salary. Soothed by the knowledge that her financial and employment status were not like her mother's, she peacefully went back to sleep.

Before long, a second nightmare beset the woman. Now she envisioned herself surrounded by golden treasures that she had worked hard to accumulate, but she was unable to do anything with her wealth. She couldn't lift it, move it, spend it, or use it for her own needs. Covered in sweat, she woke up again and pondered the significance of both dreams.

Many younger and midlife women have committed themselves to carving an identity outside of the family. But unfortunately, like the woman above, many of them have concentrated on their career but have never explored the possibilities for what to do with their money once they started earning it.

For a woman to gain power and control over her financial destiny (to be able to "lift it, move it, or use it for her own needs"), she must plan what to do with her money, and for long-term growth this must involve investing it.

Collectively, women today actually have a great deal of financial control; they just aren't taking full advantage of it. Consider the following statistics.

- Women currently control more wealth than at any other time in the history of the country.
- Forty-two percent of households with gross assets of $600,000 or more are headed by women.
- Nearly 60 percent of women now earn their own incomes; their total earnings in 1995 came to $931 billion, or 35 percent of the U.S. economy.
- Women now own one-third of all U.S. businesses, and these businesses constitute one of the fastest-growing segments of our economy.

Still, family and society are not yet preaching to women what fathers tell their sons early on: "Money talks." As the above statistics show, women are beginning to accumulate the power of money, but they don't yet know how to control it.

However, it is an indisputable fact that having money "buys" you control over your life. On a personal level, consider the increased power of the following women.

- The teenager who puts away money may increase the options for her college education and may also enjoy the luxury of assuming fewer student loans.
- The college graduate who manages her money carefully can start paying off her college loans. When the loans are paid, she assumes control over money that no longer has to be used to offset debt.
- The young adult who takes charge of her money buys control

over her lifestyle (buy or rent?) and her job (a small nest egg permits her to be more discriminating and to hold out for employment that includes a good pension plan).

- The married woman who brings home a paycheck and works with her husband to decide how to invest their pooled savings is taking control of her future.
- The midlife woman who plans and saves has earned the right to help make choices. Whether she's contributing to the cost of day-to-day living, paying for a child's education, or going back to school herself, she has the right to decide.
- The senior citizen who has saved and invested all her life can afford the retirement she imagined—without depending on anybody.
- And women of any age who maintain their own savings are not quite so victimized by widowhood or divorce.

But despite the very clear advantages of taking charge of one's own money, women, thus far, aren't 100 percent comfortable with the concept. Respondents to the Women Cents Study expressed varying degrees of ambivalence about wanting to be the one in the family who makes financial decisions. And if they are reluctant to participate in financial management for the family, it would be unusual to find them off wheeling and dealing in the market on their own.

Paradoxically, women are now expected to be wage earners, but gender roles within the household still often leave men with the power and control. Women need to realize that a by-product of earning one's own money is the right to do more than supervise the checkbook and pay the bills; they need to have a say in how that money is spent and invested.

Interestingly, the Women Cents Study found a parallel between feeling in control of your life and a willingness to take charge of your money: **If you're assertive and feel in control, you're far more likely to be planning ahead financially and contributing regularly to a savings program.** (Women must first have a perception of control before being able to plan financially.) The study showed that those women who displayed assertiveness in life (they were the respondents who were willing to return a product, make a customer complaint, or move ahead with their own plans even if they displeased others) were those who were already taking positive steps with their money.

The study showed that these women generally knew how much income they needed in retirement and what they would have to save in order to supplement Social Security or their pension program; they knew the basics of financial planning and made savings and investing for retirement a top priority; they planned to make some investments during the coming year; and they felt that financial planning was worthwhile even if they didn't have a lot of money.

But if you frequently feel you have little or no control over your personal circumstances, you are probably reluctant to do anything about managing your money. Women who have little self-confidence about life in general find it all but impossible to take control financially. The study showed that these women generally did not place any priority on saving; they had no idea how much income they needed for retirement; they knew little or nothing about investment types and financial planning principles; and sadly, they had been led to believe that financial planning was pointless unless they had a lot of money to work with. (Keep reading. Even if you've never saved in your life, you can surely manage to set aside $1 per day, and I'll show you how to invest it so that you'll have $50,000 in thirty years. If you can increase your saving to $50 per month, the strategies contained in this book will help you obtain $100,000 within thirty years.)

To help you take more control, we'll explore:

- Why it's so important that you take charge of your own money
- Why women have not generally been in a position to take control
- How assertiveness in your personal life will help you take more control over your finances

Even Uncle Sam Wants You to Take Control

The government and private industry alike are encouraging people to take more and more responsibility for themselves.

Having peeked at the balance needed for Social Security payouts in the coming years, the federal government is sending out a resounding message: Don't depend on us to meet all of your financial retirement needs. Congress is currently discussing ways for Americans to invest a portion of their Social Security contribution in the stock market, as well as the feasibility of each individual's having a "health care savings account."

Private businesses are drifting away from company-managed pension programs and opting instead for retirement programs that employees themselves can take charge of. Individual retirement accounts (IRAs) and Keogh plans are other forms of saving that allow individuals to plan on their own for their later years.

Major financial institutions have also become proponents of self-choice. As the world has become more complex, with an increasing number of choices for everything from what to watch on television to how to invest your money, advertisements for the Prudential Insurance Company now trumpet "Be your own rock" instead of "Own a piece of the rock." After test-marketing to make certain that consumers understood that Prudential was there to offer advice and guidance, the company became comfortable espousing the benefits of self-control, reminding consumers that *the only person who can really look after you is you.* (This differs sharply from the strategies of financial companies in the fifties and sixties, which stressed the paternalistic "we'll take care of you" approach.)

Even financial planners make it clear that individual responsibility is part of any good financial planning picture. Professional planners have stressed the importance of reevaluating the "three-legged stool" (Social Security, pensions, and savings and investments). In the current economic climate, the stool is becoming lopsided because Social Security and pensions aren't what they used to be. To make the "stool" level, Americans (not just women) must take on more personal responsibility for their savings and investments, or the stool will tip over when they need to sit on it.

When all is said and done, your government, your employer, your financial services company, and your financial planner are all in agreement: Each person must become knowledgeable enough about money to take control of his or her own future. If you're hearing a message more than once, it's time to listen.

What Do We Really Mean by "Control"?

The very term "control" is a frightening one. By submitting to control, we may have to submerge our own will. Conversely, if we *take on* control, we may be asking someone else to subvert his or her own wishes or desires—a demand that women (who tend to put the wishes of others ahead of their own) find extremely uncomfortable.

For this reason, perhaps it is best to view "financial control" as "financial choice," which really is the essence of control, because it gives you a say in your own future.

Actual Control vs. Perceived Control: Knowing the Difference

In my work as a psychologist, I wanted to come to a better understanding of the dynamics of control. Over the years I've learned that the psychology of control includes both "mindful involvement" and "mindless responding."

This is an important distinction when it comes to managing one's money. *Mindless responding* describes a woman who takes investment advice from others without thinking it through or really understanding all the implications. She may make the actual decision about what to do with her money, but she did it because someone told her what to do. Though she is making decisions, this woman is not really "in control."

If you were to study control theory, you would learn something very gratifying: "Believing" one has control is more than half the battle, for it is the *perception* of control that is important to a woman's self-esteem. For instance, a woman may have an impressive and substantial financial portfolio, but if she doesn't *believe* she is in control, she fails to take charge of her finances, and her self-esteem suffers: She does not believe she can make a difference, and she feels financially incompetent.

When a woman perceives that she is in control, she feels on top of her financial situation and is willing to engage in *mindful involvement.* She knows the value of her assets and liabilities and also takes the time to familiarize herself with important household records such as investments, debts, real estate holdings, and insurance. Her strong sense of financial responsibility is reflected in the way she keeps records up to date, pays monthly bills, and meets other obligations in a timely manner. In addition, she works at being a good consumer of financial products and services by doing comparison shopping and by furthering her financial education. Most important, she recognizes the value of saving and investing for long-term needs.

When belief in one's control is threatened, the result can be incapacitating (something we see a lot of at our seminars) and may lower one's feelings of self-worth.

But why are we still discussing what is at heart an assertiveness issue? Good question, for which there is an equally good answer.

When I speak to groups, young women frequently comment, "But that was our mother's generation." That's true. And while we would like to think that financial control comes easy to young women five to ten years out of college, I can tell you that the financial control picture is improving, but it's not good enough yet. Part of the reason is that the whole concept of women in control is very recent, and anything new takes getting used to.

Looking Backward: Women's "Rights" Revisited

Up until recently, women have had few opportunities for exerting control over their lives. Historically, women (especially married ones) had no control over their economic, legal, and social lives. Consider these rules, which were brought to the American colonies as part of English common law. Some of them remained in existence in some places until the late 1800s.

- Married women could not own property (though single women could).
- Married women had the same rights as idiots and children—none.
- The legal "existence" of a woman was suspended during marriage, so she was barred from making contracts or suing.
- A woman's dowry and inheritance became the property of her husband.
- A husband could sell a wife's property without her consent, and she did not control her own wages (if she earned any).
- A married woman could not buy or sell anything without her husband's permission.

- If a husband died before his wife, any inheritance bypassed her and went to the eldest son or the closest male relative.

By 1850 a widow had finally been given the right to own up to one-third of her husband's estate, but she was denied the right to sell any of the property connected with it. As for the vote, women were disenfranchised until 1920, and of course, as women are well aware, the right to reproductive control is still very much at issue.

Chronic lack of control, which has been the societal norm for centuries, is not easily resolved. It's still a part of women's unconscious psyche. When people feel a chronic lack of control, they don't take risks, and they often retreat into predictably rigid behavior patterns. Times have changed, but women's belief systems have not completely caught up with the actual changes that have occurred in women's lives.

As you recall, part of the definition of "control" is believing you have control. Women today certainly have the opportunity to control the money they acquire and earn, but first they have to believe they have the power.

Recent Voices Have an Effect Too

The women's movement of the 1970s has helped somewhat to change society's message. Fully 82 percent of women in the Women Cents Study strongly agreed that "when it comes to understanding money and investing, women can be just as capable as men"; however, most women aren't yet taking control of their financial destiny.

Among the obstacles to taking control are lingering voices from the past. The women who come to the NCWRR's financial seminars represent a range of ages, and they carry with them a range of old messages.

Older Women (aged sixty-five and over). Raised at a time when money matters were solely the domain of fathers and husbands, these women are eager and interested in finding investments that will help to supplement their Social Security without eroding their nest egg, but are often hesitant to move forward. Part of what holds them back is misplaced guilt. Taught that the accumulation of wealth was the result of hard work, they often don't feel they deserve the money they have inherited.

In the NCWRR Money Matters in the 90s Survey, we found that 60 percent of the women aged sixty-five and over were not actively looking for ways to invest money—a higher proportion than any other age group. In addition, this age group, whose attitudes were largely shaped by living through the Depression, were least comfortable with the idea of borrowing money on short notice, and were the most concerned about debt.

But this older generation has the opportunity to start taking charge if they choose to. A gift of aging is the freedom from responsibilities to others, so that, as a group, these women actually have more time than ever to concentrate on themselves. Many have picked up careers late in life and are beginning to realize that if they had the knowledge, they could possibly take the power. To brighten their outlook, they must assume some risk and put some of their money in the stock market. Stay tuned!

Midlife Women (aged thirty-five to sixty-four). These women are in conflict—both in their lives and in their attitude toward control. Many still live the very hectic lifestyle of the "sandwich" generation, which has been caught between the needs of children and the needs of parents. This is an added stress for the baby boom generation, which is just beginning to turn fifty; brought up as the "me" generation, with a heavy investment in materialism, most boomers have done very little financial planning.

Many have been in the workforce and know that perhaps they ought to be focusing more on their money, but they are still caught in a time squeeze. What's more, financial planning fails to become a priority, largely because of their conflicting "inner voices." On one hand, the women's movement has urged these women to control their destiny (and they have done so); on the other hand, society has told them (and this is particularly true of women aged fifty to sixty-four) that it is still appropriate to earn less than one's spouse. In addition, they have been raised by mothers who may not have worked, and who still live by the old notion that women should not "bother their heads about money." This is all the more surprising when one considers that their mothers would have lived through the Depression, when saving was such an important ethic.

But women entering midlife are coming into a very positive phase of self-development. According to the Money Matters in the 90s Survey, women thirty-five to fifty-four are the largest group concerned about their future and the ones who are the most motivated to attend financial planning seminars. If they make financial planning a priority, they can and will quickly make up for lost time.

Younger Women (aged eighteen to thirty-four). While this generation of women holds great promise for recognizing the importance of attaining financial independence, many have not yet started to save and invest, and they spend little time thinking about pension benefits. This problem is compounded by the fact that Generation Xers have become disillusioned about their ability to land well-paying jobs and duplicate the lifestyle of their baby boom parents.

As a college professor, I continue to be very concerned about the overall lack of financial preparedness among female students aged eighteen to twenty-four. Often they have no idea how to balance a checkbook or go about establishing credit for themselves. They are very interested in how much money they will earn after graduation, but no one (not their parents or the educational system) has given them any reason to pay attention to the benefits package included with that first job. As a matter of fact, in a 1994 NCWRR study of men and women aged eighteen to seventy-five entitled the PREP Poll), female college students were the least prepared of any group to understand basic money management skills. (This is not to say that college men are all that much better prepared—they scored second out of five groups in lack of financial management skills.) Unfortunately, many have come back to visit me two or three years after graduation heavily in debt after "maxing out" on their credit cards.

What Level of Control Do You Have?

Whether you're married or single, you may have someone with whom you divide financial tasks. (If you're single, that person may be a roommate with whom you share bills, a parent who still advises you on finance, or a professional to whom you've delegated some of your financial chores.) This exercise will help you determine whether you ought to be exerting more control so that you'll be prepared to become a proactive investor.

DIRECTIONS

Place a 1 next to the functions and tasks you take a primary role in accomplishing; place a 2 next to the functions and tasks your spouse or partner handles exclusively; place a 3 next to the functions and tasks you and your partner handle *together;* place a 4 next to the functions and tasks that are not handled *at all.*

- [   ] Paying the bills
- [   ] Depositing checks
- [   ] Requesting investment material
- [   ] Analyzing investment return statements
- [   ] Updating your will and estate planning matters
- [   ] Making investment decisions
- [   ] Working with your accountant
- [   ] Meeting with a financial planner
- [   ] Establishing short- and long-term financial goals

ANALYSIS

To analyze the above, ask yourself the following questions: For all your 1 responses:

- How comfortable are you with taking on these responsibilities?
- Do you have enough information and knowledge to adequately perform the task or function?
- Are there any tasks you feel would be better delegated to someone else (such as a professional) or shared with a partner?

For all your 2 responses:

- Why is your spouse or a paid professional handling this task or function alone?
- Would you like to play a greater role in handling this task or function?
- Have you discussed this desire with your spouse or partner? Or, if you are single, have you discussed it with your children or others interested in your financial affairs?
- If you were given this task to perform, would you know how to handle it?

For all your 3 responses:

- Although you and your partner handle these together, are there specific aspects of any one of them that you want to learn more about together?
- If you are single, and completely dependent on someone else to perform these functions, which ones would you assume as your responsibility?
- Ask yourself whether "together" means that you are *informed about the results* or are really *involved* in working together.
- Do you feel that you have enough input and control over the outcomes of these functions?
- Are there specific aspects of these tasks over which you would like to have greater control because of experience or knowledge?

For all your 4 responses:

- Why are these tasks not being handled?
- What specific barriers do you see to handling them by yourself?
- Are you fully aware of the consequences of not handling them?
- Is there a specific experience or "a voice from the past" that is preventing you from exerting control over this aspect of your life?

What Keeps You from Taking More Control?

So, what holds women back? Our studies have revealed that there are four primary reasons why a woman doesn't take control of her financial life. Even one of these reasons can be a stumbling block; two or more become a real hurdle to overcome.

1. She perceives herself not to have the time to fully control her financial situation.
2. She feels she can't possibly master the knowledge she would need to make appropriate financial decisions.
3. She is in a marital relationship where her spouse has traditionally handled the finances. (See next chapter.)

4. She feels that control is impossible because her financial destiny is determined by luck.

It is very important that you consider which of these issues dominate your financial life. The extent to which you believe that you influence your financial circumstance will have a profound effect not only on your financial behavior but on your self-esteem as well. We will examine each of them.

COUNTERING THE "LACK OF TIME" ARGUMENT

An astonishing 70 percent of women in the Scudder Baby Boom Generation Retirement Preparation Survey (compared to only 34 percent of men) indicated that not having enough time was a major obstacle to retirement planning. As you'll read in Section III, financial planning and investing do not require an exorbitant amount of time. Although many working women feel overwhelmed by the many roles they are juggling, there are ways to budget time (not just money) for this essential aspect of your life. Learning about investments is just as important as any other hat you wear, and it's vital that you make financial planning a priority.

OVERCOMING LACK OF CONTROL BECAUSE OF LACK OF KNOWLEDGE

Seventy-three percent of respondents to the Women Cents Study indicated that they lacked enough knowledge to make investment decisions. While we will discuss ways to become more knowledgeable in greater detail in Section III, it is important to remember that lack of knowledge is actually one of the easier obstacles to overcome.

The first step to gaining control of your money is getting a clear picture of what money comes in and what money goes out each month. Use a loose-leaf notebook to record each week your checkbook expenses as well as cash expenditures under appropriate categories: "food," "entertainment," "child care," "household supplies," "car expenses," "contributions," etc. (If you're ready to computerize, the new money management programs will keep track of this for you and provide you with an annual accounting of what you spend.)

Consider how much your access to ready cash affects your spending habits: ATMs—"metal cash cows"—are quite insidious; they can talk to you (in three languages), tell you how much you have in a variety of accounts, make you feel that you're not really spending your money because it is coming out of a box; but they can't tell you *how* you are spending your money. In response to a recent NCWRR survey, women indicated that they used ATM machines, on average, four times a week. Eighty-seven percent of respondents couldn't account for how they spent all their cash in a given week.

Try this exercise: For one month, record where your ATM money is going. Buy a small notebook (or use index cards) that you can carry with you to keep track of daily expenses. Writing down what you spend will take less than three minutes each day!

If you're married, get your spouse to do the same thing. After a set period, call for an "ATM summit" at which you both go over your lists. Place an asterisk next to the items that are discretionary expenses. With some discipline, this money could now be used for investing—most people will be able to find an extra $25 to $50 to put into investing.

After you've kept track of your expenses for a few months, you'll be prepared to analyze what you want to change. Your tabulations may prove that you are not at all extravagant on weekday lunches, but that you seem to drop a lot of money at the variety store picking up hair clips and puzzles and stickers for your kids. What if you reduced that spending by a few dollars and put it in a money market account? It will add up, I guarantee you.

Additional control is as close as your desk drawer. Look at last year's income tax statement to get a clear idea of income. Then consider questions such as these: Do you know how much life insurance you have? What stocks and mutual funds you hold? What pension benefits are provided by your employer?

If you're never going to get around to this on your own, make an appointment to do it with someone who can serve as "tour guide." Trying to read a tax return or a pension accrual form isn't easy if you've never seen one, but if you arrange to have someone walk you through it, you'll find the process simpler and more enjoyable. Two excellent outside resources for this are your financial advisor and the pension administrator at your place of business.

Or, if you are married and your spouse is financially savvy, plan a special dinner (or even a picnic) and go over the information together then.

Ignorance Isn't Bliss

Sandra B., a vivacious, attractive woman, suffered greatly for her lack of knowledge. She and her husband ran a very successful business together for many years, but Sandra was blindsided for having remained ignorant about certain aspects of the business (and never objecting to the fact that the business was held solely in her husband's name).

"My husband was raised to believe that the man in the family handled the finances," Sandra explains. *"Quite frankly, this was all right with me because I guess I didn't really want the responsibility. My father had been a weak person, and whenever the going got tough, my mother had to step in and take care of things, and it wasn't easy. I guess I didn't want to be married to a weak husband who might dump things back on me.*

"As our marriage evolved, we divided jobs. I ran the front end of the business (it was a funeral parlor), and he handled the finances and managed our personal stocks, bonds, and mutual funds. Sometimes he would try to explain something about our personal finances to me, but I really didn't pay attention. As I look back, it was all just numbers to me—I didn't see the connection. It was boring. I remember one specific occasion when he tried to get me to understand how to read our investment statement—all I wanted to know was how much money we had, not how it was made or the types of investments there were.

"When he was only fifty-five, he became ill with a heart condition and he never recovered. During his illness, I ran the business as always, hiring people as needed, and assuming that even when he was gone, I would have something I enjoyed to keep me busy.

"Shortly before he died, he made arrangements to sell the business— assuming I wouldn't be able to manage alone, since I had worked in only part of it. I begged and pleaded. I couldn't believe he wouldn't acknowledge my contributions and recognize that I could learn to handle other areas. But he held his ground and sold. It was a very difficult time for me."

Though Sandra's husband had left her with some money, she was denied something that had been a vital connection for her, and of course, she had no idea how she was to manage what was left to her.

Sandra's husband never realized how strongly her identity was bound up in the business; perhaps if she had demanded to be made a partner, her situation would have been different. Unfortunately for Sandra, the sale of the business robbed her of her feelings of self-worth, so at a time when she was grappling with grief, she had no strong part of herself to hold on to.

Eventually, she found the NCWRR and has now started another business and is beginning to take charge of her finances.

"I've learned a lot over the last few years, and I'm enjoying it. I now find myself watching stock reports instead of the Today *show, and my broker can't believe the questions I ask. I feel empowered, I'm learning, and I'm having fun. Maybe if I had shown interest in finances earlier, my husband wouldn't have sold the business. I don't know why I avoided it for all those years."*

If there has been a reason why you have resisted becoming interested in your financial situation, consider the following. What messages did you receive from your friends or parents (and later your spouse) about personal finance? Were you ever encouraged to read the business pages? Were investments ever discussed? Is time a current obstacle to learning more? That's frequently the case, but if you're intent on learning more, there are easy ways to start slowly. How much time can you afford right now? Five minutes a day? Start by reading the business section of the newspaper. Forty-five minutes a week? Purchase some personal finance magazines and read them, selecting the one that is most interesting to you. Two hours a week? Look for a financial planning course and enroll.

According to the Money Matters in the 90s Survey, women appeared more comfortable than men with asking a friend or coworker for investment advice, so this kind of networking will stand you in good stead. If you just can't understand what any of this is about, invite a financially savvy friend to lunch and pick her brain. What makes it interesting for her? How did she become interested? Was she nervous about making her first investment decisions? How did she overcome it? View this person as a role model, for somehow she has managed to take charge of finances and enjoy it.

MARITAL TRUTHS

A troubling finding uncovered in the Scudder Baby Boom Generation Retirement Preparation Survey is that only 29 percent of both men and women indicate that they share the responsibility of making financial and investment decisions with their spouse. For the most part, men are still controlling investment decisions, either with the wife's full consent or because these couples lack the ability to change their traditional division of roles. Clearly, as we discuss in the next chapter, this arrangement has serious consequences for both the relationship and the woman's ability to achieve financial autonomy.

OVERCOMING YOUR FAITH IN LUCK

Some women believe luck or chance controls their financial destiny; and, therefore, they see little connection between choices in life and financial circumstances.

Ida M. is an intelligent, charming woman who currently works as a financial planner. Had someone told her fifteen years ago that this would be her fate, she would have laughed in their face.

"I grew up in a male-dominated family, where my father stressed that he alone should manage the money. However, because my parents divorced when I was only eight, my fate took a turn for the worse. Instead of the luxurious life we had formerly led, I saw that my stepsisters and stepbrother now lived that life while my mother and I lived on much less. I was very resentful, and I guess I started feeling hopeless about my situation then.

"I married in my twenties, and because my husband was still going to school, I worked two jobs trying to come up with enough money for medical school tuition as well as money for us to live on. Eventually, my husband finished medical school and went on to do his residency. Then a year later, he announced he was leaving me. I certainly had no reason to feel that fate was ever going to look kindly on me, but hard work didn't seem to be helping either.

"I'd never finished college myself, and one of my friends kept encouraging me to do so. I guess the fact that someone began to believe in me gave me the first confidence I had in myself. After going through three tough years of working full-time and going to school, I finally finished and actually landed a good job with great benefits. Somehow, symbolically, that meant a lot to me—someone somewhere believed my future was worth investing in. I worked there for ten years and slowly began to take an increasing interest in finance, and finally I decided to become accredited

as a financial advisor so I could help other women understand what it took me so long to learn."

Only a person who believes she can win against the tables in Vegas or Atlantic City would leave her savings and retirement money to chance. If you fit this profile, you need to become more comfortable with taking some control in day-to-day life. As you see that life really isn't a game of chance, you'll begin to take more control over your money.

Make a deal with yourself. Select something (costing between $500 and $1,000) that you've long denied yourself, then select a sum ($5, $10, $15) to put aside every week. When you've saved the needed amount, go purchase your "dream item" as a symbol to yourself that dreams can be realized by setting a goal and working toward it.

Use the same reward system to start a modest "pay yourself first" investment program. After you've proved that you can save by having accomplished your first goal, begin setting aside money for investing; the key to getting that money put away regularly is to *pay yourself first.*

Most people who leave their fate to luck suffer from low self-esteem, seldom taking control of even simple decisions in their day-to-day life. Do you let others decide things for you? If you do, there are some simple and fun ways you can experience a more take-charge attitude, and, believe it or not, by becoming more assertive personally, you will begin to gain skills that will serve you well financially. (Women who have become accustomed to deferring to others share a common trait: They don't listen to their own desires so that they won't have to feel disappointed.) If these exercises feel high-risk to you because they are so counter to your current behavior, start slowly, but do start—it's vital that you do.

- Two of you have agreed to meet for lunch. "Where shall we meet?" says your friend. Instead of letting her choose, *you* decide. (If the service is slow or the food is bad, don't worry. That can happen anyplace. It's not your responsibility.)
- You and your spouse are going to a movie, and you usually let him decide because he doesn't really like to go. This time, you select the film. If he rebels, explain that you'd really like to see this film, and you'll go to his choice next time.

- Fix what *you* would like to have for dinner tonight. Forget about the likes and dislikes of the family for once, and don't do short-order cooking if they don't like your choice. Those aged eight or over can make themselves a sandwich if they don't like what you've fixed; those under eight will not die if they are served cheese and crackers for dinner.

By learning to be more assertive in your personal life, you will find it is easier to take charge financially.

THE IMPORTANCE OF OWNERSHIP

No matter how much the novice you feel, it's important to take an "ownership" position in the process. Taking control of how you invest your money will give you a whole new perspective and make it a lot more fun. Perhaps these comments say it best:

"When I opened my first brokerage account, I was so intimidated that I let the broker pick all the stocks," says Cheryl P. *"In the weeks that followed, I watched as some of the stocks went up and some of them went down, and the only emotion I had was anger—I kept thinking, 'These aren't* my *stocks.'*

"When my tax refund came six months later, I called the broker on the phone and told him exactly where I wanted the money invested, and now I'm having a good time. When the stocks are up, I'm elated, and when they are down, I'm disappointed, but I find it's educational. I start trying to find out whether I picked badly, or whether it's just a temporary circumstance.

"I'll hold on to some of the stocks the broker originally purchased for me, because they are doing pretty well, but I'll never again turn the decision-making over to anyone else."

8

MARITAL MONEY DYNAMICS
Working Out Control Issues with Your Partner

"My husband takes care of the big money decisions. I never wanted to be bothered with them, but now I realize how important money is. A friend of mine just went through a divorce and ended up with nothing. Even though I'm happy in my marriage, Sarah's experience showed me that women who don't exert some control over their finances are putting their futures in real jeopardy."

I'd like to share with you the following letter, which so well depicts one of the main problems that occur when it comes to matters of money and marriage.

Dear Dr. Hayes:

You don't know me but I have kept a local newspaper article about your Center's work on behalf of women in my desk for the last year. I am writing this letter to you, not anticipating that you can solve my problem, but because I want to let you know how some married women (such as myself) are facing finances and saving for the future with a spouse.

I have been married to my husband for fifteen years. We have two children and live a comfortable lifestyle—my husband is an executive for a major oil refinery here in Ohio. Since the beginning of our marriage, my husband and I have had totally different opinions on what to do with our money. Although he earns a very good salary, Herb can't hold on to money. If there's a new gadget, he is first on line to buy it. I came from a very modest upbringing and want to save more of what is coming into the house.

Although I love my husband dearly, we seem to be constantly fighting about money. A year ago, Herb came home one afternoon with a giant motor home that he bought "on sale" for $45,000. I hit the ceiling. Although we love camping as a family, this metal monster parked outside our home represents our security. Every time I stare at it, I see our children's college education trapped inside. When he steps on the gas of the thing, all I can think about is our future running on empty.

Based on the article I read about how you think women need to get more financially involved, I asked my husband if we could meet with a financial planner. Although Herb initially thought it was not necessary, he finally agreed. During the meeting, I started asking some basic questions, and for the first time in my life I felt as if I was "invisible." Neither my husband nor the planner felt comfortable with me in the room.

Dr. Hayes, it is one thing for you to preach that women take a more active role in their finances, but you assume that your spouse welcomes this involvement. Between my husband, the rolling gas monster outside, and the experience with the broker, I feel like some pushy broad that has put her nose into something she doesn't belong in. Don't get me wrong. I love my husband, but he does not seem to understand why I am so concerned about money!

Thanks for listening. If you pass us on the highway, I'm the one in the passenger seat fighting for the wheel.

Jennifer Hill

Here is my reply:

Dear Ms. Hill:

Your letter gave me much to think over. Many couples such as yourself struggle with different savings and investment goals. Although you feel helpless about what is happening with the family finances, I know you have done the right thing by getting involved.

An important aspect of your letter is that you recognize that there is a problem—an important first step. Don't minimize this—many women fail to voice their frustrations and concerns. Second, because you indicate that you love your husband, you have a foundation to work from in changing the situation. Although it would be easy to blame your husband for his "live for today" perspective, he is also a victim of a society that spends for today and leaves the future to chance. Thank goodness at least one of you recognizes the trap this creates!

What I am about to tell you may not be easy to do, but I believe it is the only way to proceed. By the tone of your letter, you seem to understand that you cannot sit idly by and watch your future unravel. If marital counseling cannot help you create a saving and spending balance in your marriage, you have little recourse but to take your future into your own hands and "grab the wheel."

I recommend that you start by becoming more educated about different financial savings and investment options. Inform your husband that you are taking the initiative to find a financial advisor you feel comfortable with and one who acknowledges your right to be involved in the planning process. Invite your husband to go with you—if he declines, go alone.

Although I recognize that you love your husband and don't want to do anything to jeopardize your relationship, you must take action that will ensure that you will have the funds needed for your children's education and your retirement.

I wish you luck.

Sincerely,
Christopher L. Hayes, Ph.D.
Executive Director, NCWRR

Jennifer Hill's situation is not uncommon. Just as women are beginning to understand the importance of future planning and the need for financial security, they encounter another obstacle: Are they betraying their spouse or jeopardizing their marriage by getting involved in financial decision-making? Decades of socialization have made some women feel that they are treading on forbidden territory if they start to take an active interest in the family's financial goals or savings practices.

Some differences of opinion over money are only natural. Marital partners come from different backgrounds, and they may hold different views of spending, saving, and investing. What's more, marital conflicts over money often have little to do with money itself and a lot to do with emotional issues such as a desire to control, fear for personal security, or a desire to replicate the family atmosphere one experienced growing up.

Changing the money dynamics within a marriage is difficult, but it can be done if you remember that you and your spouse promised to support, cherish, and uphold the union. To uphold that union is also to ensure family security. If you love your husband, you have an obligation to take actions that will benefit your own welfare as well as the welfare of your husband and your children. Although in the short term this may be difficult, it can be accomplished if it is done in the name of love and concern.

In a recent survey undertaken by Dr. Finnegan Alford-Cooper, formerly at Long Island University's Southampton College, it was revealed that couples whose marriages had lasted fifty years or longer attributed their lasting union to the ability to mutually agree on how their money and discretionary income was spent. Similarly, researchers have found that couples who controlled their finances through mutual goal-setting, record-keeping, and planned savings were less likely to argue about finances. Communication and shared decision-making seem to lead to a more tranquil relationship.

If you spouse feels uncomfortable with your growing interest and involvement, realize that there is light at the end of the financial tunnel. You'll read of women who have successfully renegotiated their financial marital relationships, and this chapter will provide you with guidelines for getting from here to there. We'll examine the following issues.

- The economic dynamics of marriage
- The financial "hot buttons" that create tension between the sexes
- How to open a financial discussion with your spouse

Marital Money Dynamics

The very nature of marriage creates new social and economic dynamics, and when it comes to issues of financial control, marriage is affected by three separate dynamics.

1. *Marriage as a resource:* One of the best aspects of a strong marriage is the fact that it broadens and enriches both partners' lives by bringing to the partnership more friends, more interests, more experiences, and, if both people work, more money.

   "No doubt about it," says Miriam. *"If I weren't married, I'd never think of traveling to Australia, let alone be able to afford it."*

2. *Marriage as a limit to autonomy:* Single, divorced, separated, or widowed persons have more autonomy than married people, since in a marriage all financial decisions should be made for the benefit of two (or for the family.)

   "Even though I'm at home taking care of our children right now, our financial advisor pointed out that we should carry a life insurance policy on my life as well as my husband's," says Suzanne. *"We have no relatives nearby, and if something were to happen to me, my husband would have a new major expense in paying for child care."*

3. *Marriage as it contributes to unequal power:* In general, American marriages are established with a lack of equality when it comes to power, and in most cases, husbands have more control than do wives. Married women who work are still more likely than married men to be responsible for the majority of housework and child care. Because these tasks are not rewarded economically, the more housework and child care a woman does, the lower her level of *perceived* control.

   "Harry always knew about financial issues, just like I knew about grocery shopping," says Linda. *"I guess we just slipped into traditional roles."*

The McCall's Financial Literacy Survey, which I conducted, indicated that married women were considered the most "at risk" group for impoverishment because of their lack of perceived financial control. In contrast, marriage has less effect on men's sense of control simply because men have been raised with the strong understanding that they must always look out for themselves.

Whose Money Is It Anyway?

From my experience, there appear to be three major obstacles to married women's having control over money.

1. "IT'S MY MONEY"

Some women have a spouse or partner who subscribes to the belief that what he earns is "my money," not "our money." While the money may be spent on mutual or family needs, there is still no doubt as to who ultimately has the final word.

Another obstacle that is given little attention (but is often the source of much marital stress) is created when a woman takes a leave from her paid employment to either have a child or raise one. Although some men may not be willing to admit it, when a woman stops bringing home a paycheck there is an unconscious shift in the balance of power. Some men feel that the wife is not really working (by being a caregiver) and unconsciously revert back to the "my money" mentality. Some of my male friends often joke about being more than willing to become "Mr. Mom" because it would be so much easier. Again, it is in the best interests of both women and men to discuss their feelings about control of money when they are ready to start a family.

Women have to learn that although they may have taken time out to raise children, they have an equal right to "our money." And men must realize that just because they have been raised to believe that money is part of the male domain, things are changing, and their mates need to participate as equal partners.

2. THE MONEY IS UP FOR GRABS

In this situation, neither partner is interested in taking control.

Our studies have shown that financial control is not necessarily a "piece of cake" for either gender. In many instances, women report that their husbands aren't *interested* in taking control of their finances. Either their money is languishing in a savings account, or it has been handed over to a stockbroker with instructions to "manage this for us" (which just creates a new dependency). As you'll see, both of these solutions are extremely dangerous ones. The money in a savings account is destined to be eroded by inflation, and the money turned over to the broker could well be mismanaged. By giving up control, these men and women are, in effect, letting "luck" create their destiny.

3. THE MARITAL MONEY TWO-STEP

Although financial seminars for women are now the "in" thing, these workshops create a marital dilemma that must be addressed. One partner's desire for financial education will affect the other partner as well.

At many NCWRR financial planning seminars, I have observed an increase in attendance by male partners. Some of these men attend because they want to support their wives' financial education. Others, however, attend because they are worried about the consequences of having to share money decisions after their wives become more knowledgeable or because they want to make sure that the experience does not upset the status quo. The implication is that *both* partners must communicate and slowly learn to handle in tandem the "marital money two-step."

If you're planning to attend a seminar and your spouse expresses interest in attending, talk about how he's feeling. (Or perhaps you've bought some books on the topic, and he's curious about your plans.) If your desire to learn more makes him feel insecure, this early communication will permit you to begin talking things out. Or you may be pleasantly surprised to find him supportive. One fellow whom I talked to at one of our seminars said it best: "For years I've been trying to get my wife more involved, and I'm so delighted that she is finally interested. I came along to support her. When we go home, I'm ready to answer any questions she has because I heard what you were talking about, and I learned a thing or two myself."

Power Struggles over Job or Salary

Some couples find themselves embroiled in financial struggles because of unequal incomes. When the wife earns more than her spouse, it creates conflict, guilt, and competition. Recently I have counseled many women who are troubled by their husbands' poor response to this earnings imbalance. If you fall into this category, you must realize that just because you earn more, you needn't feel guilty.

But earning less money is no solution either. There is a big problem with the word "earn"—it implies that a woman may not have worked as hard if she brings home a lower salary. Women need to realize they have the right to spend money, and learn about money, and have their own discretionary money, even if they earn less than their husbands.

"Job priority" also causes conflict. Whose job or career should be given priority in a marriage? In many instances, women are now being offered terrific jobs for more money in different parts of the country. This means that a husband may have to grope with his ego or worry: "Must I give up my financial security so my wife can spread her career wings?" Many times, couples compromise with commuter marriages, but that presents its own set of problems.

More often, however, women find themselves uprooted because of a spouse's job transfer. It is assumed that the man's professional growth takes priority. Unfortunately, this can create marital disharmony unless the situation is clearly discussed beforehand.

I know this from firsthand experience. My wife and I lived on the West Coast and had been married for four years when I was offered a dream job at a major university on the East Coast. At the time, my wife was working as an administrator for the county health department and had to give up her well-compensated position for me to accept this opportunity.

As I look back on this experience, the upheaval of going from the West Coast to the East Coast was not as great a problem as my inability to realize what my wife was giving up. Although she agreed to go, it took seven years before she was able to land a job that came anywhere close to the status and compensation she received in her former position.

Although part of my insensitivity can be chalked up to youth, I have come to realize that my lack of attention to her career had to do with priorities—my priorities. I can see now that certain men may not realize the importance of what a spouse has to give up, not only in paid compensation but in self-esteem and job role identity.

In our very mobile society, this type of conflict will continue. Although there is no easy answer, I think both partners need to feel that they have an equal say in the decision-making. To this day, I am haunted by my wife's jokingly proclaiming that she "arrived on the East Coast kicking and screaming."

Losing Control by Default

In my work with married women, I invariably have to switch into my psychologist role to understand how couples get off the track with their money. What I find is that women often step into a financial pitfall early in the marital union, without even realizing it.

"I don't know exactly how it happened, but somehow Stephen has absorbed all the major decisions that need to be made, and I take care of the day-to-day issues," says Greta. *"We didn't ever intentionally make a decision, but when we needed something like a new car, I was busy ferrying the kids around, and he was the one who had time to go car shopping. Only recently have I come to realize that I resented his freedom. But it wasn't his fault—we never talked about it."*

Many women lose their financial independence by not paying attention to what's happening financially—many don't even give a second glance at their paychecks before depositing them in the joint checking account. Husbands sometimes "control" the money by default, because women have expressed little interest in getting involved. As soon as one person (either male or female) controls the money and makes the investment decisions, there is a radical (often unconscious) change in the power structure of the marriage, and the struggle to regain an equal share of that power can be a difficult one.

Recently, I met Ruth T., a financially savvy fifty-four-year-old who had an interesting story about changing the dynamics of her marriage. Ruth is a great example of someone who lost control by default but took corrective action to remedy her situation:

"At the time we were married, it was typical for the wife to stay home with the children and for the husband to 'wear the pants,' and we certainly fit into that stereotype," Ruth begins.

"My husband was finishing college, and when I received an inheritance from an aunt during those early years, I immediately put it in the bank in both our names. By the time he finished college the money had been spent. I didn't think a whole lot about it at the time—I just trusted that this was how marriage was supposed to be. He is a very strong-willed person, and I wasn't about to argue with him."

Life proceeded on course. When Ruth was twenty-five, she had her first child, and then two more during the next four years. Together she and her husband had agreed that she would be a stay-at-home mother, and for many years she was quite busy with her responsibilities.

Ten or twelve years ago, Ruth hit a series of circumstances that made her reevaluate how the control in her marriage operated.

Because of the manner in which Ruth's husband had set up their finances, she had no money she could control herself. *"If I wanted to buy him a present, I had to ask him for money. It was ridiculous.*

"Certainly, a contributing factor to the action I was to take was the fact that I was reading Gail Sheehy's Passages. *It made me begin to think about changes I wanted to make, and the book gave me a good 'you can do it' feeling."*

In 1979 another aunt died, leaving Ruth some money:

"This was my chance. I was sick of asking him for money, so this time I put the money in my own name. It was more money than I needed for day-to-day spending, so I started looking around for what to do with it, and I saw an ad for a financial seminar.

"After the seminar I started making a few investments on my own without consulting my husband. Although this initially felt great, and it was a very heady experience to have this much control, I realized that something was wrong. I didn't really want to go it alone. What I wanted was to be able to decide together and share involvement with investments. But I didn't want to return to the place where we started.

"The answer was getting counseling. For about six months, my husband and I saw a therapist who specialized in couples whose problems often started with financial issues. Initially, it was very painful because we realized that our problem was more than just money. It involved how my husband perceived me, how I perceived him, and what we had in common concerning future financial goals. We struggled to find a balance— both financial and personal—and we ultimately did, but we still have to keep working at it for the sake of our marriage."

Today Ruth has become an active and knowledgeable investor. However, she fully admits that it took years for her to feel comfortable with the idea that she was no longer going to be a "financial doormat," as she describes it. At the same time, she continued to work on the issue of communicating with her husband two very powerful messages: (1) Taking more control of the family finances does not imply that I don't love you; (2) we need to mutually grow to understand each other's needs and priorities when it comes to saving.

Ruth has a strong marriage today because she realized that she had to renegotiate their arrangement. As I interviewed Ruth, I couldn't help thinking how courageous she was, although she doesn't see it that way: *"I was just doing what was important for myself and my marriage at the same time. I didn't want to give up because both were important to me."*

The World Is Changing for Both Men and Women

While women are becoming more financially involved, men are also struggling to redefine their own roles. The nineties man is going through some radical adjustments. Throughout his youth, he has been socialized to believe that finance is his domain and territory. Often he refers back to how financial decisions were made when he was growing up.

Yet recently, men are hearing another message—the importance of marital role diversification and of supporting a wife in her care-giving, career, and financial roles. With time, married men will grow to understand the necessity of having a partner who is a financial equal, but it isn't always easy.

In my own case, my wife's growing interest in becoming an engaged, active financial partner has taken a great weight of responsibility off me. We now share the responsibility of our future together. But I must confess that it was a little difficult for me to accept at first. (And I travel the country telling women how important it is that they do just what my wife did!)

The aspect of our new relationship that frightened me the most was when my wife started poring through our brokerage statements—I was afraid she would be critical of what I had done prior to her financial awakening. No matter how much financial expertise your husband has, he will still feel vulnerable to a negative opinion from someone he loves. Rest assured that even men have feelings of insecurity—"I could be doing better," they think. If they feel threatened, it can be difficult.

I've also sometimes thought how much more quickly I could make a decision when there was no one to consult, but my strongest emotion has been that of relief: It is a pleasure to be freed of the burden of being solely responsible for our later years. On the whole, this experience has strengthened our marriage.

When Your Husband Is Risk Averse or Disinterested

"In my family I handle the money. My husband won't even write checks, which is a problem when I'm away on business. Sometimes it

really annoys me. I wish he would take more of an interest. He reminds me of what a wife of the fifties must have been like. He turns over his salary and asks for an allowance. In fact, we recently had to buy a car, and I made certain we bought it in his name just so he could establish credit."

Are you married to someone who takes no interest in finance? If so, you've got to do something. Married women cannot afford not to proceed if their husbands don't take responsibility for their financial future.

For some men, focusing on the present is a way of coping with the possibility of premature death. Although they may be reluctant to express this fear, men have unconscious anxieties about their own mortality.

At the same time, women must ensure that their need for security is being addressed. If a marriage is based on love and trust, a spouse will learn to understand why his wife is taking charge in the financial arena. By such action, you are not betraying your marital vows; you are actually strengthening them by taking responsibility for the welfare of your children and your family's future.

Opening a Marital Dialogue About Money (and Staying Married!)

How do you renegotiate your financial relationship with your spouse? Over the last ten years, I have traveled the country listening to women describe their financial situations. The statements below are typical. Following each one is a suggested way to approach your significant other. Of course, it can be adapted to meet your personal needs.

Keep in mind that the purpose of your dialogue will be to communicate the importance of your becoming an active member of the family financial team. In addition, your significant other must perceive your involvement as coming from a position of caring, not as constituting a threat.

Janice

My husband takes care of the big money decisions. I never wanted to be bothered with it, but now I'm realizing that money is power, and I should have taken a bigger role in handling our finances. I really can't make any decisions because he believes that I don't have the knowledge, so I just go along with what he says. But I'm beginning to wonder if this is best for everybody's good.

Here's how Janice might introduce the idea that she wants to get involved:

OPENING 1

John, I just got a mailing for one of these financial seminars for women, and Mary's going. I'd like to go along with her, because I think it's time that I started learning about some of this stuff. After I go, will you sit down with me and explain a bit about where our money is? You've always done a great job for us, but I really think it's time I learned more.

OPENING 2

John, I read something in the newspaper about saving for retirement and how much money people need—it really worried me. And it made me worry that I wouldn't know what to do if anything were to happen to you. Do you think we're doing enough, and will you explain to me where we are on all this? I'd like to work with you on some of the planning for our future.

Janice, like many women, is ready to move from a position of financial naiveté to one of financial cooperation with a spouse or partner. I call this period the beginning of the "money dance"—a period in which one partner is inviting the other partner to join together in equal partnership. The goal is to have both partners dance in financial unison so that one doesn't dominate or control the direction of the other.

Keep in mind that these suggested openings are just the first step in the process, and change may not happen overnight. Occasionally stepping on your partner's toes is part of learning new financial roles in marriage.

In the above openings, Janice is stressing the following.

1. By acquiring some financial knowledge, she wants to prepare to become her spouse's financial partner.
2. She is using her new interest as an opportunity for John to reevaluate the role she can play in helping with the family decision-making process. In essence, she is removing an im-

portant barrier to her becoming more involved in the family finances.

3. Note that in opening #2 Janice is asking her husband to look at the emotional and financial consequences that would occur if she had to take over the finances due to his untimely death or long-term disability. If they have a strong marriage, John should respond to this issue.

4. Finally, Janice is not saying that John has done a bad job handling their finances; she is simply asking to be a part of the process.

Harriet

No matter what I say or do, my husband will not divulge any information about our assets or financial situation. I think it's his pride. He thinks this is his territory, not mine. The other night, when I asked about something, he said: "This has worked fine for fifteen years, why should we change now?"

OPENING 1

Bob, I don't want to take financial control away from you, and I don't doubt the good you've done for us. I just think it's wrong in this day and age for a wife to be shut out. I'd like to review our wills again, and I'd like to know the name of our broker. If you care about our future and our kids' future, we've got to talk about money.

OPENING 2

Bob, let's be honest. We've had our ups and downs, but we've always managed to find a way to resolve our problems. We need to use this same flexibility in addressing our money and investments.

Harriet needs to use some financial "tough love" here. She has a number of alternatives if her husband will not cooperate.

1. Establish her own savings/investment account.

2. Begin to educate herself by attending a financial seminar and using the services of a financial professional without seeking her husband's approval (out of her need to take care of herself if he dies prematurely). Or she should seek counsel from a

financial advisor and invite her husband to participate. If he says no, then she should go alone.

3. She should avoid signing any tax returns without understanding their content. By asking questions, she'll also begin to learn more about their financial situation. (All women need to understand what they are signing. You are as liable as your spouse if the IRS comes knocking on the door.)

Karen

I hear about these women who have spouses that don't involve them in making decisions about investments. This certainly is not my problem! It's just the opposite. My husband doesn't want to take any responsibility for making investment decisions or planning for the future—it's all on my shoulders, and I don't want to do it alone.

OPENING 1

George, I now realize that I can't do it all. We've got to find a way for you to help out. I worry about being fully responsible. What if something happens to our savings? Will you go with me to a financial advisor? He might be able to help us set some mutual goals.

OPENING 2

George, why don't you want to be involved in our financial planning? I really feel alone in this area of our marriage.

Karen's spouse may be busy, or he may be intimidated, and her overtures may lead them both to learning more about personal finance. But if Karen does not receive an adequate response from her husband:

1. A poor answer may reflect what is going on in the marriage in general. The inability to get a spouse to participate in planning may indicate that the couple could benefit from marriage counseling. Once in therapy, they each might have the opportunity to understand the other's perspective.
2. Karen must decide how far she is willing to go to involve her spouse. Ultimately, she may realize that *someone* needs to

plan, and she is evidently the one in the marriage who is prepared to do it.

Lisa

I'm trying to learn more about finances, but I find it hard to find the time to read the articles I collect, go over our investments, and do any planning. I have made it a priority, but I still can't find enough time.

OPENING 1

John, I'm really trying to catch up on learning more about money, but I am having trouble balancing it with work and taking care of the kids. Could you be responsible for everything on Monday night so that I could stop at the library and have some quiet time to do the reading?

OPENING 2

John, so far, this financial material is hieroglyphics. Could we set a time once a week to sit down and go through everything? I'd like to know where our money is now, and maybe you could teach me some of the reasons you follow the strategies you do.

Once the communication lines are open, continue talking:

- Discuss with your husband or partner your feelings about money, and ask him about his. (Chances are you never knew that he saved for two years to buy the motorcycle he so cherished when he was sixteen.) And talk about how he feels when you spend $2,000 on a piece of furniture. By sharing your histories as well as your current attitudes toward spending and saving, you'll each gain a greater respect for the other's feelings.
- Both partners should write down, or discuss, short-, medium-, and long-term goals. From these you should be able to create a joint set of goals as well as a way for either spouse or partner to achieve a personal goal that may not be a mutual one. For example, if you save $5 out of your spending money each week and put it in savings, there is no reason you shouldn't eventually spend it on a weekend away with a former college roommate.

- Each of you should establish your own bank account to use for expenses you don't want to ask permission about.
- Share family financial tasks. Some couples alternate responsibilities every six months so that both have exposure to all aspects of the family's money management; others let one or the other handle bill-paying or investments, but both understand all aspects and make major decisions together as a team.
- If you're recently married, learn about your partner's spending habits and review your own to see if you are destined to run into trouble. And put any cash wedding presents you received into long-term investments for the future.

Ultimately, this type of financial sharing is the most loving thing you can do for each other.

Are Young Women Doing Better?

Although some younger women indicate they want equal control, a sizable number of them are still groping with the "Cinderella complex." I have found that many of my female college students harbor the misguided belief that they will ruin their chances of finding and marrying Prince Charming if they assert their financial independence within a budding relationship.

This whole issue continues to fascinate me. Why—with what we know today about marriage and divorce and relationships and women's independence—would these young women hesitate to learn about money? To explore this further, I decided to ask both my male and female college students how they would feel about signing a prenuptial agreement. My surveys, conducted over the past three years, show that 80 percent of female students fear that such an agreement would interfere with the relationship and erode trust between the two partners. The majority of male students (60 percent on average) feel comfortable with the idea of a prearranged financial understanding.

These findings imply that women believe they gain emotional security in the marriage by *not* having a prenuptial agreement (and rock the boat if they request one) and that men feel confident they would not have to lose their financial advantage if they had such an agreement.

When necessary (or practical), men are able to see marriage and divorce as business relationships (which is not to imply that love is not a part of the equation). Women see marriage and divorce as the beginning and end of an emotional attachment. Because of these different perceptions, money matters become that much more difficult to resolve.

Women must go into marriage with the understanding that regardless of who earns what, they are going to have a certain degree of equality in deciding how the money is spent. This means that partners must communicate their money needs and issues *before* getting married. If you ask most couples, prior to marriage, whether money decisions will be addressed equally, you will get one of two answers:

1. "Of course they will." The problem with this answer is that neither partner has established a process for how this will happen. It is an automatic response that assumes love will solve everything.
2. "We never really talked about it." Here, both women and men think that by some magic formula, the marital union itself will take care of how money is handled.

Couples, especially first-timers, often don't take into consideration the fact that they bring to the union very different perspectives on money. Discussing such issues before the wedding will make the marriage stronger in the long run.

If you're already married, talk to your daughters and nieces, and encourage them to get started on the right foot.

9

WHAT COMES
FIRST—PRESENT-DAY OR
FUTURE PLANS?
Your Outlook on the Future

*"I work, I have three kids, and my mother, who lives
two hundred miles away, has been ill. I'm so busy with
'today' that I don't have time to plan a family
vacation, let alone sit down to plot out my
financial future."*

There's an apocryphal story about a middle-aged woman who
wanted to know her future, so she consulted a Gypsy fortune-
teller who came through town with a traveling carnival. While the
woman waited anxiously, the Gypsy peered into her crystal ball and
then announced: "You will be surrounded by millions of women
just like yourself!"

Feeling gratified by thoughts of friendship and happiness, the
middle-aged woman said, "Tell me more."

This time when the Gypsy looked into her crystal ball her face
became grim. She raised her dark eyes to the woman and said, "My
vision is becoming clear. I see many just like you. Most are in good
health, but you are clustered with a group of women who have few
resources and very little money!"

Horrified, the woman rose up, threw down a pouch of money, and fled.

All that evening and late into the night, the woman pondered: Why was *she* with a group of women who had so little? She'd done all the right things. She'd helped put her husband through college, and once his career was launched, she'd taken good care of their home and children and the grandparents. She'd also worked part-time ever since her littlest started school. What had she done to deserve this dismal future? And whatever could she do *now* to change it?

Throughout her life, the woman had been a solution-seeker, so she tried to think what to do. At last, the answer came to her. If the problem was money, she'd better look into what she had and start focusing on her financial future.

Though her husband had always taken care of their money, she knew from her father that savings was a first step, so she began to put away something from her paycheck each week. Her next step was to reach out to a financially savvy friend: "You've got to show me what to do to make my money grow," she said. And the friend helped by teaching her about investing.

Several years later, the carnival came back to town. The woman revisited the Gypsy to see if her fortune had changed.

"You've come back," said the Gypsy, who remembered her because no one carries pouches of money anymore. "Let's see what your future holds now." Peering into her crystal ball, the Gypsy said: "You are with another group of women, but there are fewer of you. They look strong. Your health is still good, and . . . I see it now. You are living well; you seem to have some money."

The woman smiled a self-satisfied smile: "I thought so. You showed me a future I didn't like, so I started saving for another one." She stood, and instead of leaving a pouch of money in payment, she pulled out her billfold and took out the $5 she owed. She went home that night and slept very well.

The Gypsy wouldn't have needed a crystal ball to make her first prophecy if she'd been aware of the following statistics.

- Of the elderly poor, nearly 75 percent are women.
- The median monthly Social Security check for women in 1995 was $588.

- Only 20 percent of women receive any benefits at all from private pension plans.

All of the NCWRR studies conducted to date indicate that the "bag lady syndrome" (a fear of being left destitute) is alive and well in the psyches of women. In the Women Cents Study, over 85 percent indicated a fear of not having enough money when they grow old.

What remains to be seen is whether women in general will respond as the Gypsy's customer did—by coming to grips with what might be and creating a new future. Thus far, women have not done that; they've been immobilized by the future:

- Over 48 percent of women indicate that they don't have the time to invest, and they perceive the process of investing as overwhelming.
- 93 percent of women indicate that fear of not having enough money in old age is a motivator to save and invest, yet they haven't moved ahead to do so.
- 64 percent of women have not established a specific savings/investment goal.

Because the NCWRR had high hopes that baby boomers might be more savvy about the future, we undertook a special survey of the baby boom generation (underwritten by Scudder, Stevens & Clarke). Unfortunately, it seems that baby boomers are doing little better than the previous generation when it came to financial planning. Through over 70 percent of boomers are worried about their financial future, they aren't doing anything about it:

- Only 19 percent use their disposable income for investing (47 percent have a "spend rather than save" attitude).
- 58 percent have no idea how much money they will need for retirement.
- When asked about their anticipated pension benefits, only 22 percent anticipated benefits between $20,000 and $50,000; 22 percent are not covered by any pension benefits; and 19 percent do not know whether or not they will even have a pension.

If current investment trends continue, female baby boomers will

most likely have to work well into their seventies (though 48 percent of boomers want to retire before sixty-five), because their savings will be woefully inadequate, and their pensions will have to be
double what they currently are.

This chapter will help you understand:

- What makes a present vs. a future thinker
- How simply thinking of the future can help you be better pre-
  pared
- How you can become more oriented toward the future

The Promise of Hope

If women are so worried about their futures, why aren't they
doing something about it? For a time, those of us who worked at the
Center were puzzled by this paradox.

However, through the NCWRR's collective studies and our work
with seminar participants, we've determined that **one's outlook on
the future usually shapes one's preparation for financial well-
being.** "Future thinkers"—those people who just naturally keep one
eye on what's ahead—are generally optimistic about upcoming
events and enjoy planning ahead. In contrast, "present thinkers"—
people who focus more on the day-to-day—perceive that they have
little control over the future (often because they fear that the
amount of money they could put away would never be enough to
make a difference), so they fail to plan.

Yet we have good news for present thinkers. We have found that
they can evolve into future thinkers by taking some small steps that
are extremely effective in bringing about a change. **Putting away
some money—even a small amount—can immediately bring
about a change in attitude. Just by starting to save and invest, a
woman begins to reduce her anxiety about the future.**

If you're concerned about your future, do something about it
right now. Put this book down and go to your pocketbook and take
out a ten- or twenty-dollar bill and put it in an envelope. If you're
short of cash today, write yourself a check. Write on the outside of
the envelope "My Future," and seal it. In Section III you'll learn
about places where you can invest as little as $20 to $50 and begin
to make a big difference in your future. (Every time you're tempted

to remove the money you've put in the envelope, reread the story about the Gypsy.)

How do you feel about taking a concrete step toward a better future? It's a little like getting organized. Have you ever faced your house or your desk when it was an absolute disaster? Do you remember that as soon as you saw an improvement in one small area, you were inspired to keep going? This is what can happen with saving and investing. Even when you start small, you'll begin to see—and feel—a difference *as long as you keep going.*

Present Thinkers and Future Thinkers: What Makes Them Tick?

If it makes you feel any better, most Americans are present thinkers. That's why, as a society, Americans have the worst savings rate in the industrial world. Consumerism is more popular than saving, and what people want, they want today.

Women present thinkers are generally involved in providing for their families' immediate needs and wants, and because they are so busy coping with present needs, they have little thought for the future. If they do save, it's likely to be for a vacation or an appliance—not for their children's college education or their own retirement.

When it came to money characteristics, our studies reveal that present thinkers:

- Don't set specific dollar amounts for saving and investing, and do not establish specific financial goals.
- Indicate that investing for retirement is a top priority but feel it is pointless without a lot of money to work with.
- Have no confidence (or interest) in learning more about investing and are not making particular plans to become more knowledgeable.
- Invest, if at all, in conservative ways. They place a high priority on keeping the money liquid in case they need it for an immediate expenditure.

In contrast, future thinkers see the merit of delaying gratification and can visualize attaining satisfaction through planning for the future. They know that the actions they take today can make a difference in the quality of their lives fifteen to twenty years from now, and they are not unduly fearful about not having enough money in old age.

Future thinkers also displayed specific money characteristics:

- They are able to establish a specific dollar amount as a savings/ investment goal.
- They save and invest with regular monthly contributions.
- They place a high degree of importance on saving and investing and intend to actively invest during the coming year.
- They understand that saving and investing are worthwhile even if they don't have a lot of money to work with.
- They are more risk tolerant in their investment choices because they focus more on future growth and total return than on current liquidity and safety of principal.

Future thinkers often balance many tasks in life, but their approach to juggling is different from that of present thinkers. They are able to compartmentalize. Whether it's booking a sitter so that they can play tennis or going to a financial seminar, future thinkers have realized the necessity for sometimes focusing on themselves and closing out the needs of others at that time.

WOMEN WHO HAVE BEEN THERE

Women tend to be present-oriented because they are balancing so many elements of day-to-day life. Every day they must operate with a detailed "to do" list covering all aspects of life: baby is sick, needs to be taken to the doctor; report due at work, need to check to see if all the data are in; out of dog food, need to stop at the store; need to visit Mom to help her reset her VCR—the list never stops! Because the key to this type of life is keeping all the balls in the air at once, women are sometimes reluctant to add an extra one—that of planning for their financial future. If they lose control of the present (dropping one of the current balls), the stress is so great that it becomes impossible to think of the future—coping with present problems takes up all their time.

For the most part, the women we see continue to be present thinkers for the following reasons:

- They are already doing so much, they feel they can't handle one more thing.
- They've been raised to have a "live for today" attitude.
- Their fear of the future—primarily their fear of not having enough money when they are old—immobilizes them.

Let's examine three women who represent these categories. Perhaps you'll identify with one of them.

1. Too Much to Do, Too Little Time

"I came to investing late and for all the wrong reasons," laments Barbara F., who is in her early forties and divorced, with college-age children.

Barbara grew up as one of four children in a traditional family; her mother stayed home with the children and her father took care of all financial matters. She married at nineteen and had three children shortly thereafter. *"Those years were so hectic. We both worked. Paying for child care was a stretch for us, so we were always patching together our schedules, trying to reduce costs. I just remember never having time for much of anything except taking care of the kids and trying to get to work on time.*

"Our lives really never slowed down. My husband had the better job with better benefits, so he just naturally assumed responsibility for financial matters. I never thought to question it, because I certainly had plenty to do."

Fifteen years after they were married, Barbara's husband asked for a divorce, leaving her with three adolescents and not much money: *"After all those years of focusing on the day-to-day, I suddenly had to think about the future,"* explains Barbara. *"A friend told me about a financial seminar she planned to attend, and it was a real eye-opener for me. It made me realize I had to get started and that planning could make all the difference.*

"One thing I learned at the seminar was to check on what savings and investment plans were available through my employer. It turned out that there was a company program where they would invest money for you. I started by requesting that $50 be withdrawn from my paycheck monthly, and I've really done quite well. Based on the success of my program at work, I've also tried to save a little money on the side during the week— sometimes as little as $5. I saved until I had enough to buy a few shares of stock.

"When it came to picking a stock for my first purchase, I bought one that I knew about through the company investment program, and I've made some money on it. I just wish I'd started sooner."

Barbara's marriage was no different from many others. Financial planning is usually viewed as a male domain. Retirement benefits have been skewed toward men and fail to address the unique needs of women. (Keep in mind that, statistically, a high percentage of women are employed in situations where there are no retirement benefits or programs.)

Like Barbara, other women have also been socialized to put the needs of others ahead of their own. Women who have little opportunity to find personal satisfaction in things not related to the family suffer from not diversifying their roles. Just as one needs a diversified portfolio, women—from as early an age as possible—need diversified roles that go beyond the family. The woman who goes back to school for retraining will gain confidence in her abilities in the outside world, and this will likely provide her with both the skills and the confidence she needs to take charge of her future (which may include finding a job that provides a decent salary and good pension benefits).

However, our studies reveal that Barbara's early adulthood was not wasted: The very skill of juggling all the day-to-day tasks is strong preparation for money management. Whether it's scheduling and rescheduling family life or setting up a diversified investment plan, women are quick to grasp the process of focusing on more than one thing at a time.

If women like Barbara start putting away something for the future, they'll find that they'll be able to "juggle" a diversified portfolio with ease. (In Section III you'll learn about various ways you can invest your money that require little time and a starting base of $50 per month.)

2. Living Dangerously: Living for Today

Naomi K. was an only child, and her family, though not wealthy, was very comfortable. *"My parents had trouble conceiving, and when I finally came along, they—as well as two sets of grandparents—were just thrilled,"* explains Naomi. Because of the difficulty in having her, Naomi was very much treasured by everyone, and the resources the family enjoyed were happily spent taking care of her. From the best backyard playhouse in the neighborhood to a dazzling Sweet Six-teen party, Naomi lived a very special life.

Naomi, now only thirty-four, went to school with friends who had plans for big careers, but, she says, *"Maybe because of the way I was raised, I never was particularly motivated. I wanted a house and kids and to spend days at the pool or playing tennis. Why should I push? There was nothing I particularly wanted that I didn't have."*

Naomi's husband owned his own business, and for the first ten years of their marriage, everything went as Naomi planned. *"I love decorating, and I spent a lot of time planning the look of each room in our house. We had two children not long after we married, and so I was busy with them too. I never worried about working, and I hardly thought about asking what things cost—I'd never had to growing up."*

But her husband's business hit hard times, and all of a sudden both Naomi and Phil needed to be asking what things cost. *"Once I began to understand the magnitude of what had happened, I was horri-fied. I still had several thousand dollars' worth of charges on my credit card, and we were wondering where we would get the money to make our house payments. I'd never really paid attention when Phil talked about business. It turned out that the business had been failing for a couple of years, and he had used our savings and investments trying to bail it out.*

"Phil is working at another company now. I've also taken a job, and we're beginning to catch up on our bills, but it's been terrible. After we've finished paying off all the credit cards, we're taking the money we'd been allotting to payments and putting it directly into savings. Believe me, I'll never say 'charge it' again, without thinking ahead about where the money to pay for it will come from."

Together Naomi and Phil are working to start over, and this time Naomi will be very much a part of the process. They met with a financial advisor, and now both Naomi and Phil review and discuss their financial statements when they arrive in the mail. They say that this joint responsibility has provided them with a new bond, and they are enjoying the new feeling of trust that is emerging in their relationship. Naomi knows that "live for today" will no longer be part of her philosophy. *"I'm beginning to see that I can have some effect on our future by delaying the things I normally might want today and setting aside the money for what the two of us have decided we would like for the future.*

"A few years ago I cared desperately about driving a status car. Today

I'd rather invest that money." (For additional information on how couples negotiate money relationships, see Chapter 8.)

According to the Women Cents Study, many women start out as Naomi did, with a "spend now, worry later" philosophy: Forty-one percent of respondents did not feel that controlling their spending in order to save was very important, and only 56 percent reported any hesitancy to buy on credit.

Our culture has created a population that feels entitled to the American Dream, and if it seems too far out of reach, they look for ways to make it come true.

A recent study has indicated that low-income families buy the greatest number of lottery tickets—an average of $90 worth per month. What a pity! Had all these people placed that money in a long-term investment (where the odds of a payoff are much more favorable), they could have created their own nest egg. If a family were to save $90 per month for twenty years, they could have accrued $21,600, and had they invested it at 6 percent interest during that time, they would have gained $19,777.24 in interest, giving them a grand total of $41,377.24. Having this money invested, instead of buying lottery tickets each week, holds the promise of a decent start toward retirement.

3. Concern About Aging

Louise M. was born into a well-to-do family. *"Growing up, we had household help and never had to worry about how we would pay for anything. We had riding lessons and skating lessons—every advantage."*

However, Louise's path was crossed with some bad luck. A first marriage produced a son, but the marriage ended in an unpleasant divorce. *"My husband walked out on us and rarely sent support checks, so obviously, I had to work to support us both."*

About the time her son was leaving for college, Louise met and married a very successful business executive. *"Stan commanded a very good salary, and we lived well. I was thrilled to finally quit work and live the life I'd always felt I deserved. I couldn't have been happier. We were all set for good years through our fifties and right into retirement."*

Unfortunately, their luck didn't last. Stan's company downsized, and he was out of a job. Only then did Louise learn that what they had lived on had been all he made—he'd never participated in retirement plans, and they'd lived from paycheck to paycheck. With great reluctance, Louise returned to work. *"I used to look forward to our retirement, but I don't anymore. I'm sixty-eight; I'll work as long as I can because we need my benefits, but once I retire, we're going to have to get by on Social Security and a small pension plan. It won't be the retirement I had in mind."*

Like most present-oriented women, Louise didn't think about retirement, and therefore, it never occurred to her to ask about her husband's pension plan. Only when a crisis occurs do women like Louise get involved.

Though it is commonly believed that it is gray hair and wrinkles women fear, our studies show that, like Louise, women don't fear aging—they fear being poor. Our Money Knowledge Survey indicated that 71 percent of women want to live to age ninety or beyond—yet the Women Cents Study revealed that 80 percent of women are extremely concerned about the state of their finances for retirement.

While it is appropriate for women to be concerned about their financial future, they also have reason to look forward to their later years: For women now between thirty and forty-five, the retirement years will be far better than they were for their mothers' generation:

- As a result of increased emphasis on healthy living, women are going to be far more active than previous generations were. In the Money Matters in the 90s Survey, three out of four respondents between the ages of sixty-five and eighty reported good or excellent health; only 4 percent reported poor health, and a significant 12 percent reported that their health actually improved after retirement!
- Women will have more opportunities to continue to work in occupations they enjoy.
- Although many women will live out their remaining years without a spouse, they will have thousands of peers who will want to travel, play sports, and join investment clubs with them.
- Those women who are fortunate to remain married will have mates who also want to enjoy "living" rather than resting in a rocking chair.
- When we asked female baby boomers to describe how they envision their retirement, they had a very optimistic outlook,

which included new opportunities, leisure, and more freedom. (Less than 2 percent of respondents characterized their later years as a time of decline, boredom, or insecurity.)

There is little doubt that women have tremendous opportunities for the future; they just need to be sure they have the cash to finance them.

How Far Ahead Is "Future"?

Does planning for the future mean that from the time you graduate from college you should have been focusing on retirement? Not at all. Beverly M., a forty-seven-year-old African American who was raised in a small town in Alabama, tells a story that illustrates how you can be future-oriented without focusing beyond what you can envision. She learned the art (and realized the benefits) of always focusing a step ahead of where you are, and in the process, Beverly learned to balance present and future thinking.

Beverly grew up in a middle-class family. Her mother stayed home while the children were growing up. Both her father, a church deacon, and her mother stressed the importance of education. The children were encouraged to have part-time jobs and to save their money. However, Beverly broke from her family temporarily when her parents began to "match" her with some of the young men in the church congregation whom they found "acceptable."

"In our community, the women were subservient in their marriages, and I just wasn't going to buy into that," says Beverly, who, upon graduation, moved to Birmingham to be in a larger community. A brief marriage left her with a daughter to raise, but she was fortunate because she quickly obtained a very good job.

"I knew that I needed to provide a safe and secure financial environment for myself and my daughter, and I accepted the job partly because of the excellent benefits, including a pension plan and stock options, that would allow me to feel comfortable with the position for the foreseeable future."

Beverly stayed in her position for twenty years but was laid off when the company was downsized: *"It wasn't a devastating experience because I had savings as well as the money I had invested with the company. I also took with me a good pension plan. I was able to take tempo-*

rary jobs for a while without worrying because I knew that things would work out and that I was still in good shape for the future."

Beverly's assessment was correct, and before long she was hired by the software company where she works today.

But Beverly had to reckon with one additional change beyond her job switch: Formerly, her investing had been done in the form of contributing to her company's plan. In other words, the money was invested for her. In her new job, Beverly had to take charge herself.

As a future thinker, Beverly was very measured in her approach. She knew that her child would soon be self-supporting, so at forty-five, Beverly began to focus on saving and investing for her own future—her retirement. Beverly outlines the steps she took to begin to learn more about investing:

"I gave myself a year to become better educated about my finances. "I've always been one to turn to people more knowledgeable than I am when I need help with something, and that's what I did. I looked for outside sources where I could learn more and did the following: attended financial seminars; read a couple of books on money management; started watching investment programs on television; read the Wall Street Journal, Newsweek, *and* Fortune *to acquaint myself with investing and the stock market; and finally, I joined a women-only investment club."*

Does she have any additional advice? *"Use a financial advisor— that's how I got connected to the investment club—but do so wisely. What I liked about the advisor I found was that she had a specific method for planning ahead, taking into account my current salary and how I wanted to live in the future, and she was a good teacher—she could really explain to me what we were doing and why. In addition, she emphasized that I had to learn about what was happening with my money myself; she wouldn't just take it and manage it for me. I think that's important in the long run."*

Beverly is a good example of how present thinking and future thinking blend together for optimum planning. While you may consider yourself either a present thinker or a future thinker, most of us have both qualities. We need a balance between the two. We need to reward ourselves for today's labors while also investing for tomorrow.

Those who have tried dieting realize that to be truly successful their diet must be integrated into a lifestyle change that is gradual—

one step reinforcing the next. Like dieting, moving from present to future thinking does not happen overnight. In addition, you're doomed if you start the process with expectations that are too ambitious, or expecting instant gratification. Take comfort in seeking a slow, gradual shift to future orientation instead of the unrealistic hope for an instant transformation.

Are You a Present or a Future Thinker?

You probably have some idea where you fall in terms of present or future thinking, but your answers to this quiz may still surprise you.

DIRECTIONS

Below are statements concerning personality attributes. As you read each statement, be as honest as possible about whether it reflects your general outlook or perspective.

1. I am the type of person who sets a goal and completes it.
   ☐ Exactly like me
   ☐ Somewhat like me
   ☐ Not at all like me

2. I am impressed with people who have more education or more experience at something than I do.
   ☐ Exactly like me
   ☐ Somewhat like me
   ☐ Not at all like me

3. When it comes to money, I make decisions based on what feels right to me.
   ☐ Exactly like me
   ☐ Somewhat like me
   ☐ Not at all like me

4. Before I go see a movie, I like to read a review or ask others what they thought of it.
   ☐ Exactly like me
   ☐ Somewhat like me
   ☐ Not at all like me

5. What will be, will be . . . I keep both feet planted in the here and now.
   - ☐ Exactly like me
   - ☐ Somewhat like me
   - ☐ Not at all like me

6. When I cook, I follow a recipe exactly.
   - ☐ Exactly like me
   - ☐ Somewhat like me
   - ☐ Not at all like me

7. I feel that my future is filled with great opportunities that I'll be able to take advantage of.
   - ☐ Exactly like me
   - ☐ Somewhat like me
   - ☐ Not at all like me

8. If I don't understand something, I'm not afraid to ask a question.
   - ☐ Exactly like me
   - ☐ Somewhat like me
   - ☐ Not at all like me

9. Financial planners have a much better grasp of how to make my money grow than I could ever have.
   - ☐ Exactly like me
   - ☐ Somewhat like me
   - ☐ Not at all like me

10. If I read a book like this to increase my money knowledge, I know I'll move forward with it and apply what I've learned.
    - ☐ Exactly like me
    - ☐ Somewhat like me
    - ☐ Not at all like me

11. If I were to invest in a mutual fund, I would select one based on what type of return it produced this year.
    - ☐ Exactly like me
    - ☐ Somewhat like me
    - ☐ Not at all like me

12. When it comes to major financial decisions, I often make snap judgments.
    ☐ Exactly like me
    ☐ Somewhat like me
    ☐ Not at all like me

13. In analyzing a problem, I like to play the role of devil's advocate to see all sides.
    ☐ Exactly like me
    ☐ Somewhat like me
    ☐ Not at all like me

14. When I think about investing in the stock market, I'm not worried about my investments going up and down—if I've done my homework, that's the best I can do.
    ☐ Exactly like me
    ☐ Somewhat like me
    ☐ Not at all like me

SCORING

For each "exactly like me" statement: 3 points
For each "somewhat like me" statement: 2 points
For each "not at all like me" statement: 1 point

Now total your scores for questions 2, 4, 5, 6, 9, 11, and 12. And for questions 1, 3, 7, 8, 10, 13, and 14.

ANALYSIS

Questions 2, 4, 5, 6, 9, 11, and 12 reflect your *present orientation.* Questions 1, 3, 7, 8, 10, 13, and 14 represent your *future orientation.*

Which score is higher? If you have a more *present* orientation, consider the following.

1. Present-oriented thinkers usually like predictability, want to know what is expected of them, prefer fewer options, and take a wait-and-see approach to important events. Although these are not negative qualities, they can prevent you from planning for the future.

2. To become more *future*-oriented, ask yourself the following.
    a. Are you guided by authority figures from your past who prevent you from looking beyond the present?
    b. Do you tend to trust others rather than believing in your own intuition and feelings?
    c. Do you have a tendency to accumulate knowledge and then not act on it for your future well-being?

3. If you answered yes to several of these questions, contemplate the risk you are taking by *not* looking ahead. For example, if you attend a financial seminar but do nothing about what you learned, is that really benefiting your future? If you recognize the importance of planning financially for the future but don't take time to invest in a financial product, what good is simply being aware?

4. To help you move to a more future-oriented perspective, consider the following steps.
    a. For a one-week period, focus on a particular piece of financial knowledge you want to obtain.
    b. Identify as specifically as possible what you want to do with this knowledge. Write this goal down on a piece of paper and establish a deadline.
    c. Outline the steps you will take toward achieving this goal, so that you will be taking some form of *action* with the knowledge.
    d. Apply this process to developing other future-related goals.

Your Future Priorities

Here's a final "future-oriented" exercise for anyone who is hoping to retire within the next twenty years. (If you're thirty-five and want to retire by fifty-five, this means you too!)

Part of the reason it is difficult to think ahead to retirement is that society emphasizes the accumulation of money in the abstract, which is much more difficult to visualize than a particular lifestyle. This exercise will help you focus on how you see your lifestyle changing after you retire. When you realize what it is you'd like to have, it will be much easier to figure out ways to pay for it.

DIRECTIONS

We have listed various options and lifestyle possibilities you may want to consider for the future. Place a number next to each item, reflecting its priority level for your future: 1 is highest priority; 2, somewhat a priority; 3, not a priority.

- [   ] Travel
- [   ] Return to school
- [   ] Start a business
- [   ] Perform volunteer work
- [   ] Take enrichment courses
- [   ] Develop a new hobby
- [   ] Maintain current job and career track
- [   ] Relocate
- [   ] Spend time with your children or grandchildren

ANALYSIS

Look at all your number 1's. These priorities paint a picture of your future self. Research on aging indicates that there is a three times greater likelihood of achieving a satisfactory lifestyle in your retirement if you envision what you want and *plan for it*. At this stage of your life, it is important to begin planning in order to make sure that you have the financial resources to implement your goals.

10

DECIDING WITH YOUR HEAD OR YOUR HEART?
Financial Decision-Making

"I'm good at saving money, but I'm having trouble making decisions about investing. I get nervous when I think about the possibility of losing what I've worked so hard to save."

A real estate agent once told me a wonderful story about two cousins who were clients of hers. Both lived in a major city, but because they were starting families, they were interested in moving to the suburbs. Here's how my friend related their story:

"I got to know Jan—a very delightful, methodical person—quite well, because over the course of two years she and I looked at many, many homes!" explained the real estate agent good-naturedly. "Jan's style was a careful one, and she and her husband investigated everything—if we found a house, she then visited the school and called all the neighbors. A year into the search, she still hadn't purchased a house, and we'd missed out on one or two because of all the legwork she did on each property before she would make any sort of commitment.

"Then one day she made an appointment with me, but this time she was bringing Kathy, her cousin, and Kathy's husband, Doug, since they were also interested in moving to the suburbs. That day we looked at six houses. Kathy and her husband fell in love with the third house we visited, and they made an offer the very next day."

The difference between the two women lay in the fact that Kathy had made one key decision—to move to the suburbs—and she was prepared for the other necessary decisions to follow in rapid sequence. My friend explained to me that Kathy had grown up in a neighboring community and was convinced of the rightness of their plan, so when she and her husband looked at houses, they were open-minded, and they happened to really like one of those that were on the market that day. (And remember, too, that Kathy had benefited from all of Jan's careful investigation of the neighborhood and the community.)

In contrast, Jan was a methodical, organized person who would never make a major decision without carefully examining every aspect of the purchase, and because she was more ambivalent about her basic decision to move, her methodical nature sometimes got in the way of making a decision.

P.S. Jan did finally buy a home, and my friend reports that both couples are very happy.

Two Women: Two Decision-Making Styles

Two women with very similar backgrounds started from one central point—both wanted to buy a house. However, they took very different approaches to the process of decision-making: Kathy was an emotional decision-maker and Jan was cognitive.

Cognitive decision-makers base their decisions on facts. Generally speaking, their decisions are well thought out and supported by research and planning. As a result, they tend to worry less about their choices after they are made.

Jan and her husband made plans for their move, and she set about looking for a good house in a comfortable community with a good school for her children, doing all the vital research along the way.

The difficulty Jan faced was one that sidetracks many cognitive decision-makers: She got bogged down in the "process." Instead of enjoying the very exciting prospect of her move, Jan got wrapped up in "doing it right," and found it difficult to get beyond the information-gathering stage. She and her husband had lost out on several homes because they were sold before Jan had time to finish her investigation.

The cognitive decision-maker is at her best when she learns to know when enough is enough and it's time to make a decision.

Emotional decision-makers base their decisions on feelings. The ideal emotional decision-maker is one who absorbs the basic facts of a situation and then is willing to take a leap of faith that her decision will be the right one.

Emotional decision-making does not work well when it is used simply to "get a decision over with." Sometimes this kind of impulsive decision results from a lack of confidence: "I'll never come up with the right answer, so I'll just pick any answer." Other times, the emotional decision-maker may not know how to look for the information (such as finding out about a stock) to back up her decision. Or sometimes she'll put the needs of others before her own and wind up making a decision based on what is good for someone else.

In the real estate agent's story, Kathy represents emotional decision-making at its best. She is comfortable with her basic decision to move. She has confidence in her choice because she knows the area and has listened to Jan, so when her "heart" tells her she's found a great house, she is ready to act.

Now refer back to the Self-Test in Chapter 2. What did the test reveal about your decision-making style? Are you emotional or cognitive, or some balance of the two?

When the NCWRR first started studying women and money, we assumed that we would be able to identify the "perfect" decision-making style. Instead, what we learned was that there *is* no single correct style. If you're too emotional, you may invest impulsively based on an unresearched "hot tip"; if you're too cognitive, you may get bogged down in the process instead of realizing that there is a time when you just have to go for it. The ideal style would seem to be finding a balance between the two.

What Our Studies Reveal About Financial Decision-Making

If you're like most women who took the Women Cents Survey, you are careful about making investment decisions (80 percent of our respondents perceive themselves as doing a lot of research and planning prior to making an investment); and once you're ready to make your decision, you may ultimately go with a hunch (56 percent of respondents use intuition when making investment decisions). However, getting to the ultimate decision point isn't easy: Fifty-four percent of you procrastinate on financial decisions because of fear of making a mistake, and 58 percent worry once you've made the decision.

And what about financial "hot tips"? Would you (or most of our respondents) buy on one? The answer is a resounding no. Of those women surveyed, 87 percent reported that they were not likely to make an investment based on a hot tip.

Another study (the Dreyfus Gender Investment Comparison Survey) provided us with deeper insight into the decision-making process. Our most significant finding was that, when it comes to making a decision, women are much more likely than men to consult others—a financial planner, a friend, or a spouse. There are two primary reasons for this. One is to gather information, because, by nature, women utilize their support systems to their advantage by frequently consulting others. The second reason is to seek validation. Women are often fearful of making a mistake, so talking to others provides them with an opportunity to confirm that what they are doing makes sense.

While networking can offer decided benefits, one danger lies in the continual pursuit of information or validation from others. Women often fall victim to information or opinion overload, which turns something simple into something very complicated and cumbersome. That is why *you* must ultimately be the sole judge of what is in *your* best interests.

There's a terrific secret to knowing when you've gathered enough knowledge and are ready to make a decision: *When the information or advice you're seeking becomes repetitive, you've done enough—go ahead and make your decision.*

Gender Differences in Decision-Making

Ever since the NCWRR was founded, the media have been extraordinarily interested in how men and women differ in their approaches to money, including their decision-making styles. As a result, we've visited and revisited this issue in our studies, to see if there were any puzzle pieces in the gender differences that might help women to become more comfortable with the financial decisions they make.

When the NCWRR looked at the genders separately, we found that men tend to be speculative investors, always looking for that pot of gold.

Because a boy's upbringing includes competitive sports (watching if not playing) where winning and losing are part of everyday life, men are more likely to see investing as a game: How can I beat the market? How can I get a better rate of return (so I can brag to my friends)? Their decision-making involves a competitive dynamic, and they generally have fun with the process because they perceive it as a sport.

A man's decision-making is also more focused on doing what is right for *him,* partly because of the competitive aspect, but also because boys are raised with the knowledge that they must take care of themselves. If you want to tell a man something about investing for his later years, he's ready to listen; or he'd be glad to hear about a long-term investment with a good rate of return. From the beginning, he's known that the only person taking care of him is going to be him.

Women's decision-making tends to be based on security and concern for others. A woman is more likely to worry about how to accumulate money to take care of her family *as well as* herself.

A woman might make a decision to start planning for her financial future because she doesn't want to be dependent on her family for help. And this is actually a very positive first step. While on the surface the decision may seem to be made to spare her family from having to spend money on her, intuitively she also knows that the minute she accepts support, she loses her independence.

Since women are very security-oriented, their decision-making tends to be directed toward gaining enough money to get by rather than to get rich. This desire for security also means that most of their decisions favor safe investments rather than those that might return more but hold some degree of risk.

Because of their different motivations, men and women also

huve different attitudes toward seeking expert advice. Men may consult a financial advisor, but they make their own decisions. Women, on the other hand, feel inexperienced at investing, and because they are concerned about making a mistake and losing their security, they are less sure of trusting their own instincts. Instead, women are more likely to trust a financial advisor, a work associate, or a friend. This reluctance to trust their own abilities starts early. As you will recall from Chapter 4, girls are not encouraged to trust their mathematical/analytical intuition and as a result, later on they turn to others for the "right" advice on investing.

And unlike men, who may play the market with a gamesmanlike attitude, women often say, "I want to know that I have a financial plan in place, but I don't want to spend my weekends or all my nights reading and analyzing financial charts. I don't see that as fun, and I really don't have the time."

To increase understanding of gender differences in decision-making, I often use the following exercise in my classes to open up a group discussion.

A man had a wife who was dying of cancer and needed a specific medication from the pharmacy. Although he had very little money and no health insurance, the husband still wanted to investigate how much this drug would cost.

When he went to the pharmacy, he found that the medication was so expensive he couldn't possibly afford it. Over a two-day period, he tried to plead with the druggist to give him the medication, promising he would pay for it over time. The druggist repeatedly refused. In complete desperation, the man broke into the store late at night and took the medication for his wife.

Was the man right in what he did?

The responses to this ethical dilemma are fascinating. Most of the men in my class are unequivocal in their belief that what the man did was wrong. He committed a crime and should be punished for it.

Most of my female students take a very different approach. In their opinion, the man was justified in his decision, because his wife was dying and he had a more pressing commitment to his wife than to society.

This illustrates an important gender difference in decision-making. Men are often guided by principles and rules. Women are guided by the emotional and interpersonal aspects of a problem.

MEN LEARN EARLY TO BE COGNITIVE THINKERS

One interesting result of our study was the discovery that few women were able to articulate their decision-making style, while men were more likely to be able to explain it and describe the cognitive process. The cause of this gender difference seems to lie in the fact that boys are rewarded from birth for this type of thinking; girls are not. And by the time they have grown up, men have gained confidence in their decision-making style and are therefore able to articulate what it is they do.

My work at the NCWRR has shown me that women often underestimate their investment prowess, their decision-making abilities, and their intuitive common sense. If women were to give themselves more credit for their decision-making skills (and women exhibit plenty of them—for example, they beat men hands down when it comes to the research process), they would find subsequent decisions easier and easier to make.

Underestimating financial talents seems to start very early. A high school in Massachusetts tested the money knowledge of their coeducational student body. After taking the test, the majority of boys indicated that they knew most of the answers. The vast majority of girls indicated that they did not feel they had done well. When the results came in, the girls had done just as well as the boys.

I've also come to realize that men often have the luxury of time; women usually don't. Cognitive decision-making requires time to investigate and consider what's being presented, and the process goes more quickly for those who can compartmentalize their lives and focus on one thing at a time. Women, who so often have to cope with the demands of so many others, rarely have this opportunity.

I've also learned another valuable lesson: It is not so critical for women to understand how they arrive at their decisions or be able to verbalize the process. What is important is that they take the steps to ensure their financial future. For this reason, it is logical—and preferable—for women to create a decision-making system that works for them, not to worry about whether there is a right or wrong way to make a decision.

IF YOU GET RIGHT DOWN TO IT, NEITHER SEX FINDS DECISION-MAKING A CINCH

Ultimately, one of our most interesting findings is that both men and women find financial decision-making a challenge (Should I sell the stock today? Tomorrow? What if it goes up after I sell it?). While most of the survey respondents acknowledged that certain steps do take place in the decision-making process, they felt that no two decisions were made in exactly the same way.

The reality is that whether you are male or female, it is extremely difficult to be a confident decision-maker. Today's investor must wade through hundreds of potential mutual funds, stocks, and annuity plans. Every analyst has a different opinion, and no two financial magazines or newspapers agree on the best way to invest. In addition, the industry has hundreds of financial experts forecasting each turn of the market and what it means to the individual investor. Small wonder people feel overwhelmed!

Sifting through so much information isn't easy, but everyone becomes more skilled—and more comfortable—with practice.

Making Good Decisions

Good decisions all rest on the framework of a step-by-step system. Along the way there will be variations, but to begin, think of it as a three-step process:

1. Recognize that a decision needs to be made.
2. Research the decision and evaluate the alternatives.
3. Make a choice among the alternatives.

Once you understand the basics, your system can—and should— take on a life of its own. Financial decision-making is an art, not a science. The more you practice, the more comfortable you'll be with all types of decision-making.

Consider, too, the aftermath of any decision. Good decision-makers also take time for a postmortem to evaluate the result of their decision. In this step, consider:

- Was the decision valid when made?
  If not, what went wrong?
- Is the decision valid now, and will it continue to be valid?
  If yes, take no further action.
  If no, can the decision be undone? Is a new decision necessary?

Once you feel comfortable going through the decision-making process (using both your cognitive and emotional skills), it will become second nature, and you'll no longer see it as a step-by-step process. It will flow easily and naturally as part of your new money personality.

Trusting a Hunch or Your Intuition

I'm a firm believer that many good decisions are ultimately pushed in one direction or the other by a hunch or intuition. A hunch is generally based on data that may not be quantifiable but are often based on sound judgment. Consider the experience of one of the women who visited the Center:

Mary P. was having lunch with a friend who had just invested $10,000 in a limited partnership. Her friend was so excited about the investment that she told Mary she should consider it too. Mary, looking for a new investment, called her friend's broker. *"I immediately got a sales pitch about how big a return I was going to get . . . that it was a sure thing."*

After hearing the sales pitch, Mary became suspicious and called her accountant to ask if he knew anything about this particular investment. When he said he didn't, Mary read a bit about limited partnerships and found that this specific type of investment was very speculative and far from the promised "sure thing." She called the broker again to get a list of other investors, but he never returned the call.

Later Mary learned the outcome: *"My friend told me that the limited partnership went belly-up and she lost everything. I'm glad I followed my instinct and didn't take the broker's word for it."*

Mary used her intuition and won. When it came to trust, she just didn't feel comfortable with what was happening. But intuition was not the only component that made Mary turn this offer down. She was unable to come up with the answers she needed to make a well-reasoned, cognitive decision to invest. Mary is representative of many women who don't feel comfortable making decisions without concrete information.

The financial advisor also lost out by not taking Mary more seriously. Our studies indicate that women want to work with a financial advisor who will help to educate them on investments and listen to *their* needs.

Think about some of the personal decisions you've made recently. List three instances when you just "knew" what had to be done—you couldn't explain it, you couldn't analyze it, but it was clear nevertheless. (Despite protestations from your mother, did you stop by her house and find that, as you suspected, she didn't feel well? Or have you ever phoned a friend who said she was fine, but then after you sensed distress and encouraged her to talk, went on to share with you some bad news she'd just received?)

If you evaluate these decisions, chances are you'll see that you were actually information-gathering all along. You made the decision when your subconscious sent up a red flag about something, or when your deep knowledge of another person permitted you to make a correct decision about something affecting him or her.

Women have always been credited with doing well by following their instincts in the caregiving arena: "It was mother's intuition; she just knew it was something more than a cold bothering her child." Historically, however, these intuitive feelings have been used to nurture others, not to benefit themselves. How many mothers of young children do you know who would climb into bed to get over the flu? Not many, I suspect.

Start listening to your intuition about yourself. Being in tune with your own feelings will let you listen to financial hunches and help you to develop a very important money management skill—whether it's an intuitive feeling about trusting (or not trusting) a broker, or following your hunch about getting out of a particular investment.

Here are some suggestions for using your intuition to facilitate your financial decision-making:

- If it seems too good to be true, you're probably right.
- Test your intuition by watching for the results of a particular investment to see if your hunch was correct.

- Bounce your financial hunch off a trusted advisor, friend, or spouse.
- If you don't feel right about a financial decision, wait. There is no opportunity that cannot wait for a clear and rational decision.
- Don't ever make financial decisions on the basis of emotion alone.
- Use the intuition you have cultivated in your personal life to pick out the financial roses from the thorns.

Procrastination: A Natural but Avoidable Pitfall

As a psychologist I've learned that there is always an underlying reason for procrastination. Over the years, I have helped many women overcome financial procrastination by getting them to examine their feelings and determine why these emotions surface at certain stages of the financial decision-making process. When it comes to overcoming financial procrastination, half the battle is simply recognizing that it is a problem. If you can identify the feelings you experience, you can solve the problem by changing the financial dynamics.

Think of two decisions that you made recently that were money-related and that caused you to procrastinate. You might have had difficulty deciding upon a major purchase, or perhaps you were wrestling with where to invest your money. Now ask yourself the following questions.

1. If you procrastinate about making money decisions, can you identify at what "decision point" you have a tendency to get bogged down? Is it when you are
   a. Gathering information?
   b. Getting the opinions of others (the more you hear, the more confused you feel)?
   c. Calling your financial advisor and worrying if he or she approves?
   d. Failing to make a decision because you place others' needs before your own?
   e. At the point where you ought actually to be making the decision to move forward?

2. What feelings do you experience when attempting to make a financial decision?
   a. Frustration
   b. Anger
   c. Indifference
   d. Boredom
   e. Uncertainty

3. Based on the above, can you identify why you feel this way?
   a. Are you angry that you have to make such a financial decision?
   b. Does the financial information cause you to feel frustrated?
   c. Does making this decision make you feel bored and disengaged?
   d. Are you unsure how to move forward even if you have all the information you need?

Here are some possible strategies to make decision-making easier. Check off the ones that seem as if they would be the most helpful to you.

☐ Take advantage of the support of an advisor, spouse, or friend.
☐ Find other ways to understand the information.
☐ Join an investment club.
☐ Attend a financial seminar.
☐ Evaluate the root cause of the emotions you experience.

And to ensure that you'll make a decision:

☐ Periodically review where you are with the issue.
☐ Set deadlines for yourself.
☐ Evaluate the necessity or importance of the decision.
☐ Make sure that your decisions are being addressed in order of priority.

The Decision-Making Process, Personally Speaking

Lila T. is a forty-one-year-old married woman with two children. She works as a vice-president for sales in a computer technology company, and her down-to-earth approach to decision-making is an excellent example of how most women go about the process.

"My awareness about finances and the need to plan hit me gradually," says Lila. *"One day I received my 401(k) statement and realized that I didn't have a clue as to how to read it or understand the asset allocation. I decided that I was going to learn more about my finances even though my husband had a good handle on such matters and he often took the lead when it came to investing.*

"I took an investment seminar and was handed a complimentary financial book explaining how to understand and make investments. To be honest, I let the book sit on the bookshelf for almost a year without picking it up. In retrospect, I now understand why: The idea of filling out a cash flow statement and writing out my financial goals sounded boring. Another aspect that bothered me was that I make a sizable salary and I felt kind of stupid that I didn't know this stuff already.

"About two years ago we were at a party and my husband made a joke that 'my wife is learning finances by osmosis.' That was it! I made the decision to start making some investments through a broker. I started by purchasing some stock. You will never believe how I made the decision as to what to purchase. I called up a female friend in the investment business and asked her for some hot tips. Without thinking twice, I just picked up the phone and placed the buy order. In retrospect, my decision was based on my desire to show my husband that I could do it. However, I would be lying if I told you that I didn't lose sleep that night over my decision. Certainly, many of my friends would not have purchased a stock on a hot tip."

The tip was no ticket to instant riches, but it wasn't a disaster for Lila either. She says: *"Now I do a lot more research and reading prior to making an investment. But it would not be accurate to say that I follow a set formula for making investments. There are some things I understand, and some things I don't.*

"Part of me is impulsive and part of me wants to think through what I am doing regarding investments. This may sound funny, but I also believe that intuition plays a great role in finances. (You can't tell me that all the millionaires in the world followed a recipe for their success.) And anyway, my system must be working. I am beating out my husband in terms of overall return for the last two years."

Too many women get hung up on the process of making a decision and never get around to *doing* anything. Just as long as you're not being reckless, you should plunge in, make the best decision possible, and then move on.

As Your Confidence Grows, So Will the Side Benefits

A woman who becomes comfortable with her financial decision-making and savvy to the world of investing will enjoy these additional benefits:

1. The financial markets are gender neutral; nobody cares if you are male or female.
2. All you need is money to invest and knowledge—you don't have to depend on others to make decisions.
3. There is no "glass ceiling" in the financial marketplace. As long as you have money (even a modest amount), no one will prevent you from reaching your goals and financial potential.
4. You have no boss to control what you do, just the forces of the marketplace. To "personalize" the process, you can network, find an investment club, or locate a financial advisor to help you along.
5. Investing does not have to be a full-time job, and you can choose your level of participation in terms of both time and money.
6. You can steer your own financial ship by setting your own goals to be as ambitious or as cautious as you want.
7. Absent a crisis, your success or failure is a private matter. No one needs to know.

11

FINANCIAL TRUTHS
Doing Away with Myths and Misperceptions About Money

"My family never talked about money unless it was to preach things like 'Money doesn't grow on trees' or 'Do you think I'm made of money?' or 'You'd better put something away for a rainy day,' none of which is very helpful when it comes to deciding whether to buy a certificate of deposit or to invest in a tax-free money market fund."

No matter how bright or well educated a woman is, myths and misperceptions arising from the family and societal messages that start in early childhood are so deep-seated that they can easily skew her view of the world. A woman I met a few years ago is a great example of someone who simply couldn't escape a recurring financial nightmare:

"For as long as I can remember, I have feared being penniless and poor," says Cynthia G., forty-two, who recently married for the second time. *"My parents divorced when I was eight, and because my father didn't make good on any support payments, my mother worried about money constantly. Fortunately, I got a scholarship to college, but as soon as I graduated, I began a nonstop mission to find financial security. My*

*goal was to get into television broadcasting and become an anchorwoman
for a major network. I now realize that this type of position symbolized
power and security to me.*

"To get into the business, I volunteered as an intern at a local television station while working two part-time jobs to support myself. Finally after five years, my break came. I was asked to anchor a 6 A.M. community affairs program on Sunday mornings. Although I earned peanuts, the position was a major stepping-stone for me, and for three years I devoted all my energy to it. Then, in 1986, my next big opportunity came. I was asked to coanchor the weekend news. This was not only a major jump in pay, but it brought me closer to the financial security that was so important to me. Three years later, I became the full-time anchor of the weekday news, making more money than I had ever imagined.

"I thought that attaining my professional goal would erase these feelings of financial insecurity—but it didn't. Regardless of how much I brought in, I still felt driven to make more money and attain more status to rid myself of these feelings. It's hard for me to take time off to enjoy myself. Although I save everything I can, my fears don't abate. Unfortunately, the bag lady within keeps chasing me, and I don't seem to be able to escape her presence."

This nightmare is one of those most often described by the women who come to our seminars, and it is obvious that the fear runs deep. This type of irrational fear is a prime example of a normal concern (not having enough money) being taken to abnormal extremes (that you will have nothing more than the possessions you carry with you).

Though the bag lady syndrome is a prevalent and haunting fear, it is just one of the financial myths that are the result of childhood family dynamics, gender issues, and societal messages. Occasionally, these fears breed workaholics who strive to bring in great sums of money, but as Cynthia's story illustrates, no amount of money will resolve the fear until the psychological issues are addressed.

Like sex, family discussions about money are often taboo, meaning that children grow up with no reality check when it comes to finance. As a result, myths and misperceptions about money abound. This leaves children with little natural understanding of money to help them separate myth from reality, and as a result, misperceptions—or misguided emotional reactions to money—are common.

This chapter is going to examine some of the most common myths concerning women and money, and we'll address what you can do to move beyond them.

The Bag Lady Syndrome

What woman hasn't seen a homeless woman, a "bag lady," and said to herself, "There but for the grace of God go I"?

The bag lady fear is so pervasive that there is even a World Wide Web site called the Bag Lady Syndrome. Of course, those who use it aren't true bag ladies who have gone into libraries to access the Web on public computers; they are working women who are putting money away but can't get rid of that overwhelming, bad feeling in the pit of their stomach.

Ironically, the bag lady syndrome even extends to the rich and famous. Sherry Lansing, currently chairman of Paramount Pictures, has had a stellar career in the film business, but in an interview with the *New York Times,* she revealed a recurring dream:

"An attractive, well-dressed man drives along a Beverly Hills street in a white Rolls-Royce, a glamorous blonde by his side. They see a tattered homeless woman sitting forlornly in the street and the man seems to recognize her.

" 'You know her?' the blonde asks disdainfully.

" 'Just someone I used to know,' he replies."

In this dream, Lansing herself is the homeless woman.

Certainly, not every woman fears becoming a bag lady, but I have counseled and worked with enough women to know that many unconsciously fear becoming impoverished regardless of how much money they make or how much their spouse makes. And unless the average American woman today makes significant changes in her savings and investment patterns, her bag lady worries will not be so far-fetched. As I have said in many of my speeches: "We are well on our way to duplicating another generation of impoverished older women in our society because of a lack of financial planning." In my opinion, many women recognize this possibility.

When I talk with women, their fears come out in different ways. For some, it is a feeling of uneasiness about the future. For others, it is a need to hide money inside a picture frame to make sure they have enough "just in case." In my own life, I can see this syndrome at work in my wife, who protects her savings account like an armed guard. She openly admits that the account serves as her security blanket. I also see it in my eighty-two-year-old grandmother, who has accumulated a significant nest egg but still lives in a run-down apartment building because she doesn't "have enough money."

Why has the bag lady syndrome become so prevalent? There are many contributing factors, beginning with the way girls are raised. Instead of the "you can do it" messages boys traditionally receive, girls are buffeted by messages like "You've got to be careful," "You can't go out alone at night, it isn't safe," "You're going to get pregnant," "I wouldn't risk it if I were you." These messages are heavily exaggerated to make sure that girls will conform, but they create undue anxiety about the future. Women rarely hear that "the world is your oyster," nor are they traditionally exposed to the type of "atta boy" messages young males receive on the playing fields. And while marketing professionals, intent on maximizing sales, are beginning to broaden their sales pitches to depict female athletes and women leading more active lifestyles, our culture's gender bias is so deep and so subtle that these new messages barely scratch the surface in beginning to change how girls and women are perceived.

Times are changing, however, when it comes to the security of marriage. Gone are the days when a woman could wrap herself in the cocoon of marriage or her femininity and confidently say, "I've got myself a good man—he'll take care of me for the rest of my life." Women today know subliminally that they really can't count on a man to provide for them, and they fear living impoverished and alone as a bag lady.

The Dreyfus Gender Investment Comparison Survey provided some fascinating insights about women's need for financial security. Women were twice as likely as men to agree with the statement "I insist on knowing where every penny of my money goes." In follow-up interviews, we found that this desire to track money had less to do with budgeting than it did with the fear of not having enough money. What is interesting to note is that this "need to know" crossed all age and income groups among women.

As a result of these factors, when a woman sees a homeless woman, she conjures up images of herself wandering the urban streets alone with a shopping bag full of odds and ends and perhaps a few worn reminders of a past that might have included a home and intimate connections. Women tell me: "We see 'her' and we see 'us' sitting alone on benches, on office building steps, propped up against buildings begging for money. We see 'her' and we see 'us' sleeping in doorways or in subway tunnels. Our bodies are covered with sores, our hair is matted and greasy, our skin is weathered and red." The image of the bag lady is personal and horrifying, for it strikes a chord so deep and primal that even the most secure woman is affected by it. The bag lady is a physical, nightmarish reminder of what can happen to any woman at any time.

MEN SEE THE WORLD DIFFERENTLY

Despite the fact that you see more homeless men than homeless women on the street, men do not often share women's fear of homelessness.

When a man sees a homeless person, he is more likely to look at the differences than the commonalities: "This guy is sure different from me" or "What did he do to get where he is?" A man will look for concrete explanations for why this person is homeless, and this process of rationalization distances him from the homeless man.

I believe men's resistance to "bag man syndrome" is largely because they feel more in control of their financial environment than women do. The Dreyfus Gender Investment Comparison Survey demonstrated the importance of financial control in creating a healthy attitude toward money. Results of the study showed that twice as many women as men felt they didn't have enough control over the direction of their financial life. Because men tend to be more comfortable with risk-taking and more secure about their financial prowess, they believe that they have the ability to avoid impoverishment.

Men and women view "home" differently, too, and for that reason, the term "homeless" takes on a gender-specific meaning. To a woman, the home is where she raises and nurtures her children; it is a place to display her aesthetic taste; it contains her private and personal treasures. It is a shelter that physically and emotionally protects her life and that of her family. A woman can look out from her kitchen window and view the bounty of her garden; she can glance at a piece of heirloom china that brings forth memories of older generations or look at the rocker where she once nursed her babies. A home and the things within it reflect a woman's identity, what she is all about.

In contrast, men have historically defined themselves and gained status through public life—their work, travel, politics, business, and explorations. The home is rarely as important to a man's sense of self.

Therefore, stripped of the physical and emotional shelter of home, a woman is more likely to feel exposed and vulnerable. The fact that her home and all it represents could be reduced to a bag filled with string, empty cardboard coffee cups, an old brush, a tattered blanket, a torn sweater, and perhaps some food is the stuff of which true nightmares are made.

OVERCOMING THE FEAR

The answer to overcoming this syndrome is what we've been discussing all along. Women must take responsibility for their own future as independent individuals. Part of the bag lady fear stems from issues related to self-perception and self-esteem. Though outwardly the syndrome concerns a fear of not having enough money, it also reflects a need on the part of some women for validation, acceptance, and self-fulfillment. As you saw in the story about the television anchorwoman, chasing money is not the answer to the bag lady syndrome. The answer lies in addressing the psychological issues that will help women feel more secure. By doing so, they will develop the traits they need to feel comfortable about acquiring a financial education.

Ideally, parents should be instilling both their sons and their daughters with positive money attitudes. In the Dreyfus Gender Investment Comparison Survey, we found that parents encouraged their sons to work for money at far younger ages than their daughters: Boys on average started earning money before the age of thirteen, while girls started much later (sixteen to eighteen). When responding to the question "How important was it to your parents that you saved your money?" twice as many boys as girls said they were encouraged to do so.

When I work with women to help them overcome the bag lady syndrome, I recommend several steps that have proved to be very effective:

1. **Verbalize what money symbolizes to you.** For some, it is validation of self-worth; for others, it is filling a hole left by an absent father or a poor upbringing.
2. **Address the part of you that is so fearful.** Confront the fear head-on by validating that it is real, and identify *specific* actions that will increase your level of economic security. By all means, don't run away from it or negate it!
3. **Concentrate on what makes you feel secure.** When women are asked to do this, few of them mention money. Most talk of relationships or the solidity of family and children.
4. **Take stock of what you've accomplished in your life.** If you realize that you have many ways to validate who you are and what you represent, you'll see that money is only part of the total picture.

The next important step toward overcoming your fears is to begin planning for the future as early as possible. According to the Dreyfus Gender Investment Comparison Survey, most men and women start talking seriously about retirement planning between the ages of thirty and thirty-nine. Starting as soon as possible is one sure way for a working woman, married or single, to develop the financial resources over a period of time that will enable her to be independent, self-sufficient, and secure as she enters her later years.

If you are currently very close to retirement age and find yourself lacking economic security, you still have options to consider. Many older women have taken part-time employment to supplement their Social Security income; others have reduced their living expenses by moving to more affordable housing; still others have found a roommate to share costs. The earlier you start planning, the better, but no matter when you start, there are always options to consider.

Over the last several years, we've found that when women begin to work on taking charge of their money, their fear of becoming destitute diminishes over time. This is the result of developing a new mind-set by making a serious commitment to financial planning—not a result of acquiring more money. If you believe that you can control your financial destiny, you are more likely to create situations where you flourish financially. By reducing the fear of becoming impoverished, you spend more energy on taking positive steps toward securing your financial future. Women demonstrate a tremendous ability to adapt. By believing in your financial self, you will be able to adapt to the difficulties created by inadequate pensions, credit problems, and other potential pitfalls along the way.

Women must learn to use their bad dream as an impetus to move into a new financial reality.

The Financial Advisor as Knight in Shining Armor

Another of the myths that women live with is that someone is going to rescue them from the burden of financial concerns the way knights in shining armor once saved damsels in distress. Whether that knight comes disguised as a family friend, a spouse, a business manager, or a stockbroker, you mustn't let yourself become the helpless damsel. Here's why:

"Practically everyone in the film industry uses business managers who take care of everything from bill-paying to investing," says Jennifer M. *"We'd used this business manager for ten years. Over time, we'd delegated more and more of our financial responsibilities to him and had no reason not to trust him.*

"Today we're in court trying to get back a small percentage of what he took from us. Times got bad, and I guess he started borrowing from one client to satisfy another, and he finally had to file for bankruptcy—it totally wiped us out except for current income."

Sheila S. is thirty-two and is well paid as a corporate attorney. When she got a phone call from her brother, who had gotten a "hot tip" from his broker, she barely hesitated before handing over her savings to her brother's broker, who promised that they would all triple their money "fast."

I spoke to Sheila two months later. She and her brother had both lost 50 percent of what they gave the broker. No gains; just one big loss on a hot tip.

Ironically, many men are waiting for that knight too. A good number of them appear to have taken control of their money, but, in fact, what they have done is to turn their money over to brokers or financial advisors and then more or less forget about it. Thirty-nine percent of the men who participated in the Dreyfus Gender Investment Comparison Survey indicated that they do not follow their stocks or mutual funds on a regular basis.

The myth of the financial advisor as knight is one that has

molded my own beliefs about financial responsibility, because I saw the danger of this practice within my own family. Although this book is about the financial needs of women, these stories convey a moral for either gender.

My Uncle's Knight. Uncle Ben, whom I always admired, made a startling revelation to me a decade ago. Fifteen years before his retirement, he entrusted all his savings to a financial advisor with the directive to "invest my money for me so that it will produce income for my retirement." Believing that his major task was completed (he'd built up his savings and now he'd found someone to take care of the money for him), Uncle Ben forgot all about it, to the point that he even neglected to follow the statements that periodically came in the mail.

When it came time to retire, Ben contacted his financial advisor only to find that over the years he'd actually *lost* money. The investment had been a terrific one in the eighties, but over time it went downhill.

Ben admitted to me that his post-retirement lifestyle is certainly not what he would like it to be. "I can only blame myself," he said recently. "The financial advisor who initially set me up with the investment was doing the right thing at the time. My fault was expecting him to constantly monitor this investment—that was my responsibility."

My Father's Knight. As I explained earlier, my own parents failed to plan adequately for their retirement, and they've suffered too, because my father put his faith in a knight who came into our lives via the phone lines. (Read Chapter 12 to learn the questions my father should have known to ask anyone selling financial investments by phone.) As my father recalls, he was contacted by a broker who was selling shares in a new mutual fund. The broker indicated that by making regular monthly contributions to the fund, my father would potentially see a 20 percent return annually.

Over the next ten years, my father faithfully sent in his check, but his life as a busy doctor kept him involved, and he failed to monitor his investment. Recently, I tracked down the investment and found that the shares, which had originally been valued at $18, were now worth only $2.10.

"I never once thought to check out the advice," he explained to me. "I blindly trusted that I was going to make the return I was quoted on the phone. That investment was a loser from day one, and I should have been more vigilant."

These experiences serve to illustrate that *you must remain in control of your own money.* You may have found a wonderful broker or a financial advisor who comes well recommended by friends or family. The advisor may be trustworthy, smart, loyal, and always in the know financially, but you still *cannot* afford to neglect your own responsibility by passing it off to someone else.

"When I first started investing, I was too intimidated to buy stocks that interested me, so I let my broker make all the decisions," says Abigail N. *"I hated having put control over my hard-earned money in the hands of someone I hardly knew. If the stocks went up, I was happy, but when the stocks went down, it just made me angry at the broker.*

"Gradually, I became brave enough about making some selections, and the whole process became more interesting—and more fun."

As Abigail learned, being in control of your financial destiny means having an ongoing relationship with your investments. This means tracking how your stocks, bonds, and mutual funds are doing and taking corrective action when needed. Being in control also means soliciting advice when you don't know how to properly evaluate how your returns are doing compared to other similar investments. Once women get involved, they actually tend to do very well with this: In the Women Cents Study, 76 percent of women reported checking on their investments at least once a month, with 33 percent watching even more frequently.

Ten Misguided Myths About Money

Based on my experience, the following myths, which originate from many different sources (our upbringing, societal messages, etc.), play a very significant role in shaping how we feel about money and our investment practices. Unchecked, they act as impediments to developing a proactive investor mentality.

At first reading, you may not think a certain myth applies to you, but don't discount its significance immediately. Also consider whether these myths remind you of any others you grew up with that might be affecting you now.

MYTH 1

Winning the lottery would solve all my problems.

Fifty-three percent of respondents to the Women Cents Study indicated that this quick-fix solution was a possible answer to their financial problems.

Reality: There is nothing wrong with looking for quick fixes, but long shots should be viewed for what they are. Although the slogan for the New York lottery is "Hey, you never know . . ." the odds of winning lotto are 1:25,827,165. And the odds of winning the grand prize in Pick 10 are hardly much better: 1:8,911,711. Unfortunately, this type of fantasy thinking is counterproductive, since it lets people avoid the serious issue of planning for the future. As we observed in Chapter 9, people who buy lottery tickets would be better off saving and investing their money.

MYTH 2

Money is the root of all evil.

Many midlife women harbor feelings of guilt about earning money. This myth prevents some women from asking for a raise in salary or wanting something for themselves. The guilt stems from the fact that women have been brought up to be caretakers and not to be concerned with commerce, the "dirty" aspects of the world.

Religious beliefs and culture also contribute to our view of money as bad. We live in a society that delivers two conflicting messages: (1) that our materialism is dragging us down, and (2) that we should enjoy ourselves today because the future is so uncertain.

Since almost everyone enjoys having money and spending money, this "root of all evil" adage is most likely to rear its head when we're feeling financially deprived. You want a bigger raise, but an inner voice keeps you from speaking up for yourself because you don't want to appear selfish. You've just attended the reading of your stepfather's will, and you're hurt by some of the provisions that obviously weren't "share and share alike." Your good friends are buying a bigger house in a better neighborhood, and without being able to control it, you feel envy. At times like these, we too frequently repeat the words our mothers may have said: "It's wrong to think so much about money. Money is the root of all evil."

Reality: The accumulation of assets is *not* a selfish endeavor, and you shouldn't chastise yourself for taking the time to think about and plan what to do with your money. This not only ensures a better quality of life down the road but also ensures that you will not be a financial burden to your loved ones.

MYTH 3

I'll have enough money later on . . .

Many women practice this kind of wishful thinking without considering how they will reach their goal.

Reality: Remember the story about the ant and the grasshopper? The ant worked hard all summer putting away food for the winter, and the grasshopper spent the summer enjoying himself, never heeding the ant's warnings. Well, some people are grasshoppers. They live in denial that anything bad will ever happen to them, and they comfort themselves with the belief that somehow they won't become a statistic. Yet, as the fable is told, the ant is the one who fares best because he spent time planning for the future.

Unless women take a greater stake in making better investment decisions, there is a tremendous likelihood that they will be poor in their later years. Remember:

- The median monthly Social Security check for women in 1995 was $588.
- Only 20 percent of women receive any benefits at all from private pension plans.
- Of the elderly poor, nearly 75 percent are women.

MYTH 4

I will have a spouse or partner to help me with my financial needs.

Reality: Women have got to start planning for themselves because a sizable number of them will face a future that may not include a mate. The average age for widowhood in the United States is fifty-six, and one out of two current marriages will end in divorce.

In our seminars, I recommend that women plan with the hope

and anticipation that they and their partner will retire together, but that they should make backup plans in case they find themselves alone.

MYTH 5

Financial terminology is intimidating.

Fifty-four percent of the Women Cents Study respondents reported that they were intimidated by financial jargon.

Reality: Learning about finance is no different from learning anything else. When you start out, it is confusing, but it becomes clearer over time. Think about the first time you played tennis. Did you know the rules of serving when you first started? Or perhaps you're a piano player. Did you know what "pianissimo" meant at your first lesson? Probably not.

Whenever you're learning something new, there are logical avenues to pursue—you might take a class, check out a book from the library, consult a friend, or talk to a financial advisor. And if the class, the book, the friend, or the advisor is talking over your head, just keep looking. There will be someone or something that can explain it in plain English. (Section III of this book will serve as your first guidebook.)

One other piece of news: Acknowledging the importance of reaching an increasing customer base, the financial industry is making great strides toward "dejargonizing" a lot of the information they produce. So, as you become more educated, you'll also find more printed material for people who lack backgrounds in finance and personnel who understand the importance of conversing clearly with them.

MYTH 6

Conversations about money and investing are boring.

Though fewer and fewer women report that they find financial conversations boring, they are still reluctant to be active participants. Until recently, few women had the opportunity to talk about money or investment, so many still feel uncomfortable talking about investments in a social setting. Some women even feel un-comfortable discussing money in financial planning sessions. Thirty-four percent of women in the Dreyfus Gender Investment Comparison Survey indicated that they were very uncomfortable answering specific questions put to them by a financial advisor. (Al-though women in general are more likely than men to admit that they don't know something, we've learned it depends on the cir-cumstances. Within a seminar, investment club, or in a one-on-one setting, women are *more* likely than men to admit not knowing something. However, when women are in an environment where they don't feel comfortable—such as a meeting with a financial ad-visor and a spouse or in a coed seminar setting—they are more likely to clam up and will be reluctant to ask questions freely.)

Reality: Many women are finding investment clubs the perfect setting to begin conversing comfortably about money. Over time, many women will learn to enjoy talking about their triumphs and failures as much as men do.

"I don't find financial management particularly enjoyable," says Madeline B. *"I joined an investment club, and it's been a good place to learn more in a nonthreatening environment. It's important for a cautious person such as myself to be able to listen and learn and not feel pres-sured."*

As for whether or not the subject is compelling: Anything you don't understand can seem boring, but think about it—what *are* people interested in? People are interested in *things that affect them* or *things they know about.* By purchasing this book, you have shown that you know the subject affects you; now what you need to do is add knowledge to that awareness.

MYTH 7

Financial planning is pointless unless you have enough money to work with.

Forty-eight percent of female baby boomers feel that a major im-pediment to financial planning is lack of funds. This is creating a major stumbling block for younger and midlife women.

Reality: Saying "Why bother? It's not enough" is a defeatist atti-tude. The truth is that you don't need a great deal of money to begin an investment program. Once you open a mutual fund account, you can make contributions of as little as $25 to $100 a month. Obviously, the more you set aside, the better your financial situation will be in a few years.

If you're puzzled as to how you'll ever be able to increase your savings, here's a simple strategy: Use money you never counted on anyway. If you get a raise, put the difference into savings; if you finish paying off a loan, put the amount that formerly went toward the loan directly into savings (you won't miss it, because you're used to that money leaving your account to pay off your loan). Refer to Chapter 14 for additional strategies for saving. As you begin to see your money grow, you'll probably become more aggressive about trying to put money away.

MYTH 8

The secret to investing is to "keep it easy to manage and easy to understand."

A shocking 94 percent of women reported that they prefer their investments to be "easy and simple."

Reality: This attitude puts women on treacherous ground because CDs and savings accounts are the most logical "simple" investments—no complex rules or intricacies of timing one's investments. But these simple choices don't compensate for inflation, growth of principal, or long-term needs, making them poor long-term investments.

Knowledge can make other investments seem equally simple and easy, so keep reading!

MYTH 9

I can do financial planning on my own without the help of an expert.

According to the Scudder Baby Boom Survey, this generation intends to be increasingly self-reliant; only 27 percent of baby boomers have consulted with a financial professional, 45 percent have no plans to consult one, and only 28 percent plan to do so in the future.

Twenty-eight percent of women surveyed in the Women Cents Study indicated that lack of trust in an advisor was the primary reason they had never consulted one.

Reality: While self-reliance is admirable in many ways, when it comes to financial investing, the ideal is to use a financial professional to establish a system of checks and balances. Picking the best investments for the long term can be complicated, and because there are always risks involved, the ideal situation includes one or more financial professionals to help you along the way. A good financial team—with you at the helm—can help you work through selecting investments that are tailored to your risk level, long-range goals, and desire for liquidity.

As for reliability, although there are bad eggs in any profession, you can find a planner you trust by interviewing several you've learned about through referral. Or you can request and evaluate their credentials while also asking for references. If they are affiliated with a major institution with which you are familiar, this, too, offers protection.

Credentials are important, but don't forget about the human element—selecting someone you like. You'll want to select as your advisor someone who is smart and sensitive as well as knowledgeable about personal investments. He or she should also enjoy providing the services you need, such as considering new financial goals and reevaluating your retirement plan. For more advice on selecting a financial advisor, see Chapter 19.

MYTH 10

It is better to make no investment decision than to make one and have it be a mistake.

Fifty-four percent of respondents to the Women Cents Study put off financial decision-making because they were afraid of doing the wrong thing.

Reality: All investors make mistakes—that's how you learn. (The only catastrophic mistake would be if you encountered a scam, and we'll discuss "scam detection" in Chapter 12.) Otherwise, dollar cost averaging (investing your money periodically to average out your per-share cost) and diversification (spreading out your money) will prevent you from suffering terribly if an investment should go bad.

Strategies for Developing More
Reality-Based Money Attitudes

Over the years, I have observed that the women who seem to have a realistic grasp of money and can rise above family myths and misperceptions follow some common rules and strategies. Now that you've read about the obstacles, you should be prepared to take the following steps:

1. Evaluate the basis of your past perspectives on saving and investing. As we have emphasized before, the more you understand about the powerful influences that shaped your attitudes, the more you'll be able to control them.
2. Take steps to change these attitudes. Simply becoming aware of these barriers will help you begin to eradicate them.
3. Learn from other women who are knowledgeable, and take those you admire most as role models. One reason female investment clubs are working so well is that women are learning from other women and using them as role models.
4. As you refine your financial goals and begin to make investment decisions, constantly monitor your "attitude creep." The phenomenon of attitude creep is experienced by all of us—as new knowledge is incorporated, we replace old attitudes with new ones. We need to make sure that these new attitudes are realistic and can be applied in a positive manner. A perfect example of this is what is happening with investors today. They have gone from "cautious indifference" concerning the stock market to what Federal Reserve Board Chairman Alan Greenspan has dubbed "irrational exuberance"— meaning that they seem to believe that stocks will maintain their upward momentum indefinitely. Particularly in this economic environment, investors must constantly monitor whether their investments are realistic and their goals achievable.

Benefiting from Your New Reality-Based Attitude

Our research findings demonstrate that women are becoming more realistic about money, and that those who are more reality-based in their money and investment attitudes are more likely to:

- Understand the relationship between risk and reward
- Have clear and identifiable short- and long-term financial goals
- Make regular contributions to a 401(k) or other retirement plan
- Recognize how much money they will need to retire with a "comfortable lifestyle"
- Use and *apply* the information obtained from financial publications and educational seminars
- Are much more optimistic about their future
- Don't believe that their destiny is determined by fate
- Indicate that they have a "trusting relationship" with their financial planner
- Are not unduly anxious about making a financial mistake
- Have a tendency to be consistent and deliberate in their financial decision-making

The most exciting aspect of my work is witnessing the transformation that occurs when women begin honestly to believe that they can triumph over their fears of insecurity and build a life predicated on belief in their financial abilities. This is the last step in women's development—the belief that they can control their financial destiny.

One final word of wisdom. I'm sure you've heard this financial adage: "Money can't buy happiness." Though, of course, money does not directly purchase happiness, women do quickly discover that those who are financially secure have more options in life, particularly in their later years when age, health, and marital status can otherwise severely limit their choices.

Financial planning simply must become a top priority.

12

"HEAD IN THE SAND" SYNDROME
Lack of Knowledge About Planning and Investing

"I've always been afraid of asking questions for fear of sounding stupid. Then I saw that I wasn't the only person who didn't understand, and that helped me overcome my fear of asking basic questions. Since then it's been easy to move ahead and find out what I wanted to know."

This chapter represents a critical fork in the road. Which path you take will have a very definite impact on how you approach the next section of this book. Either you will let this new financial information sit there unused or you will begin to apply it to improve your financial future.

At the conclusion of our seminars, I often say to the participants: "Some of you will leave today ready to move ahead and change how you've been handling your money; others will be unable to do so, though a good number of those will gradually become prepared over time."

I say this to you too, but I'll add something that I hope will speed you along: Regardless of how long it takes you, what happens after this has less to do with money smarts than with having the right attitude. A lack of financial knowledge is a choice—women can put their heads in the sand or choose to change their attitudes.

Unfortunately, up until now, many women have put their heads in the sand, hoping that these issues would go away or be taken care of by someone else. Twenty-nine percent of the respondents in the Women Cents Study reported that they knew "little or nothing" about investment types and financial planning principles, and another 58 percent reported that they knew only "the basics." Only 13 percent described their level of understanding as "advanced" or "expert." Nearly one half of the respondents indicated that not knowing enough about investments was an obstacle to their involvement in financial planning activities.

Yet the Women Cents Study, in addition to other NCWRR studies, clearly demonstrates the benefits women experience when they seek financial knowledge to address their particular needs and circumstances. Women who had a better understanding of investment types and financial planning principles were:

- More likely to have realistic attitudes toward money
- Considerably more risk tolerant
- Far more confident about their financial decisions
- More likely to be engaged in financial planning activities including setting goals, consulting financial professionals, and purchasing stocks, bonds, and mutual funds

It's a worthy goal. Refer back to the Self-Test in Chapter 2 and see how you fared in Section E, which concerns financial planning and investment knowledge. While this chapter will help make financial information more accessible to everyone, it will be particularly helpful to those who were in the Caution or Danger Zone.

This chapter presents a plan for becoming more knowledgeable about financial planning principles and investment types. We'll discuss the fact that each person processes information and knowledge differently. By understanding how you utilize new information, you will be better able to overcome the barriers you encounter in your pursuit of knowledge.

In addition, I'll present you with four steps that will help you to move ahead with learning what you need to about finance. By following these steps, you will soon begin to view accumulating financial information as a pleasurable endeavor; what seemed impossible to understand will become much easier over time and through exposure; and your worst fear (of being scammed) will be entirely eradicated.

The most important message in this chapter is, "Knowledge is power." I have no doubt that you can be like the thousands of other women who have used these steps to their financial advantage. Keep on reading!

How to Process Financial Information

After years of teaching personal finance, I have come to realize that each woman has a different way of absorbing the information she receives. If we have twenty participants in a seminar, they will each use the information differently, depending on their developmental progress. One will start making phone calls to brokers the very next day; another will take away a good base of knowledge but little interest in implementing it immediately; a third may emerge with little understanding of exactly what she should do next.

The reactions of these participants has little to do with intelligence and a great deal to do with the way they process information, but it tells me something about the barriers and strengths they bring to the financial table. Each reaction is based on a woman's money personality. No one type is good or bad. What is important is to recognize which type you come closest to so that you are better prepared to acquire the financial knowledge you need.

As you read about the following learning styles, reflect back on your life and think about how you responded to learning something new in an adult education course or when beginning a new hobby. As you start investigating financial information, remember that the material presented to you is only half the picture. How you process it is the other half.

SILENT LISTENERS

"I attended the financial seminar not so much for the information but to get my husband off my back. I sat and listened, but my heart really wasn't into learning about the material. It was only much later that I

realized I needed to understand this information for myself—not for my husband."

Silent Listeners will often sit in a financial seminar or counseling session and listen to everything but make few attempts to apply the information they have acquired. They often defer to a more powerful external voice and ignore their own inner voice. They buy a financial handbook or attend a seminar because others have told them it's important. However, they are there in body only and have not yet connected the information to their own financial circumstances. Silent Listeners need to empower themselves to take charge of their own situation. They have not yet come to grips with the idea that the information is for *their* benefit. By taking personal ownership of the ideas presented, Silent Listeners can move from disinterested spectator to active learner.

To find out whether you are inclined to be a Silent Listener, ask yourself why you're reading this book. Are you doing it for you, or are you reading it for someone else?

If you feel you're a Silent Listener, try listening to your own voice; you may not be ready to speak up for yourself yet, but by learning to hear how you feel—what interests you as well as what scares you—you'll be ready for the next step sooner.

READY-FOR-CHANGE LEARNERS

"My husband refused to baby-sit, so I hired a sitter, but I was bound and determined that I was going to get to the seminar tonight."

After spending a lifetime living up to the expectations of others, Ready-for-Change women are now moving ahead. Though they are not quite ready to make the full leap, they are taking a first step toward financial independence by attending a seminar. As they gain knowledge, they'll be poised to make some financial decisions by themselves. When I meet these women, there is a certain sparkle in their eye. They have come to the seminar because at last they realize they can change their financial situation. I call these women "financial cliff-hangers": They want to become financially literate, but a little nagging voice of uncertainty holds them back. This type of woman is often finally rescued by her own desire to move forward.

If you recognize yourself here, start with small steps. Reading this book or attending a financial seminar is a perfect way to begin. If you're nervous about investing, start by making certain you have a bank account of your own, or if you've already done that, move some money out of savings and into a money market fund, where the money is also very safe but you may be able to get a slightly higher interest rate (see Section III). As your confidence builds, you'll be able to do more.

Generally, Ready-for-Change Learners are an eager group who really want to get started. Not knowing what steps to take keeps them temporarily immobilized. If you already know what step you'd like to take next (invest in a mutual fund, select a broker, etc.), write down what your goal is and then list the steps that will get you there. If you're considering a mutual fund, reading one of the personal finance business magazines that list the top performing funds would be a good first step. Other steps will follow logically from there.

KEEP-IT-SIMPLE LEARNERS

"I get confused. I keep attending more financial seminars because I can only digest one or two concepts at a time."

I can always spot Keep-It-Simple Learners in a financial seminar. They want information explained so that it can be digested immediately. They have a tendency to take it all in, but they discard immediately any information they don't understand. They like predictability and clarity, and if what they learn is likely to create a substantial change in their portfolio, they sometimes resist because they don't like uncertainty.

The principal danger in this learning style is that many financial concepts (dollar cost averaging, the Rule of 72—see Section III) take time to understand and apply, and you need to practice using the concept. By immediately discarding any piece of financial knowledge, you greatly limit your potential.

Keep-It-Simple Learners will be heartened to hear that both genders have trouble understanding certain concepts immediately. I have witnessed many women who have benefited from adopting a more patient approach to the learning curve and being totally amazed at how savvy they can become.

There are four ways to go beyond being a Keep-It-Simple Learner:

1. Don't *expect* to totally comprehend a new concept the first time (not because you're dense; simply because most people do need to have concepts explained more than once). Give yourself the time to review the information or ask questions until you grasp what's being discussed.

2. Begin to develop perspectives and opinions about the facts and information you accumulate so that you can relate the material to your own circumstances. This allows you to practice using the concepts to see how they can change your financial situation.

3. Use outside resources—everything from the business section of the newspaper to your accountant or financial advisor—to help you sift through all the facts to determine what is financially best for you.

4. Slowly and patiently move from "practice" mode to application mode so that you actually use the financial concepts you've learned. As you realize that what once seemed so complex can be both easy to understand and financially rewarding, you'll be eager to learn more.

BLOCKBUILDING LEARNERS

"The investment club I joined has given me the opportunity to build on what I know, and at last I'm feeling more comfortable about where to put my money."

Though some women start out as Blockbuilders, they more often start out as Keep-It-Simple Learners and develop into Blockbuilders. Blockbuilders are at the next stage of development. They are gaining an increasing sense of control and the world is becoming easier to manage. Many of these women are novices who have experienced an investment gone sour or have consulted a financial professional who gave them poor advice. However, realizing what has happened has given them a stronger belief in themselves. They are determined to learn from the past and develop a "building block approach" to digesting new information. They are tenacious at grappling with what they don't understand. One of the major barriers this group has to address and overcome is that the world of investments is not always consistent—every situation is a little different. They need to concentrate on the basic rules of investing and spend less time trying to find the perfect investment. Their financial education is really twofold: to acquire new information that they can understand and control, and at the same time, to recognize that the rules for making good choices must be adapted and changed in accordance with circumstances. For example, a thirty-year-old Blockbuilder who came to the Center wanted to learn more about investing. After learning something about mutual funds, she started out by investing in a conservative-growth fund. Later, as she learned more and acquired more savings to invest, she moved a portion of her money into a more aggressive growth fund so that she could increase her return.

What I find fascinating about this group is that because they are comfortable with their own identity, they are not easily dismayed when something goes wrong; they use the information and experience as new financial learning tools.

Those of you who are Blockbuilders are well prepared to move on to the next step. You may still be nervous and lack the confidence you will acquire over time, but you know that you must take care of yourself, and you are able to balance the voices of others with your own wants and needs. You are at a good stage. Keep going!

CHEERFUL EXPERTS

"I'm having a great time. I'm not winning with every investment, but I'm certainly learning by doing."

These women have confidence in themselves. They are risk-takers and still feel comfortable with what they are doing with their money, even if someone else sees it differently. This is where all investors—male and female—would like to be.

I recognize Cheerful Experts because they are always the first to raise their hands in a seminar. They are very opinionated financially, and have a very clear and focused idea of what they want to do with their money. Most will admit that they were not born with this outlook—rather, they are constantly on the lookout for new ways to build on their financial foundation.

What fuels their attendance at a financial seminar is that understanding money and investing has become a game. To them it's all fun. An important characteristic of this group is that they are not unduly confident or guided by gender stereotypes about money.

Their motto: "There's always something new to learn about investing."

Steps to "Higher Learning"

Because you can't afford to keep your head in the sand and ignore your finances, following these steps will make it easier for you to absorb and take advantage of the financial information presented in Section Three.

STEP ONE: GATHERING FINANCIAL KNOWLEDGE EVERYWHERE YOU CAN

Although understanding financial terminology can be intimidating at first—and moving beyond the basics can seem overwhelming—if you start learning slowly, and at your own pace, you can overcome these hurdles. Step One is to realize that the information you need can be found in easily accessible places. You don't have to wade through boring textbooks or sit through endless seminars to find out what you need to know.

Just as there are hundreds of consumer products to choose from, there are hundreds of financial publications and investment products from which to select. This alone can be daunting. I recommend that women start the process of finding helpful literature by sitting down in their own living room where they are likely to have a copy of their favorite women's magazine. Most of these publications now have finance sections that are targeted to women's needs, and these sections often refer readers to other user-friendly materials.

Next, if you attend a financial seminar, ask for recommendations of both books and magazines. Some organizations may have reading lists, as the NCWRR does, broken down by financial topic and investment product. Or you can even do an Internet search based on a specific topic area.

Also consider the following points:

Take a proactive approach to educating yourself. Although the temptation is to bury your head in the sand and say "forget it" or wish that someone else would take responsibility for you, the reality is that you must play a leading role in your own play. Based on what I've said above, there is no reason you can't learn at your own pace, and find the publications and resources that are right for you.

Accept the fact that financial advice is loaded with contradiction. When we had our first son, my wife and I ran out to the store and loaded up on books about proper child care. By the end of the fifth book, we were more confused than when we started. It was a great relief to us to recognize that experts were all well intentioned but that they didn't always agree or have the same formulas or perspectives. Recognize that you will be chasing windmills if you are searching for the "perfect" solution to or source of financial knowledge.

Use all the information on finances and investing to your benefit. Although there is so much financial information that one can easily feel snowed under, use this as a positive. In surveying the vast material, *start simple.* In addition to the basics presented in this book, you're going to want a good reference book on money and investing. Read it in small, digestible sections.

When we asked women throughout the country what they wanted in a financial reference book, they gave us some criteria you can use to make your own choice:

- Material presented in a clear, understandable fashion with minimal jargon
- Financial terms easily explained
- Investment options presented objectively with an explanation of how they can be beneficial or why they should be excluded from a particular portfolio. (Stay clear of an author who claims to have a foolproof way of beating the market or "making a million like the big boys.")
- Material that gets right to the point (since time is of the essence)
- A resource list of financial organizations that can be contacted for further information

Subscribe to one financial magazine that is educational in nature and covers a broad range of consumer issues. Newsstands are filled with a wide variety from which to choose. I recommend that you take home several to evaluate before writing out a check for a subscription:

- Do you like the way the material is presented?

- Are the articles on topics that are of interest to you?
- Can you relate to the people and situations discussed?

I also recommend that you select a financial magazine that specifically addresses women's investment and money needs on a regular basis.

Start reading your newspaper with a different slant. Although the business section of the paper can be a wonderful source of financial information and knowledge, don't discount what you're reading in the other sections either. This year the stocks my wife selected did better in total return than the ones I selected. After putting my male ego on the shelf and humbly asking what crystal ball she was using, I found that she had selected stocks based on consumer trends. The news is full of trends that speak to what consumers are buying, and how a particular industry or product is positioned for the future.

Join an investment club. Women are joining investment clubs in staggering numbers for one simple reason: These clubs provide women with a supportive atmosphere to learn about the world of investing. The knowledge they gain is then applied by selecting and purchasing investments that are carefully researched by the members of the club.

Attend a financial planning seminar. Another good way to gain critical information on money and investing is by participating in a financial planning seminar. A word of caution: If you decide to attend a financial planning seminar, make sure the information is educational in nature and not intended to be a come-on for a particular financial product. During the last five years, the number of financial seminars for women has grown tremendously—fueled by women's having disposable income to invest and their growing awareness that retirement planning is critical. Just make sure the information is unbiased. (See Section III.)

Network with other women interested in personal finance. A growing number of women's organizations include members who, like you, are interested in exploring the world of finance and investing. The next time you attend a meeting, see whether you can identify the level of interest in starting an investment club or sponsoring a financial planning seminar. Or decide to meet informally with several friends to discuss money matters.

STEP TWO: YOUR MIND-SET· BEING OPEN TO NEW IDEAS AND APPROACHES

Being open-minded about your ability to learn about finance is the single most important step toward getting started. If you've ever moaned, "I'll never understand all that," it's time to come up with a new approach.

Another unique finding of the Women Cents Study is that one's level of schooling does not necessarily have anything to do with one's becoming a good investor. You don't need a college education or a Ph.D. It's more important to be motivated, to have an open mind, to gain awareness of those aspects of your personality that assist or deter you from investing, and to expose yourself to unbiased financial information.

Women can become intrigued with understanding financial information if they view it as a vehicle to gaining what they want (power)—something men have understood for a long time. Learning about new financial investments can become a game in which you dare yourself to conquer unknown territory (very similiar to the feeling one experiences by finally understanding how to operate a new gadget or a new program on one's computer). By changing your mind-set, you'll see financial terms and investments as personalized tools you can use to improve your financial situation.

STEP THREE: APPLY WHAT YOU HAVE LEARNED

Once you feel comfortable with your new financial mind-set, it's time to become more active. Women who perceive themselves as being active and knowledge-oriented investors don't need a lot of capital to be competent investors. As we will show you in the next section, there are good investments suited to everyone's pocketbook. Women with modest means can make themselves secure by properly using the resources they have.

STEP FOUR: KNOWING WHEN TO CONSULT OTHERS AND WHEN TO STAND ON YOUR OWN

Make your own decisions, or rely on the recommendations of others? That is always difficult to determine. And unfortunately, there is no easy answer. Sometimes you'll want to go it alone; other times it will be better to listen to others, and remember, you can always use your financial advisor as a sounding board. You'll benefit by doing so.

Investors today are facing financial planning options overload: Should you invest in mutual funds? Put together your own stock portfolio? Do bonds provide greater security, or should you go into your company's 401(k) plan? This generation can't look back to see "what my dad did," because the world today offers a mind-boggling variety of investment options.

The Dreyfus Gender Investment Comparison Survey provides two fascinating findings: (1) The majority of both males and females were unable to indicate what criteria, if any, they would use in selecting a financial advisor. (2) The majority of both males and females had "no opinion" on whether they were more likely to purchase a load or a no-load mutual fund. What this says is that the financial industry has a long way to go in terms of helping consumers make informed decisions.

In the Dreyfus Gender Investment Comparison Survey, when asked what resources they had used during the past year for making investment decisions, the majority of the sample indicated "no one—I did it on my own" (50 percent of females; 57 percent of males).

This trend toward greater self-reliance is of concern for the following reasons.

- Women are twice as likely as men to be dissatisfied with the rates of return on their investments over a three-year period.
- Women are three times as likely *not* to know what types of investments offer the best rates of return.
- Women are more likely than men *not* to know what size nest egg they need to retire comfortably.

Baby boomers, for the most part, seem more comfortable trusting themselves to secure their future than they do using the professionals. This is surprising when you consider their level of knowledge and experience:

- 84.5 percent describe their level of investment experience as "somewhat experienced" or "novice/beginner."

- 58.9 percent are not sure how much money they will need for retirement.
- 15.4 percent fear they will need to lower their standard of living when they retire.
- 42 percent say they don't have time to manage money for their retirement future.

The current financial world is extraordinarily complex—and changing daily—and while you must be knowledgeable, it's important not to act in a vacuum. There are excellent professionals to whom you can turn for advice and who will act as a sounding board in your quest for investment knowledge.

"I finally took my portfolio to a financial advisor whom a friend recommended," says Natalie C. *"I liked her immediately, because she left my original investments in place until we'd been working together for a time. Initially, we worked only with some additional funds I wanted to put into the market. Only after a few months when I'd begun to trust her did she start to talk about other possibilities for the investments I'd made on my own. I liked that. If she'd torn into and criticized everything I'd been doing, I don't think I could have stayed with her."*

Friends—an Important Source of Knowledge and Support

When it comes to being self-reliant or going it alone, friends can provide a bridge between total independence and reliance on a professional to manage your money for you. Friends can be a source of knowledge, and at the same time, they can provide support as you start investing.

In all likelihood, your first line of support will come from a loved one—someone who takes an interest in you and your financial future. Sometimes that's your spouse; other times—even when you're married—you may find that you're more comfortable consulting your friends. (The Dreyfus Gender Investment Comparison Survey showed that women were twice as likely as men to use friends for financial advice.) Here are the qualities to look for in the people you turn to for financial advice:

- *Risk tolerant:* The person(s) you call should be someone who will be rational when the financial news is bad and who will celebrate with you when it's good. This is sometimes where a spouse lets you down; if you have a husband who is going to be devastated when the stock market drops 25 points, look elsewhere for your support.

- *Future-oriented and open to change:* If the person you call is going to say "I told you so" when you're worried about one of your investments, look for someone new.
- *Interested in you:* The best financial advice comes from financially savvy people who know and love you and care about your financial future.

As you talk to friends about investments, always remember that you're your own person and have got to filter this information and decide what's right for you.

STEP FIVE: KNOWLEDGE KEEPS YOU SAFE: THE ART OF AVOIDING A SCAM

Fraud is big business. According to the U.S. Office of Consumer Affairs, Americans lose approximately $100 billion a year to fraudulent schemes—many of which are presented as "investments."

Two years ago, I received a call on the Center's 800 line from a woman who was extremely upset. She was an intelligent woman who listened to a religious radio broadcast every morning. One day there was an announcement on the program indicating that if listeners would send $15,000 to a certain address, they would have their money returned in six months with 18 percent interest. The pitch was particularly appealing to this woman because the money was going to be used to set up a mission in Africa to feed and clothe children. She sent her money without signing anything; the announcer had indicated it was a totally safe investment.

When ten months had passed, the woman called the religious organization to inquire about her money. To her shock, the number had been disconnected. In desperation, she wrote a detailed letter to the address where she had sent her money. When she received no reply, she called the NCWRR in a state of panic, and after talking to her, it became quite clear to me that she had been victimized. What made the story memorable for me were three factors that are at the heart of any scam: (1) She had acted on her emotions without appropriate information; (2) she had nothing in writing from the company that collected her money; (3) she asked for no references that would allow her to check on the legitimacy of the operation.

I found out later that she had been one of eight thousand people taken in by this particular scam. When she contacted the state attorney general's office, she found out that the company traveled from state to state acting as an investment charity that preyed mostly on women and those who were religious and wanted to do something good for themselves and others at the same time.

To help you separate the legitimate from the fraudulent, here's what to watch for:

- Beware of telephone, mail, or in-person solicitations that sound too good to be true. Whether it's a "free" vacation, a "sure deal" in gold mine investing, or the opportunity to double your money within a short period of time, don't agree to anything on first contact. A good deal can wait; a scam artist can't.
- If the solicitor indicates that "time is of the essence" and that waiting will cost you, ignore the plea. Any worthwhile investment will still be there after you've had time to check it out. "Tomorrow will be too late" and "Act now because others may take your place" are good tip-offs to a fishy deal. Some con artists have become smarter, and they are now using a "three call" approach, so just because they call back, it doesn't mean they are legitimate. Check references.
- Don't rely too heavily on one person's recommendations. Some of the most distressing stories of fraud concern people who have persuaded someone who trusted them to enter into a financial deal. Even if the get-rich-quick offer comes from someone you know, take the time to check it out.
- Resist even the "penny ante" pitch. Some bogus sweepstakes state that you'll be eligible to win big bucks if you buy something small, like a $10 jar of face cream. While losing $10 is no big deal, the problem is what happens afterward. Your name and telephone number will be sold to other scam operators, and because you'll be deluged with "good offers," you may fall prey to another scheme on a grander scale. State attorneys general cite many cases of people who started out investing only $5 or $10 and ended up losing $50,000 to $100,000.
- Be suspicious of "inside" information, "hot tips," and rumors that supposedly will give you a big advantage over other investors.

- Check out investment "professionals." While the process for selecting a good financial advisor is covered in depth in Section III, it is important that you know that scam artists do come disguised as advisors. Stories abound of insurance policies that were canceled when a victim made a deal to trade up for a "better" policy or get-rich-quick condo investments that never broke ground. You've got to be skeptical at all times, and you've got to check references.
- Before agreeing to anything, get a professional opinion from your attorney, financial advisor, or accountant.

SEEING THROUGH A SCAM

Whenever you receive a telephone call offering any form of investment opportunity, whether unsolicited or in answer to a request for information, be sure to check out the following information. (In the NCWRR PREP Poll, we found that 43 percent of women indicated that they routinely received such calls.)

- Don't withdraw cash from a bank or an ATM at a stranger's suggestion.
- Don't give out your credit card number to an unsolicited caller.
- Never make hasty spending decisions.
- Be wary of filling out mail solicitations that say you have won a prize. Most mailings of this type are looking for potential victims to call.
- Don't discuss your personal finances with a stranger.
- If you are considering a possible investment, be certain to ask the following questions every time.
  Do you have references? Be sure you get more than one (one could be the caller's partner). Then be sure to check them out.
  What are the risks in this investment? There are no sure deals, so if that's the answer, keep looking for something else.
  Can you give me (or send me) something in writing? Scam artists will find this makes you an undesirable mark, and most will move on to another victim. However, bear in mind that written documents can easily be faked, and you still need to scrutinize them carefully. With a legitimate investment, there should be a prospectus or other acceptable document describing the exact nature of the company and operations involved and the nature of the risks and potential.

Could you explain this to my financial advisor? If they are illegiti-
mate, they won't have time.

*Can you give me information about the company's principal offi-
cers?* Obtain the name, address, and phone number of the principal officers. In addition, get the name, address, and phone
number of the person who is making an investment offering
on the phone. Ask what their background is in the field and
why they have a particular interest in this venture.

- Whenever possible, deal with established businesses whose
  reputations are known and trusted in your community.
- If someone is too persistent, be suspicious. You don't owe this
  person anything, and don't be afraid to hang up without explanation.
- And fraudulent or not, don't ever invest in anything you don't
  really understand.

If you are suspicious about a company or individual, check their
licensing and legal history by calling the Better Business Bureau, the
state securities administrator, the Securities and Exchange Commission, the local district attorney's or state attorney general's consumer fraud unit. For false mail solicitations, call the postal
inspector's office. (See Appendix C for helpful addresses.) There are
many con artists, so don't sit back; take action. The steps you take
may protect the next person.

The biggest mistake any woman can make is believing "it could
never happen to me" or "I could never be so gullible."

If you emerge from reading *Money Makeovers* with a proactive
stance, you'll find yourself among a group of women I greatly admire. These women are confident in the investment decisions they
are making because they understand the fundamental nature of the
stock market and don't lose any sleep over the twists and turns. By
nature, they are not "market timers"—they research an investment
as much as possible and then make a decision and take an active
role in monitoring their investments. They don't invest money in
financial products they don't understand, and, as a group, they are
three times more likely than men (who are more inclined to move
in and out of the market for "quick hits") to call themselves long-
term investors. Since they have done their homework, they usually

use a financial advisor or seminar or club for assistance in selecting stocks, bonds, and mutual funds. Otherwise, they seek out information from TV and radio programs, newspapers and magazines, classes, and books on an ongoing—but not all-consuming—basis.

SECTION

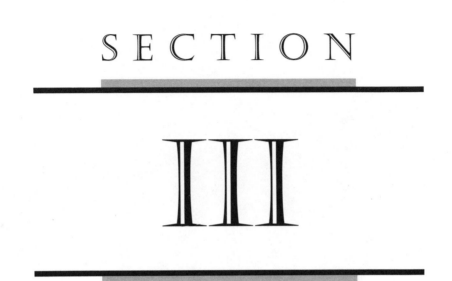

III

13

YOU'VE COME A LONG
WAY ALREADY

Congratulations! If you've read this far, you've already come a long way. Simply by bringing your self-analysis far enough to recognize your strengths and weaknesses, you've proved that you have the will to take charge of your money. That in itself is a major accomplishment.

Now I want to make this next step—obtaining the financial knowledge you need—as simple as possible. Since I've been able to observe the thousands of women who go through our seminars covering this information, I know the following guidelines will help you.

1. Don't be upset with yourself if you don't understand something the first time. The goal of this section is for you to enjoy learning about finances. You will be much more successful if you just relax. The beauty of a book is that you can reread what you want when you want to. Use a highlighter, write in the margins, and turn down the corners if that makes it easier for you to find relevant material again later.

2. Some people actually enjoy reading cookbooks although they rarely go into the kitchen and prepare the recipes; others like reading travel guides in place of traveling. Well, I never hear of anyone reading financial advice for pleasure or as a replacement for doing something. So, as you read through these

chapters, always remember that the goal is to *apply* the information so that you can build a solid financial future. Keep asking, "How can *I* use this information? How does this apply to *me*?"

3. Not every piece of information will apply to you now. However, I still recommend that you read, or at least skim through, every chapter. By doing so, you'll know where to find the information when you need it.

4. The information in this book is a launching pad, a beginning from which you'll move on. Later, as you start to invest, you may become interested in picking your own stocks. That's when you'll decide to purchase another book devoted entirely to selecting stocks, or you'll go on-line and do some reading on the Internet.

Throughout this book, you have read stories about women who have turned their lives around by overcoming psychological barriers and taking charge of their money. Remember that not one of these women accomplished this feat overnight. If there is any common denominator to their stories, it is that they persevered, and by adopting a positive attitude, they were able to understand the basic financial principles that led to success over a period of time.

For many, it takes time to absorb the implications and take small steps that lead to financial independence. During the writing of this book, I received a letter from a woman who attended one of our seminars over two years ago. She wrote:

> For over a year I procrastinated about moving forward with all the financial information I needed to learn. However, when I left your seminar I knew that my life would never be the same again; the financial handbook reminded me of how much hard work I'd be doing soul-searching. After your talk, I felt reassured that learning about finances is filled with all kinds of possibilities—a milkweed pod just opened. As I learned more about the financial information you touched on, the seeds went flying up and were swirling in the air. To make it all manageable, I focused on planting and nurturing one or two seeds at a time.
>
> I also want to share with you some of my mixed feelings, because it took me a while to overcome the idea that making

and investing money is a bad thing, done by people who aren't concerned about others. When I began to understand this was a wrong perception, it made me angry that women have long been taught that money is unholy. I was socialized to accept that women don't deal with or handle money. Because of this message, I chose the teaching profession—as a server type of person who could make a difference to children. Now I realize I can still uphold the values I've lived by in working with children, but I can also learn about my financial needs and take care of them.

Each new piece of financial information I acquire is a "seed." I decide whether I should use it in my garden now to blossom later or keep it in the shed to germinate for another season. Thank you, Dr. Hayes. Your information helped me understand the tools I need to cultivate my garden.

As I look out over the sea of faces at our financial seminars, I always have two conflicting thoughts, and I feel the same way now: I feel a tremendous responsibility to provide you with the information you need to take charge of your money—it's so critical that you do. But as an educator I am also aware that growth and change can be accomplished only by the participant. I cannot force you to hear the "financial call to arms" and to begin a prudent savings and investment plan. Only you can do that for yourself, and I believe that you can.

If, while you are reading the information presented in this section, you become nervous about the risk involved, worried about making a change, have difficulty making a decision, or encounter any of the other difficulties we have discussed, just turn back to the relevant chapter and think again about why it's so important for you to invest in yourself. Good luck.

14

FINDING THOSE INVESTMENT DOLLARS

"My money comes in, but by the end of the month, I really have no idea where it has gone. I never have anything left over to save."

A vital part of taking charge of your money is tracking where your current income goes. Unfortunately, when this topic comes up at the NCWRR seminars, most women groan because they know that tracking cash flow often precedes the unpopular task of budgeting. If I'm fortunate, I'll find at least one woman in the audience who has discovered the merits of both. Marie P. was one of these.

"My husband and I had never worked with a budget before, but we were having trouble making ends meet, so we decided to give it a try," says Marie P., the mother of three children nearing college age. *"We read about how we needed to track our income and expenses before developing a budget, so we started by doing that. Income was pretty easy because our money comes from only two sources—his paycheck and mine—but going over all our expenses took time. Most revealing was when we started tracking our weekly cash. I found I didn't spend very much wastefully, but I was constantly doling out money to the kids. We resolved that it was time to put them on allowances that would supplement what they made through occasional work like baby-sitting and lawn care.*

"Overall, setting up a budget after tracking our cash flow for a few months has been a really worthwhile experience. Once we had a map of where our money was going, it gave us an opportunity to close off some of the roads where we didn't want it flowing so freely anymore! We've never felt we had 'two nickels to rub together' before, and now, thanks to this plan, we're actually doing some goal-setting for what we'll do with our savings."

This chapter is going to focus on ways to take control of what you have, including tracking cash flow and budgeting. You'll also read about new and interesting ways to save money painlessly. The following steps are part of the process, and we'll cover them in the following order:

STEP ONE: Getting organized

STEP TWO: Creating a cash flow worksheet

STEP THREE: Establishing a budget

STEP FOUR: Establishing credit

Step One: Getting Organized

You have to know what you've got financially in order to gain control over it. A vital step in this process is locating and organizing your financial papers and the relevant phone numbers.

In order to assess your current situation, you need to locate the following. Check off each item after you locate it; draw a line through those items that aren't applicable.

- ☐ Life insurance policies and records
- ☐ Other insurance policies and records
- ☐ Stock certificates (if you're holding them)
- ☐ Bond certificates (if you're holding them)
- ☐ Money market records
- ☐ Brokerage house statements
- ☐ Bank statements
- ☐ Deed to property
- ☐ Mortgage agreement
- ☐ Other loan agreements and payment books
- ☐ Notes receivable (does anyone owe you money?)

- [ ] Employee benefit information and statements
- [ ] Company profit-sharing and bonus plan information
- [ ] Pension information
- [ ] IRA, Keogh, 401(k) records
- [ ] Annuity records
- [ ] Premarital contract
- [ ] Divorce agreement (financial terms)
- [ ] Trust documents

Don't forget to take the time to organize the financial information you deal with regularly:

- [ ] Mortgage payment book
- [ ] Current bills and related information (For your current bills, purchase an expandable folder, using dividers for each month. Mark one section for unpaid invoices; the other sections of the folder can be for storage of paid bills—filed by month—and related documents.)

While you're at it, also gather together the items that constitute your "important papers." Included in this category are family birth certificates, wills, marriage and divorce certificates, Social Security cards, military discharge papers, passports, death certificates, tax receipts and old tax return information (for the last seven years), home-related receipts and documents (insurance policies, a household inventory list, receipts from capital improvements to home and property), and funeral information. These papers should also be stored together so that they are easier to locate.

WHERE TO STORE YOUR DOCUMENTS

Safe-Deposit Box

Copies of the following:
  Your will
  Your living will (if you have one)
  Power of attorney

Originals of stock and bond certificates

Inventory of personal property
List of insurance policies and their numbers
List of important telephone numbers re your holdings
Legal documents
Mortgage papers
Passports
Titles to property/real estate
Trust documents
Copy of funeral instructions

Fireproof Box at Home

Originals of the following:
   Your will
   Your living will
   Power of attorney
Your safe-deposit key and the location of the box
Insurance policies

Filing Cabinet

Automobile records
Employment records
Funeral and burial instructions
Important telephone numbers
Investment statements
Loan agreements
Mortgage information
Tax information

Basement or Closet Storage

Tax returns must be saved for seven years. These can go in "deep storage," high in a closet or in the basement, as easy access isn't important.

At the time of the owner's death, a safe-deposit box is generally sealed, making it awkward if family members need any of the papers that are stored there. That's why it's better to keep originals of these documents at your attorney's office or in a fireproof box in your home.

If you are married, do not list the safe-deposit box in your husband's name only. List it in both your names so that you'll have access to what you need when you need it.

When I first started presenting seminars for women, I encountered Ann M., a soft-spoken middle-aged woman who came to the seminar in a very distressed state. During a break, she came up to me and confided that she had lost her husband to cancer a month before and had no idea whether he had even taken out a life insurance policy. She was particularly concerned for her financial future because their two daughters were still quite young.

When I asked her if he had left a will, she sheepishly admitted that they had never taken care of that. As we talked, it became clear that she had no idea where they were in terms of their assets or insurance coverage.

"Go home and locate every document you can and bring everything back to the Center," I told her. When she appeared at my office the following day, we spread everything out on the conference table. After about fifteen minutes, I discovered a $500,000 life insurance policy her husband had taken out after the birth of their first daughter. This discovery eased Ann's burden immeasurably, and she simply sat and cried for a while, she was so relieved. Imagine how much easier the last few months of her husband's illness would have been for Ann if she had only known that she would have some money to work with once he was gone.

This is just one illustration of why it's important to be organized so that you'll know what you have. I can't tell you how many women who visit the Center are like Ann; they don't have any idea what they own or would have the right to if their fortunes changed. Take the time now to get organized. It can make all the difference in the world to your sense of well-being.

GATHERING IMPORTANT TELEPHONE AND ACCOUNT NUMBERS

In addition to these papers, your financial life will be simplified if you gather and list telephone numbers of your employer's personnel office (for information on company benefits), your insurance agent, bank, lawyer, accountant, and financial advisor or broker (if you have one).

Also sift through your papers and make a single list of the following: brokerage and bank account numbers, credit cards, and insurance policies. This list should go with your important papers.

THE BENEFITS OF COMPUTERIZING YOUR FINANCES

While a pencil, calculator, and a yellow legal pad can serve as your worksheet for all financial figuring, these calculations can be done more quickly and easily on a personal computer once you invest the time in setting up and learning the system. Visit a software store and ask for information or a demonstration of some of the personal finance programs. Also talk to friends about what they are using.

For example, if you set up a budget on your computer, you need simply enter your expenses each month and the computer will categorize them and routinely give you an annual report on how you're doing. (This also saves time on tax preparation, as the categories are already created and tabulated for you.)

Step Two: Understanding Your Cash Flow by Tracking Income and Expenses

BUDGETING GETS A BUM RAP

"I couldn't bear the thought of budgeting because I thought it would mean living this terribly constricted life," says June K. "Then a friend showed me what she was doing, which really had more to do with tracking her expenses, and I felt I could do that."

The thought of "budgeting" brings with it all sorts of negative connotations—watching every penny, doing without, not having enough money to eat out occasionally . . . You name it, budgeting has been blamed for it.

A budget is none of those things. A good budget is nothing more than a *plan*. What's more, it's a plan based on your current spending habits. That's why the first step in devising your budget is creating a *cash flow statement,* an accurate picture of where your money goes during the month.

After you monitor your expenses for a period of time, you will be able to set up an intelligent budget for yourself and/or your family. The beauty of a budget is that you can actually allot more money to the things that make you happy. For example, you may decide that one of your priorities is having dinner out as a family once a month. You may need to reduce expenses in another area in order to come up with the money, but the control—and the choice—are yours.

How many times have you said, "I just don't know where my money goes?" We hear this over and over from NCWRR seminar participants. Though "budgeting" and "planning where your money goes" are familiar concepts, few people—men or women— have much understanding of how cash flow (what comes in and goes out) or budgeting (planning for what comes in and out) applies to them.

In our Women Cents Study, we learned the following.

- Only 30 percent of respondents followed a monthly spending plan or budget.
- 40 percent said they had a general plan they carried "in their head." (Despite this general plan, these respondents generally did not understand how to account for all their money at the end of any given month.)
- 30 percent had no spending plan at all.

Regardless of these dismal statistics, 83 percent of respondents indicated that one of their financial goals was to control spending so that they would have money to save and invest.

If you truly want to take charge of your money, then take the two to three hours that you will need (it shouldn't take much longer if you've pulled together your financial papers) to set up a cash flow statement.

Next, take at least three months to track your expenses so that you have an accurate picture of where your money goes. (Once you set up a system, keeping track of expenses requires less than five minutes a day.)

After that, you'll be prepared to establish a plan—a budget—for how you'd really like to see your money spent, and of course, top on the list of priorities should be finding money for saving and investing.

WHO SHOULD FILL OUT A CASH FLOW STATEMENT?

Everyone. Whether you're a novice or an expert money manager, it is always helpful to create a cash flow statement to identify discretionary income for investing. When you realize your family is spending $135 a month at fast-food restaurants, you may well decide to teach your teens how to heat up the stove.

FILLING OUT A CASH FLOW WORKSHEET

To begin to track your cash flow, fill out the worksheet on page 240. (Surprisingly, many people don't even know exactly what their actual income is.)

As you work through it, you'll note categories for both income and expenses that occur only once or twice a year. You must prorate annual, biannual, or quarterly income and expenses so that you'll know how they affect your monthly cash flow. For example, if you receive a $1,200 annual bonus and want to create an accurate picture of your monthly income, you need to divide 12 (months) into $1,200. Your company bonus, spread across the course of a year, increases your monthly income by $100.

The same should be done with expenses. If your annual insurance payment is $900, again, you divide 12 into $900, meaning that you need to set aside $75 a month in order to save up for that $900 payment each year. Even the cost of a vacation should be prorated as an expense across twelve months.

"Why do I have to do that? Why can't I just deal with it when I get the bill(s)?" is a question we hear frequently at the Center. Here's why: The money has to come from somewhere, and unless you're tapping into savings for costs such as quarterly or annual bills, you need to make certain that money is not spent on something else during the year.

By prorating these expenses on a monthly basis, you will get an accurate picture of your income and expenses for the entire year. (While another solution would be to prepare an *annual* budget, that isn't very practical because it's not the way we live. For example, you may have budgeted $60 per month for a haircut, but that amount changes its meaning when it's translated into an annual figure of $720.)

TRACKING YOUR CASH EXPENDITURES

As we've already noted, cash slips through most people's fingers quite quickly. A $2.75 greeting card for a favorite aunt, $5.50 for lunch every day at work, $8.95 for a new paperback novel, $15 for a CD, and extra cash spent on anything from nail polish to impulse purchases for the kids can really add up!

If you have not yet tried carrying a small notebook or index cards to record your daily expenses, do so now, and try to keep it up for three months. Chances are you'll be stunned at how much "wandering around" money you spend.

Tracking these cash expenditures will not only help identify what you are spending; it will also provide you with a picture of your spending patterns, habits, and priorities—the dollars you spend will tell you a lot about yourself. Some women are shocked to find out what they spend on cosmetics; others walk into a bookstore and can't resist spending $20 or $30. There is nothing wrong with spending money on something you enjoy or value, but you should be aware of the fact that you're spending it.

Once you have a figure for the miscellaneous cash you've been spending each month, look over the list and see how you feel about the expenditures. You may decide every penny you spend on a new book is worth it, but you may also decide that you're tired of lunches from the employee cafeteria anyway, so you'll save some money by bringing your lunch twice a week instead.

The very act of writing down your expenses will also help curb some impulse purchases. If you're just about to purchase yet another type of garden gadget, chances are you'll think twice when you remember you have to write it down.

But austerity is rarely a route to successful budgeting—it's too demoralizing. That's why the cash flow statement we've devised includes allowances for all family members. Both adults and children should be allotted a certain amount of money each month to spend on personal needs, with a little built in as "mad money." If you really want that garden gadget, you ought to be able to have it if you've been watching other personal expenditures that month. To decide on the appropriate allowances, review each person's spending habits after documenting expenses for the three-month period. This will give you an idea of their needs and wants, and you can adjust it based on what seems right.

Make two photocopies of your cash flow statement. The first copy will be used to record current spending practices for three months. The second copy will be used to create a budget—your target amount for what *should* be spent in each of the categories you've identified.

THE PROOF IS IN THE EXPENDITURE

One woman who came to the Center found the entire process of creating a cash flow statement educational—and beneficial:

"After doing some detective work on my spending habits, I was shocked to find that I was a 'compulsive catalog shopper.' After two months, I realized that I spent over $178 on catalog purchases for items that really weren't necessary. I also found a pattern to it all. To relax at night, I would thumb through catalogs while watching television. When something struck my fancy, I would pick up the phone (which was also right next to me) and put the items on my credit card. I didn't realize how expensive this habit was until I started examining how much was going out each month. The shocking thing was I was spending money without even moving—other than using my fingers to dial the telephone!"

MONTHLY CASH FLOW STATEMENT

	MONTH 1	MONTH 2	MONTH 3
Income			
Wages/salaries (gross)	_____	_____	_____
Bonus (prorate to per-month figure)	_____	_____	_____
Dividends	_____	_____	_____
Interest	_____	_____	_____

Rent income
Tax refund (prorate)
Loans owed to you
Other (pension, trust income,
    etc.)

Expenses

Savings and investment
    money
Taxes (see your check stub
    from work or last year's
    tax filings)
    Federal
    State/local
    Social Security (if self-
        employed)
    Personal property
    Real estate/other
Insurance
    Auto
    Disability
    Homeowners
    Health
    Life
    Long-term care
Loan payments

_____

_____

Credit card payments

_____

_____

Consolidated debt payment
Home operation
    Rent or mortgage payments
    Maintenance/
        improvements
Utilities
    Gas and electricity
    Water/sewer
    Telephone
    Garbage
Family maintenance
    Food
    Clothing

Health costs (incl.   _____   _____   _____
  prescriptions)
Child care   _____   _____   _____
Tuition/lessons   _____   _____   _____
Books/supplies   _____   _____   _____
Personal care (haircuts, etc.) _____   _____   _____
Allowances (for all family
  members)
  Names:

  _____   ____   ____   ____
  _____   ____   ____   ____
  _____   ____   ____   ____
  _____   ____   ____   ____

Dry cleaning   _____   _____   _____
Automobile/transportation
  Gas   _____   _____   _____
  Maintenance/repair   _____   _____   _____
  Parking/public transit   _____   _____   _____
  Boat/camper   _____   _____   _____
Discretionary
  Alcohol/tobacco   _____   _____   _____
  Entertainment   _____   _____   _____
  Vacations   _____   _____   _____
  Hobbies   _____   _____   _____
  Contributions   _____   _____   _____
  Gifts (holiday expenses)   _____   _____   _____
  Lunches (work)   _____   _____   _____
Miscellaneous
  Books/magazines/   _____   _____   _____
    newspapers
  Fees/dues   _____   _____   _____
  Alimony   _____   _____   _____
  Dependent support   _____   _____   _____
Other

  _____   _____   _____   _____
  _____   _____   _____   _____
  _____   _____   _____   _____

Month 1

Income _____
Expenses _____
Net difference _____

Month 2

Income _____
Expenses _____
Net difference _____

Month 3

Income _____
Expenses _____
Net difference _____

Step Three: Creating Your Budget

After tracking expenses for three months, you'll be ready to plan where you'd *like* your money to go.

If you are married or have a "significant other," go out to one of those new coffee bars where you can sit for a while uninterrupted and begin to plug in appropriate numbers for monthly expenses (use a copy of the cash flow statement for easy reference). Certain costs, like your rent or mortgage payment, cannot be changed. Others, like utilities, will vary slightly, but you'll have a general idea of how much must be set aside each month in order to be certain you'll have enough money to cover the bill.

As you turn to the expenses that are optional, categories such as clothing and personal care expenses, as well as all the listings under discretionary expenses, you'll get a good view of your overall cash flow.

Take a look at your final income figure for each month and subtract from it your total for expenses. If you're lucky, you'll have more income than expenses.

However, you may be surprised. While it seemed as if you were living within your means, you may find that by the time you prorate any annual or quarterly expenses (such as insurance payments) and spread them throughout the months, you are actually spending more than you are bringing in.

If so, your next task is to trim expenses. Go through each line item and see where you can cut back. Perhaps your home-decorating expenses have gotten a bit out of line. Can you reduce or eliminate those expenses for a while? And what about recreation? Why not take the family to the movies once a month and rent videos the other weekends? When you get other expenses under control (perhaps paying down your credit card debt), you can loosen up again. (Later in this chapter there is additional information on what to do if you're carrying a lot of debt.)

Now go through it all again for one more belt-tightening. You've got to find some additional money for saving and investing. Keep in mind that's one of the main reasons you're doing this in the first place. If you can't find as much as you might like by reducing some of the expenses you've listed, keep reading. There's more information on finding the savings you need.

Another woman who finally learned the benefits of tracking income and expenses was a financial sophisticate, a former Wall Street trader. Deciding she wanted a slower-paced lifestyle, she moved to the country without doing any research on the job market:

"I spent the proceeds of my pension, all my savings, and the money from the sale of my house, and I finally had to file for bankruptcy—my lifestyle was way above my earning capacity in this new location. I credit my return to financial soundness with finally learning to plan and budget, concepts I'd ignored in the past. Now I'm living a comfortable lifestyle with much less than I lived on when I worked on Wall Street, but I'm perfectly happy and have what I need."

PAY YOURSELF FIRST

Are you surprised to see "Savings" at the top of the expenses category in the Monthly Cash Flow Statement? You shouldn't be, because what is your most important expense? You—and your future. That's why you have to pay yourself first.

There are several ways to be certain this first payment is made promptly each month. When you pay your rent or mortgage bill at the first of the month, write a check to your savings account (or preferably to a higher-interest investment account) at the same time. Also check into your options at work. Many employers offer automatic savings plans, and before you see a penny of your paycheck, the money can be transferred to a savings account, mutual fund, or savings bond program.

How much should you be saving? Trying to save 8 to 12 percent of your monthly income is a worthy goal. If you absolutely can't manage that high a figure, then start with a percentage you can handle and vow to increase it by 1 percent each year. Or set a modest dollar amount, perhaps $50 a month, and resolve to boost it periodically. Just start saving.

FOR THE PERSISTENTLY RESISTANT

There are always a few seminar attendees who are evidently not paying attention when tracking cash flow is discussed. "I don't have a head for numbers," "I'm too impatient to keep track of all this," "It will never work for me," are some of the protests we hear, and these are the same women who later report that they "just couldn't monitor" their cash flow.

After ten years of conducting financial seminars, I have come to the conclusion that some women will never progress beyond having a budget in their head. Instead of heaping guilt on you, I'm going to share with you a secret that won't replace a good budget, but it will help:

Write a check to yourself for savings every month without fail.

This will still permit you to participate in the rest of the program outlined in this book.

While tracking your cash flow might help you find extra money to put away or help you redirect your cash flow toward something more beneficial than how you're spending it now, the most important thing is to set aside money for saving and investing. If you do that, you've taken care of the most important aspect of budgeting.

SAVINGS TIPS AND TRICKS

"I can't save," you may be moaning. Yes, you can. You have to, because, as we've discussed, if you don't, you're putting your own needs last. The money you save and invest will be put to use later for both short-term and long-term goals, both of which will be set up to make your life better and happier. Here are some suggestions for coming up with some big bucks and small change that will put you ahead:

- When you finish paying off any type of loan, keep writing a check for the same amount, but this time send it directly to an interest-bearing investment account.
- The next time you get a raise, just earmark that extra money for savings.
- Use cash as much as possible. This technique will restrict your shopping to the items you really need, and by not running up debt on your credit card, you avoid the risk of having to pay interest on the monthly balance.
- If you have money in savings and are carrying a large balance on your credit card (for which you are probably being charged 18 to 21 percent interest), withdraw your money from savings to pay off the credit card debt. While reducing your lump-sum savings is frustrating, no one should be paying almost $20 for every $100 borrowed. By reducing the debt, you're already saving—just don't run up a big bill again.
- If you're in debt and are paying off high-interest loans, consolidate your loans and refinance the debt. For example, if you have three store credit cards and one bank card on which you owe money, total the amount owed and visit a bank to talk about borrowing money to pay off the high-interest loans. Some people take out a debt consolidation loan; others use a home equity line of credit (where the interst is fully deductible on your income tax return). Either of these loans will almost certainly be at a much lower interest rate, saving you money in the long run.
- Shop strictly by list at the grocery store. Think back to your last trip to the supermarket. Do you recall the number of items you (or other family members who may have accompanied you, particularly the under-age-eighteen set) may have added to your cart as impulse buys? If you make a sensible list and stick to it, you'll save money weekly.
- Buy in bulk. Throughout the country, people are benefiting from the proliferation of "membership" warehouses, where you can buy staples in bulk at radically reduced prices.
- Calculate the worth of the coupons you use at the supermarket and earmark that money for investing. Whether it's $2.50 or $10 a week, it all helps.

- "Recycle" your money. Every time you take soda cans back to the grocery, earmark the deposit money for savings.
- Pick one area of your life where you're prepared to make a small financial sacrifice: Have lunch out one time fewer per week. Reduce your fall clothing expenditure by $50. Don't splurge on something because it's for the kids (and if your children are grown, keep your splurges small—it's time they learned to stand on their own feet economically). Invest the money you save or put it in an interest-bearing money market account.
- Profit from impulse. Next time you're at the mall deciding "should I or shouldn't I?" decide no, and put that money in the bank instead. Or limit the size of your splurge to $25 to $30 and save whatever else you might have spent.
- Look for petty cash. Pull all your loose change in a jar at the end of the day; by the end of a month or two, you'll have between $20 and $50 to save.
- Move your savings into instruments you can't touch immediately. If your money market account comes with a checkbook, consider locking up the checkbook so that you use it only in an emergency. And don't ever leave savings in an account that's accessible with your ATM card!
- Reward yourself. When you meet a savings target for a month, reward yourself. The reward could be a new paperback book or taking the family out to dinner, whatever will make you feel good without violating your savings plan.

These are just a few ideas. If you keep looking, you'll find other ways to trim expenses.

Step Four: The Importance of Women and Credit

The importance of establishing credit cannot be underestimated. Here's what Linda R. said: *"Shortly after I divorced, I made it a priority to establish my own credit, and I've never had a problem with it—in part, I think, because my parents were very cautious people and not into consumerism. I've always been satisfied to live within my means. If you can't do that, I think that's where you get in trouble with credit."*

If you have not established credit in your own name, you are a "financial nobody" and it is vital that you do so now.

One wealthy woman whose husband left her when she was sixty-six was upset when she applied for her first Visa card in her own name: *"I was shocked! They gave me a spending limit of $500—certainly not enough to take care of a month of my normal charges,"* says Frances C. *"It was a financial and emotional setback for me. My husband had always taken care of everything for us, and I felt he left me with no way to carve out a new life."*

In adidtion to the inconvenience of not being able to get a credit card with an adequate spending limit, without established credit you won't be able to rent your own apartment, take out any type of loan, or buy a home.

Even if you have no plans for doing any of these things, take steps now to establish your financial identity. No one should be relegated to being a nobody; it greatly reduces later options. To begin:

- Visit a bank and set up your own checking and savings accounts.
- If you have had jointly held credit cards or loans, write to the credit card issuer or the institution granting the loan and request that your joint account transactions be reported in your name in addition to your husband's (the report should be in your legal name, not as Mrs. John Smith). You are both responsible for keeping payments up-to-date, so make sure you're establishing a good track record for yourself as well.
- Request your credit report from a credit bureau to ascertain that the reports are being made the way you requested. (See Appendix C for names and phone numbers of credit bureaus.)
- Apply for a major credit card to begin to establish a credit history. Shop for one with no annual fee. (Most cards will require that you have your own income. Alimony is considered income, but if you were to apply for a loan specifying alimony as your primary source of income, the bank would also check the credit record of your ex-spouse.) Then you need to use the card regularly for a year or two, making the monthly payments promptly to establish your creditworthiness. (For your sake, you're better off paying in full every month.)

Your bill-payment record will go on file with companies who maintain credit reports. Later on, if you want to apply for additional credit cards or take out a loan, your history will be checked before you receive additional credit.

If you are contemplating purchasing a home or starting a business in the near future, you might also consider taking out a small bank loan, for as little as $5,000.

The cost of this credit-building exercise (you'll pay interest on the money you borrow) will be less if you invest the money you borrow in a safe interest-paying investment. This way you'll pay only the percentage difference between your borrowing rate and the interest rate you're getting as income. The fact that you qualified for and paid back a small loan will be very meaningful when you attempt to borrow major money.

CREDIT DEFINED

Keep in mind that there are two types of credit. The first is credit-of convenience. This is when you carry and use credit cards regularly, paying them off when the bill comes each month. Whether you're buying something over the telephone or you simply prefer not to carry large amounts of cash, the use of a credit card is simply part of the American way.

The second type of credit involves borrowing money, usually in the form of a loan (or simply overspending on your credit card), to buy something you couldn't otherwise afford. Always keep in mind that this form of credit has a psychological component. You're purposely deciding to spend money you don't have for something you cannot afford. With housing prices what they are today, few could afford homes without credit; some couldn't purchase cars without a loan. And if you budget for monthly payments, there is nothing wrong with assuming a reasonable amount of debt. But always keep in mind that a loan—or an overextended credit card—is nothing to get involved in lightly. When you decide to borrow money, you should plan exactly how and when you'll be able to pay it back.

REPAIRING A POOR CREDIT HISTORY

If you and your spouse (if you've been working with mutually held credit cards or a joint account) have missed payments or been late in making payments on any of your household bills or your credit card or loan payments, you're going to need to invest some time in cleaning up your credit history.

Start by establishing a better payment pattern to demonstrate that you can handle the payments properly.

If you have actually failed to make good on some type of debt, you may have to invest five years in creating a more positive credit history for yourself. One alternative during this time is to visit a bank and set up a secured credit card for yourself. You deposit a certain amount of money in the bank; this money acts as security and establishes your credit limit.

If you are concerned about your credit history, don't apply for credit and risk being turned down. Credit refusal goes on your credit report and will predispose other institutions to turn you down as well. If you're in a precarious situation, visit your bank and discuss whether you can prequalify for the credit, so that when you apply you'll know a "yes" is assured.

15

WHAT DO YOU WANT? WHAT DO YOU NEED?
Setting Realistic Financial Goals

"What do I want? Oh, there are so many things . . . but I've never really let myself dwell on it, because most of the time we're just getting by."

6 6 I'm a saver," says Marge C., who came to the NCWRR seminars because—despite her efforts at saving—she knew she
wasn't getting ahead financially. *"When we were first married, we were
in our late twenties, and I had a decent nest egg saved. Steve didn't have
anything because he'd just finished struggling through medical school and
still had bills to pay."*

Marge's first nest egg went for a down payment on a modest condominium, a luxury that most of Steve's doctor friends, who also
had acquired major debt during medical school, couldn't afford.
After that, Marge established a strict system for paying off Steve's
student loans, and they gradually did so over a period of several
years. *"This prevented us from saving during this time because any extra
income went to offset the loans."*

But as Marge describes it, she and Steve just couldn't get ahead:
*"I wish they taught a financial basics course in medical school, because it
certainly would have helped us out. Everyone imagines that all doctors*

251

rake in big money, but they don't always. Steve went on staff at a hospital, and while he does well enough, we are by no means wealthy."

After their two children were born, Marge took time off to stay home and raise them. *"During those years we were always dipping into savings. Steve wanted a boat, and then the kids needed braces, and my mother got sick, and we had to help her out—it was just one thing or another.*

"So here I am—a saver with nothing," says Marge with a trace of bitterness. *"I'm fifty-two years old, with two children in college. They are receiving some financial aid, but Steve and I had to take out loans to supplement the package that was offered. Now we're ten or fifteen years from retirement, and we've got virtually nothing. When I let myself think about it, I'm just beside myself with worry."*

At the financial seminar Marge attended, she saw how her natural interest and ability to save were thwarted because she didn't set goals and stick by them. Whenever a family member needed something (a boat for Steve, orthodontics for the kids), Marge and Steve simply dipped into savings. While there is nothing wrong with any personal expenditure you decide to make, the art of it is always keeping part of your nest egg intact. Whether this means waiting to buy the boat until after you've saved the money for this type of luxury, or whether it means taking out a small loan to cover the orthodontics (so that you don't have to disturb your long-term savings), you've got to set goals and then do all you can to preserve the money set aside for those goals.

One of the most gratifying moments in my work is when I see women identify goals that are truly meaningful to them and then make those goals a reality. Women are wonderful at goal-setting once they are given the opportunity to reflect on what they want to accomplish.

It is my hope that every woman who reads this book will make financial goal-setting a priority. Just by doing so—by putting your desires into words—you immediately increase the odds of achieving whatever it is you want. What's more, by specifying what you want to accomplish with your money, you've accomplished a critical aspect of creating a financial plan—a task that both men and women tend to view as daunting, but one that is really no more complicated than deciding what you want financially and mapping out how you're going to get there.

"When I first came to the NCWRR seminar and took the Women Cents quiz, I scored poorly in every section," says Rachel F. *"I was particularly weak in investment knowledge and general planning.*

"Since then I have come back for more financial instruction, and along the way I set some goals. I recently purchased my own condominium and am feeling more optimistic about the future. I also feel much more confident, and I have no doubt that it's because I've taken the initiative and started to plan."

This chapter will help you learn how to set both short- and long-term goals. The decisions you make here will affect your investment strategies for today as well as the future, so take the time to go through this information carefully.

This chapter is of utmost importance. Don't skip it or skim it. It is vital that women, no matter how young, begin to plan ahead—even as far ahead as retirement. While Social Security and employer pension plans were not devised to discriminate against women, they usually do, because they are designed for the traditional male who has made a decent wage and maintained an uninterrupted employment history over the years. Women who ignore this chapter may find their Social Security income less than they expect, and will find that the system has failed to keep up with the changing roles of women.

LIFE EXPECTANCY—WOMEN LIVING EVEN LONGER

One thing that may affect your goal-setting is your current life expectancy. Few people think about how many years ahead they may need to plan. Here's what you should know:

In 1940, a sixty-five-year-old man could expect to live about two more years. In 1996 he could expect to live about 15.5 more years, and women have experienced an even greater increase in their life expectancy. In recent years, the life expectancy of sixty-five-year-old women has been going up a month a year. If you analyze the month-a-year trend, eighty years from now, sixty-five-year-old women will have twenty-five or twenty-six years remaining. This statistic alone should motivate the parents of younger girls to teach their daughters the virtues of saving as quickly as possible.

The following table will give you an idea of how many more years you can expect to live (and therefore need to plan for).

AGE AND AVERAGE REMAINING LIFE EXPECTANCY

Age	Average Remaining Life Expectancy
20	59.9
25	55.1
30	50.3
35	45.5
40	40.7
45	36.0
50	31.5
55	27.1
60	22.9
65	19.1
70	15.4
75	12.1
80	9.1

Source: Life Tables from the Centers for Disease Control and Prevention/National Center for Health Statistics.

Dreaming the Dream

At heart, this chapter is about dreams, and of course, the proper setting for talking about dreams is a relaxed one. If you're single, pack up this book and take it to the beach or curl up in your most comfortable chair at home. If you're married, tell your spouse you're bringing in your favorite take-out food tonight, and the two of you are going to spend some time dreaming together about your financial future. You should both also do some dreaming on your own. Your husband may aspire to take up portrait painting, and you may want to go back to school; and your dreams should reflect what is important to each of you. Use the worksheet on page 257 for noting down your goals.

One of the major findings of the Dreyfus Gender Investment Comparison Survey is that at every stage of life, women are three times more likely than men to visualize, identify, and articulate their goals and aspirations. So take advantage of this ability and focus on the hopes and dreams you have for the future.

Your dreams, of course, will be affected by your age and stage of life. Some of you will use the Financial Goals Worksheet to write about buying your first home, paying for your children's college education, or being able to afford to retire and travel extensively once you have the time.

Planning ahead isn't easy, but don't get discouraged. Everyone struggles with this task. It isn't easy facing the great unknown. You can't help wondering if your retirement years will in any way mimic those of your parents. Corporate downsizing, the instability of Social Security and health care, wage stagnation, and the increased cost of living have created widespread disillusionment about the future.

To come up with dreams that will provide you with fulfillment, you must create a mind-set that allows you the freedom to question whether you want to continue taking on certain roles or whether you would feel more fulfilled doing something else. From my experience, what prevents women from dreaming the dream is that they feel trapped in a "bad movie."

If you've recently felt hopeless about ever getting anywhere with your life, think again. If you establish a series of goals and have factored these dreams into your plan, you will increase your ability to realize them, largely because you'll have the opportunity to figure out ways to afford them.

"I always dreamed of going to graduate school, but I gave up my aspirations after college and got married," says one woman.

"As the kids got older and my husband sensed my unrest, he encouraged me to 'go for it.' I'm a psychologist now at forty-eight, and I couldn't be happier."

Right now, you can begin by asking yourself the following questions.

- What do you really want to do? Think back to some of the hopes and dreams you had growing up, and see if any of them apply now.
- Do you want to stay with your present employer for the next decade, or do you have the urge to strike out on a new career path? If you want a new job or career, begin to think about any training that might be required, and consider the impact a switch might have on your retirement planning and employee benefits.

- Do you want to take a "time-out" sabbatical in the future to travel, write a book, investigate a new hobby, start a family? If so, begin to think about what it will cost in terms of dollars and begin planning.

Only your imagination can hold you back. Though it isn't easy to rewrite a life script, many women have found a way to have their dreams come true through one word—planning.

And if you're a "present thinker," this is a particularly important task because it's an easy way to think about the future (and your eventual retirement) without having to add anything to your "to do" list just yet!

The worksheet shouldn't be completed quickly, though it will need to be filled out if you are to benefit fully from the information in the following chapters. Start by using it to stimulate your thinking, and as a discussion point if you're married. Whether it takes a week or a month to fill out doesn't matter, it's just important that you do it.

"I'm only forty-nine, but I'm already a widow, so when I was presented with the idea of setting some financial goals, I decided to do it with a friend who was in a similar circumstance," says Jean H. *"We set a date for dinner, and I made photocopies of the goals sheet so that we could each fill one out. Having someone to talk it out with really helped, and when we got to the part about retirement, it was far less frightening, because being with a friend for the planning somehow made each of us feel that we'd have friends in retirement too."*

PLANNING ON THE PC

You'll find this process is greatly simplified if you have a financial planning program on your home computer. While you have to enter all the appropriate data, the computer program can do the math for you. For example, if you want to know how much you'll need to save each year in order to have enough money for your three-year-old to go to a private college, you simply enter current-day cost, adding in an estimated figure for inflation, and the computer will spew out the dollar amount you'll need to pay for four years of schooling.

Note: As you'll see on the worksheet, I want you to write down an estimated figure for what you expect each goal to cost. If you don't know the cost of some of the goals you list, take time to do the research. This may be as easy as phoning a travel agent to get the average price for a trip to Hawaii or talking to your child's school guidance counselor about what a year of college tuition will run. Or it may be quite complex. Perhaps you know you want to start a business, but you aren't quite certain what it will cost. Take the time to do the research by calling a local small business organization or contacting the Small Business Administration (SBA) for some leads as to what start-up costs for various types of businesses will run. Even a ballpark figure will do to begin with; you can refine it as you go along.

FINANCIAL GOALS WORKSHEET

Short-Term Goals

In the upcoming year, I have or can foresee the following major expenses. (These could range from a badly needed car to an anniversary vacation.)

Item   **Expected Cost**

_____   _____

_____   _____

_____   _____

Long-Term Goals

In the next five years, I anticipate the following major expenses. (These might include college tuition for a teenager, a larger home for a growing family, renovating your kitchen, or starting your own business.)

Goal   **Expected Cost**

_____   _____

_____   _____

In the next ten years, I anticipate the following major expenses (returning to college, starting a business, providing financial support for or relocating an aging parent.)

Goal   **Expected Cost**

_____   _____

_____   _____

How I Envision the Future

Describe the way you would like to spend your retirement years by recapturing that "can do" spirit of adolescence and dreaming of how you'd really like to spend those twenty to twenty-five years of your life. (Do you plan to travel? Work part-time? Move to a condo in Arizona?)

_____

_____

_____

_____

_____

As you go through the worksheet, you'll emerge with several figures: some specific dollar amounts for what you'd like to do in the short term, as well as some figures for the long term. But before you start saving for either of these, you have one other matter to attend to: You've got to be prepared for an emergency.

Reaching Everyone's First Savings Goal

When it comes to savings, you need to provide for four separate categories:

1. Emergency savings
2. Savings for upcoming major expenses
3. Retirement savings
4. Money earmarked for investing

As you can see, the second, third, and fourth categories are established for building toward your future. However, the first must be reckoned with before you move on.

Look at your cash flow sheet. What is the total for three months of expenses? Every individual *must* have enough money set aside to cover three to six months' worth of living expenses in case of an emergency. Only after you've saved that money can you move on to your other three goals.

Many experts want you to have six months of savings readily available, but this generally steers people toward keeping too much cash in a low-return investment. Some experts are now recommending that you restrict your savings fund to three months. Beyond that, in a true emergency, such as a job loss or a serious illness, you will be able to put your hands on money that is less liquid. One way is through a home equity line of credit. By establishing one now (and paying it off immediately so you're not paying interest on money you don't currently need), the line of credit will be available to you if and when you need it for a family emergency. You need pay interest on it only when you actually borrow against it.

And if unemployment hits, you will actually have access to part of your nest egg: If you've made contributions to your company's retirement program *on which you've been taxed,* you'll get this money back when you leave your employer, so when you're making those after-tax contributions, you are both saving for retirement and building an unemployment fund. (Your pretax retirement plan contributions, the company's contributions, and all your investment earnings must go directly into an individual retirement account at a brokerage firm or mutual fund company if you should switch jobs or else you'll pay a heavy tax penalty. This acts to safeguard part of your retirement fund.)

Your three-month fund should be kept in some type of liquid (readily available) investment such as a money market mutual fund.

Reaching Your Other Goals

Saving for short-term goals is generally a lot more fun than saving for long-term ones. If you and your spouse would really like to purchase a small condo or a time-share at your favorite ski resort, that is more than likely an achievable goal. You simply have to dedicate yourself to setting aside some money toward it over the period of a year or two that it takes you to amass enough for the down payment and the first year's carrying expenses.

Saving for long-term goals such as your children's education or your eventual retirement can take a decade or longer. However, you can amass thousands of dollars—even hundreds of thousands of dollars—over time simply by saving a few dollars a day and letting it earn interest in something more profitable than a savings account. For example, you could save $5,000 in five years by investing only $68.55 a month at 8 percent interest.

MONTHLY CONTRIBUTIONS OVER FIVE YEARS

Goal to Save ($)	Interest Rate		
	6%	8%	10%
5,000	$ 71.96	$ 68.55	$ 65.31
10,000	143.91	137.09	130.61
15,000	215.87	205.64	195.82
20,000	287.83	274.18	261.23

Compound interest means that interest is paid on both the principal in your account and previously earned interest. It's often referred to as "magic" because the money you earn turns around and earns more money for you.

The Magic of Compound Interest

One of the most important aspects of goal-setting is that your money can benefit from compound interest. When interest on your savings earns interest, this reduces the amount of money you need to put away to reach your goal. For example, if you dream of starting your own home-based business in approximately five years and know that you'll need at least $10,000 to get started, you need to invest $137.09 per month at 8 percent interest in order to have $10,000 in five years. However, if you were merely to save $137.09 under your mattress where, obviously, no interest at all would be earned, much less compounded, you would be able to save only $8,225.40—still a nice piece of change, but not as good as if you'd been getting interest, especially if compounded.

For this reason, the earlier you start to save for goals such as college tuition and retirement, the easier you make it on yourself. By putting money away now, your money will grow through interest, as well as additional savings.

Take the example of college costs: If tuition continues to increase at an annual rate of 7.2 percent (the average yearly increase for the nine-year period ending in 1995), by 2011 it will cost an average of $154,425 for four years at a state school and $332,287 for four years at a private institution.

By starting early, families can put away a respectable amount of the money they will need, and with compound interest, the college fund will grow even fatter.

Everyone Has the Same Long-Term Goal: Start Saving for Retirement Today

One of the new problems for baby boomers (as well as for younger people who delay childbirth) is that while college costs are skyrocketing, you can't afford to save sequentially (first for tuition costs and then for retirement) because your youngest child may not get his bachelor's degree until you're well into your fifties—only a few years away from when many people retire.

For that reason, whether this is your first year of employment or your twenty-first, you ought to start saving for retirement *today*. People are living longer, and regardless of your age, no matter what your current circumstances, it's vital that you start to save. Actually, the younger you are and the fewer financial demands you have, the more aggressively you should save and invest so that the money will be working for you.

There's one indisputable fact: **There's no such thing as saving too much for retirement.** If you have millions and millions when you're sixty-five, I'm sure you'll find ways to enjoy the money!

OUR USE OF THE WORD "RETIREMENT"—A DISCLAIMER

The word "retirement" has caused me great consternation. As I'm trying to motivate individuals to plan for their future, the youth-oriented baby boomers balk when talk turns to the "r" word. Even the American Association of Retired Persons (AARP) is downplaying use of the word, realizing that while baby boomers might join an organization known as AARP (the way we talk of AT&T), they are going to turn away if what's being offered sounds like it's for "old" people.

Without question, during the next several decades the retirement experience as we currently know it will be radically redefined by the baby boom population. Each of us has his or her own ideas and definitions of what this transition will be like. So please don't turn off or tune out. You and you alone will define what your own retirement experience will be. Many women (and men too) have failed to focus on planning for the future because of the stereotypical images retirement conjures up in their minds. But you don't have to sit on a porch in a rocker; your retirement years can be whatever you want them to be—so long as you can finance them.

STEPS YOU CAN TAKE TODAY

- Create an "event" time line for your family that will show when you are likely to need money for significant occasions: down payment on a home, private school, college, wedding. If you have a way of visualizing when your bank account will take a big hit, it will be easier to prepare for it.
- Maximize your 401(k) contributions and set aside any additional money you can for your long-term future.
- If you're self-employed, set up a SEP or a Keogh account.
- If you're near retirement age, shop now for your retirement home. You're more likely to get a better price if you buy before the rest of the boomers.
- If you're thinking of starting your own business after you retire, get it off the ground now, before you need to depend on it. Lots of people start businesses and moonlight until they feel they are ready to retire from their regular job and go it alone.

16

PROTECTING WHAT YOU HAVE

*"I neglected to review my employee benefits over
the years, and after being reminded to do so,
I discovered I was using just a fraction of what
was available to me."*

This is the chapter about what insurance coverage you should
have, and I don't want you to skip or skim it, especially if you
are inclined to be a present-oriented rather than a future-oriented
thinker. It may not be as exciting as reading about how to make
your money grow, but in order to put your financial house in order,
you really must take the time to evaluate what insurance protection
you need.

This topic is a special one for me because of an event that occurred over four years ago. I was in relatively good health until one
day I started having problems breathing. After two days with no
improvement, my wife convinced me to go to the doctor. I was diag-
nosed as having congestive heart failure and was rushed to an emergency room. During the next six months, I was unable to work.

I mention this experience not because of the health implications,
but because of what went through my mind during the first month
following my diagnosis. I immediately began to think of how I was
going to pay the bills and handle the monthly expenses. I was
scared, very scared—not so much for me, but for the ones I loved,
my family. Fortunately, my wife had encouraged me to take out life

and disability insurance several years prior to this. Without this protection, our life would have been severely disrupted.

Today I talk to women about my experience because I am concerned that so few of them know what protection they have. I understand that it is difficult for many people to think about their own death, disability, or long-term-care needs, but a few moments spent focusing on the topic can protect you and your family from the possibility of unnecessary financial hardship. The story below is just one of many I have heard over the years.

"We married when we were in our early forties, and it was a first marriage for both of us," says Nina H. *"We were both financially savvy about our own money, and we each had good health benefits through our employer. For a long time it was easier to keep things separate, though we began to comingle funds over time.*

"What never occurred to me was having a general financial review of all that we had. Unfortunately, Sam died at fifty-five, and when his estate was settled, it turned out he had an excellent life insurance policy through his job—the only problem was he'd never updated it after we were married, and his eighty-year-old mother was the beneficiary."

We cannot foresee what will happen in the future, but we can rest more comfortably in the present knowing that we have a certain degree of protection. Whether you are married, single, or divorced, an important part of financial management is evaluating all the types of life and health insurance coverage you have. It can make a tremendous financial difference to you later on. This chapter is filled with information on life insurance, health insurance, disability insurance, long-term-care needs, and estate planning.

What You Need to Know About Life Insurance

The intent of life insurance coverage is to provide money for a family in the event of the death of someone upon whom the family has depended economically. It is a family safety net to provide help when you need it most.

Understanding this definition will help you assess what you need and when you need it.

Your first thought is probably to insure the family breadwinner. If your family were to suffer the loss of its primary income, you would definitely need the life insurance payout to help until you got your lives straightened out.

Now let's consider a tougher question: Using the definition above, should a stay-at-home parent have life insurance coverage?

Absolutely. Should anything happen to him or her, the other parent (presumably the father) might be hard-pressed to come up with the extra money it would take to pay for full-time household help. Unless you are *certain* you have a willing relative who would pitch in, the few dollars paid out each year for a term policy on the primary caregiver is money well spent.

Even if your children are grown and you and your spouse both work, life insurance may be a good investment. (Use the worksheet on page 266 to assess how much each of you should carry.) At the very least, it will be ready, tax-free cash upon the insured's death, providing the survivors with money to cover funeral costs and outstanding debts. If you decide to carry more than a minimal amount, it can provide a financial base for the surviving spouse.

HOW MUCH IS ENOUGH?

Because each person's needs are different, it is difficult to present a formula that will answer the question for each reader. Your best bet is to talk to your financial advisor or an insurance representative who can help you come up with an amount that is right for you. However, here are some guidelines to help you begin the process:

- Life insurance is generally intended to provide enough money so that, if the sum is managed properly, it will supplement a family's needs for approximately ten years following the income-provider's death. (By that time it is assumed that a family will have made other arrangements for income.)
- When you calculate replacement income, figure the replacement of *after-tax* salary.
- Be sure to add in a lump sum for any extraordinary costs such as college expenses. Though it might have been difficult to pay college costs out of normal expenses, this is your opportunity to do some prudent financial planning.

At the Center we offer the following formula to help women calculate how much insurance they would need:

A. Enter your monthly wages (after taxes).   _____

B. Multiply by .75. (This is to calculate 75 percent of   _____
    income, which is the standard benchmark used by the
    industry to arrive at the amount of money that would be
    necessary to supplement a family's needs for a ten-year
    period.)

C. Enter any income your survivors have without your   _____
    income.

D. Subtract C from B. (This will be the monthly amount your _____
    survivors will need.)

E. Multiply D by 12 to calculate yearly amount needed.   _____

F. Multiply the years your dependents will need this   _____
    coverage.

G. Adjust for inflation: Multiply by the annual inflation rate _____
    (e.g., 4 percent) and add this amount.

H. Calculate any additional costs for dependents, other   _____
    expenses, or debts (mortgage, college costs).

I. Add G and H. This is the total amount of insurance you   _____
    need.

Sample Calculation:
A. $2,000
B. $2,000 × .75 = $1,500
C. $1,000 (Social Security benefits to children under eighteen or nineteen
    [if a full-time high school student])
D. $1,500 − $1,000 = $500
E. $500 × 12 = $6,000
F. $6,000 × 10 years = $60,000
G. $60,000 × 4% = $24,000 + $60,000 = $84,000
H. $30,000 (college costs) + $50,000 (other) = $80,000
I. $84,000 + $80,000 = $164,000

   Once you have this figure, it's time to take into account any preexisting insurance policies. For example, if you have $100,000 life
insurance through your job, then, working with the sample given
above, you would need to purchase only $64,000 more coverage,
and that will help contain your costs.
   Don't wait until "later" to purchase your insurance. Health problems can make it difficult to buy an affordable policy, so take care of
this while you're still in good health.

WHAT KIND OF INSURANCE SHOULD YOU BUY? PERMANENT VS. TERM

There are two main types of life insurance: permanent and term.

Term life insurance provides pure life insurance protection (death benefits) for a specified period of time. It is much less expensive for a high level of insurance than permanent life, but it pays death benefits only—there is no cash payout if the insured outlives the term. Term insurance can be purchased for almost any amount of time; one, five, ten, and twenty years are common. If you stop paying premiums, all benefits cease, so it's important that "pay annual insurance premium" be placed right up there with your other high-priority fixed expenses. *Renewable term* allows you to automatically extend the policy for another specific period until a maximum age. However, every time you renew, your premiums will increase because you are older.

The cost of term insurance is based on life expectancy, so the closer you get to a probable time of payout (death of the insured), the more expensive the insurance will be. It is an ideal form of life insurance for young families because of its low cost.

Permanent life insurance offers death benefits plus the accumulation of cash value and is more expensive than term insurance because of this added benefit. Whole life and universal life are the two primary types of permanent insurance.

Whole life insurance (also called cash-value or straight life insurance) offers death protection for a person's lifetime, plus a savings program. Premium payments on whole life insurance tend to be fixed for the duration of the policy; this makes them higher than term premiums when you're younger, and generally lower as you get older (when the cost of term insurance rises). The distinctive characteristic of whole life is that its cash value builds according to a predetermined annual schedule, and its investment earnings are tax-deferred. Thus, in addition to the death benefit, there is an investment aspect to the policy, and it serves as a form of enforced savings. In addition, you can borrow against the policy up to its current cash value.

Universal life might be considered a combination of whole and term insurance. Universal policies are split so that part of the premium pays for yearly renewable term insurance while the rest is invested in a fund consisting of short-term, often high-yielding securities.

Many consumer advocates say the best value is in term insurance. While generally speaking, your investment return on a life insurance policy is lower than what you could get elsewhere, you've got to take into account your objectives before making a decision. For example, universal life may be the best bet for people in the highest tax bracket who want to shelter some investment income from taxes.

Shopping Guidelines

- See if you (or your spouse) are eligible for group life insurance through your employer, union, or professional, fraternal, or alumni association. These group policies are almost always less expensive than insurance purchased individually. Group policies are usually for term insurance. Read the fine print about cancellation: If you switch jobs or drop out of the organization, will you still have coverage? If not, then use this type of policy to supplement your other insurance coverage, which will remain stable through the years.
- Talk to two or three insurance representatives for advice and price quotes. You'll be surprised at the variations in cost.
- Look for a "good buy"—the most coverage for the best price.
- Investigate the payment schedule. Some companies charge more per year if you need to spread out the payments.
- Keep your insurance up-to-date. Review it every few years to be certain you have the right amount of coverage, and be sure to change the beneficiary when necessary.

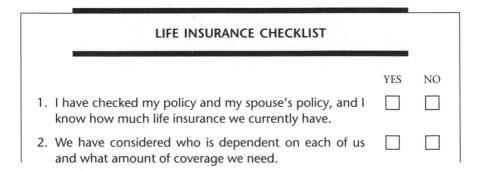

LIFE INSURANCE CHECKLIST

	YES	NO
1. I have checked my policy and my spouse's policy, and I know how much life insurance we currently have.	☐	☐
2. We have considered who is dependent on each of us and what amount of coverage we need.	☐	☐

3. We have calculated how much more insurance we each need to supplement what we get through work. ☐ ☐

4. We have shopped around to get the best price for the life insurance that is right for us. ☐ ☐

Health Insurance Coverage

In order to keep family medical bills low throughout your lifetime (whether it's for a checkup or a minor surgical procedure), participating in some type of health care plan is vital to your family's financial health.

An interesting finding of the Scudder Baby Boom Survey is that women who have focused on the possibility of health problems (having the appropriate insurance; understanding their disability and medical coverage; and learning about long-term-care insurance for themselves or elderly parents) are the most prepared of any group to have a financially secure retirement. The findings again demonstrate the rewards of being a future-oriented thinker.

Stay alert for news on employee-sponsored health packages. The Health Insurance Portability and Accountability Act, which took effect with some employers in July 1997, makes it easier for employees who are changing jobs to benefit from the best health coverage available for a longer period of time. The law also provides for more than a million people to become part of an experiment to test the concept of medical savings accounts. These are private, tax-favored accounts that are to be used to pay for routine health costs. The accounts are then coupled with high-deductible medical policies, which would cover major medical bills.

Good health insurance or membership in a managed care program can provide you with extra money for savings now by reducing current health care costs and protecting you from extraordinary costs later on. Here's what you need to know today (even if you're perfectly healthy):

VITAL STEPS TO TAKE FOR ANY WOMAN TWENTY TO SIXTY-FOUR

Chances are your medical coverage will come through either your or your spouse's place of employment. Group plans such as these offer good prices, partly because most employers help offset some part of the cost. If you do not have access to a group health care plan through an employer, check with your church, a political group, a professional organization, or a union, all of which sometimes offer group health care plans. (Buying an individual policy can be prohibitively expensive.)

Employers generally offer one of two types of plans for health care:

Traditional reimbursement (indemnity) plans. In these programs, you may use the physician of your choice, and the insurance covers a predetermined part of the cost of your medical care. For example, insurance will pay 80 percent of the fee for outpatient costs after you pay an annual $500 deductible. Payment is generally made at the time of service by the consumer, who is then reimbursed by the insurance company after submitting a claim. Plans can be comprehensive, offering both inpatient and outpatient benefits, or they may just offer hospitalization. Indemnity plans are becoming increasingly rare, and are quite expensive when available.

Managed care programs. In today's health care environment, there are numerous types of managed care programs where one health care provider oversees (manages) patient care. All these programs emphasize prevention, early detection, and treatment of illness. Though consumers may pay a small fee (copayment) at the time of service, the paperwork entailed in filing a claim is no longer necessary, as the health care provider is responsible for filing the claim and is paid directly by the insurance company or medical plan. Managed care plans include HMOs, PPOs, and point of service plans (POS).

Health maintenance organizations (HMOs). By paying a monthly fee (premium), you obtain access to all types of health care services—from family checkups to mental health care.

An HMO is generally the most restrictive of all managed care plans. It is also the oldest form of managed care. Health care providers contract with, or are employed by, the HMO and provide services to all people who participate. Many HMOs have their own health centers, hospitals, and even pharmacies, and your plan provides coverage only at these specified locations and with HMO physicians. In this setting, you may be asked to select a primary care physician to coordinate your care.

If an HMO program is a benefit offered through your employer, chances are your company is paying the bulk of the expense, though you may be contributing monthly toward the payment. A prime financial advantage to an HMO is that your costs are restricted to this annual fee plus minor expenses for special services. What's more, you no longer need to worry about deductibles and tracking the payments between you and your insurance company.

Preferred provider organizations (PPOs). These plans came about as a compromise between reimbursement (indemnity) programs and the HMOs. In this type of plan, the insurance company contracts with health care providers for services at a discounted rate to the insurance company. You are given more latitude and are able to obtain care from a provider who participates or from one who does not. However, when you seek care from a participating provider, you generally have lower out-of-pocket expenses. When you see a nonparticipating provider, the plan works very much like a reimbursement plan. In many of these plans, all care must be coordinated by the primary care physician you have selected (if you are using the participating provider option). If you want to see a specialist, you must first either see or be referred by the primary doctor or the care will not be covered and you will be responsible for payment.

Point of service plan (POS). This is one of the newer plans being offered and is very similar to a PPO. The key difference is the point at which the service is initiated. If you obtain outpatient care from a participating physician and are referred to a hospital by that physician, all inpatient and outpatient care will be paid at participating provider levels. If the initial care is rendered by a nonparticipating provider and hospitalization is needed, benefits will be paid according to the nonparticipating provision of your insurance policy.

WHAT TO LOOK FOR IN REVIEWING
HEALTH INSURANCE OPTIONS

1. What coverage is provided for hospitalization? How many days? Is there a lifetime or annual maximum? What must you pay out of pocket for each hospitalization? What hospitals participate (if looking at managed care) in the plans you are reviewing?
2. What coverage is provided for physician service? What is the

copayment per visit (if managed care)? Are there any limits to the number of visits per year? Must you go through your primary care physician to see a specialist? Must you pay for preventive care (annual physicals)?

3. What coverage is provided for mental health/substance abuse services? Are there both inpatient and outpatient benefits? How many outpatient visits are allowed annually? Lifetime?

4. What is the yearly deductible, and what percentage must you pay out of pocket for outpatient services (when applicable)?

5. Is there a lifetime maximum benefit allowance? That is, once you have used X amount of dollars for health care you receive no more.

6. Is there a "medical necessity" provision in the health insurance contract? (That is, does the insurance company have the right to determine if the treatment was medically necessary?)

7. How does the insurance carrier determine its usual, customary, and reasonable fees? For example, in a reimbursement (indemnity) plan or when using the out-of-plan option in either a PPO or POS plan, each insurance company will pay only a percentage of the "usual, customary, and reasonable" allowance. You are reponsible for anything the provider charges above that. It is important to know how that allowance is determined.

8. Will you be subjected to a "preexisting condition" provision if you select this health insurance coverage? That is, if you have a chronic condition or are currently being treated for a problem, will coverage for that problem be excluded permanently or for a period of time if you change insurance?

9. Will you be eligible for health insurance if you change jobs or if you or anyone in your family has an ongoing health condition? (Request this information from the insurance company or ask your employer about applicable state laws.)

10. What is the premium or fee you must pay?

If possible, try to get health coverage in your own name. Check with your employer. If you are covered through your spouse's program, check to see what will happen if you divorce or if he retires. Also ask if surviving spouses get any health benefits when the retiree dies. Statistically, you're likely to live longer, and it's vital that you have adequate health coverage.

If you have a group policy and lose connection with the group—change jobs or drop out of an organization—see if you can convert your policy to an individual one. You'll pay more money for it, but at least you will have some kind of health protection until you are able to join another group.

And if you're considering an HMO:

- Is the HMO accredited? (This is not required, but it's a good sign; it means the organization has joined a group that monitors standards.)
- How many doctors are board-certified (meaning they have passed a test in their specialty)? The average certification rate is about 70 percent.
- How long do patients wait for appointments?
- Is preventive medicine encouraged?
- What is the staff turnover rate? (A high one is a bad sign.)
- What is the member retention rate? (A high one is a good sign.)
- For referrals, contact the Group Health Association of America, 1129 20th St. NW, Suite 600, Washington DC 20036; 202-778-3200.

Disability Insurance

Disability insurance provides payment if you are disabled and unable to work for a period of time. (Individual policies will specify the time frame.)

During the first year I began to conduct research on the financial planning needs of women, I found that disability insurance was one of the most overlooked types of insurance. Many financial advisors and insurance agents told me that it was very difficult to convince women of the need to investigate whether they had disability insurance at their place of employment and whether they needed additional coverage.

The importance of disability insurance for women came to me

not just from research but from an experience I had the first year we started conducting financial seminars. I remember the story even today, seven years later.

Beverly W. was a forty-two-year-old single parent with three children. On a rainy day in New York she was walking to work and crossed a street when the light was green. A taxicab hit her and she was hospitalized for seven weeks with multiple injuries. It took Beverly over a year to recuperate. During this time, she was eligible for and received only limited funds from the state. Since she did not have a comprehensive disability policy, she lived hand-to-mouth during the entire period of her convalescence. Her inability to work made it very difficult to pay the bills and care for her children.

"I never thought about ever getting hurt or sick," she told me. *"It just never occurred to me. Now I recognize how important it is for women who are single parents to consider whether they are covered in the event that something happens."*

Women between the ages of forty-five and sixty-five are three times more likely to be disabled than they are to die. And actually, both men and women in their thirties and forties are more likely to become disabled than to die, making disability an important kind of insurance for the young.

Women are often under the mistaken belief that they are covered by disability insurance through their employer or that they would be eligible for disability through the Social Security system. Unfortunately, if they do become disabled, they find that their coverage is woefully inadequate, and they often learn that it is extremely difficult to qualify for disability under Social Security. Social Security Disability Insurance is generally intended only for severe, long-term disability. For those reasons—particularly if you are divorced or single and are the sole wage earner in the family—you cannot afford *not* to have adequate disability coverage, and this may mean obtaining private coverage.

When you shop, check first with your employer to see what kind of group disability coverage is available. Then call an insurance agency so that you can compare what your employer offers with the benefits of a private policy. Look for the following.

- How is the disability defined? Are you considered disabled if you can't continue your usual form of work, or are you considered disabled only if you can't work at any type of job?

- Does it cover partial disability, or must you be totally unable to work?
- Does the plan cover disability regardless of cause?
- What is the waiting period? The longer you wait, the lower your premiums, but you must take into account your company's sick-leave and short-term-disability policies before deciding how long you could go without receiving the additional income.
- How long would the benefits be paid?
- Is there a cost-of-living escalator, and if so, what is it? If you pay for benefits equaling $1,500 a month in today's economy, what will you be paid ten years from now if you become disabled? There should be a cost-of-living escalator to allow for inflation.

When you shop, be sure your coverage is guaranteed renewable and noncancelable. (Most companies do cancel a policy once you turn sixty-five.)

Long-Term Care

From the time I was a junior in high school right through my years in graduate school, I worked in nursing homes to help cover my tuition. To this day, my mind is filled with images of the women (the predominant patient population) I cared for. I worked in a wide spectrum of facilities ranging from disgraceful "holding tanks" for the unfortunate elderly to those that provided compassionate, excellent care. My experience taught me several painful lessons: If people need institutional care, having money makes a big difference. I also became a staunch believer in the right of the elderly to live out their remaining years with dignity.

Although nursing home standards have changed since I worked in them over two decades ago, it is still a system based on the haves and have-nots. Those with adequate private resources can afford private-duty nurses to supplement their care. Those who don't must rely on the help that is available. During my orderly days, I was often assigned fourteen to sixteen patients a day who depended on me for bathing, feeding, and other basic needs. It was impossible for me to do justice to all who required my attention.

This experience left a lasting impression on me. I say fervently to all readers that it is critical for you to have an economic foundation to support your long-term-care needs. For many, a long-term-care plan may fill the bill.

Long-term-health-care plans provide insurance coverage if you need nursing care over a prolonged period of time, whether it is due to aging or a debilitating illness such as Alzheimer's, Parkinson's, or a stroke. Right now, women between the ages of sixty-five and sixty-nine have a 52 percent chance of using a nursing home at some time in their lives, and, needless to say, paying for long-term health care can be exorbitantly expensive. That's why it's important to provide for this kind of insurance even while you are still in midlife or younger.

Because long-term care is not considered a pleasant topic (whether it's providing care for a sick parent or your own long-term care), few people plan for it, and that's a mistake.

Many Americans are under the mistaken belief that Medicare provides for these costs. The reality is that Medicare was never intended to cover anything but acute care, and while Medicaid is intended for long-term needs, it is available only to those who are near or below the poverty line.

Another misunderstanding concerns what constitutes long-term care. It is often thought to consist only of institutional care, but home-based care provided by a professional caregiver is included as well. Unfortunately, these policies rarely cover all the costs, though they are certainly a worthy start. Nursing home care costs range from $30,000 to $70,000 a year, while home health aides may cost $10,000 a year for only three visits per week; as you can see, these costs really mount up.

Talk to your financial advisor or insurance agent about various policies. (With most companies, you are not eligible for this type of policy until you are fifty, but you should start soon after that to keep your costs low.) There will be many options, and here are some of the things you should look at:

- This type of insurance can be costly and you may never need it. However, you must weigh this against the possibility of depleting your financial resources if you or your spouse has a long-term illness. (Couples are advised to try to come up with the money for this type of coverage; often the well spouse suffers a financial reversal because, with no coverage, all resources go to pay for the suffering spouse.)

- Check with your personnel office to see if your employer offers any long-term-care policies. Any sort of group coverage is preferable to an individual policy.
- If you cannot buy a policy through your employer, shop around. This is a relatively new type of insurance, and you need to listen carefully and read the policy carefully as well.
- Be sure to consider the company. Stay with a well-known insurance company to be sure it will be around to pay out in the future.
- Look at the types of coverage provided by the policy. Ideally, it should cover all levels of care, including community-based care such as adult day care.
- Do not buy a policy that is disease-specific or nursing-home-specific. You want a broad-based policy that covers you whatever your illness and wherever you opt to stay.
- Does the policy have a built-in home health care or post-confinement benefit or a rider to provide this service?
- Compare the benefit amounts for nursing care and for any home health care, both the amount it would pay per day and any maximum it might pay per stay or related stay. Some policies pay just the costs incurred; others pay the amount the policyholder elects to receive even if actual costs are lower. Some policies provide benefits for emergency medical response systems, home modifications required by a medical condition, or temporary professional care so that the burden of in-home care doesn't fall entirely on a spouse, children, or other unpaid caregiver.
- Determine the daily benefit amount desired. This is the maximum benefit that can be received for any one day. Before choosing a benefit amount, you should find out the going rate for nursing homes or home health care in your area. Typically, individuals choose an amount in the range of $100 to $150 a day.
- Determine the length of time the policy is to last. The average nursing home stay is about two and a half years, but if a family

is particularly long-lived, it may be best to provide for a lifetime of care.

- Determine the desired elimination period. The elimination period is like a deductible and should be selected based on the amount one is willing to pay out of pocket before benefits begin. The most common choices are twenty days, fifty days, and one hundred days.
- Look carefully at what are called "gatekeeping" restrictions. Is a hospital stay required before qualifying for benefits? Is it possible to be admitted to any level of care? Is an organic mental illness covered based on a doctor's diagnosis and clinical testing? What preexisting conditions are covered?
- Is the policy one that can be canceled by the insurer or does it have guaranteed renewability?
- Does it offer inflation protection and how is that calculated?
- Will the policy pay for alternate care options under the primary benefit or just under a home health care benefit?
- Is there a waiver of premium option while benefits are being paid? (This would mean you wouldn't have to pay for the insurance during the time you are receiving benefits.)

LONG-TERM-CARE INSURANCE COST

Can you afford coverage? It is important to look carefully at cash flow planning in retirement.

You can reduce premium expenses by lowering the daily benefit amount, choosing a shorter benefit period, or increasing the elimination period. No two policies are written the same way, so they need to be analyzed to put them on an equal footing.

Some employers are beginning to offer long-term-care insurance as part of an overall compensation package or as part of a "cafeteria" plan (long-term care is offered as one of your possible options). An employer-sponsored group plan will probably offer you the best price option. Women under fifty-five may be interested in purchasing LTC protection for their parents, or for themselves when the price is low.

Estate Planning

Estate planning involves making provisions for what happens to your assets when you die.

Every adult, regardless of age, should have a will. State laws vary as to how estates are divided when someone dies intestate (without a will), but you can be sure that no state would make the same decisions you would.

If you have minor children, it's vital that you provide for their welfare by specifying a guardian and describing how you want any money distributed. When you select a guardian, choose someone who is young enough to keep up with kids and who is likely to raise your children in a way that is consistent with your style. Many people select a "guardian of the body" to be the caregiver, and a "guardian of the property" to watch over the money. Your father-in-law might be the perfect guardian of the property, while your loving but financially not-so-responsible brother might make a better substitute parent. This type of arrangement can give you added peace of mind.

If you're single or childless, you still ought to plan ahead to see that your relatives and favorite charities are remembered.

Trusts can help your heirs to circumvent some of the oddities of our legal system. When a person dies, a will must go through probate, a legal process for administering and implementing the directions in a will. This can be a lengthy process, but if you create a living trust, your assets can go directly to your beneficiaries without going through probate.

That's why it's important to consult an attorney now. The charges for making a basic will are generally only a couple of hundred dollars, or you can use a software package on your computer to draw up a will. What makes any piece of paper a valid will is having it witnessed and signed by three people.

Many people are now adding "living wills" to their estate planning. A living will tells your family and doctor what, if any, life-support measures you would accept or would not accept. A medical power of attorney grants authority to someone you trust to make decisions with a physician regarding your medical care options.

Once you have taken care of your insurance coverage and estate planning, you can relax. Every two or three years, you'll want to review the provisions you've made, but your basic work is done.

17

LOOKING AHEAD
Life Planning for All Ages

"Time has been my best ally. I started putting away $100 per month when I turned forty, and now I'm sixty-two and I'm amazed at what long-term savings and investing can do."

Most people assume that retirement planning is something you start doing in your late fifties or early sixties. By this time, I trust you know that it's not. The earlier you start planning, the better, and that's why I think "life planning" is a better term. The best type of financial planning is when you are saving and investing as a lifelong endeavor that will benefit you at each stage of your life—all the way through old age.

Other people are put off by "retirement planning" because they've read just enough about it to have noticed that the figures bandied about for what people will need in the bank at retirement hover around a million dollars. Those figures are, indeed, discouraging, and if you've read those articles, please don't close the book now. I'm going to show you that time and compound interest can help you save far more than you ever imagined. In addition, NCWRR research has revealed solutions that will permit you to feel comfortable with your planning—and you won't have to constantly worry: "How am *I* going to save enough money?" You'll find the solution later in this chapter.

If you are already in midlife, there's still time to prepare. In many ways, you are coming upon this information at the perfect time psychologically. If you're like most midlife women, some of your caregiving responsibilities are lifting, and many of you are rededicating yourselves to paid employment. We've found that women who thrive during their later years are those who develop four personal characteristics during midlife:

1. They begin to focus on their own financial security.
2. They develop a strong and secure personal identity, knowing who they are and what they want.
3. They have or develop secondary employment skills, providing them with something to fall back on if they have job-related problems or wish to change career paths.
4. They live a healthy lifestyle, which preserves their good health for old age.

As you can see, these are not impossible tasks, and not one of them involves having a bagful of money for retirement. What you see here is that those who are destined to thrive during retirement are those with the mind-set and personality traits to do what is necessary to provide for themselves. In cases like these, they are *thinking ahead financially, setting goals, and saving*—the prime requirements for being able to afford retirement.

As you'll read in this chapter, your retirement years really can fulfill the goals you wrote down on your planning sheet. You just have to plan how you're going to pay for them. First, you'll learn:

- How to determine how much money you may need at retirement
- What you need to know about the "retirement reality," or "Why Will I Need So Much?"
- What you will get from Social Security
- The latest on pensions and other types of retirement plans

This chapter is going to tell you what you need to do based on the goals you've set for yourself, and the next chapter will introduce you to some of the investment concepts that will help you maximize all your savings dollars.

What Do Women Want?

As I listen to the women who come through the Center, I find that today's midlife women are looking for a unique retirement experience. When I hear them talk of goals, I pick up the following.

- They would like to have more freedom to pursue hobbies, exercise programs, and leisure activities.
- Although women perceive this period as an opportunity to spend more time with a mate, there is a distinct desire to test their own career limits and nurture friendships.
- Women see this period filled with "self-improvement" activities (which range from adult education classes to developing new skills).
- Many women want to travel and see more of the world.

Women have been so inundated with caregiving tasks prior to retirement that this is the first real opportunity for them to spread their wings. Specifically, here are some women speaking for themselves:

Sixty-one-year-old Marge R. summed up her retirement plans this way:

"I've always been athletically inclined and have fantasized about using this period of my life to explore and hike some of the great mountain peaks in the United States. I recently received a flyer in the mail from a women-only hiking and travel club that designs trips with groups of females who enjoy the wilderness and the outdoors. I am really excited because I can meet other women from different parts of the country and enjoy my sport at the same time. My husband is already joking about how he will need a cell phone just to keep in touch with me after we retire."

Betty Anne T., a forty-four-year-old eighth-grade teacher in the Bronx, has a different slant on her retirement dream.

"I am a mystery novel addict who must go through four books a month. There just never seems to be enough time to really enjoy all the reading I want to do. What am I going to do with my retirement? I want to live out a murder mystery. It's not as weird as it sounds! I want to take a couple of years and go on some specially designed cruises and trips that cater to mystery lovers—dinners, plays, and clue hunts that are all part of relaxing. Also I want to take some side trips to where some of the greatest

mystery novelists of the twentieth century were born. I want to create a retirement that is like reading a good novel—as you progress through the book the excitement builds and you're inclined to cheat and leap forward to the end page because you can't stand it."

Selma N., fifty-eight, says:

"I've always dabbled in art as a sideline, painting and selling furniture to friends and friends of friends. I could never have lived solely on that income, but I'm taking early retirement, and between my retirement income and the business, I should do quite well. I love doing it and I just can't wait to have the time to market my work more extensively and make it a viable business."

Finally, Susan F., a forty-eight-year-old administrator of a high-pressure corporate sales division for the last twelve years, views her retirement in an entirely different way.

"My vision of the 'golden years' is lying on my couch until 11 A.M. and doing whatever suits my fancy. A big sign on my front door will read: NO STRESS ALLOWED! Because of my job, I've traveled and experienced many different things. I just want to stop and smell the roses. Playing with my two grandchildren and walking on a moonlit beach with my spouse is exactly what I want. No phone calls, reports due, and no personnel headaches. To those who tell me I'll get bored of this, I respond, 'Different strokes for different folks.' For me this is exactly what I want."

How Much Will You Need for Retirement?

THE UNDER FORTY-FIVE SET

If you're between twenty and forty-five, retirement seems very far away, and the best answer to how much you will need for retirement is "A lot."

At this stage, your primary *long-term* financial objective is to build savings for retirement. Even if you can only afford to set aside $10 a week right now (something you can achieve by bringing lunch one day a week instead of buying it), it's vital that you do. According to some experts, a forty-five-year-old who is earning $60,000 a year would need an annual income of $144,321 to maintain the same standard of living in retirement twenty years from now. (Although I wish I could change the numbers, this is what the experts are saying.

While starting to save now and changing one's spending habits during one's retirement years can make it unnecessary to have this much money, these figures indicate why it's so important to start saving *now*.)

Because traditional retirement savings formulas don't work for younger people, I have developed some retirement savings goals for this age group:

1. Women in their twenties and thirties should try to save at least 5 percent of their income for retirement. This percentage takes into consideration that you are at a stage of life where you may be trying to reduce college debt, purchase a house, or save for other short-term goals. Women in their forties should try to increase their savings to at least 10 percent.
2. If your retirement program at work involves contributions from your employer, run, don't walk, to sign up for it; getting matching money from your employer is one of the best investments you can make.
3. Another strategy I recommend at this time involves developing a "flexibility savings pot"—a savings account that will be used down the road to start a new income source such as acquiring training for a new career. This retirement strategy is great for younger women, who may be working part-time because of child-rearing responsibilities and who could use the money to launch a full-time career later on that would provide economic security for retirement.

At this age, you can look forward to many changes in your life, and it is important to remember that successful financial planning is also a very fluid process. In the ensuing years, you may find that for several years you have to divert part of the money formerly earmarked for retirement into paying for your children's college tuition; that's to be expected. Remain flexible—and adamant that you *will* put away at least $25 per month for retirement. It will pay off in the end. Later on, it is vital that you increase your retirement savings again.

PEOPLE IN MIDLIFE

There are two methods experts offer for determining how much you'll need at retirement. One involves estimating the cost of the retirement lifestyle you envision; the other involves saving so that you'll have 70 to 80 percent of current income at your retirement.

First, the working-backward approach: If you know you want to retire in Arizona, talk to financial experts about realistic estimates of the income you'll need to maintain a certain lifestyle in that area in the next ten or fifteen years. That estimate gives you a figure to work with.

Assuming that you want to continue your current lifestyle, you'll likely need 80 percent of your current household income. If your current income is $50,000, you'll need $40,000 to be comfortable; if your current household income is $80,000, you'll want $64,000 in retirement; if your current income is $150,000, you're looking for as much as $120,000 so that you won't feel you're "coming down in the world."

And remember how long you have to provide for: In the next two to three decades, average life expectancy could rise to eighty-three years for women and seventy-seven for men. In my opinion, this is a very conservative projection. (Look at the people around you—you could live for a very long time.)

A critical step to retirement preparation during these years is cutting living costs and budgeting. You can use the money you save to put into retirement savings, and you will be preparing yourself for a more affordable lifestyle by watching your expenses. Cost-cutting measures might include:

- Evaluating car expenses. Getting rid of a second car or lowering insurance premiums will save money. (While you'll always want liability coverage, older cars sometimes aren't worth insuring for collision damage.)
- Cutting back on credit card debt. Payments on credit card balances really eat away at the potential to save for retirement.
- Minimizing entertainment and restaurant expenses. Scrutinize this budget item carefully for potential savings.
- Reducing clothing, gifts, and incidental expenses. Most experts believe that midlife adults can save as much as $2,000 a year by cutting back on these purchases.

Your next task is to assess your retirement income, which will likely be from Social Security, a pension plan, your IRA or Keogh, or any income-producing investment you might have.

What You'll Need vs. What You'll Have: Calculating Your Retirement Gap

To fill out the following worksheet, you may need to refer back to Chapter 14 for current lifestyle figures, and if you don't have figures for what your pension or Social Security income will be, take the time now to find out. (Keep reading this chapter for more information.)

Projected annual retirement expenses to _____
maintain current lifestyle:

(This figure will come either from your projected expenses in a new retirement location or from your 80 percent projection based on current lifestyle.)

Now draw up a list of future retirement income (yearly figures). (If you don't know these figures, keep reading for more information on the various programs.)

Social Security	_____
Pension or retirement fund	_____
Investment income	_____
Dividends	_____
Interest from savings	_____
Annuity income	_____
Rental property income	_____
Other	_____
TOTAL	_____

Now look at the difference between (a) the retirement income you project you will *need* and (b) the retirement income you will *have*. That gap is the amount you will need to bridge through saving and investing.

This is an important warning call. Many people don't consider what their true retirement needs will be.

To find out how much you should be saving for your retirement depends on many things, your stage of life and your future expectations among them. A financial advisor will be happy to help you come up with a monthly savings figure based on the information you provide. Or if you're working with a financial planning program on your computer, you may be able to get an idea of your needs by plugging in figures there. Or you can take a stab at it right now.

"WHY WILL I NEED SO MUCH?"

In our seminars, women are always quite taken aback by the figure they come up with as the "gap" between what they will have and what they will need at retirement, and I am always asked, "But, Dr. Hayes, why will I need so much?" This is an understandable question, and the answer is twofold:

1. **You need to have enough retirement savings so that you will be able to withdraw a measured amount of money from the account over the course of your retirement years and still have enough to last through your lifetime.** And because you do not know whether you will live five years or twenty-five years after your retirement, you need to have plenty put away so that your savings—combined with Social Security and any pension you may be eligible for—will permit you to live a comfortable lifestyle.

2. **Your savings must be able to withstand the effect of inflation.** Inevitably, your savings are going to lose buying power over time. Even with a low rate of inflation, it is estimated that the purchasing power of a 1996 dollar will be only 28 cents in twenty years. Look what has happened to a few specific items in the last twenty-five years. Fill in the last column with what *you* recently paid for each of the following.

	1970	1980	TODAY
Postage stamp	$0.06	$0.15	_____
Loaf of bread	0.23	0.43	_____
Automobile	3,400	6,900	_____
Average home	25,600	64,000	_____

Inflation is manageable as long as the money you invested is at a rate that stays ahead of inflation.

These are the reasons why the amounts the experts tell you to save are so astronomical. How will you manage? Better than you think if you keep on (saving and) reading.

RECKONING WITH WHAT SEEMS IMPOSSIBLE

Even if you have not yet done the calculations to learn how much you'll need in your later years, you know the media are telling us that it is going to be near the million-dollar mark. Well, that's a shocking and unsettling figure to anyone—whether you're twenty-five and focused on trying to make enough money so you don't have to have a roommate (though with steady savings and compound interest most twenty-five-year-olds could easily save that amount of money by starting now), or whether you're fifty-five and getting so close to retirement that the million-dollar figure is simply unthinkable. The figure is stunning, and for that reason, I would like to share this story with you:

One day in 1996, near April 15—tax deadline time—I was sitting in a diner waiting to be served when I couldn't help overhearing a conversation between two women in the next booth. The woman sitting closest to me was lamenting to her friend that she and her husband were having to pay Uncle Sam $1,400 in taxes. Her friend turned around and responded with the following, a quote that sticks with me to this day: "Yeah, and then all those financial experts tell you that you have to save half a million dollars before you retire. What a joke."

To explain what happens when people become overwhelmed in this way, I have coined the term "learned financial helplessness," an emotional response that occurs when a person feels he or she is incapable of altering a given outcome. According to the Scudder Baby Boom Survey, the average American hearing this information tunes out and turns away. Apparently, we have been so inundated with unrealistic savings and investment expectations that we feel completely helpless.

Even the financial planning industry has unknowingly created this feeling of learned financial helplessness. Two years ago my wife and I consulted a financial advisor to get some investment advice. The advisor punched our earnings, our investments to date, our financial goals, and our anticipated retirement date into a laptop computer. In the blink of an eye, the computer spit out an unbelievable number we needed to save each month to reach our goal. Instead of being elated that we had some concrete data to work with, we looked at each other in horrified disbelief. Unfortunately, neither the computer nor the financial advisor gave us much consolation or hope.

Although I am not an advocate of putting the blinders on, I am very concerned that these reports have traumatized people at the very time they need to be saving and investing so that they *can* have some control over their future.

But don't despair. I am here to *promise* you the following:

- Ignorance is your worst enemy, which is why it's vital that you evaluate your situation and take some type of action.
- Some savings are better than no savings, so please put something away.
- Time is your best ally; if all you can put away is your loose change some weeks, you'll be amazed at how even those nickels and dimes can grow (through accumulation and compound interest).
- Statistically, long-term (more than five years) investments do well. (See the following chapter for more information.) This bodes well for any employer-sponsored retirement plan as well as your own investing.

But there's also another solution, and this one has to do with lifestyle, not money.

Redefining Retirement: The Solution to "Learned Financial Helplessness"

As a result of the research studies I have overseen, I have come up with a solution to learned financial helplessness that is here for the taking.

To better explain this, let me share with you a little more of what I've learned. Like everything else they have done, the baby boomers are going to transform yet one more aspect of life—retirement. For this generation, retirement will be a period of life filled with recapturing old dreams and opening new doors. Note the following statistics from the Scudder Baby Boom Retirement Preparation Survey.

- 47 percent of baby boomers want to retire before the age of sixty-five. (It is also significant to note that for the last decade, the retirement age has been gradually slipping to an average of fifty-nine and a half.)

- Only 10 percent of baby boomers want to work full-time after their main career is over.

Yet reality may leave baby boomers with the task of reinventing their retirement dream. While they may want to retire before sixty-five, they may have to interpret this as retiring from full-time or corporate employment. And they may not want to work full-time after retirement, but they may find themselves starting their own businesses or accepting part-time employment of some type because of two major factors, and these factors are the key to avoiding the doom-and-gloom scenario:

1. They will remain professionally active because they *want* to remain involved. Baby boomers may well live twenty-five years beyond the age of sixty. Whether they return to school or retrain for another type of job, they may find that part-time employment or entrepreneurial pursuits are emotionally and financially rewarding.
2. They will realize that Social Security and their retirement plan just won't cut it when it comes to paying for that cruise to the Bahamas, so they will find ways to remain financially healthy. One of the glorious aspects of the baby boom generation is that they do, indeed, march to their own drummer. As soon as they realize that funding a twenty-five-year retirement is going to be quite expensive, they'll start finding ways to cope.

To further improve their situation, they'll become more frugal. The Dreyfus Gender Investment Comparison Survey found that in midlife, women exhibited greater financial realism than men. This bodes well for midlife women who will need to find creative ways to stretch their income dollars as they grow older.

(STILL) WORKING (A LITTLE BIT) HARD FOR A LIVING

In the Dreyfus Gender Investment Comparison Survey we also found that women were more likely than men to seek paid employment after retiring from their present job. The traditional view of retirement (the complete cessation from any form of paid employment) will be changed by boomers who want a more flexible part-time job that more closely meets their interests and desires. For example, some will start income-generating jobs based on a hobby or a new interest.

Future retirees will want to select jobs that accentuate or support their "active lifestyle." They will want jobs that are stimulating, challenging, and allow them to maintain a quality of life that typifies the boomers' perceptions of themselves. The new prototype of retirement is based on what we can't have now (especially women)—balance, or what I call the "blended life course," an ongoing mix of work, leisure, and education. Baby boomers aren't likely to drop their thirst to embrace what interests them, and the chances are good that the majority will want to stay active and involved— and still be able to stay up late enough to catch the Rolling Stones when they're in town.

Women (and men) who continue some type of part-time job or begin an entrepreneurial undertaking they enjoy (from selling real estate to teaching piano part-time to spending March and April of each year helping people with their taxes) will find they have the best of both worlds—a commitment to something that provides some structure in their lives and the added income that will ease the burden of financing those years.

Women are perfectly suited to do this because of their employment/work patterns. Since child care often prevents women from utilizing their full potential until later in life, they come into the labor scene with a high degree of pent-up desire to get their careers on track; they are given the opportunity to supplement their savings with specialized loan programs to start their own businesses; and they have been groomed early in life to be multi-role-oriented.

In the meantime, there is one important step that only a few women who come to the NCWRR financial planning seminars have taken. That is making sure that anyone who can contribute to retirement (the government, employer, one's own investment plan) is doing so—to the full extent possible.

Here's what you need to look into:

"Pennies" from Heaven; or, What to Expect from Social Security

I'll never forget the new twenty-three-year-old employee I met one day who was so excited that the government was providing Social Security for his retirement in forty-two years . . . Don't be similarly deluded. While Social Security will help, a comfortable retirement will require a much more well-rounded package than just these "pennies."

Having a Social Security number does not guarantee you income from Social Security. You or your spouse (for spousal benefits) needs to have earned enough "work credits" in a job covered by Social Security to qualify. (Your job is covered if you have been paying into the Social Security system via payroll deductions.) The maximum number of credits you can earn per year is four, and you are fully insured under Social Security and will receive full benefits at retirement once you have earned the necessary forty work credits.

Approximately every three years, you should check on the accuracy of your Social Security Administration records. Call 800-772-1213 and request Form SSA-7004, "Request for Earnings and Benefit Estimate Statement." When you receive a copy of your record, compare this with your W-2 forms and tax returns. If there are errors, contact your local Social Security office to have your records reviewed. Any error that occurred more than three years ago generally cannot be corrected, so be certain to take care of this regularly, or your retirement income may suffer.

If you lack a full forty credits, you still may be eligible for some benefits if your spouse (and sometimes a former spouse) earned the required work credits. When you are sixty-two or older, if your spouse is receiving Social Security, you will be eligible to receive 50 percent of the amount he receives.

A widow can collect Social Security benefits at age sixty or older if her husband earned forty work credits and was fully insured under Social Security.

Until 1985 it was more difficult for a divorcée to receive spousal benefits, but a change in the law has made it easier for a woman who was married for ten years or more to collect, regardless of whether her former spouse is collecting.

Can you collect your own Social Security and also as a dependent spouse? No. A working woman can collect only one benefit—the higher of the two amounts. However, you can switch if and when one will pay you a higher income. For example, you might retire on your own benefits at age sixty-two but switch over to benefits on your husband's work record after he retires if that amount will be higher.

Social Security benefits are adjusted for the rate of inflation. The rate of increase varies to reflect changes in the cost of living, but new amounts are never less than those paid the year before. The cost of living adjustments (COLAs) start when you are sixty-two, even if you're not yet drawing Social Security. The amount is then added to the base amount on which your benefit is figured.

Beyond obtaining an estimated earnings form from Social Security, you should study the following table, which illustrates how much you would receive if you retired in 1996.

FIRST YEAR SOCIAL SECURITY INCOME
Starting in 1996 at age sixty-five, spouse at same age

Salary in Year Before Retirement ($)	Wage Earner's Benefit ($)	Spousal Benefit ($)
15,000	7,104	3,552
20,000	8,460	4,224
25,000	9,828	4,908
30,000	11,160	5,500
35,000	12,372	6,180
40,000	13,200	6,600
45,000	13,608	6,804
50,000	13,944	6,972
55,000	14,256	7,128
60,000	14,556	7,272
65,000	14,808	7,404
70,000	14,964	7,476
75,000	14,976	7,488

The age at which you choose to retire will affect your benefits. People who choose to retire earlier than age sixty-five will receive a *permanently reduced* benefit spread over what is assumed to be a longer period of time; those who retire later than age sixty-five will receive a higher benefit over a shorter period of time.

Please note: In 1983 the Social Security Administration increased the age for getting full benefits. If you were born before 1938, you still qualify for full benefits at age sixty-five. Anyone born in 1938 has to be sixty-five and two months, anyone born in 1939 has to be sixty-five and four months, etc. Full retirement age inches up to sixty-six for people born between 1943 and 1954 and to sixty-seven for anyone born after 1960.

A BIG CURVE IN THE ROAD:
THOUGHTS ON THE SOCIAL SECURITY CRISIS

If you've been following the news over the last few years, you've almost certainly spotted the stories predicting the end of Social Security.

A good analogy to the impending Social Security crisis is driving in a car at sixty-five miles per hour and all of a sudden seeing a big sign that says, "Danger—Curve Ahead." Because of such factors as increasing life span, legions of baby boomers headed for retirement, and the "baby bust" (a period following 1964 that saw a radical dip in births, which will result in a dip in the number of workers paying into the system), the Social Security trust fund is projected to be exhausted by the year 2030. Instead of jamming on the brakes to avoid the curve or pretending it doesn't exist, women, I believe, need to anticipate and plan for the possibility of change. It is highly unlikely that there will be no form of Social Security; however, there is a strong likelihood that there will be a continuing upward movement of the eligibility age, and for some people there may be a decrease in benefits. While there is no way to know exactly what the changes will be or how they will affect any one individual, there are ways to protect yourself:

- Increase your savings rate, even by a small amount.
- Contribute to your company-sponsored retirement plan to the fullest extent possible.
- Consider a part-time job or some type of freelance work you might enjoy doing post-retirement.
- Communicate your views on Social Security for the future to your senator or congressional representative. Advocacy never hurts.

And always remember, **it's impossible to save too much for retirement.**

A retirement program represents the single most important safety net for women, yet few women understand its importance:

"I've worked for the last twenty-five years—ever since my youngest child entered kindergarten—and I wish I had known to pay attention to this benefit," says Barbara L., who is currently fifty-nine. *"I worked part-time at first, so I wouldn't have even been eligible then, but I never took advantage of any of the savings or retirement programs later on, and now I wish I had. I won't be able to retire until I'm seventy as a result."*

I sincerely hope that reading this book has impressed upon you the importance of planning ahead and taking advantage of any retirement programs your employer offers.

If you're married, talk to your spouse (or ask that he contact his personnel department for information) about what is already due him (and also whether the pension or plan would continue to pay out anything if you live longer than he does).

As you explore what is already due you and consider what you need to know about improving your current situation (your employer may have options you haven't taken advantage of), you'll need to have a basic understanding of the different types of retirement and pension plans.

What You Should Know About Company-Sponsored Retirement Plans

Though not all employers provide retirement plans, if your employer does, be sure to enroll. These plans offer a way to contribute to your plan via payroll deductions, which ensures that your money is saved regularly. In addition, companies that provide plans often offer some sort of "match" to the money you put in. Always take advantage of this—it's free money that you'll need one day.

With all of these plans, what you are eligible for depends on what your employer offers and what rules the company sets for eligibility.

The types of retirement plan offered may include the following.

DEFINED BENEFIT PLANS

Defined benefit plans (often called pension plans) provide a specific monthly payment when you retire; that is, you will know exactly what you will receive (generally based on a formula of salary earned and years worked) and you can plan your lifestyle accordingly. A percentage of your regular paycheck is paid into the plan by you or by your employer, or by both.

In the old days, pensions were the norm. You or your spouse may still have one of these plans in your employee benefits program, though increasingly, companies are moving away from them because this type of plan has proved very costly. Instead, they are substituting defined contribution plans for defined benefit plans.

Once you vest (become eligible to benefit) in a pension program (generally in five years), you have the right to receive, upon retirement, whatever pension benefits have been earned up until the time you left your job. Over a lifetime, you may have vested in more than one pension program and will earn the right to receive several small pensions. Keep careful records of your earnings, so that you'll know what you are due and how to collect benefits.

Spouses can often receive pension benefits—known as a joint and survivor annuity. A joint and survivor annuity is an annuity that pays a lifetime income to the person for whom it was purchased and to another person, generally a spouse.

One particular caution to women who are expecting spousal benefits: Prior to 1984, a spouse—generally a husband—could, without permission from his wife, sign for a higher benefit payment during his lifetime by giving up his claim to a survivor benefit. As of 1984, a new law states that the couple must *both* sign in order to waive these benefits. This change was a positive one for women, as a widow is placed at an additional disadvantage if pension benefits are wiped out by her spouse, without her consent.

In the case of divorce, a court may award the woman a share of her former husband's private pension and allow her to begin collecting her benefit while he is still working, after he retires, or after he dies. State laws guide the courts' decisions about how much she will get, and about whether the pension is to be divided as marital property or used as a source of alimony or support. (Or the couple may decide these issues as part of their property settlement.)

DEFINED CONTRIBUTION PLANS

Defined contribution plans depend on a specific amount being deposited into the plan (either percentage of salary or a stated dollar amount contributed by you and/or your employer). You will not know the amount of your benefit before you retire because the returns on investment cannot be calculated in advance. The contribution—not the benefit—is what is consistent in this plan, and the amount of money you receive will vary according to how much is invested and how well the investments perform.

There are several types of defined contribution plans:

401(k) Plans

Employees contribute pretax salary (income earned by you but not subject to taxes until a later date) to the plan; the employer may also contribute, based on a set formula. No tax is paid on the contributions or their earnings until distribution. Employees are generally given a choice as to the level of investment (conservative to aggressive) they want to pursue, making it a retirement plan that offers individuals a great deal of control over their money.

The name 401(k) refers to the section of the Internal Revenue code that explains this type of retirement plan. Government documents sometimes refer to it as a *cash or deferred arrangement* (CODA) retirement plan, but the name that has stuck with the public is 401(k).

When baby boomers were asked (in the Scudder Baby Boom Survey) what finally motivated them to begin thinking about their retirement, the single most important factor was receiving literature from their employer concerning their 401(k).

At some point during your life, the majority of you will work for an employer who is offering a 401(k) plan, since this is the most popular program being offered today. For that reason, it is worth spending the time to learn more about it. Here is some key information:

How much can I contribute?

There is a cap, which is adjusted each year for inflation. During 1996 the maximum was $9,500 (on your contribution, not on the matching contribution from your employer). The government determines the amount you can contribute based on a nondiscriminatory formula. The cap imposed by your employer can be lower, though not higher, than the government cap.

Is my money safe in a 401(k) plan?

It's not insured by the federal government the way savings accounts at FDIC banks are. However, employers are required to set aside 401(k) money in a separate account that management cannot touch, in order to protect your money if your employer runs into financial trouble. Incidents of financial mismanagement have occurred in the past, but regulatory agencies have tightened up regulations in order to prevent them from occurring again.

What information should my company give me on the plan?

Employees should receive a Summary Plan Description that provides the overall scope of the plan. In addition, you should receive the following (sometimes it is in the overall description of the plan; other times it's distributed separately):

- A description of each investment option and the goal and risk-return ratio of each
- The identity and location of your plan's investment manager
- An explanation of how you are to make your investment choices and how often you can change them
- A description of any transaction fees or expenses
- A copy of the prospectus (a legal document explaining the fund) for each mutual fund in which you have invested, and an explanation of your investor rights

You should also be able to obtain, on request, financial statements, reports, assets owned by each investment, information on the values of the shares you already own, and other pertinent information.

How much risk is associated with a 401(k) plan?

The risk you incur is with the investments you choose to make within the 401(k), not the 401(k) itself. There are many safeguards to ensure that your funds are not misappropriated by your employer. However, stock funds are more volatile than bond funds or money market funds, but even if you select the safest option, there is some risk. As you've learned in previous chapters, if your investment grows too slowly, it may not keep pace with inflation and you may end up with less money than you need to live comfortably in retirement.

When should I begin contributing or participating in a 401(k) plan?

The sooner the better. Because of the power of compounding, if you contribute regularly in the early years of your career, you will have a big head start on those who procrastinate. Even if you have to stop contributing temporarily because of a major expense such as buying a home or financing a child's education, the money you already have in the plan will continue to grow.

How should I invest my 401(k) fund?

Your company will provide you with a menu of investments to choose from. Financial planners generally recommend that you divide your retirement savings among several different options, so that it will not be vulnerable to the losses of any one category.

What is the most common mistake people make with their 401(k)'s?

They invest too conservatively. Instead of remembering that this is money for the long haul and that they can afford to take some risks, people worry about losing it all, so they keep it "safe." The end result is that inflation hurts their long-term buying power.

When should I shift my funds from one investment to another?

Financial planners agree that you shouldn't try to anticipate market trends. However, you may want to shift some of your 401(k) funds if your employer offers you new options and they match your overall plan. And as you approach retirement, you will probably want to reallocate your funds. Although you need to know something about how your investments are performing, don't become fixated on short-term performance.

Can I put more money into my 401(k)?

Forty percent of all workers are enrolled in 401(k)'s that permit them to make *after-tax* contributions to their account. After-tax pay is counted as part of your income and you will be taxed on it, however, the advantage of after-tax contributions is that the earnings are tax-deferred, and you are taking some additional, excellent steps toward planning ahead for your future.

Can I borrow from my 401(k) plan?

It depends on your plan, so check with your plan administrator. Two-thirds of all plans allow participants to borrow against their funds, but there are restrictions. You can borrow 50 percent of your money up to $50,000. In most cases you must repay the loan in five years, and you must pay interest on the loan, although the interest goes into your own account.

Can I withdraw the funds whenever I want?

Not before age fifty-nine and a half, though there are exceptions to this, in case of death, medical expenses, or a disability.

What happens if I am laid off or change jobs?

You are entitled to all the money that has accrued to you. If you are not yet fifty-nine and a half and decide you want to withdraw from your plan, you will be hit with a 10 percent penalty. If you want to roll the money over into another retirement plan, you need to be sure to instruct your company to transfer the 401(k) funds directly to that other account so that the transfer can be made without incurring the penalty.

According to *Money* magazine, a good 401(k) plan offers the following features.

- The opportunity to sign up as soon as you are hired
- An employer match of at least 50 percent of some or all of your contribution
- At least six funds with a broad range of investment styles
- Timely account information via an 800 number
- The freedom to make transfers or change allocations at least four times a year
- Total expenses of no more than 1 percent of assets
- The ability to borrow and make hardship withdrawals

403(b) Plans

The 403(b) plan is similar to the 401(k), except it has been created for employees of nonprofit, tax-exempt organizations such as educational or religious organizations or charitable foundations. As with the 401(k) plan, the employee contributes pretax salary, and the employer may contribute an additional amount. Taxes are deferred until withdrawal.

Profit-Sharing Plans

Rather than providing a pension plan, some companies have adopted a profit-sharing plan. Your company determines its total contribution. One variable here is how well your company does during a particular year. A rise or drop in profits can create a proportional increase or decrease in the amount contributed to the plan. Another variable is how well the investments of the plan perform. At retirement, you receive payments equal to your allocated share of the plan's investments.

ESOP (Employee Stock Ownership Plans)

An ESOP is a plan that invests primarily in the securities of the employer. Like a profit-sharing plan, an ESOP provides a formula for allocating the contributions among the participants. The purpose of the plan is to give employees a vested interest in the company, thereby providing them with an additional incentive toward greater productivity. You have the potential for gaining from this type of investment if the company stock value increases over time. Keep in mind that ESOP plans are not always pretax or deferred from tax.

SEP-IRA (Simplified Employee Pension)

This is a simplified employee pension that allows an employer (or yourself, if you're self-employed) to contribute to your IRA (individual retirement account) without having to offer a more complex type of plan. You can have a SEP-IRA in addition to a regular IRA.

When you track down the type of plan offered by your employer, ask:

- What happens to my retirement plan benefits if I am laid off or take early retirement?
- Will my retirement plan benefits be reduced by any Social Security payments I receive?

- What survivor options are available, and how might they affect my monthly benefits?

MAKING WISE CHOICES: RETIREMENT DOLLARS "IN WAITING"

The money you set aside for your retirement is invested so that it can grow. With company-sponsored plans, you are sometimes given a choice of investment options, and it is left to you to apportion your savings among the options that seem best for you. (Chapter 18 contains a chart that is applicable for general investing as well as long-term retirement planning.) Your choices will depend on the type of plan you enroll in. With a 401(k) your employer will offer you a few alternatives—to invest in your own company's stock, to put money in a stock mutual fund, a bond mutual fund, a balanced mutual fund (a mix of stocks and bonds), or perhaps a money market fund. The literature presented to you by the benefits department will indicate which investments are conservative and which are designed for greater growth. Every time you contribute, your money is divided according to your specifications.

Approximately four times a year (this is easy if your program issues quarterly review statements), check the status of your accounts. Remember that it's a long-term investment, so you needn't panic over a temporary lull or dip in a particular area. If, however, you feel the account just isn't performing up to par, you'll want to do some shifting. You might want to consult with your financial advisor on this.

BEING YOUR OWN WATCHDOG

Though most company programs are very safe, you sometimes read news stories about pension and retirement plans that have gone belly-up as a result of fraud, misuse of employee contributions, and so on. For that reason, women who are covered by a plan should be aware of how solvent the fund is and how her dollars are being invested.

Any of the following should be considered warning signs.

- Late or irregular statements, or statements that regularly reflect wrong selections
- An inaccurate balance in your account (keep track of your pay stubs so that you can compare your year-to-date contribution figures), or

wild fluctuations in your balance, beyond the normal market fluc-
tuations
- Employee rumblings about problems with their accounts
- Unusual expenses (such as a loan to a company officer)
- A delay in your company's matching contribution
- Indications that your company is experiencing severe financial dif-
ficulties

If you have any concerns, contact your company benefits office. If
their answers are unsatisfactory, contact the federal Pension and Welfare
Benefits Administration (PWBA), 202-219-8776, or check your local
phone book for a regional office.

WHY WOMEN HAVE NOT PARTICIPATED IN RETIREMENT PLANS IN THE PAST

Despite the fact that women live on average five to seven years longer
than men, they have not always participated in their company's retirement programs. My research shows that many women don't even know
these programs exist or what their benefits would be if they did participate. Here's what women say are their reasons: "I couldn't afford to set
anything aside"; "Oh, my husband's working. He has a plan, and we need
the extra money"; "I can't think about growing old now." Or they participated for a while and then decided to take the money out. Or they depend on someone else to take care of the finances.

Other Forms of Retirement Savings

You may want to examine other types of savings plans to supplement the money you'll receive from company-sponsored plans and
Social Security. The government has provided two key instruments
(IRAs and Keogh plans) for this type of additional savings; annuities
offer another option for some.

INDIVIDUAL RETIREMENT ACCOUNTS (IRAS)

Anyone with earned income can open an IRA, though the tax-
deferred benefits are available only to some (see next paragraph),

and you can also open one for your spouse As of January 1, 1997, married couples filing a joint return may contribute up to $4,000 annually to an IRA (even if only one spouse is employed). The deductibility of contributions remains subject to existing limitations, so consult your tax advisor. The money you put into your IRA must be money you are prepared to sock away for a long time, as penalties must be paid if you need to withdraw the money before you are fifty-nine and a half. The amount you will eventually realize from your IRA depends on how much you have put away and how well your investments have done.

Earnings on IRAs are not taxed until you withdraw the money, and for many people, the contributions to an IRA account are also tax-deductible. For some, this benefit has been taken away. You can no longer deduct your full IRA contribution if you (or your spouse) are covered by an employer-sponsored retirement plan and your adjusted gross income is more than $25,000 for singles, or more than $40,000 if you're married. If you fall into this bracket, check with your accountant to see if some of your contribution may still be deducted. Current laws provide a scale of income level and deductibility.

Investments in these accounts are self-directed, meaning that you and your financial advisor can decide where the funds are to be invested, taking into account your personal financial plan, risk tolerance, and other investments.

If your retirement savings will primarily be in the form of an IRA, you have some additional choices:

Where should you open your IRA? If you choose certain banks, your investment options may be limited to conservative investments like CDs and money market accounts, neither of which are likely to keep you ahead of inflation in the long run. You may prefer putting your IRA in a mutual fund company where you can move your money around among funds within the mutual fund family.

You cannot withdraw from an IRA without paying severe penalties. This money is there for you for a certain reason and for a certain time when you're going to need it. When you reach retirement age, you certainly don't want to learn that "the cookie jar is empty."

KEOGH PLANS

A Keogh plan is a retirement vehicle for the self-employed. Keogh plan contributions are deducted from your gross income and the tax is deferred until you withdraw the funds.

If you own a business, are self-employed, or earn money as a freelancer, a Keogh plan may best suit your needs. It differs from an IRA mainly in that you can set aside more money each year (since a self-employed person may have no other retirement plan from which to benefit). All the money put into your Keogh plan must come from your self-employed income. If you lose money in your business in any given year, you will not be able to contribute any-thing to your Keogh plan.

ANNUITIES

You can buy an annuity either with one lump-sum payment or with monthly contributions. Your money grows, tax-deferred, until you need it. Annuities are issued by insurance companies and sold through financial institutions such as banks, insurance companies, and brokerage firms.

Annuities are a nonqualified retirement account. They are best understood when compared to IRAs. The dollars you put into an annuity are after-tax dollars, but they grow tax-deferred like an IRA. There is no limit to the contributions you are allowed to make to an annuity, but, like an IRA, there is a penalty if you withdraw the funds prior to age fifty-nine and a half. The amount withdrawn from an IRA prior to fifty-nine and a half will be taxable at your current tax bracket, and a 10 percent excise tax will be applied as well. A withdrawal from an annuity prior to fifty-nine and a half will have a 10 percent penalty, but you will be taxed only on the amount that has been *earned on the principal* that has been contributed—the principal itself has already been taxed. Unlike IRAs, you do not have to begin minimum distributions at age seventy and a half; you do not need to take the funds out until they are needed.

There are two types of annuities: *single premium-deferred* annu-ities, which offer a fixed interest rate for a specified period of time, and *variable* annuities, which offer mutual funds as investment op-tions.

Most people think of annuities as a guarantee of future income.

There are many options for how you receive the money you've set aside, and one of them is to receive a "guaranteed" stream of income during retirement. For people in a high tax bracket, who are starting late on retirement savings or who are frustrated by the limits on the amount they can save through other types of retirement plans, an annuity may be a solution. Keep in mind that an annuity is not the type of investment that provides ready access or liquidity.

Based on your particular financial situation, you may want to discuss this investment alternative with a financial advisor, especially if you are risk averse and want a "guaranteed" payoff at a special maturation date. But stick with well-known, reputable companies if you buy an annuity. They aren't FDIC-insured, and should the insurance company or mutual fund company fold, your money (if invested in a single premium-deferred annuity) could be tied up, earning little, for years. Variable annuities would not be at risk, as they are separate accounts.

Saving like Crazy

In addition to taking advantage of every program possible, keep in mind the seriousness of your retirement planning, and, after reviewing some of the savings tricks outlined in Chapter 14, keep saving systematically for your retirement. The tables below will give you an idea of how your money will grow.

HOW A SINGLE $1,000 INVESTMENT WILL GROW

Percent*	5 Yrs.	8 Yrs.	10 Yrs.	12 Yrs.	15 Yrs.	20 Yrs.	25 Yrs.	30 Yrs.
3	$1,159	$1,267	$1,344	$1,426	$1,558	$1,806	$2,094	$2,427
4	1,217	1,369	1,480	1,601	1,801	2,191	2,666	3,243
5	1,276	1,478	1,629	1,796	2,079	2,653	3,386	4,322
6	1,338	1,594	1,791	2,012	2,397	3,207	4,292	5,744
8	1,469	1,851	2,159	2,518	3,172	4,661	6,848	10,064
10	1,611	2,144	2,594	3,138	4,177	6,727	10,835	17,449
15	2,011	3,059	4,046	5,350	8,137	16,367	32,919	66,212

*Percent annual net rate of return (compounded)

HOW A $1,000 INVESTMENT EVERY YEAR WILL GROW

Percent*	5 Yrs.	8 Yrs.	10 Yrs.	12 Yrs.	15 Yrs.	20 Yrs.	25 Yrs.	30 Yrs.
3	$5,310	$8,890	$11,460	$14,190	$18,600	$26,870	$36,460	$47,580
4	5,420	9,210	12,010	15,030	20,020	29,780	41,650	56,080
5	5,530	9,550	12,580	15,920	21,580	33,070	47,730	66,440
6	5,640	9,900	13,180	16,870	23,280	36,790	54,860	79,060
8	5,870	10,640	14,490	18,980	27,150	45,760	73,110	113,280
10	6,110	11,440	15,940	21,380	31,770	57,280	98,350	164,490
15	6,740	13,730	20,300	29,000	47,580	102,440	212,790	434,740

*Percent annual net rate of return (compounded)

A *Primer for* Handling Financial Scare Tactics

From my years of working with women, I know that "scaring" is no way to encourage action (it doesn't work particularly well with men either). Whenever you read something about your financial situation that scares you and discourages you from being proactive, here are six things I want you to do:

1. **Don't let the numbers speak for themselves.** When you see headlines that warn of a bleak future if you don't have $300,000 saved, recognize that there is always something you can do that will help.
2. **There is more positive news than reaches print.** Although I am not minimizing the serious implications of women's savings and investment predicament, most of these doom-and-gloom stories fail to acknowledge the positive. Our NCWRR research clearly shows that women are *aware* of the need to plan for the future and want to take steps to change their financial situation. By purchasing this book, you are already responding positively.
3. **Respond to reality, not fantasy.** Don't worry about what can't be done, and focus on what can be done now. Certainly, some readers may be at a stage of life when it would have

been helpful to start earlier, but move on, and don't dwell on what might have been. Just start putting away as much as you can today. Although we know the future won't take care of itself, we *can* control the present.

4. **Simply starting is good enough.** It is human nature to compare ourselves to others or to worry about whether we are living up to other people's expectations. If you can only put away $50 or $100 a month for your future, that's a good start. Although somebody or some magazine article may tell you that you have to save X dollars, don't be discouraged. Just keep saving. If you remember the story of the turtle and the hare, you'll recall that "slow and steady" wins the race.

5. **Take advantage of all the help you can get.** It is absolutely vital that women take advantage of any employer-sponsored retirement plans. If you're currently employed and aren't sure what's available, call your personnel department immediately. Employers are required by law to provide their employees with a detailed explanation of any program that is in place and how it is funded. And if you're job seeking, ask about benefits at the same time you inquire about salary.

6. **The impossible can become the possible.** Over the years, I have seen wonderful, inspiring cases of women with modest means who became financially secure through planning and saving. It's easy to become disillusioned by the financial news, but so long as you keep working at it, you shouldn't let the doomsayers get you down!

18

NOT-SO-RISKY BUSINESS
Basic Investment Strategies

"I like investigating investments and making informed decisions. I find myself watching stock reports instead of the Today *show. I feel empowered because I'm learning, making money, and having fun. I just love it!"*

What's so great about investing? Hear it from some new converts:

- "It's like any hobby. The more you learn, the more interesting it is, and I'm really having a good time."
- "I have my stocks listed on my on-line service, and I love turning on my machine in the morning to see how I'm doing. On boring days when things are slow, it's great to feel part of this big financial adventure when something is *always* happening."
- "Yes, there are ups and downs with investing, but name me one thing in life that doesn't have its highs and lows."
- "When I read good news about the companies I've invested in, I take a little pride at having selected those for an investment."
- "Watching my investments grow gives me a sense of accomplishment and a feeling of control—that I made this money!"

There is nothing more gratifying to me than witnessing the

"birth" of an investor. I trust by this time you are well aware that I believe each of you has the potential to take charge of your finances—all you need are the tools and information to get started. Plunge into this chapter with confidence and you will emerge feeling even better about yourself because you'll feel that you have a new level of control over your future.

However, a word of caution is in order here. Read this chapter with this underlying thought: To become a savvy investor takes time. Financial education is a lifelong endeavor, so don't expect it to happen overnight. Remember, you are learning about how to invest for the long term, so take your time to digest the material fully.

As you might guess, this is, in my opinion, the most important chapter of the book. Although I am unlikely ever to meet many of my readers, my fantasy is that when I read a success story about a woman who is happy in her later years, partly because she is financially secure, I will hope that she may have at some time encountered and adopted the investing principles put forth in this book.

Certainly, this will not be the only resource you use in becoming a savvy investor, but it contains the very essence of what you need to know to start your financial journey.

This chapter will present the following information.

- How to understand different investments and their relationship to risk and return
- How to use specific investment strategies to develop a sound investment plan
- How to use information from annual reports, Value Line, and other sources
- Investment trends that take into account women's longevity, singleness, and other demographic realities

If you are going to stay ahead of inflation and maximize the money you save, it's important that you "put your toe in the water" and start learning about investing.

SWIMMING UPSTREAM

By this time, I trust you're more than willing to take the investment challenge. As you know, you need to. With luck, you'll also be an inspiration to others, because the statistics are not encouraging. Here's what we've learned about women's investments through the Women Cents Study:

- 40 percent have never purchased shares in a mutual fund.
- 63 percent have never purchased individual stocks.
- 83 percent have never purchased corporate, municipal, or mortgage-backed bonds.
- 88 percent own savings and money market accounts.

However, it isn't just a gender problem. The 1996 Scudder Baby Boom Generation Retirement Preparation Survey highlighted a variety of serious and alarming trends concerning boomers' present and future investment and savings practices:

- Only 19 percent own mutual funds.
- Only 10 percent own individual stocks.
- The majority have funds in bank accounts.
- Over 65 percent of female boomers want only to invest in safe or guaranteed investments (compared to 55 percent of boomer men).
- Over 58 percent have not established savings goals.
- Over 70 percent are worried about their financial future.
- Only 19 percent use their disposable income for investing (47 percent have a "spend rather than save" orientation).
- Only 19 percent are strongly confident about their investing.

Even if making this bold step into the world of investing sets you apart from those you know, it's important that you do it. Then turn around and encourage others. An entire population is at risk.

Getting Started

At this stage, I hope you have done the following three things.

1. Set aside money for an emergency fund and placed it somewhere safe and accessible, such as a money market fund.
2. Contributed the maximum possible to your company's retirement plan or your IRA. (Even if you have other financial

goals, the benefits of this money compounding over the long term make it too important to neglect taking this step.)

3. Assessed and taken care of your insurance needs in order to protect what you have.

When people invest in financial instruments, they tend to worry about these things:

1. *Stability:* Will the money I invest still be there when I want it? A stable investment will fluctuate very little; a riskier investment fluctuates more, and with fluctuation there is the possibility that you'll lose some of what you invest (for the opportunity to make even more).

2. *Accessibility:* Will I be able to get my money if I need it? Some investments are very liquid (you can get the cash right away if you need to), and some are tied to a timetable, with penalties for an early withdrawal. Still other times, your investment will be stronger if you can leave it alone. A strong, stable stock may be a wonderful investment if you buy it and hold it for five years (the minimum number of years recommended for holding long-term investments), but if you need the money in six months, buying that particular stock may be a waste of your time. When developing an investment portfolio, you need to find investment vehicles appropriate for your short-, medium-, and long-term needs. That way you will not have to access your retirement account, for example, when you plan to purchase your first home or when it's time to send the kids to college.

3. *Return:* The return on an investment is what you make on it—what it would sell for plus its income (interest or dividends). Generally, stability decreases as return increases. Rates of return vary according to the economic climate and the strength of the investment. (Even a good stock may be down somewhat in a bear—down—market.) When figuring return, it's also important to consider inflation and taxes. Look at what you will actually make on the investment, subtract the percentage you will lose to inflation and taxes, and this will help you determine your net return on the investment.

The Investment Pyramid

The investment pyramid represents an investment vehicle's earning power combined with its degree of risk. The pyramid offers a handy tool for you to use when deciding what type of investment to make and how to balance your portfolio.

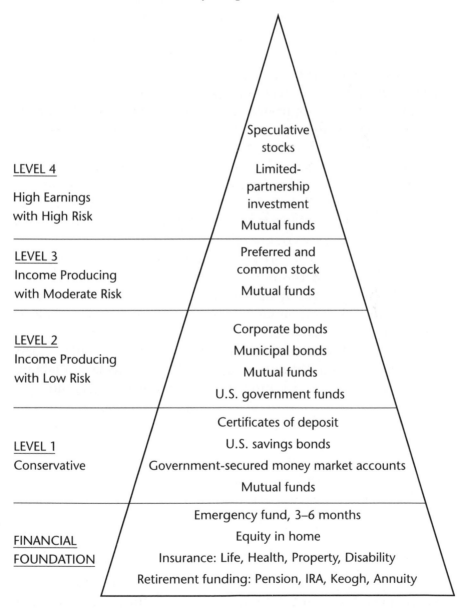

LEVEL 4

High Earnings
with High Risk

Speculative stocks
Limited-partnership investment
Mutual funds

LEVEL 3
Income Producing
with Moderate Risk

Preferred and common stock
Mutual funds

LEVEL 2
Income Producing
with Low Risk

Corporate bonds
Municipal bonds
Mutual funds
U.S. government funds

LEVEL 1
Conservative

Certificates of deposit
U.S. savings bonds
Government-secured money market accounts
Mutual funds

FINANCIAL FOUNDATION

Emergency fund, 3–6 months
Equity in home
Insurance: Life, Health, Property, Disability
Retirement funding: Pension, IRA, Keogh, Annuity

Also refer to Chapter 5 for help in assessing your comfort with various risk levels.

The foundation of the investment pyramid consists of the items—ownership of your home, your emergency fund, insurance needs, and retirement plans—you were to take care of before you even considered investing.

Level 1 on the pyramid progresses to conservative investments—certificates of deposit, U.S. savings bonds, Treasury bills, government-secured money market funds, and those mutual funds that virtually assure the safety of your investment capital while offering modest earnings. These types of investments are useful for money you know you're going to need in less than five years. If your son will be college age in a year or two, then these types of investments would be a good bet for your money.

Level 2 on the pyramid contains income-producing investments with minimum risk. This group includes government bonds, municipal bonds, and bond funds. Retired people who need to keep their money safe and would like it to kick off some income (via interest or dividends) often seek out Level 2 investments.

Level 3 offers moderate-risk investments that hold the potential for investment growth—stocks of well-known, well-managed companies that are familiar by name and most growth mutual funds. If you want to make your money grow, you're going to want to learn more about these investments.

Level 4 investments are high-risk. They are speculative ventures, such as limited partnerships, small-capitalization stocks, initial public offerings (companies selling stock for the first time), and commodities. Many of these vehicles are acknowledged risks in new industries with unproven earning capability for the opportunity of great pain. If you're a risk-seeker, you may well find it exciting to put a limited amount of your funds into one of these higher-risk investments, preferably in consultation with an adviser who has knowledge about the particular field in which you're investing your money.

The Most Important Pieces in Your Investment Puzzle

As you piece together what you'd like to do in the way of investing, the most important thing to do now is to focus on two important pieces of this project:

- *Your goals:* What are your short- and long-term aspirations for how you'll use the money?
- *Your risk tolerance:* What's your risk comfort level? Are you conservative? Middle of the road? Aggressive? Keeping this in mind will help you select your investments. Having worked through the information and exercises in Chapter 5, I trust that you now realize it's important to do *some* risk-taking, but there's no point losing sleep over your choices. Diversification will let you keep some money safe while taking small risks too. The important thing now is that you learn to enjoy investing enough that you'll continue and work to learn more.

You also need to identify your *investment objectives*—what it is you want each investment to do for you. It's perfectly all right to have more than one objective. For example, look at the goals you set in previous chapters. If you're thirty-five with plenty of years between you and retirement, you might decide to place part of your IRA in a moderate-risk investment where you hope your nest egg will grow.

You may, however, have another objective: If you have an ailing mother and may need to use some funds to help cover the expenses of her illness, that money might be placed in a much lower risk investment.

Keep your own goals in mind when you consider the following objectives.

- Security of what you've invested. No one wants to lose what she invests, of course, but some people place a premium on not risking the possibility of any loss. If you're in a situation where you simply feel you can't afford to lose anything, then security will be a prime objective.
- Building wealth. People who are hoping to maximize their investments, even if it means taking some risk with it, have set "growth" as an objective.
- Stability of income (stability of the interest and/or dividends paid out by certain investments). Some people, particularly people who have already retired, need to have their investments produce income. If stability of income is an objective, then you are looking for the types of investments that pay interest or dividends regularly.

As you review the possible objectives you might have when investing and compare them with your financial goals, you'll soon see what's most important to you. For example, if you're investing for your three-year-old's college education, you can afford to go for growth of capital, because you can afford to take the risk because you don't need the money soon. If, however, you're helping your mother with her investments, and her income is little more than Social Security, you must go for safe investments that offer stability of income so that she'll have some supplementary funds coming in regularly.

The next principle you need to keep in mind is the risk vs. reward ratio: **The greater the risk you are willing to take, the greater the possible reward.**

If you look back at the investment pyramid, you'll see that the higher you go up the pyramid, the greater opportunity you have for return and the greater your exposure to loss.

The Four Most Important Rules of Investing

1. **Invest for the long term.** Statistics show that long-term investors do well.
2. **Do your homework, and look for investments with a track record.** If a company or a fund shows long-term stability, it's a very good sign for profitable investing.
3. **Diversify.** As discussed in previous chapters, you'll sleep better if you don't have all your eggs in one basket. (Keep reading for more information about a diversified portfolio.)
4. **Practice dollar cost averaging.** This is the strategy of investing regularly and buying shares during market ups and downs. By accumulating an investment at different intervals, you average out your cost. This helps protect you against price fluctuations for longer-term investing. For example, let's assume you're setting aside money monthly to invest, and in month one, you purchase Coca-Cola at what turns out to be a market high. By purchasing more shares of Coca-Cola during subsequent months, you average out the cost of your shares, providing you with a solid investment over time.

Your Investment Options

Though they come in all types of packages, there are really only three different types of investments:

1. *Cash and cash-equivalent investments:* These include savings accounts, money market accounts, and mutual funds. As discussed previously, these types of investments are appropriate for emergency money or for money needed short-term. It's also a perfect place to park money until you decide on a different investment.
2. *Stocks:* With stock ownership, you are investing in a company. Ownership of stocks can be very profitable in the long run, but casual investors should expect to leave the majority of their money in a particular stock for three to five years. Historically, the longer you hold a good-quality stock, the better you're going to do.
3. *Bonds:* When you buy a bond, you are loaning money to another entity: the government (government bonds), a corporation, or a municipality. When you are loaning money to someone, you are concerned about the quality of that person's credit. In this case, you are lending money to a corporate or government entity, and you want to be sure you will receive the interest payments promised, as well as the return of the money you loaned. The longer the period of time the entity wants use of your money, the higher the interest rate it must be willing to pay you. The safest bonds are U.S. government bonds; the riskiest are corporate "junk" bonds.

A common variation on each of these options is the very popular financial instrument, a mutual fund. Because mutual funds are one of the most popular forms of investing right now, we'll take a look at them first.

Exploring Mutual Funds

A mutual fund is the packaging of cash, stocks, bonds, money market funds, or some combination of these. A mutual fund is a way to invest in a professionally managed portfolio that pools the money of many investors. Mutual funds offer an excellent way for people with limited amounts of money to increase the diversification of their investments.

Like stocks and bonds, mutual funds can experience downs, offering you an opportunity to buy more or to stop and reevaluate.

Though there's fun to be had in buying shares of a specific company, unless you have the ability to fully diversify your portfolio, you should consider building the core of your portfolio with mutual funds, and complement those funds with stocks in individual companies. Some of the aspects investors like about mutual funds are the following.

- *Professional management:* Mutual funds are managed by full-time securities analysts with years of experience and access to the market information necessary to manage a portfolio of stocks or bonds. Investing on your own, you could not match the research resources available through professional management.
- *Diversification:* By investing in many different securities, in many different industries, you can significantly reduce the volatility of your portfolio.
- *Flexibility:* There are mutual funds suited to every investor's needs, from the conservative to the aggressive. Because investment companies would prefer to keep your money under their umbrella, many have created "fund families"—different funds with different investment objectives, managed by different professionals, but still within the same major company. With only a phone call, you can easily transfer portions of your investment within a family of funds if and when your needs change. However, as a consumer you still need to judge each fund on its own investment merits.
- *Low cost:* The expenses of the mutual fund are spread over many thousands of shares of stock, resulting in lower costs per share than those you would incur if you tried to purchase the securities on your own.
- *Liquidity:* Mutual funds allow investors to withdraw their money at any time.

The past performance of a mutual fund can be researched by contacting the fund directly for a prospectus (the legal document about the investment) and the latest annual report, or by asking your financial advisor for a prospectus and a report from one of the outside fund reporting services (Morningstar, CDA/Weisenberger, Lipper, or Value Line). You'll also find quarterly or annual analyses done by the financial magazines.

When you buy a mutual fund, you can do so directly through the mutual fund company or through your financial advisor or broker.

Some funds are "load" funds, meaning that you pay a fee when you make your initial purchase (with a "back-end load" fund, it's paid when you sell). Others are "no load"; there will be no up-front charge. With all funds, however, there will be management fees embedded in the fund. Management fees vary considerably among firms. A funds management fee must be listed in its prospectus. You can determine what fees are charged by reading the prospectus. If you don't understand it, call someone in your financial support system and ask for help.

Mutual funds are categorized by their investment objective. They may be "growth" funds (they take on greater risk with the hope of long-term reward) or "income" funds (stocks are selected for their ability to pay good dividends), or they may specialize in an industry, such as health care, utilities, or entertainment.

When you're ready to buy, decide on an amount of money you can invest for the long term, and divide it among several mutual funds with different types of investment objectives so that your portfolio is diversified. How you allocate your portfolio will depend on your goals, age, and tolerance for risk.

FUNDS FOR ALL NEEDS

Once you've set your goals, developed your timetable, and determined your risk tolerance, it is time to select the mutual funds that are right for you. The following are the major asset classes and the style categories for each.

Money Market Funds

Money market funds deal in short-term, high-quality, cash-equivalent securities such as Treasury bills.

Domestic Stock Funds

Growth Funds. These funds are comprised of large company stocks, including blue chip stocks, and the funds contain a mix of "growth" and "value" stocks. Growth stocks are companies with earnings that are expected to grow quickly. Value stocks are companies whose stock price is low, relative to earnings, book value, or cash flow. These funds fluctuate with the market, so there is risk; however, they are generally considered an investment that will deliver long-term appreciation.

Growth and Income Funds. These funds deal in the stocks of companies that are well established in their industries, still in a growth stage of development, and able to share their earnings with their shareholders through paying dividends. People who are looking for investments that produce ongoing income while there is still some growth of capital tend to invest in these funds.

Aggressive-Growth Funds. These deal in small company stocks that tend to be more volatile than those of most established larger companies. These are high-risk stocks, intended for people who are trying to maximize their money in a short period of time, but also can be beneficial as a long-term investment to minimize their volatility.

Bond Funds

Taxable bonds are issued by governments or corporations to finance expenditures and operations.

Municipal bonds are issued by state and local governments. These bonds are exempt from federal income taxes, making them a potentially attractive investment. They can also be free of state income tax if the bond is issued by the state in which you reside, thus making its interest both state and federal tax-free. Bond funds tend to suit people who are looking for income from their investments.

Balanced Funds

These funds invest in both stocks and bonds. Stocks are part of the mix for their higher return, and bonds are included for their higher yield. Traditionally, these funds hold 60 percent of their assets in stocks, 40 percent in bonds. In general these funds will have more risk than an all-bond fund but less risk than an all-stock fund. These funds produce some income while preserving principal.

International Stock and Bond Funds

The stocks and bonds of foreign countries would have the same investment objectives as domestic funds. Because many foreign markets are not as developed as that of the United States, and because of currency risk, international stocks and bonds are considered more volatile than U.S. stocks and bonds. However, because the movement of foreign markets is independent of the U.S. market, foreign stocks may be high when U.S. markets are low and vice versa. For this reason, balancing your portfolio with U.S. and foreign securities lowers volatility by increasing your diversification.

Specialized Funds

There are funds with many other investment objectives to choose from to complement your core portfolio—from funds with a socially responsible objective to those that invest in a certain sector, such as biotechnology, telecommunications, and precious metals.

EVALUATING A FUND AS AN INVESTMENT

When looking for a mutual fund, here are some questions to keep in mind:

How long has the fund been around and how has it performed?

Here you're looking for the fund's track record over the last three, five, or ten years, if possible.

Who is the fund manager, and how is his or her track record? Or is there a team approach to managing the fund?

If the fund undergoes a management change later on, you may want to reevaluate whether this investment should remain in your portfolio.

How frequently does the fund "turn over" its portfolio?

In a tax-deferred retirement account, you don't have to be concerned with the taxability of the fund, but if it's a taxable account, you need to determine how much you have made on your investment after taxes. The higher the turnover, the higher the tax implications.

What is the fund's investment objective?

Be sure the fund's objectives fit with your own goals for investing.

What are the top ten holdings?

Do they sound solid to you?

What is the minimum required to open an account?

What are the subsequent investment amounts? What are the fees?

If you are looking at a bond fund, ask about the credit quality of the portfolio and ask about its track record. What have its three-, five-, and ten-year returns been?

You're looking for preservation of capital and consistency of the interest being paid.

Is there a money market fund within the family of funds?

You want as much flexibility as possible. Is it a family of funds with one star fund, or are there different types of funds within the family that can meet all your needs?

READING THE MUTUAL FUND TABLES

The value of your mutual fund is not set by supply and demand the way a stock price is established. The value of your mutual fund depends on the value of the underlying securities. At the end of the trading day, the value of the securities held by the fund is tallied and a share price is determined. When you place an order to buy or redeem a mutual fund, the price quoted you will be the closing price for the fund on the previous day.

When you check the status of your mutual fund in the newspaper, the listing reports several pieces of information:

NAV (net asset value): This is the price of one share of the fund. This figure is computed by totaling the value of all the securities and cash and dividing it by the number of shares the fund has issued.

Offer Price: This information tells you whether or not there is a fee to buy into this fund. "NL" indicates a no-load fund, but if there is a number in the offer price column, it tells you what it would cost to buy a share of the fund. For example, if the value of a share is $18.25 and the figure in the "Offer Price" column is $18.78, that indicates you will pay a 53-cent premium to purchase shares in that mutual fund. (While the cost of buying into a fund is a factor, remember that what's important in the long run is the fund's track record. Will you make money on your money?)

NAV Change: This last column will indicate a plus or minus figure, and that indicates how much the per-share value has gone up or down from the previous day.

Let's suppose you put $1,000 into XYZ Mutual Fund. They will send you a statement telling you how many shares of the fund your $1,000 bought on that day, and for our purposes, we'll say that each share was worth $9.45, so you will own 105.82 shares of XYZ Mutual Fund. A month later, if the fund does well and the net asset value goes up, say to $9.95, simply multiply 9.95 (the new value) by the number of shares you own (105.82), and you'll find that your investment is now worth $1,052.91, so you'll be ahead almost $53 for one month's "work."

Be sure to track your returns. The Mutual Fund Alliance has an easy formula for calculating the *total* return on a mutual fund: Multiply the number of shares you own by the current net asset value per share (price per share). Then subtract your original investment amount from the result. Add any capital-gain or dividend/interest distribution that you did not reinvest. Divide the total by the original investment and multiply it by 100 to convert the decimal answer to a percentage.

WHEN TO SELL A MUTUAL FUND

1. If the fund has changed its portfolio mix and no longer meets your investment objectives
2. When a new management team or manager is assigned to the fund, and there is no established track record for reference
3. When the fund contains many stocks that are the same as or similar to those represented in the portfolios of other funds you own.
4. When the fund is consistently underperforming other funds with similar investment objectives and risk parameters. Be sure to take a long-term perspective when evaluating performance. If you have made your purchase decision based on the fund's long-term performance, be sure you are not making the decision to sell on a poor quarterly performance.

Exploring Stocks

The stock market was created so that the general public could invest money in companies they believed in (and possibly gain financially as a result), while the companies benefited by having additional cash to invest in their business. The price of stocks rises and falls based on supply and demand. When demand is high (if, for example, the company announces good news), stocks command a higher price because shares are harder to come by; when demand is low (based on bad news), the prices drop. The actual method of buying and selling stocks used to be handled as an auction; today the principles of an auction are still in place, but most orders are "auctioned" and exchanged within a computer.

So how do *you* make money? There are essentially two ways: dividends and capital gains. Some companies take a portion of their profits and share them with stockholders in the form of *dividends,* or cash payouts. Although some companies pay dividends year after year, this is not guaranteed. If the company experiences problems, it can cut or even eliminate the dividend.

Other companies plow their profits back into the company so that it will grow more quickly. If that happens, the stock should gain in value, creating *capital gains.* If you sell your stock for more than the price at which you purchased it, you will have experienced a capital gain.

New investors are always puzzled by the different exchanges. Why is one stock traded on the New York Stock Exchange and another on NASDAQ (National Association of Securities Dealers Automated Quotations)? There are about 150 different exchanges worldwide, and where your stock is listed has something to do with its prestige and acceptance into one exchange or another. Most major "blue chips" are listed with the New York Stock Exchange, although the American Stock Exchange has a good number as well. The NASDAQ is not actually an exchange in and of itself, it is a recording system for the over-the-counter (OTC) market, which includes many regional exchanges with smaller companies. There is no secret to knowing on which exchange a particular stock is listed other than asking your broker.

More important to an investor are the types of stocks there are to consider:

Blue chip stocks are the largest and strongest companies. These stocks are considered safer than most because of the enormous resources of these companies and their long tenure. Though the stocks do fluctuate, they are more likely than stocks of smaller companies to rebound quickly.

Secondary issues come from firms that are smaller and less well known, but they are still large, well-established companies. Like blue chips, they usually have a diversity of holdings, making them less vulnerable to a downturn in a single area of the economy.

Income stocks are the stocks of companies that are well known for paying dividends, often utilities such as telephone, gas, and electric companies.

Growth stocks are those from newer, smaller firms such as biotechnology and Internet companies. Investments in these stocks are generally made for their appreciation potential as the company grows.

Penny stocks are the securities of smaller companies that are thinly traded, and traded infrequently, making them illiquid at times. They are long shots—high-risk but offering the possibility of great rewards if they should "make it."

GUIDELINES FOR PURCHASING A STOCK

Once you are considering a possible stock to buy (it's been recommended by a friend, or you've noticed continuing good news
about the company in the newspaper), more research is necessary.
You'll want to learn if there are any "shadows" in the company's
background. Call your financial advisor and ask for some information on the company. Or take the following steps.

- Call the company for a copy of its annual report or ask your
  advisor to get you one; the annual report will tell you about
  what goals the company had set and how well they've done at
  meeting them. (See page 333 for information on how to read
  an annual report.)
- Visit the library and take a look at *Value Line Investment Survey,
  Moody's Handbook of Common Stocks,* or *Standard & Poor's Reports,* any of which will provide more insight into the company's track record and how the analysts feel about it. (See
  page 333 for information about using these research tools.)
- The on-line services offer a wealth of financial information. If
  you subscribe to one, find out what information is available to
  you.

If there doesn't seem to be any bad news on the company, and it
is expected to continue to do well, call your advisor. If he or she has
no major negative information, you're probably ready to invest.

When you make your stock purchase, ask your financial advisor
how the company is listed and on which exchange it is traded, if
you haven't already picked up that information in your research.
Also ask what commission you will be charged for the purchase.
(Costs vary, so you have to ask.)

As you've already learned, you don't need big bucks to get started
in the stock market, but you may be wondering what you should do
if you can't yet afford 100 shares of a particular company. The solution lies in what is known as a DRP (dividend reinvestment program) through the company itself. (Not all companies have this
program, but a good number of the blue chip companies do.) You
can buy as little as one share of stock through your advisor or
through the company to start this program, and it's a wonderful
way to continue adding shares to your portfolio. Your dividends are

automatically reinvested in the company and are used to purchase additional shares as they accrue. You can also purchase additional shares directly from the company for a minimal transaction charge—often as little as $1.

My one wish for all women is to at least start by purchasing a few shares of a company that has a DRP program and watch what happens as your dividends are reinvested. I often recommend to women who have built up to 100 shares of a particular company through a DRP that they then move on to another company that offers a DRP. Women can get more information on DRP programs by contacting the National Association of Investors Corporation (see Appendix C), which disseminates information on participating corporations.

BLUE CHIP STOCKS

If you've ever played poker, you know the derivation of the term "blue chip." Like the most valuable blue chips used in poker, this market term is used to describe the stocks of the largest, most consistently profitable companies. Despite their nickname, blue chip stocks can also go down, so don't be deceived.

THE IMPORTANCE OF GOOD RECORD-KEEPING

Every time you buy or sell stocks, mutual funds, or bonds, you will get a confirmation slip listing all of the details—including dates of trade and settlement (the settlement date is the date on which either cash, for the buyer, or a security, for the seller, must be in the hands of the broker in order to satisfy the conditions of a security transaction), price per share, commission, tax, and the total dollars invested. It is important to retain these slips not only because they are useful in matching your buy and sell orders but also because they have the information you will need when filing your income tax return.

Though you could certainly keep everything in a file folder, you may find that a loose-leaf binder works better. In the loose-leaf, you can keep your monthly statements as well as the confirmation slips, and by filing them chronologically, you'll find it easy to flip through to find what you need.

If You Do Little Else . . .

Even if you're not yet in the habit of following your investments regularly, you *must* read your brokerage statements when they come, to check for general accuracy. For example, if you have $10,000 in your brokerage account, and you suddenly receive a report that shows only $3,000, you're going to want to make a phone call right away. Chances are a clerical error has occurred, and your advisor will be able to take care of the matter immediately.

If you've not invested before, call your financial advisor when you get your first statement. He or she should be willing to walk through it with you.

FOLLOWING THE STOCKS

When you want to check a stock, you need to ask your financial advisor which exchange the stock is listed on and then look at the alphabetical listings in the newspaper. (These listings are alphabetical by full name. For example, IBM is listed as if "International" were spelled out.)

To follow the stock, you'll need to understand the stock listings:

52-Week				Yld		Sales				
High	Low	Stock	Div	%	P/E	100s	High	Low	Last	Chg
25 1/4	15 5/8	BoisCOff	...	...	25	325	21 1/8	20 3/8	21	+ 9/16
9	3 1/4	Bombay	...	...	dd	2368	8 3/4	8 1/4	8 3/8	− 5/16
12 1/4	8 1/8	BordCh	.80 e	8.6	13	882	9 9/16	9 5/16	9 5/16	− 3/16
27 1/16	15	Borders s	...	...	35	1449	27 1/16	26 1/2	27 1/16	+ 9/16
58	33 1/4	BorgWAu	.60	1.1	14	561	56 1/4	55 15/16	55 15/16	− 1/8
18 9/16	9 1/4	BorWSc	...	...	25	139	18 5/16	18	18 1/4	− 1/8

The figures in the far-left column report the high and low of the stock price for the previous fifty-two weeks. The high and low figures just to the left of "Last" and "Chg" show the market activity for the stock price for that day. Prices are reported in $^1/_8$-point increments ($^1/_8$ of a dollar is 0.125 cents).

Div (dividend): the latest annual dividend paid by that stock on each share owned

Yld (yield): the stock's latest annual dividend expressed as a percentage of that day's price

P/E (price-earnings ratio): the price of the stock divided by the earnings reported by the company for the latest four quarters

Sales 100s: refers to the volume of shares, in hundreds.

Last: the closing price for the day

Chg (net change): the day's closing price compared with the previous day's

The "When" of Buying and Selling Stock

If you're just beginning in the market, forget about market timing. No one has successfully timed the market for the long term. Instead, invest in good solid companies and hold on. If you're ahead of the game in a few years when you're ready to sell, then your money has done its job.

The secret to buying stocks and mutual funds is to evaluate how a particular investment fits into your overall portfolio. In general, to build a solid portfolio, you'll want to invest across various industries. This type of diversification will ensure that something in your portfolio will be blooming at any given time. Another thing to keep in mind in building a portfolio is to select stocks that represent large, medium, and small companies. The objective of your portfolio will determine whether it is weighted more heavily toward large blue chip companies or smaller companies that are more volatile but can potentially provide greater growth.

Although every financial advisor has different rules about how many individual stocks should be in any one portfolio, I recommend that you have no more than ten. I've arrived at this number because I know it is very difficult to track and monitor more than ten stocks and do a good job of it. Within a portfolio that contains ten stocks, I will bet you that over time, five will perform exactly as you expected, two will be disappointments, and three will perform beyond what you ever could have anticipated or imagined. However, your combined net gain from all ten will usually put you ahead of the game.

So what do you do with those stocks that are not performing to your expectations? Some in the financial industry would advocate selling a poor-performing stock after it depreciates in value 15 percent. Rather than using a set formula for a sell order, I recommend that women use this figure as a reminder to do some additional homework.

First, you need to evaluate why that particular stock is dropping. Find out the following: Is the stock in a particular sector that is out of favor at the moment? If so, you might want to hold on to it, because every sector has ups and downs.

The more important question to answer is whether the stock is performing poorly because of some underlying company problem (lack of anticipated sales or poor earnings growth, for example). If the problem is poor earnings, you need to determine whether this is a temporary or permanent phenomenon. If it looks like earnings will be stalled for the foreseeable future, it may be a signal to sell that particular stock.

On the flip side, should you sell a stock that has appreciated in value more than 15 percent? Again, you need to do your homework in consultation with your financial team to determine the answer. A critical aspect of the decision will be based on what your expectations were when you selected the stock in the first place. If you bought a stock for the purpose of generating a certain level of appreciation, then perhaps you do want to sell it. However, when you sell a stock, keep in mind that you will probably want to reinvest the money. Are you going to be able to find an alternative that is able to perform in the same manner as the one you sold? Also before selling, factor in the capital-gains-tax consequences in addition to the commission you paid for the purchase. Ideally, you want to make sure that you are truly coming out ahead in this transaction.

If you decide to hold a stock that is performing well, be sure you continue to monitor the quarterly earnings of the company. You want to make sure that the long-term trends on earnings are positive. The biggest danger is complacency—the belief that just because a stock has traditionally done well, and is meeting or exceeding expectations, it will continue to do so.

Exploring Bonds

Bonds are a good investment when you are looking for income. Bonds have various maturities (from one to thirty or more years), and bonds held to maturity have no growth potential or protection against inflation. If interest rates go up, the fixed rate of interest on your bond will not be affected, but the current value of your bond will go down. However, if interest rates have gone down since you bought your bond, the value of your bond will go up, because you will have a higher interest rate than is currently available.

Tax-free municipal bonds are popular with those in high income tax brackets in high-tax states. While the yields on these bonds are less than for other types of bonds, the tax-free aspect makes them attractive because by not paying taxes on the income, you effectively receive 2 to 3 percent more income from the "munis." Remember, it's not what you make, it is what you keep that counts.

Your tax bracket will determine if this is a good investment, so check with your advisor.

A NEW VIEW OF A DOWN MARKET

Someone once said, "The stock market is the only place where a sale [dropping prices] causes people to run the other way."

As an investor, next time you hear the market is down, think of it as a buying opportunity. That blue chip that's been a little out of your price range may now be within reach and "on sale."

Three Handy Investment Tools

The Annual Report. While reading through the text and looking at the pictures in the front section of an annual report might be a leisurely undertaking, what you're really looking for are the two tables in the back of the report: the balance sheet and the income statement. The *balance sheet* shows how strong a company is by subtracting what it owes (liabilities) from what it owns (assets). A conservative investor might look for companies that have ample working capital, with current assets at least twice as large as current liabilities, for example.

The *income statement* (also called the earnings report) shows how much a company makes or loses during the year. It will show the amounts received from selling goods or services and other items of income balanced against the costs incurred to operate the company.

Figures given in the income statement can help you determine a company's profit margin and whether or not its operation is profitable. To determine this, take the operating profit and divide it by sales. For example, if a company has $900,000 in sales and shows $90,000 in operating profit, we would get a ratio of 10 percent. This means the company makes 10 cents on every dollar. To get a better picture of this, you need to compare this profit to the profits of previous years to see if it is improving.

A company's earnings per share (EPS) can also be determined from the income statement, and this is another figure you want to see grow over the years. Divide the net-profit number by the number of common shares outstanding—this will give you the earnings per share.

A financial report also reveals how much money a company is putting into growth (research and development), how its cash flow is changing, and whether or not the stock value has changed due to increased dividends or stock splits.

The most important thing to remember about any of these figures, however, is that what really counts is comparison. Is the company doing better than it was before? How will it perform in the future?

Value Line Investment Survey. The *Value Line Ratings and Reports* is a reference tool (available in almost all libraries) that reports on individual stocks to provide investors with information about the timeliness of purchasing a stock, the risk level, historical performance, and other factors. It is designed so that it can be updated constantly by adding inserts and is the most widely used resource for individual investors.

It is a vital tool for selecting stocks. One thing even novices can check for is Value Line's weekly ranking of stocks. Stocks are ranked from 1 to 5, 1 representing the stocks most likely to outperform the market, and 5 being those most likely to underperform in coming months. As your knowledge grows, you'll find it fun to be able to read so much in-depth information about a company's financial standing. The reports quickly reveal a company's strengths and weaknesses.

The Prospectus. This is useful if you're considering a mutual fund. It indicates the minimum amount of money required to open an account; the investment goal of the fund; the fees; the fund's past performance; the risk; how to purchase and redeem shares; and what services are offered to shareholders. The prospectus is a legal document, so it also contains the names of the funds' managers, the fund company's address, and other pertinent background information. Most important, the prospectus identifies the types of instruments (stocks, bonds, etc.) in which the fund invests its money.

THE SINGLE BEST MATH TRICK YOU'LL EVER LEARN

Do you know the Rule of 72? It's a terrific way to find out how long it takes invested money to double. By dividing 72 by the interest rate you're earning, it will give you a rough idea of how many years it will take your money to double.

It works similarly to show you how quickly your money is losing value. Divide 72 by the current inflation rate to find the number of years it will take prices to double.

How to Pick Investments Based on Shopping for Eggplant

I want to share with you a personal story about my eighty-nine-year-old grandmother, whom I have always known as Nana. She has lived in the same apartment in Hell's Kitchen in New York City for sixty-four years, ever since she immigrated from Sicily. Although Nana has never really liked to share her finances with anyone, I have been the exception, because, as the oldest grandson, "I walk on water." (Those of you who know the Italian culture know what I mean.)

For years I have suspected that Nana was a "mattress stuffer," because she pays for everything in cash, can't speak English well, and doesn't trust banks.

One day when I visited her, I was talking about my work at the NCWRR seminar that I was conducting in the city, and with a twinkle in her eye that I hadn't seen in years, she went into her bedroom and brought into the kitchen a shopping bag full of documents for her current year's taxes. She pulled out a year-end statement from a brokerage firm that indicated she had earned 19 percent on her investments that year. I was amazed . . . I never thought she knew anything about purchasing securities, let alone making a 19 percent return on her money.

I asked Nana how she had earned so much money. She said that over the years, she had made investments using the same rules she uses for buying eggplant. I have gotten her permission to share with you what her rules are:

1. If the eggplant has just come into the store, don't buy it—you can't tell if it will get ripe later. In stock terms, don't buy an investment that doesn't have an established track record.
2. If the eggplant has bruises on it, don't immediately disregard it—it may get ripe later. Certain stocks may look "battered," but that doesn't mean they won't come back.
3. Don't immediately pick an eggplant because it looks "perfect"; it may be rotten inside. Be cautious of any investment that looks too good to be true.
4. Before you finally buy your eggplant, give it a good pinch to make sure it feels right. In making a decision to buy an investment, check it out and then follow your instincts.
5. Once you slice it open, and it's not "white like snow," bring it right back to the market. Make sure the investment you buy is what you wanted and what you expected. If not, sell it.
6. When you finally cook your eggplant, use just a little heat—it will come out more tender. Don't rush a good investment. Time will work for you if you let it.
7. Finally, have a good relationship with the grocer who is selling you your eggplant—he or she will steer you toward the bargains. Having a trusting relationship with your financial advisor will result in better information.

As Nana has certainly proved, one's age or background has little to do with one's ability to maximize finances and investments.

Planning Your Portfolio

As you consider your investments, you might think of balancing your portfolio the way you go about planning a meal. You need small helpings of several items to make it a balanced meal—or a balanced portfolio.

Financially, you must always keep in mind three words: *stability, accessibility, return.* These will be your watchwords when it comes to balancing your portfolio. Some of your money should be stable, some should be accessible, and some must pay a good return.

Savings needed in four years or less should be put in an absolutely safe place—money market mutual funds, savings bonds, bank CDs, or Treasury bills. Although these investments earn low returns, your money will be there when you want or need it. In this category, also put emergency savings, money for the down payment on a house, and for college tuition payable within four years. This is your cash portfolio.

Savings you won't touch for five years or more should be invested in stock and bond mutual funds. The stocks of large companies have returned an average of 12.6 percent annually since 1950, assuming all dividends were reinvested; government bonds earned 6.2 percent. This is the kind of growth you need for a retirement nest egg. (In this case, I mean well-defined stock-owning mutual funds. Individual stocks are a much higher risk.)

Why is the five-year rule important? It is based on the length of time it has taken in the past for the stock market to recover after a drop in price. By recover I mean returning to its value prior to the decline, assuming that dividends were reinvested. Since World War II, the market has come back from a sharp drop in about two years on average. The longest recovery period was three and a half years, following the downturn that started in 1972.

If you'll need your money in less than five years, there's a risk that the market will fall and not recover in time. But if you can leave your money untouched for a longer period and ride out the decline and recovery, you should wind up ahead.

In general, you need to select investments that will provide you with income to last a potential span of thirty years after the traditional retirement age of sixty-five, so consider adding some aggressive-growth mutual funds to your portfolio during your midlife years.

As you come closer to age sixty-five, move at least 20 percent from the riskiest assets of your portfolio into a solid growth and income fund. The rationale for this decision is that because of inflation, extra health costs, and the possibility of widowhood, you will not be able to depend solely on income-generating investments.

Although diversification is important to both men and women, our research indicates that women are much more likely to have savings/investments clustered in low-risk, guaranteed instruments. If you are extremely risk averse, put 20 to 30 percent of your portfolio into a conservative mutual fund. Even in a conservative portfolio, diversification reduces risk.

Important Components for Financial Success

1. *You:* The first and most important member of your financial team is you. It is your money, and you are ultimately responsible for your financial future. Don't delegate your future to anyone.
2. *Self-education:* To know how to select the right investments, you need to educate yourself by attending a financial seminar and reading financial magazines, newspapers, and books.
3. *Your financial advisor:* It is my opinion that you need a financial advisor to help you attain your goals—particularly if you perceive yourself as a financial novice.
4. *Monitoring your investments:* Putting your money into an investment is only the first step. You need to be vigilant in monitoring its performance to determine whether it is meeting your expectations.
5. *A "can do" attitude:* If you believe you can, then you can—a simple statement but an attitude it is sometimes difficult to maintain. In assembling your "team," you want people who are positive and optimistic. If you go in with the notion that you can never find anybody to trust, or will never find the right investment, you are much more likely to fulfill your worst fears.

In financial seminars I am frequently asked, "What does it take to be a successful investor?"

I tell audiences: "Money and time, both of which should be within your grasp."

If you've followed the advice set out in earlier chapters of this book, you've learned that an amount as small as an extra $5 a week can make a difference. Add time to any size investment and you'll find that it's your greatest benefactor.

What can you add to really make it work? Eagerness, intelligence, and the willingness to monitor what's going on. You'll find the process much easier than you think.

19

ALL FIRED UP WITH NOBODY TO CALL?
Creating a Financial Support System

"I didn't think I had enough investment money for a broker to be interested in me. Then I learned that many of them are willing to start with a small account, trusting that if the relationship goes well, the account will grow."

Peggy C. is an African American single mother in her mid-forties who has always been financially savvy. Throughout her teen years, she worked part-time, and though she never attended college, her work ethic, drive, and basic intelligence led her to a very successful career. Because of her need to support herself and her daughter, she watched her money very carefully and always took full advantage of company benefits, including savings and investment programs.

Despite this obviously positive track record and a high degree of interest in investing and money management, Peggy reports that one of the smartest things she ever did was turn to a financial advisor. *"I have been very comfortable with my advisor from the beginning because there was never any pressure. After eighteen years at [one company] I own a great deal of stock there, and though I've sold some over time, my advisor never rushed me to do anything.*

"She also places emphasis on education," Peggy continues. *"She suggested I keep a journal about stocks that interested me. That way I could follow them for a period of time, or ask her about them, and I could be in charge of my own decision-making—with her as my partner. She just keeps telling me, 'I don't want you to hand your money over to me; I want you to understand what I'm talking about so that you can make the decision for yourself.'*

"That's my idea of a great partnership," concludes Peggy.

Peggy's situation is the ideal. A strong, intelligent woman with an average amount of financial knowledge has found a professional who can advise and support her, and she has been fortunate to locate someone who is interested in a long-term partnership.

Unfortunately, Peggy's story is not typical; yet as more and more women take charge of their money, they (and men too) need to find professionals whom they trust. In recent years, financial products have become more and more complex, and professional advice can be invaluable. Without an adequate support system, it is difficult to make good, knowledgeable decisions about investing. Selecting a stock or mutual fund is relatively simple compared to knowing when to sell it.

Various NCWRR research studies provide an alarming picture of how inadequate women's financial support systems generally are. The following findings paint the picture:

- 66 percent of women interviewed for the Women Cents Study indicate that they don't have a financial advisor/broker they can trust.
- When those interviewed for the Scudder Baby Boom Survey were asked to rank their investment experience, over 44 percent perceived themselves as novices, yet over 44 percent of both men and women had no plans to consult a financial professional in the future.
- When asked whom they rely on for financial advice, baby boomers responded as follows: Only 6 percent rely on a stockbroker; 13 percent rely on a financial planner; 4 percent rely on a banker. The most often used source for financial advice is personal research.

Yet women particularly would enjoy having a financial advisor. The Dreyfus Gender Investment Comparison Survey revealed that more women than men want to keep their investments simple and easy to understand (56 percent of women vs. 45 percent of men). With advice, this emphasis on "simple" wouldn't be necessary.

This trend concerns me. We spend more time interviewing nannies, house-hunting, locating a physician, or shopping for a new car than we invest in building a team to help us safeguard our most important life support system—our money. Yet a good financial team, including a financial advisor/broker, accountant, and insurance agent, can help you to select investments that are tailored to your risk level, long-range goals, and desire for liquidity.

Based on our research, we have found that if women become aware of the importance of developing a financial support system, they generally follow through and create one. (With men, ego often gets in the way of asking advice. If you're lost and a man is driving, isn't it a given that you'll drive around for a long time before he stops to ask directions?) For that reason, I trust you'll start gathering some names right away.

This chapter will offer you advice on building your support system, and we'll discuss:

- Establishing a relationship with your bank (or banker)
- Selecting a financial planner or advisor
- Working with a broker
- Ascertaining whether you have a good insurance agent and accountant or tax preparer
- Gaining support through an investment club

WOMEN AND BANKING—YOU HAVE THE POWER

In most American families, women handle the majority of money management tasks, including balancing the checkbook, paying bills, and conducting the family banking. Observe any bank line and chances are you'll notice that a high proportion of the bank's customers are women. Since women also keep a significant amount of money in passbook accounts, they represent a powerful consumer group for the banking industry, and today's banks want to keep their business.

This means you can exert some control. In the Money Matters in the 90s Survey, the women we polled indicated that they wanted five things from their bank:

1. Being perceived as a valued customer
2. Having their financial and loan needs understood
3. Being provided with good value for their money
4. Lower checking and transaction fees
5. Being treated in the same manner as a male customer

If you aren't getting what you want from your bank, move your business elsewhere.

Banking Basics

There was a time when families relied on banks for almost all their financial needs, but that was when the opportunities for personal investing were less complicated, and banks—rooted in small-town decency—featured a friendly banker who knew you and knew your family.

Today, in most places, your small-town bank has been replaced by the branch office of a multistate financial entity, and the odds are that you visit the ATM machine far more often than you go into the bank. If you do step in, where is your neighborhood banker? She's there, but only until she's transferred to another branch.

For that reason, although you *do* want a relationship with your bank, that relationship will be based on the financial benefits offered, not on whether banker Mary Smith or Bob Jones went to high school with you.

While some banks may no longer offer the best investment options for your money (some have actually been quite aggressive about getting into the business of selling a full range of investment options), a bank is still an important part of your financial picture, because it offers a convenient "way station" for your money. You need a place that offers ready access to your spending money (the ATM machine) and the option of a checking account. (If you're married and share a joint account, you should have a personal one as well.)

You ought to reevaluate what's important to you, keeping the following in mind.

- *Convenience:* As they have begun to market themselves more actively, banks have learned that they need to be where people are—branch offices are opening in malls and supermarkets, and ATM machines are going in every place imaginable.

- *Electronic capability:* You may not be interested in banking through your personal computer right now (and you don't have to be), but it's the way of the future, so ask what your bank is doing in this area. If it has made no inroads into electronic banking, this may be a sign of a backward bank; you might do well to look elsewhere.

- *Fees:* Examine your current bank statement (you do this regularly, don't you?) and look to see what fees, if any, you are being charged. Some banks charge a basic fee plus a per-transaction charge (sometimes this includes use of the ATM), and the costs can mount quickly. You may want to shop around. Also examine the statement to get an idea of your banking pattern (how many checks per month you write); in shopping around, knowing how many checks you write will be a significant factor in making a decision.

CHECK OUT FREE CHECKING

Banks are aware that they need to be competitive about their fees. Many will provide free checking if you agree to keep a minimum balance—the trick is to find a situation where the minimum balance requirement (it can be as low as $500 or as high as $3,000) doesn't mean you've parked a large amount of money in a no-interest checking account. Here are some issues to consider and discuss with your banker:

1. Will the bank let you link accounts to qualify for free checking? This way you can keep your money in a savings account, money market account, or a bank certificate of deposit, where the money can earn interest while saving you banking fees.

2. Will the bank waive the fees if you sign up for direct deposit of your paycheck? Some banks do. Here's a tip: If you live paycheck-to-paycheck, have the money deposited directly into checking and specify that your employer or the bank transfer a specific amount ($50? $100?) directly to savings. If your financial situation is such that you carry a balance in your checking account, reverse it. Have your paycheck depos-

ited directly in an interest-bearing account, then transfer money into your checking account as you need it to cover your bills.

3. Remain alert to charges on your ATM transactions. Some banks charge if you use another bank's machine; others charge for all transactions—even if all you are doing is transferring money from account to account. Again, talk to your banker about what can be done to get around this fee. If you can't get around it, you may want to find another bank.

Once you're happy with your banking arrangement, sign up for overdraft privileges (and then try not to use them). Overdraft privileges cover your account if you should write a check for more than you have in the account, and though you'll be charged for using the service, it will be less money (and far less embarrassing) than bouncing a check.

WHAT YOU SHOULD KNOW ABOUT WHAT YOUR BANK WOULD LIKE TO SELL YOU

Your bank would like to have your money. Here's what they offer you:

Savings Accounts

No minimum balance is required on a savings account, though there are sometimes fees if your balance drops below a certain figure. The interest rate is low compared to other offerings, but you get high liquidity.

Consider putting some money in a savings account only if you are just starting to build up your nest egg (and you don't have the minimum needed for a higher-return investment) or if you can link it with other accounts to earn free checking privileges.

Money Market Accounts

Money market accounts generally have variable interest rates that usually, but not always, pay slightly better than a savings account. Ask how your bank's interest system operates. You generally need $1,000 to $2,500 to open a money market account and a $1,000 balance at all times to avoid paying a fee. Many accounts offer check-writing privileges so long as you maintain the minimum.

Money market accounts were created in the 1980s to woo back customers who were moving their money out of bank savings accounts to find higher-interest rates. At the time, the interest rates paid were quite high, but this is no longer the case. So, like a savings account, a bank money market account is no automatic "first choice" for your money. The account can be valuable, however, if you can use it to gain free checking privileges.

Bank Certificates of Deposit (CDs)

Bank CDs pay a higher interest rate than either of the previous two options, but as part of the bargain, you have to promise to leave your money there for a specific period of time—anywhere from three months to ten years (one year is typical)—and the longer you leave it, the higher the interest rate. CDs can generally be purchased for as little as $500 and then in incremental denominations. Some brokerage houses offer slightly higher interest on CDs; however, if you can use the bank CD to get free checking, it's worth purchasing one from the bank instead.

If a bank displays the FDIC sticker, all of the above financial instruments should be insured up to $100,000.

In order to be competitive, some banks are training personnel to sell other financial products, including insurance, and stock and bond mutual funds. Some offer a discount brokerage operation for buying and selling individual stocks. Anything purchased through this type of service would not be FDIC-insured. (If you're confused, ask.)

The Value of a Financial Advisor

Financial advisors come in many varieties including registered representatives at brokerage firms (often called stockbrokers), independent financial planners, bank representatives, and insurance agents who offer financial advice.

A good financial advisor can be a lifelong partner who:

- Listens to your needs and goals
- Assesses what you have and what you'll need. (This should involve an evaluation of everything from what you own to what you've saved, what insurance coverage you have, and

what money you'll have coming to you through any retirement plans you've established.)

- Develops an appropriate financial strategy that meets your
  goals, and helps you to understand the risks and rewards of
  investing
- Makes certain that your portfolio is diversified
- Monitors your portfolio with occasional meetings/phone calls
  with you
- Conducts a regular review of your investment goals

A good advisor will help you to avoid:

- Panic selling, when the market dips a few points—or a lot
- Failing to diversify
- Buying at the high and selling at the low. (No one can do this
  perfectly, but your advisor should be dealing with this every
  day and should have more experience than a layperson.)
- Buying investments that are off course for your goals
- Buying yesterday's hot investment (which may not have po-
  tential for the long term)

I'm a big believer in financial advisors because I've seen what
they can do, particularly when it comes to decision-making. If you
scored in the Danger or Caution Zone in the decision-making, control, or risk aversion sections of the Women Cents Self-Test, run—
don't walk—to find a financial advisor who will work with you.

A good financial advisor will help you assess what you have, clar-
ify your goals, and consider your risk tolerance, and you'll emerge
from these initial meetings with a well-designed financial plan that
will guide you in managing your income and expenses, maintaining
a good credit record, and feeling confident about your future.

When should you contact a financial advisor? As soon as possible
(but you'll be better off if you do your homework first). Pick a date a
month or two from now by which time you will want to have made
that all-important phone call. This will give you six to eight weeks
to gather some names from friends.

WHY SOME WOMEN DON'T CONSULT FINANCIAL ADVISORS

In the Women Cents Study as well as the Dreyfus Gender Investment Comparison Survey, women revealed three barriers that kept
them from consulting a financial advisor:

1. They were worried about finding someone they could trust. (Twenty-eight percent reported this concern.)
2. They feared they didn't have enough money to invest to be of interest to an advisor. Forty-two percent of women (compared to only 23 percent of men) indicated that "not having enough money to invest" was a major obstacle to utilizing the services of a financial advisor.
3. They didn't understand the commissions or transaction fees and didn't want to spend money on something they didn't understand. Seventy-nine percent cited the fees as "too expensive," yet 64 percent noted that they didn't really understand the fees/commissions charged. According to the Dreyfus Gender Investment Comparison Survey, women were far more likely than men to cite that the fees/commissions were too expensive (57 percent vs. 33 percent of males).

Women also felt that because an advisor frequently wears two hats—that of advisor and that of salesperson for investment instruments or insurance—advisors might try to peddle them an inappropriate product because of their vested interest in a certain financial instrument. In addition, respondents realized the importance of remaining involved in financial decision-making, and many reported being fearful that an advisor would simply start talking in unintelligible financialese and take control of their money.

I can't deny that you might encounter an advisor who is dishonest (some are) or who doesn't think you have enough money (some cater only to high-rollers, though most are happy to start out with whatever you bring them).

What I can do is explain that a financial advisor can be an asset to your team, and that it's easy to separate the good from the bad by doing your research.

SHOPPING FOR A FINANCIAL ADVISOR: TWO EXCELLENT SOURCES FOR REFERRAL

There are two particularly good ways to find a financial advisor who is right for you:

Ask friends, family, and coworkers for referrals. By talking to people who have a background similar to yours, you'll be more likely to find an advisor who is familiar with the type of investing that would interest you. If you have two kids to put through college, you don't want an advisor who works only with retirees, for example.

Attend financial seminars run by planners/advisors. These professionals are looking for your business, and the seminar will give you the opportunity to judge whether their knowledge applies to you. Many advisors offer you the opportunity to meet with them privately at a later date, providing you with an additional chance to make an evaluation.

FINANCIAL SEMINARS FOR WOMEN: SEPARATING THE GOOD FROM THE BAD

If you haven't noticed, many financial companies are sponsoring seminars for women. These programs range from out-and-out sales pitches for purchasing specific products to excellent educational programs that are nonproduct-oriented. Before running to the phone to register, it would be well worth your while to obtain some basic information.

- Find out who the presenter is and what his or her qualifications are. Checking the qualifications of the presenter provides you with two pieces of information: (1) Does the person have the appropriate credentials for the topic he or she is presenting? (2) Does the person have a background in education—many do. Some have degrees in it; others are adjunct professors at local colleges. While this is not a vital qualification, it can make for a better seminar because the person will probably be more skilled at teaching the material at hand.
- Ask about the content of the seminar to get an indication of whether or not the motive is primarily educational.
- Ask whether the program is oriented for the novice investor or if it's more advanced. You don't want to go to a program that will be above your head or bore you to tears.
- Finally, don't be afraid to request that you not be contacted by a sales representative afterward.

THE TWO BASIC TYPES OF ADVISOR

There are basically two types of financial advisor. One type is a stockbroker (registered representative) who may be referred to as a "financial counselor" or a "financial advisor," and may, in fact, be a certified financial planner (CFP). As in any profession, there are those who emphasize selling you financial products, hoping they will meet your objectives, and those who realize that to do a good job, they need to develop a financial plan tailored just for you. You, of course, will be happier with the latter.

Those who are stockbrokers must be registered with the National Association of Securities Dealers (NASD). NASD requires that representatives undergo regular retraining on rules and regulations, and their companies are required to provide continuing education programs. This is important to you because, with the financial world changing so much, it is vital that you have someone who is abreast of these changes.

The other type of financial planner may work for a bank, represent an insurance company, or be totally independent. Those who are on staff with a financial company (a bank or an insurance agency) may be salespeople of mutual funds, insurance, or annuities, but they will have received special training in order to advise you on the broader financial picture. Those who are totally independent (which is actually not a great number) will charge on a fee basis only, and some people prefer seeking their advice simply because they have no affiliation that might influence their recommendations.

Most states have specific requirements for financial advisors. Financial advisors should also be registered with the Federal Securities and Exchange Commission (SEC) as registered investment advisors.

WHAT YOU SHOULD KNOW ABOUT CREDENTIALS: UNDERSTANDING THE "ALPHABET SOUP" OF DESIGNATIONS

Financial planners and advisors who are not stockbrokers come with a variety of credentials. While, ultimately, the person you use should be someone knowledgeable who demonstrates concern for your specific situation, it can be helpful to know what these various designations mean.

The International Association for Financial Planning (IAFP) and the National Association of Personal Financial Advisors exist to help maintain ethical standards within the profession. While it may be difficult to remember the significance of the following designations, an advisor who lists one or several credentials demonstrates that he or she is certified and has undergone a lengthy and difficult course of financial preparation.

The *Registry of Financial Planning Practitioners,* established by the International Association for Financial Planning, has quite stringent requirements. To become a member, a planner must hold a CFA, CFP, ChFC, CPA, or a degree that has a strong financial services emphasis, must pass an examination, and must complete at least sixty hours of continuing education credits every two years.

The *CFP Certified Financial Planner* designation is earned by people who have passed a rigorous certification exam and have proved their expertise in all aspects of financial planning. The license is granted by the International Board of Standards and Practices for the Denver-based Institute of Certified Financial Planners.

The *Chartered Financial Analyst (CFA)* designation is granted by the Financial Analysts Federation to those who have demonstrated expertise in investing, though many now offer full-service financial planning.

The *Chartered Financial Consultant (ChFC)* designation is given by the American College in Bryn Mawr, Pennsylvania, to those who have passed certain courses and maintain high ethical standards.

The *Chartered Life Underwriter* designation is awarded by the American College in Bryn Mawr. The CLU is the top credential for life insurance agents.

The *Personal Financial Specialist (PFS)* designation is awarded to people who are already certified public accountants (CPAs), have personal financial planning experience, and have passed a comprehensive exam.

The *Chartered Mutual Fund Counselor (CMFC)* designation denotes someone with a specialty in mutual funds.

The *Registered Financial Planner (RFP)* designation is given by International Association of Registered Financial Planners to those who have four years' experience in planning, a business-related college degree, a securities or insurance license, and a CFP, ChFC, or CPA designation.

No single credential is crucial, but the fact that a person has undergone additional training is significant. You then need to evaluate each professional in the context of his or her ability to meet your needs.

THE ADVISOR AS PERSONAL FRIEND: WHY FRIENDS OF FRIENDS MAY BE BETTER THAN FRIENDS

What if your friend or neighbor is a financial advisor? Isn't that the advisor for you?

It depends. Some people are comfortable working only with people they know from college or met on the tennis court; others are horrified at the thought that someone they know is also the professional to whom they are baring their financial soul.

"I want to have a relationship with my broker, and I'm casually up-to-date with her wedding plans and that sort of thing," reports Pat C. *"We didn't start out as friends, and I prefer it that way. I didn't start investing until I was in my forties, and somehow I would have felt very strange about sharing my entire financial history with someone I see in town."*

Vivian R. reflects a totally different viewpoint: *"Thea and I taught in the same school for years. She finally decided to go back and retrain to become a financial advisor, and because I knew and respected her, I knew she would do well at whatever she undertook. I was happy to sign on to be one of her first clients."*

Certainly, there are trade-offs when you select an advisor you know personally rather than someone who is only a professional resource. Although it is an individual decision, remember that whomever you use, you must provide him or her with a complete understanding of your goals and financial resources. Leaving out financial information can only hurt you in developing a comprehensive plan. If you don't feel completely comfortable mixing the personal with the professional, I wouldn't advise it. It is also particularly difficult if the relationship isn't working out for either one of you.

TEN QUESTIONS TO ASK WHEN INTERVIEWING ADVISORS

Meet face-to-face with at least three of the recommended advisors. At the interview, explain a bit about yourself and your financial history, and ask the following questions.

1. Do you work with clients whose backgrounds are similar to mine? If they don't, you don't want to be their guinea pig.
2. What is your area of expertise, and how long have you been

in business? Your earlier screening should have told you that this person is a broker, is affiliated with an insurance company, or is an independent financially based planner, so this question should elicit information on what he or she thinks he does best. As for years in the business, ideally, you'd like to find someone who has weathered the crash of 1987 or an extended down market. Inevitably, the financial markets will go from rosy to less so, and back again, so you'd like to have someone who has had experience in good times and bad.

3. Are you willing to take time to teach as we proceed? Make it clear that you want to be part of the decision-making process; some advisors would prefer to work with someone who won't "hassle" them with questions. However, keep in mind that no one financial advisor can ever meet *all* your educational needs.

4. What is your savings and investment philosophy? You'll find out if it dovetails with your own.

5. How often do you generally call clients? A good advisor will promise to be in touch but will also make the offer that you can call anytime.

6. Could you explain the compensation process to me? Do you earn higher fees on some investments than on others? Ask up front so you'll know in advance what to expect.

7. How often will you review my portfolio? Is there a standard procedure for an annual review? You want reassurance that after the initial plan there will be follow-through.

8. Could you show me a financial plan you've prepared for someone else? An advisor should have a sample, with names blanked out, to show what you can expect.

9. How do you stay up-to-date? Stockbrokers/advisors with major firms draw on gigantic research departments; if the person you're interviewing has no such affiliation, you'll want to know how he or she stays current.

10. Can you provide me with the names and telephone numbers of three current clients? Then be sure to *follow through* and phone these individuals.

After the interview, make a few notes about your reaction. Did the person ask about your financial goals and listen carefully to your responses? Did he or she seem genuinely interested in you and in getting your business? Was he or she patient if you asked basic questions? Did she seem willing to explain what you didn't understand?

No matter how "nice" the person was, your gut instinct following the interview will let you know whether this is the advisor for you.

DOES GENDER MATTER?

I'm often asked whether women should go exclusively to female financial advisors. My answer has always been the same: The gender of a financial advisor is a matter of personal preference. There are some women who come to our seminars who feel less intimidated by a woman financial advisor. For others, the gender of the financial advisor matters little, and some others feel more comfortable with a man. The most critical factor is whether the person (male or female) is listening to your needs and is interested in helping you achieve your financial goals.

SO MUCH INFORMATION, SO LITTLE CONSISTENCY

Women often tell me that they are frustrated by the fact that every planner or advisor has a different recommendation, method, or plan for them.

What you have to realize from the beginning is that financial pundits will always disagree about where the market is, where it's going, what stocks are hot, and how best to position your portfolio for the long haul. Don't be intimidated by all this "noise." A financial advisor and friend once told me, "Do the basic financial homework. Next, find a financial advisor you can trust, who will help you get from point A to Z. After that, close your ears and don't be distracted by the daily noise that is generated by Wall Street—all it can do is keep you up at night."

This is solid advice for long-term investors who are not inclined to move their money around on a regular basis.

HOW DO ADVISORS GET PAID?

Investors must realize that financial advisors have a right to receive payment for the work they do. Creating a financial plan takes time, and a good advisor will do some special research to select products that are right for you.

The advisor may be paid an hourly fee, a percentage of the capital managed, or a flat fee, which is generally based on the complexity of the plan. Some advisors are not compensated at all until you invest, and then they receive commissions on the investments they recommend. Most commonly, advisors receive a portion of their compensation from fees and the rest from commissions. Sometimes the commissions are deducted from the up-front fee. One way to evaluate these planners is to ask what proportion of their earnings comes from fees as opposed to commissions. There is always a danger that planners who are very reliant on commission income will steer you into the kinds of investments that generate the most money.

Insurance agents (life and health insurance agents and property and casualty insurance agents) generally make their money through commissions.

MAKING THE DECISION

The women who visit our Center say that the most important criterion for their choice of a financial advisor is the ability to listen. Women want someone with whom they can connect on an emotional/personal level as well as on a financial level. Although women are not looking for financial advisors to become their best friends, they expect them to understand their life situation and listen to what they identify as priorities.

In Section II, we discussed two types of decision-makers—emotional and cognitive. You'll need to be both to make this decision. Use your emotional side to determine whether this person is hearing what you're saying and listening to your goals and aspirations. Use your cognitive side to determine whether the recommendations being presented meet your goals and objectives. If the chemistry is not right between you and your financial advisor, you will be less likely to turn to him or her to ask questions or obtain support when the market is going through its gyrations.

I stress constantly that each woman must use her intuition in sizing up whether a potential financial advisor is going to meet her criteria for someone she will entrust with her hard-earned money— and the realization of her financial dreams.

DO FINANCIAL ADVISORS FOR WOMEN EXIST?

Although the financial industry as a whole has been slow to respond to addressing the needs of women, there is a growing cadre of financial advisors who understand women's unique financial needs. The following story from one such person's case files demonstrates how a financial advisor can help women help themselves.

The Story of Anne Blake

Anne is the forty-nine-year-old owner of a florist shop in southern California. She has been married for twenty-six years. In relating her financial history, she began: "Shortly after I married my childhood sweetheart, I received an inheritance and I put everything in both names. Before I could blink, the inheritance had vanished—my husband had spent it all. If I wanted any money to spend, I had to put it on a credit card or ask for money, even to buy a present for him! It was then that I realized I had to become more assertive.

"In 1988 I received another set of inheritances from two aunts who remembered me in their wills. I put the money in my own name so that my husband couldn't spend it all.

"For managing this money, I wanted to get a financial advisor who would help me invest it, but I didn't want to get a name from the Yellow Pages. I also didn't want somebody that was going to talk down to me and try to tell me what to do. What I wanted was someone who cared what I needed. Lastly, I didn't want anyone to say, 'Have I got a deal for you!'

"I found [my advisor] through a seminar she was offering. When I went to her office following the seminar, the first thing she did was listen to what I had to say and provide me with some feedback. We started from there. I appreciated [her] honesty and integrity. If I ask about an investment and she doesn't know, she'll tell me where I can learn more.

"What I like most is that she checks in with me—I don't know what her schedule is, but it seems that whenever I'm thinking we haven't talked in a couple of weeks, she's on the phone. Just to touch base and see how I'm feeling about my investments and the return I'm getting.

"I would also like to tell other women that there are financial advisors out there they can trust. Just be sure to ask questions. If the broker doesn't want to answer them, look for somebody else. Have the courage of your convictions, read as much as possible regarding investments, and don't be afraid to make mistakes, because if you don't make mistakes, you won't learn."

The advisor responds: "In working with women like Anne, it is important to listen to their stories. My ability to help her was based on getting her to understand that I heard the difficulties she experienced and recognized what she wanted to do with her money. It is critical to validate what women are experiencing and gain their trust through rapport.

"In general, women are still at the awareness stage in terms of understanding the importance of financial investing. At the same time, I believe that women such as Anne have the potential to be proactive investors if they are able to get beyond their fear of risk and need for security.

"Just like Anne's case, I need to be sensitive to the different issues that husbands and wives deal with on money and investing. For example, some married men have the tendency to be intimidated when their spouse comes into a financial counseling session. My job as a financial advisor is to make sure that wives have an opportunity to be a part of the financial decision-making process.

"There are definite differences between how men versus women interact with financial advisors. Men have a tendency to go into a financial counseling session telling you what they want. On the other hand, in working with women such as Anne, it is important to pick up on their life story or financial situation and build from there.

"I am a strong advocate for educating women about different financial investment options before even talking about various products we offer. My philosophy is that the power rests in the hands of my client, and I am just one part of the team. Because women generally prefer to ease into a decision, I use a 'putting a toe in the water' strategy with most of them: I get women to start slowly and overcome their risk-aversiveness by demonstrating easily understood strategies like dollar cost averaging and the importance of diversification. I also recommend that women take a long-term perspective with their investments and put the blinders on when the market begins to dip.

"As Anne said, I believe that an important role of a financial advisor is to do a great deal of 'hand-holding' during down periods of the market. When I met Anne, I realized that it was important that I emphasize that 'someone is minding the store' when the market is going up and down. What helps also is making sure that you evaluate whether your client's expectations are realistic, based upon their investment choices and risk tolerance.

"In working with women like Anne, it is important that I don't create dependency between the two of us. My philosophy is that 'we' are jointly making the decisions. I feel women should shop for a financial advisor who has three qualities: the ability to admit when they don't know something; the ability to show caring and empathy; and most important, the ability to listen.

"Also, because women are very goal-oriented, it is critical that you lay out a long-term plan with clearly defined goals."

FIVE THINGS TO UNDERSTAND BEFORE STARTING A RELATIONSHIP

To use a financial advisor effectively, you need to do the following.

1. You must understand the role of a financial advisor. He or she is no knight in shining armor. Financial advisors are part of your financial team, and the leader of your team is *you.*
2. It is easy to feel that after choosing a financial advisor, your job is done. Absolutely not. You must continue working together to ensure that your long-term needs are met.
3. We all have difficulty with the concept that advisors make money on our money, but advisors must get paid for what they do. Would you expect to go to a doctor for an ailment and not be charged for his or her services? Of course not. As a matter of fact, if the doctor said, "I won't charge you any-

thing," you would probably question the value of the advice you got! Always remember, you get what you pay for.

4. When advisors are brokers or represent an insurance company, clients are frequently very wary. But remember, these are products that you may need—there's nothing wrong with your advisor selling them. Just like a car salesperson should sell you a car that suits your taste and budget, financial advisors have investments that will provide you with what you need to accomplish your goals.

5. A financial advisor is only as good as the information you give him or her. It is critical that you do your financial homework first. One of your most important tasks is articulating what you want to do with your money. Where do you see yourself in ten to twenty years? How much risk are you willing to take to reach your goal? Armed with this information, your advisor can help you create a map.

If You Still Need a Stockbroker . . .

As explained previously, your financial advisor may also be a stockbroker, in which case you've taken care of two "team slots" with one person. If, however, your financial advisor has another expertise or affiliation (such as being an insurance expert or an accountant), you'll want to hunt for a broker. Your advisor may have suggestions, or get recommendations from friends. Be sure to interview—chemistry is very much a part of a good relationship. Just because someone is highly recommended doesn't mean you'll get along well together.

Otherwise, the process is much like looking for an advisor. Refer back to the questions to ask an advisor. In addition to that list, also ask what his or her client-load is. (Forty to sixty is a good number for a broker.)

Be certain that this person works with clients whose needs are similar to yours. If he or she is making major trades for people with million-dollar portfolios, he is not the one to handle your first $1,000 purchase.

If you feel you don't need the advice of a full-service broker, you can purchase securities on-line or via a discount broker, but if you choose this route, always confer with your advisor to make sure your purchases are in keeping with your long-term investment strategy.

WATCH WHAT YOU SIGN

If a financial advisor or broker wants you to sign any type of agreement, take it home and read it first. And if the person should say, "I haven't filled in all the information yet; just sign it so we can get your account up and running," don't do it.

The form usually includes some information about your net worth and your investment goals. You want to be certain that anything put in writing accurately reflects your financial situation and your goals.

THE DISCOUNT BROKER: WHAT YOU SHOULD KNOW

Full-service brokers offer investment advice and generally base their opinions on a mountain of research produced by a company research department. Like everything else in life, you pay for this additional service.

In contrast, discount brokers cut commissions and do not offer advice about what to buy or sell. There are two levels of discount brokers: full-service discount and deep-discount. Some of the larger full-service discount brokers offer walk-in offices and almost all of the services offered by a regular broker, but they don't fund their own research. When asked, they may assemble materials for you on a particular stock, but they still do not make recommendations on stocks the way a full-service broker does. The commissions for this type of broker may be 20 to 60 percent lower than the commissions charged at full-service brokerage houses, depending on how large your transactions are.

Deep-discount brokers offer fewer services for an even lower price, sometimes 90 percent less than what a standard broker charges. Most deep-discounters do not have offices and deal by phone only.

While having a broker who offers advice has definite advantages, you might consider doing what some do: Have a regular account at

a full-service brokerage firm and then do the investing you want to
do on your own through a discounter. It certainly can't hurt to save.
Just make sure the trades you make are based on solid personal research. And don't use your full-service broker for expertise and then
buy through a discount broker—that's not good business.

How to Know When to End a Relationship

In our studies, we've found that among women's strengths are
the fact that they do their homework on decisions such as selecting
a financial advisor and that they are loyal. The latter is a wonderful
quality—until something goes wrong. Sometimes an advisor will
take on so many clients that he or she no longer has time for as
much individual attention, or sometimes it's just a case of a relationship gone sour.

Though women initially seek advisors who have excellent financial knowledge and provide an emotional connection, they've
got to remember that this is a business deal. Since all markets fluctuate (so it doesn't necessarily make sense to drop an advisor/broker
just because the markets—and your stocks—are down), you need
to focus on whether or not two critical components are in place:
relationship and return on investments.

In evaluating whether an advisor/broker is meeting your needs,
ask yourself some critical questions:

- Is the advisor I initially selected still providing me with the
  level of service that made me select this professional in the first
  place?
- Is the advisor still able to meet my long-term needs? (For example, after several years your investment goals may change,
  and you should be investing in new products.) Is the broker
  able to bring in other resources to meet those needs?
- In the face of adverse returns, do I feel that my broker is right
  beside me weathering the storm? (The answer to this fundamental question will tell you whether to continue using the
  same resource.) We are all happy when our money is growing;
  the true test is how well our broker has educated us to deal
  with "bad weather."
- Is the broker still sensitive to my unique concerns and issues
  (such as risk tolerance, need for control, and so on)?

Some women stay in a relationship too long out of loyalty; others reject a broker too quickly because of a downturn in the market. What you need to evaluate is the long-term potential of the relationship and the possibility of good returns. If something in these factors seems amiss, it's time to move on.

And On to the Accountant or Tax Preparer

Unless you already have an accountant, this team member might well be simply a tax preparer who comes well recommended.

Take the time to find someone who has an established tax preparation business and who will be interested in cultivating a relationship with you. You'll save time and money each year by working with someone who already knows your situation and will be focusing on how any tax changes may affect you.

THE IMPORTANCE OF ESTATE PLANNING

A good lawyer is an important part of any financial support system, as he or she can help you put together a wise estate plan. If you don't have one, start asking around.

Insuring Against Disaster Through Someone You Trust

The purpose of insurance is to protect you against loss or damage to your home, car, or property. (Life and health insurance are covered in Chapter 16.) While there will be days when paying a few hundred dollars in insurance premiums for your homeowners policy may seem like money down the drain, you need only run into someone who has experienced a fire, a furnace "puff-back," or water damage from a leaking roof to realize that having a check from the insurance company could make all the difference.

What you don't want to do is overpay for your coverage, and that's where a good insurance agent comes in. Like a good financial advisor, an insurance agent should be a good listener. He or she should assess your needs and find the policy that provides the coverage you need for the lowest premium. Look for someone who knows the business and is enthusiastic about it—someone who is "just passing through" probably won't have his heart and soul in finding you the best policy.

There are two types of insurance agent, both of which must be licensed in the state where they do business: The *independent agent* sells the policies of many companies and can shop among competing firms to get the best coverage and price. The *exclusive agent* represents only one company, but if that company is a large one, the agent will have access to a wide variety of plans.

Shop around and compare prices, and when doing so, present to the agent the full range of your insurance needs. Sometimes you can get a better price if you are buying several policies (such as automobile, disability, and homeowners insurance).

To check the soundness of your insurance purchase, you really needn't worry too much about your local representative. What matters is the quality of the company issuing the policy. Once you've been offered a policy, visit the library and ask to see one of the following investment rating books: A. M. Best; Moody's, Duff and Phelps; or Standard & Poor's. You will want to look for the track record of the company and check the ratings for an "A" or better.

Insurance agents make their money by charging a commission on the policies you purchase. Additional commissions are paid each time you renew, so it is to the agent's benefit to keep you happy. Though you may not need to speak to your agent frequently, be sure to keep him or her up-to-date about any major changes in your home or property.

WHEN THINGS GO WRONG

Ellen H. was sold over a dozen life insurance policies she didn't need.; Mary T. was advised to buy stock that had nothing to do with her goals; Jane K.'s spouse left money with a financial advisor and when Jane checked on it after he died, she found that the $30,000 he invested had dwindled down to $20,000.

Just as there are unethical doctors and lawyers, there are unethical financial advisors who will sell you anything for a commission. Unfortunately, over the last ten years I have listened to hundreds of stories like those above. To avoid getting "taken," you must:

- Do your financial homework; do not rely on someone else to do it for you.
- Trust your instinct if you become concerned about something that is being sold to you. Don't feel foolish if you have more questions about a financial product. Anytime you are told that it is a good idea to buy a particular stock, mutual fund, insurance policy, or any other financial product, ask the following: *How will this particular product or investment benefit my particular financial situation?* If your broker or advisor cannot explain it to you clearly, don't buy it.
- If you're newly widowed or divorced, don't make a financial decision during the transitional crisis; and when you do decide, solicit the opinions of your support team.

Investment Clubs

The investment club is a wonderful phenomenon that is changing the lives of many women. These clubs can be a critical component in a woman's financial network. They provide women with a nonthreatening environment for learning the basics of selecting stocks, bonds, and mutual funds. They foster a sense of female community ("we're all in this together"), which helps to dispel fears and anxieties about investing, and they thrive on the notion that ten heads are better than one.

Most clubs are not expensive to enter into, and education is a prime component. Experts on particular types of financial products will be brought in to explain the goals and objectives of the different investments the club will consider.

If you'd like to form a club of your own, start by talking to a group of friends or coworkers to find others who are interested. You'll also need to establish club guidelines. Here are the ones we use for the NCWRR Investment Clubs (those of other clubs may vary):

- Membership. Limited to twenty-one or fewer women.
- Term. The Investment Club partnership continues on a year-to-year basis. On any anniversary date after the start-up, the members may vote to terminate the partnership. A two-thirds majority of the club membership shall rule.

- Purpose. The purpose of the club is to invest the assets of the partnership solely in stocks, bonds, and other securities for the education and benefit of the members.
- Meetings. Held once a month.
- Contributions. The members make an initial contribution of $100 to the club and then make equal contributions at each monthly meeting of $50, payable by cash or check.
- Management. Each partner shall participate in the management of the club on an equal basis.
- Membership withdrawal. Members can withdraw from NCWRR clubs at any time with the following stipulations: (1) At the time the member drops out, she must provide written notice to the secretary of the club, and her share of the assets is calculated on the net asset value of the club at the time notice is given (whether or not the investments to date have shown a profit); (2) the member will not receive her share for sixty days; and (3) the club has the right to replace the member or to continue with one partner fewer in the club. (There are many different ways to provide for dropping out.)

"I recently joined a women's investment club, and I'm learning a great deal. The money I've invested is small enough that I don't worry about losing it, and it's a good environment because some people know a lot, and some know very little, but everyone is learning together," says a woman who recently attended an NCWRR seminar.

Studies have shown that after an average of ten months of membership, most members begin to develop their own personal portfolio outside the club.

Five Ways to Make Sure Your Financial Support System Works for You

Building a financial support system is like listening to an orchestra—the sounds you hear should all come together to make good music. You don't want or need to hear just one musical instrument. Adopt the following strategy to be certain that what you're getting from your financial support system is not just "noise." Ask:

- Have I done my part to understand the role each member of my financial team plays in meeting my financial goals and objectives?

- Have I adequately researched and understood the recommendations being made by members of my financial support team?
- Do I feel comfortable with the fact that I will get a variety of advice and input that may at times seem contradictory?
- Do I know how to sort through the information and pick out what is important?
- Finally, do I feel my financial team players are investing the time to look out for my best interests?

Some Final Thoughts

In coming to the end of this book, you're just starting another journey: Financial education is a life-long voyage. However, if you can begin to think of investing as "fun" and look upon it as a pleasurable hobby, you are likely destined to use the principles set forth in this book and go on to succeed with your money. If you get discouraged at any point in the process, remember that the only way you can fail is by doing nothing.

Please feel free to write me at the NCWRR and let me know how you are doing with your financial goals and investing. Your financial future is important to me.

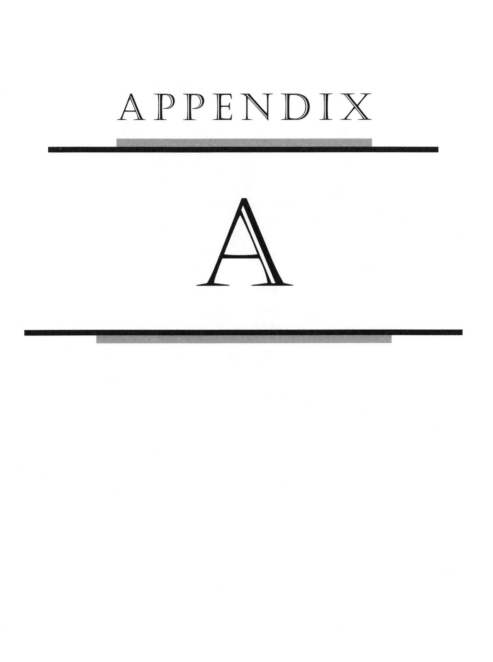

APPENDIX

A

GLOSSARY OF INVESTMENT TERMS

Asset allocation—a strategy for balancing risk within a portfolio. A predetermined percentage of investment dollars is placed in financial products that preserve principal. The remaining investment dollars are placed in financial products that seek growth. The goal is to achieve for the portfolio the highest expected return without taking on more risk than the investor wants to accept.

Balance sheet—the financial statement of a business or institution that lists the assets, debts, and owners' investment as of a specific date. Assets are listed in the order of how soon they will be converted into cash, and debts in the order of how soon they must be paid. Since balance sheets do not list items at their current monetary value but rather in historical dollars and cents (the amount paid at the time of purchase), they may greatly overstate or understate the real value of certain corporate assets and liabilities.

Balanced portfolio—a portfolio containing several different types of investment products. Most balanced portfolios are invested in stocks, bonds, and money market instruments.

Bear market—a period during which stock prices are declining.

Beta—a number that compares the volatility (movement) of a stock's price to that of the total market. A beta of 1 means that a stock price moves up and down at the same rate as the market as a whole. A beta higher than 1 indicates moderate to high price volatility. For example, a beta of 1.5 forecasts a 1.5 percent change in the return on an asset for every 1 percent change in the total market. High-beta stocks are best to own in a bull market and are worst to own in a bear market.

Bond—a long-term debt security representing a contractual agreement by a company or government to repay borrowed money by a specific date and at a specified interest rate.

Book value—a method of measuring a company's worth. To determine book value, deduct the company's liabilities from its assets, then divide by the number of shares of stock. The result is the per-share book value.

Bull market—a period during which stock prices are rising.

Capital appreciation—increase in the price of an investment; also known as growth.

Capital gains/loss—the profit/loss that results from a change in the price of an asset. A *realized* gain/loss occurs when an investment security is sold at a price above/below its cost.

Capital markets—a term encompassing all the securities markets in which stocks, bonds, and money market instruments are traded.

Capital preservation—an investment objective in which protecting the investor's initial investment from loss is the primary goal.

Cash equivalent—an asset such as property or stock that has a realizable cash-value equivalent to a specific sum of money. It is so easily and quickly convertible to cash that holding the asset is essentially equivalent to holding cash. A Treasury bill is a good example of a cash-equivalent investment.

Commercial paper—a short-term, unsecured promissory note issued by a finance company or a relatively large industrial firm. The notes are generally sold at a discount from face value, with maturities ranging from 30 to 270 days. Although the large denominations ($25,000 minimum) of these notes usually keep individual investors out of this market, they are popular investments for money market mutual funds.

Consumer Price Index (CPI)—a measure of the current cost of living when compared to that of a base year (currently 1967). The CPI is equal to the sum of the prices of a number of goods purchased by consumers and weighted by the proportion each represents in a typical consumer's budget. The CPI can be a misleading indicator of inflationary impact on any given person because it is construed according to the spending patterns of an urban family of four.

Contrarian—an investor who does the opposite of what most investors are doing. A contrarian investor often selects securities that are out of favor with the market, because the contrarian operates on the premise that when stocks are very popular they are overbought (meaning that buyers overpay).

Credit quality—a measure of the likelihood that a company will be able to make interest and principal payments on its bonds or other debt securities. Standard & Poor's Corporation and Moody's Investors Service rate the credit quality of publicly traded debt securities. Bonds with the highest credit quality ratings are known as investment grade, and bonds with poor credit quality ratings are known as speculative or "junk" bonds.

Current income—cash interest regularly received on fixed-income investments and cash dividends regularly received on stocks.

Debt—an obligation to pay a specific amount in money, goods, or services to another party. Also referred to as liability. When buying stock, you would be advised to select companies whose total debt is equal to no more than a third of total assets. Debt and asset figures can be found in *Value Line Ratings and Reports,* in *Standard & Poor's Stock Reports,* or in a company's annual report. Usually, the lower the debt ratio, the safer and better the company. A company that is reducing debt is also worth considering.

Diversification—the process of investing in a number of different types of financial products to reduce the risk of poor performance by any one type of investment's having a major impact on overall portfolio results.

Dividend—cash payment made by a company to stockholders.

Dividend yield—a percentage figure calculated by dividing the dividend rate by the market price. For example, if a stock paying $4 in dividends annually sells at $80, the dividend yield is 4 divided by 80, or 5 percent.

Dow Jones Industrial Average (the "Dow")—a trademark for one of the oldest and most widely quoted measures of the stock market price movements. The average is calculated by adding the share price of thirty large, seasoned industrial firms that represents various components in the economy. The term "Dow Jones Industrial Average" or "the Dow" is sometimes used synonymously for the "stock market."

EPS—earnings per share; a company's net income divided by the total number of outstanding shares. Investment managers use it as a measure of the firm's profitability.

Equity—the ownership interest of common and preferred stockholders in a company.

Ex-dividend—the term used to refer to a stock no longer carrying the right to the next dividend payment because the settlement date occurs after the record date determining the holders who will receive the dividend. For example, if XYZ common stock goes ex-dividend on May 31, an investor purchasing the stock on or after that date will not receive a dividend check in the next period. A stock trading ex-dividend is indicated in stock transaction tables by the symbol "x" in the volume column.

Expected return—the return investors anticipate they will receive on an investment over some future time period. The expected return often differs from the investors' actual return.

Financial objectives—what investors would like to achieve with their investments, such as building a retirement nest egg, financing the cost of higher education, funding a special project.

Fixed income security—a security, such as a bond or a preferred stock, that pays a constant income each period. Price changes in a fixed-income security are caused primarily by changes in long-term interest rates.

Fundamentals—the term used to refer to the economic factors underlying the state of a business, such as the company's industry position and its basic income and balance sheet items.

Growth stocks—stocks of companies that have many growth opportunities. They trade at a cost that is sometimes many times their earnings and book value.

Income stock—a stock that has a relatively high dividend yield. The stock's issuer is typically a firm having stable earnings and dividends and one that operates in a mature industry. The price of an income stock is heavily influenced by changes in interest rates.

Investment objectives—the investment strategy followed by an investor. Investment objectives can be designed to generate long-term growth, current income, or a combination of the two.

Investment policy statement—a summary of an individual's or group's investment objectives that serves as a guide for all investment decisions.

Junk bond—a high-risk, high-yield debt security. These securities are most appropriate for risk-oriented investors.

Liquid—a term that describes assets held in cash or in instruments easily converted to cash. High liquidity produces flexibility for an investor in a low-risk position; however, it also tends to decrease profitability.

Market capitalization—the value of a company as determined by the current stock price of the company multiplied by the total num ber of outstanding shares

Market timing—the act of selling investments before they decrease in value and buying when they are *about* to increase in value. Market-timer investors will move their money among stocks, bonds, and money market instruments based on their expectations of short-term price changes in the capital markets.

Money market—the market in which short-term, highly liquid, low-risk assets such as Treasury bills, bank certificates of deposit (CDs), corporate commercial paper, and bankers' acceptances (short-term credit instruments created by a nonfinancial firm and guaranteed by a bank) are traded.

Par value—the stated value of a security printed on its certificate. A bond's par value is the dollar amount on which interest is calculated and the amount paid to holders at maturity. The par value of preferred stock is used in a similar way to calculate the annual dividend. Par value can also be the minimum contribution made by investors to purchase a share of common stock at the time of issue.

Performance—the change in value of an investment or an entire portfolio over a specific period of time. The overall performance of an investment includes any income and capital gains/losses.

Portfolio—the combined securities held by an investor.

Price/Earnings (P/E ratio)—the stock price divided by the earnings per share (EPS). For example, a stock that sells at $100 and earns $10 per share is selling at 10 times its earnings. As a rule, a relatively high price-earnings ratio is an indication that investors feel the firm's earnings are likely to grow. Price-earnings ratios vary significantly among companies, among industries, and over time. One of the greatest influences on this ratio is long-term interest rates. In general, relatively high rates result in low price-earnings ratios; low interest rates result in high price-earnings ratios.

Principal—(a) funds put up by an investor; (b) the amount of money borrowed by a company in issuing a bond or other fixed-income security, representing the amount that must be repaid by the borrower upon maturity.

Reinvestment risk—the risk of being unable to invest the proceeds of a fixed-income investment upon maturity into other fixed-income investments having a comparable interest rate. The risk is created by the possibility of a drop in market interest rates.

Relative price strength—a gauge of a stock's price performance determined by comparing it to the price action of a general market average like the S&P 500 index or, in some cases, all other stocks. A relative strength of 70, for example, means a stock outperformed 70 percent of the stocks in the comparison group during a given period—say, the last six or twelve months.

Risk—the possibility that the actual return on an investment will be different from the expected return. Typically, the greater the risk, the greater the possible return on an investment.

Risk-free investment—a riskless investment. U.S. Treasury securities are considered risk-free investments.

S&P 500—a market value index of stock market activity. It measures the performance of five hundred widely held common stocks and is often used as a barometer for the stock market.

Securities and Exchange Commission (SEC)—a federal government agency, created by the Securities and Exchange Act of 1934, that regulates the securities industry and administers federal securities laws.

Small-capitalization stock—the stock of a relatively small firm with little equity and few shares outstanding. Because small-cap stocks tend to be subject to wide price fluctuations, the potential for short-term gains or losses is great.

Split—the division of a corporation's stock into a greater number of shares. The split may be made in any multiple: two for one, three for one, and so on. A reverse split would be one for three, and so on. Essentially, a firm splits its stock to reduce the market price and thus make the shares attractive to a larger pool of investors.

Stock, common—stock of a corporation that represents an ownership interest in the corporation.

Stock, preferred—stock that has first claim on dividends and/or assets in case of the dissolution of the corporation, up to a certain definite amount, before the common stock is entitled to anything.

Stop order—an order to sell a stock at a designated price. For example, you may own a stock that you want to sell if it reaches a certain price. If you place a stop order, it means that the stock will be sold automatically when the stock reaches that price.

Total return—the total amount a given investment returns to the investor, including any capital gain or loss and stock dividends or interest from bonds or other interest-bearing securities.

Volatility—fluctuations in the value of a security or an entire portfolio. Volatility is viewed as a measurement of an investment's risk.

Yield—a percentage that shows the dividend and interest income paid by a security over a certain period of time. Yield is not fixed. It changes as the market price and individual rate change.

APPENDIX

ASSESSING YOUR NET WORTH

A net worth statement is a tally of your total assets (all that you own) minus your liabilities (what you owe). It is of value because it provides a picture of your current financial situation. If you apply for a mortgage or a loan, a bank is going to want to see a net worth statement, and when it comes to investing, being able to assess where you stand financially will aid you in setting goals and priorities.

What You Have. The first step in drawing up a net worth statement is to list everything you own that has "ready" cash value. (You own furniture, clothing, and perhaps a pet, none of which are readily salable for cash.)

Checking account   _____

Savings account   _____

Certificates of deposit   _____

Money market funds   _____

Mutual funds   _____

Stocks   _____

Bonds   _____

Employee stock plan   _____

Profit-sharing plan   _____

Life insurance cash value   _____

Retirement accounts

  IRA   _____

  Keogh   _____

  401(k)   _____

  Vested pension   _____

Home   _____

Other real property (land, investment property, vacation

    home, etc.)   _____

Collectibles (with resale value)   _____

Money owed you   _____

   TOTAL   _____

These are your assets.

What You Owe. Now you're going to make a list of your debts—everything that you owe. (On items such as credit cards, you needn't fill out any debt if you pay it off every month, a highly advisable thing to do; it becomes a liability only if you're carrying debt from month to month.)

Home mortgage   _____

Other mortgages   _____

Loans

   Home equity   _____

   Car   _____

   Other bank   _____

   Student   _____

Charge card debt

   Bank card   _____

   Other cards   _____

Taxes

   Income   _____

   Real estate   _____

Other debts   _____

   TOTAL   _____

These are your liabilities.

Now for some extremely simple math: Take the total figure from your assets column and subtract the total figure from your liabilities column. This figure will give you your *net worth.*

So long as your assets are greater than your liabilities, you're on your way to better things. If your liabilities are greater than your assets, it means you've fallen into negative net worth, and your first job must be repaying what you owe and setting up a system so that you're not spending more than you have.

You may want to meet with your accountant or a financial counselor for help in getting your finances straightened out. If you're suffering under major credit card debt, you may want to consolidate your debt by taking out a bank loan (at lower interest than what you are paying to credit card companies) to pay off the credit card balances. (Cut up all or most of your cards right after you've paid everything off.) Some people have simply fallen into a lifestyle that is beyond their means. If you fall into this category, you may need to find ways to scale back. A good accountant or a debt or financial counselor can help you get hold of the situation.

You must take care of today's financial situation in order to plan for tomorrow. Whether you're dreaming of a short-term goal like an island vacation or a long-term goal like a comfortable retirement, you can't get there without taking care of the here and now.

APPENDIX

C

ADDITIONAL RESOURCES

The following groups, national organizations, and governmental units provide additional information on different aspects of money, investing, and consumer protection.

Governmental Organizations

Federal Trade Commission (FTC)
Correspondence Branch
Washington, DC 20580
202-326-2418

Part of the job of the FTC is to investigate consumer problems and complaints and to ascertain whether there have been any legal violations.

Internal Revenue Service
800-829-1040

Citizens can receive information on tax filings and guides to tax services.

National Association of Insurance Commissioners
120 W. 12th St.
Kansas City, MO 90034
816-842-3600

This organization provides information on specific state insurance commissioners and disseminates material on regulations that govern the insurance industry.

Pension and Welfare Benefits Administration
Dept. of Labor
200 Constitution Ave. NW, Room N5656
Washington, DC 20210
202-254-7013

PWBA protects the integrity of pensions, health plans, and other employee benefits through the dissemination of worker benefit rights, assisting pension benefit administrators, and developing and overseeing employment-based benefits.

Securities Investor Protection Corporation
805 15th St. NW, Suite 800
Washington, DC 20005
202-272-7450

The SIPC is a government-sponsored organization created in 1970 to insure investor accounts at brokerage firms in the event of the brokerage firm's insolvency and liquidation.

Social Security Administration
Office of Public Inquiries
6401 Security Blvd., Room 4-C-5 Annex
Baltimore, MD 21235
800-772-1213

The SSA operates a toll-free number 7 A.M. to 7 P.M., Monday through Friday, for information on Social Security benefits, for reports of fraud, and to address SSA's customer service standards.

U.S. Securities and Exchange Commission
Office of Investor Education and Assistance
Mail Stop 11-2
450 5th St. NW
Washington, DC 20549
800-732-0330

The SEC is a federal agency that administers U.S. securities laws and is able to assist investors with complaints or questions about their investments.

Financial Education and Advocacy Groups

American Association of Individual Investors
625 N. Michigan Ave., Suite 1900
Chicago, IL 60611
800-428-2244

The AAII is an independent, not-for-profit corporation that was formed in 1978 to assist individuals in becoming effective managers of their own investments through publications, nationwide seminars, home study programs, and participation in individual chapters.

American Bar Association
Division for Public Education
541 N. Fairbanks Ct.
Chicago, IL 60611
312-988-5735

The mission of the ABA's Division for Public Education is to provide programs, develop resources, disseminate technical information, and act as a clearinghouse for a wide range of law-related issues for consumers.

Consumer Credit Counseling Services
800-388-2227

A nonprofit community service agency with over 1,200 offices throughout the country, CCCS helps consumers who are overextended (in debt) with confidential counseling, debt repayment plans, and educational programs.

Museum of American Financial History
26 Broadway
New York, NY 10004
212-908-4519

Founded in 1988, this is America's only museum dedicated to informing the public about the indispensable contribution of the capital markets to the development of the nation and its institutions.

National Association of Investors Corporation
P.O. Box 220
Royal Oak, MI 48068
810-583-6242

The NAIC is a not-for-profit, largely volunteer organization that provides products, services, and professional support for individual investors.

National Council of Individual Investors
1828 L St. NW, Suite 1010
Washington, DC 20036
800-663-8516

The NCII is a national, self-supporting membership organization of individual investors that provides material and services to help in understanding investment products, financial services, and securities law.

National Insurance Consumer Organization
P.O. Box 15492
Alexandria, VA 22309
202-547-6426

This organization provides an array of materials and information concerning the purchase of all types of insurance plans.

National Investor Relations Institute
8045 Leesburg Pike, Suite 600
Vienna, VA 22182
703-506-3571

The NIRI is a not-for-profit professional organization whose mission is to advance the practice of investor relations and the professional competency and stature of its members.

9 to 5 National Association of Working Women
614 Superior Ave. NW
Cleveland, OH 44113
216-566-9308

This organization provides information and educational programs for working women.

Pension Education Clearinghouse
P.O. Box 19821
Washington, DC 20036

This organization provides advocacy, information, and publications related to income needs during retirement, pensions, and the need to plan for early retirement.

Pension Rights Center
918 16th St. NW, Suite 704
Washington, DC 20006
202-296-3778

The Pension Rights Center is a nonprofit public interest group organized in 1976 to protect and promote the pension rights of workers, retirees, and their families.

Investment/Insurance Trade Organizations

Association for Investment Management and Research
5 Boar's Head Lane
P.O. Box 3668
Charlottesville, VA 22903
800-247-8132

The AIMR is an international, nonprofit organization of investment practitioners and educators that grants the Chartered Financial Analyst (CFA) designation.

CFP Board of Standards
1700 Broadway, Suite 2100
Denver, CO 80290
888-333-6659

Provides referrals to CFP's in your local area.

Institute of Certified Financial Planners
7600 E. Eastman Ave., Suite 301
Denver, CO 80231
800-282-7526

The ICFP grants the CFP designation and provides referrals to financial planners in local communities.

International Association for Financial Planning
2 Concourse Pkwy., Suite 800
Atlanta, GA 30328
800-930-4511

The IAFP is a professional organization that acts as a clearinghouse for information on financial planners.

North American Securities Administration Association
1 Massachusetts Ave., NW, Suite 310
Washington, DC 20001
202-737-0900

This association provides the number of your state securities commissioner. You may check a planner's licenses and ask about disciplinary actions.

Investment Company Institute
1600 M St. NW, Suite 600
Washington, DC 20036
202-466-5460

The ICI is a national trade association representing mutual funds, unit investment trusts, and closed-end trusts. It sponsors conferences that are open to the general public.

National Association of Personal Financial Advisors
355 W. Dundee Rd., Suite 107
Buffalo Grove, IL 60089
888-333-6659

The NAPFA is a nonprofit organization that provides information and contacts for investors looking for fee-based planners.

National Association of Securities Dealers
1735 K St. NW
Washington, DC 20006
800-289-9999

The NASD provides investors with educational materials and information on securities traded on the NASDAQ stock market.

Public Securities Association
40 Broad St., 12th floor
New York, NY 10004
212-809-7000

The PSA is a trade group of banks, brokers, and dealers engaged in underwriting and trading federal, state, and local government securities.

American Society of CLU & ChFC (Insurance Agents)
270 S. Bryn Mawr Ave.
Bryn Mawr, PA 19010
800-392-6900

This organization provides a list of insurance agents in your local area with the CLU and ChFC designation.

Security Exchanges

American Stock Exchange
86 Trinity Pl.
New York, NY 10006
212-306-1000

This is an exchange in New York City that trades securities of national interest; the AMEX (or ASE) often trades in the securities of younger and smaller firms.

Chicago Board of Trade
141 W. Jackson Blvd.
Chicago, IL 60604
312-435-3500

The CBOT sponsors commodities courses, offers visits for educators, and provides current quotes at no charge.

New York Stock Exchange
11 Wall St.
New York, NY 10005

Besides being the world's leading securities marketplace, the NYSE provides investor information, educational programs, and data on securities, and acts as a major tourist attraction.

Women's Groups

National Association of Women Business Owners
1100 Wayne Ave., Suite 830
Silver Spring, MD 20910
301-608-2590

NAWBO is the only dues-based national organization representing the interests of all women entrepreneurs in all types of businesses.

Women Incorporated
335 Madison Ave.
New York, NY 10017
212-503-7752

This organization provides women entrepreneurs with information and resources on obtaining business capital, developing a business plan, and effectively operating a company.

Credit Reports

There are three major credit agencies that maintain credit reports:

TRW, 800-392-1122
Equifax, 900-685-1111, charges $8 to get a report.
Trans Union, 216-779-7200

Health Organizations

Group Health Association of America
1129 20th St. NW, Suite 600
Washington, DC 20036
202-778-3200

This organization can provide information on various health plans and their distinctions. They can also provide referrals to HMOs in your area.

APPENDIX

ABOUT THE NATIONAL CENTER FOR WOMEN AND RETIREMENT RESEARCH

The National Center for Women and Retirement Research, based at Long Island University, Southampton, New York, is the first academic entity in the country to focus on the pre-retirement planning needs of midlife women. Established in 1988 by Dr. Christopher L. Hayes, the Center addresses three broad mandates:

- *Research:* to undertake applied studies that uncover and articulate the economic, psychological, and social needs of midlife women prior to retirement
- *Education:* to foster an increased awareness of the need for women to plan for retirement during the middle adult years in order to avoid impoverishment later in life
- *Training:* to sensitize community, public, and corporate leaders regarding the needs of midlife women

THE PREP PROGRAM

A major activity of the Center, the Pre-Retirement Education Planning for Women (PREP) Program, was launched in 1986 with a $300,000 grant from the Administration on Aging, Department of Health and Human Services. PREP was established to provide women with the information and skills needed to create a secure and independent future. The overall goal of PREP is to ensure that the United States does not produce another generation of destitute older women.

By attending PREP seminars and using specially designed handbooks, women are provided with the tools to gain the knowledge and confidence necessary to build their own financial resources. Along with addressing the financial needs of women, PREP focuses on other life-planning skills about which women need to be aware, such as health and fitness, knowledge about employment, and the emotional issues associated with the aging process.

Since 1986, more than 100,000 women have contacted PREP and participated in life-planning seminars nationwide. Professional facilitators help women build a strong foundation in understanding how to navigate through the various transitions that mark the middle years of life. Special attention has been given to organizing seminars within business, union, university, and community settings.

Women can contact PREP for seminar, research, and publication information by calling toll-free: 800-426-7386. The following handbooks and audiovisual materials are produced at the Center:

> *Looking Ahead to Your Financial Future*
> *Social and Emotional Issues for Mid-Life Women*
> *Employment and Retirement Issues for Women*
> *Taking Control of Your Health and Fitness*
> *Long-Term Care Issues for Women*
> *Money Matters for Women: Setting Up An Investment Club*
> *Mid-Life Women and Divorce*
> *Women and Money: Things Your Mother Never Told You About Finances* (videotape)
> *Preparing for Your Financial Future* (audiotape)

THE PREP REPRESENTATIVE PROGRAM

To address the growing numbers of women seeking to attend financial planning seminars for women, NCWRR instituted an innovative program entitled the PREP Representative Program. The goal of this program is to recruit and train financial advisors throughout the country on addressing the financial needs of women. NCWRR selects some of the most outstanding financial professionals throughout the country to provide "Money Matters!! For Women" seminars. These PREP representatives are rigorously trained at the National Center for Women and Retirement Research to go back to their local communities and act as our liaison with women who are requesting both educational programming and financial planning assistance.

To date, thousands of women have benefited from this one-of-a-kind program that bridges the educational mandate of NCWRR and the professional financial community. Only financial advisors with extensive financial planning experience and high ethical standards are accepted into the program. By the year 2000, NCWRR will have PREP representatives in every part of the country. Those interested in finding out more about this aspect of NCWRR can contact us for further information at 800-426-7386.

APPENDIX

E

ABOUT THE NCWRR RESEARCH STUDIES

Throughout the text, references are made to various studies conducted by the National Center for Women and Retirement Research. The following summaries provide more detail about these studies.

Women Cents Study. This was the first national research study to explore women's financial decision-making process from a psychological vantage point. Sponsored by Prudential Securities, the sample of 1,100 women was obtained from NCWRR mailing lists, women's organizations, and from callers to the Center's toll-free number. The sample included women between the ages of twenty-one and seventy-five; all states were represented, with particular attention to a rural-urban mix; and all respondents reflected female employment trends and marital status in the general population. The study was conducted in 1995 by the NCWRR.

Scudder Baby Boom Generation Retirement Preparation Survey. This is a three-year national study to gather information on a yearly basis about the retirement planning actions, attitudes, needs, and concerns of individuals born between 1946 and 1964. Sponsored by Scudder, Stevens, & Clarke, the first poll (1996) was based on a 104-item mail survey developed by NCWRR and sent to a nationwide sample of 15,000 baby boomers. Analysis was conducted on 1,091 baby boomers (47 percent female; 53 percent male). (We received more than 1,091 responses but limited our analysis to this number.) The study includes three retirement planning indices (retirement planning attitude index; retirement planning action index; retirement planning wellness index), which will be used to compare investing trends over a three-year period (1996–98).

Dreyfus Gender Investment Comparison Survey. This was a one-year national study conducted in 1996 to compare the financial attitudes, financial decision-making, investment history, and financial goals and objectives of women vs. men. Sponsored by Dreyfus Corporation, this study is the most comprehensive investigation to date to analyze how women vs. men deal with financial issues. The 108-item survey was mailed to 25,000 males and 15,000 females. A total of 2,000 responses (we received a higher number but analyzed 2,000 for statistical reasons) were analyzed (equally divided between men and women). Respondents ranged in age from eighteen to seventy-five, were married and single, and represented all socioeconomic groups. The study resulted in an unprecedented look at the similarities and differences between men and women with relation to all aspects of financial behavior.

Money Knowledge Survey. Conducted in 1993 in collaboration with Sun America, this NCWRR survey polled over 2,000 women on a national basis. The purpose of this study was to evaluate women's perceptions about retirement, longevity, and their level of financial awareness. The results of this research provided an in-depth understanding of the characteristics of financially secure women who are over the age of sixty-five.

Money Matters in the 90s Survey. This was a regional study that investigated the banking and money management practices of women and men. Conducted between 1994 and 1995 and sponsored by Chemical Bank, the research was based on a 140-question survey mailed to 34,150 men and women living in the greater New York City area. An initial pilot study of 1,000 respondents (equally split between male and female) was used for analysis and reporting for this book.

Gender, Identity, and Self-Esteem Study. The purpose of this national study was to identify how self-identity changes during the adult years. A major objective was to determine how the sexes are similar and/or different in relation to sources of self-esteem. Based on the responses to a 135-question survey that covered the entire life span, the analysis (based on 215 females and 160 males ranging in age from eighteen to ninety) indicated that traditional perceptions of how self-identity is crystallized needed to be updated in order to address the realities of living in the 1990s. This study created a new concept of adult development called Life-Ties, a set of related experiences and the perceptions these experiences evoke within the lives of adults. This two-year effort was conducted between 1993 and 1995.

PREP Poll. Conducted by the NCWRR in 1992, this poll surveyed 5,000 women on the NCWRR mailing list concerning their perspectives on financial planning and the priorities they perceived as important in dealing with money. This mail-in poll was nationwide and consisted of twenty questions. The PREP Poll findings acted as a major impetus to conducting more in-depth examination of the psychological characteristics that constitute a woman's money personality.

Divorce Over 40 Survey. This in-depth national study in 1989 investigated the impact that divorce has on women forty years of age and older. The purpose of this research study was to examine how midlife women adjusted psychologically, socially, and economically after the dissolution of a long-term marriage. A total of 352 females completed a seventeen-page questionnaire and were interviewed over a one-year period.

Financial Literacy Survey. Conducted in collaboration with *McCall's* magazine in 1989, readers filled out a twenty-five-item survey and returned it to NCWRR for analysis and interpretation. Although 20,000 surveys were returned, analysis was conducted on 8,500.

INDEX

AARP. *See* American Association of
    Retired Persons
Accountants, 363
Adolescence/preadolescence, 33–52
    and attitudes toward money,
        34–50
    parents as role models in, 35–39
    school performance in, 33–34
Advisors. *See* Financial advisors
American Association of Retired
    Persons, 262
American Association of University
    Women, 57, 58
Annuities, 306–7
Apter, Terri, 40
Assertiveness, 6
Asset allocation, 27, 371

Baby boomers, 11
    and financial planning, 127, 159,
        203–4, 218–19
    Retirement for, 167–68, 290–91
    savings of, 159–60, 261
Bag lady syndrome, 159, 190,
    191–95
Banking
    accounts, 211
    ATM use, 132, 346
    basics of, 344–47
    certificates of deposit, 347
    checking accounts, 344, 345–46
    money market accounts, 346–47
    overdraft privileges, 346
    savings accounts, 74, 87, 93, 94,
        98, 106, 248, 319, 346
    and women, 343–47
Better Business Bureau, 223
Bonds, 87, 332–33, 371
    certificates, 232
    corporate, 315
    government, 87, 316, 319, 322

interest on, 319, 332–33
international, 323
junk, 319, 373, 374
knowledge about, 6
long-term, 87
maturities, 332–33
municipal, 315, 316, 319, 322,
    333
savings, 315, 316
taxable, 322
tax-free, 333
Budgets, 231–32, 236–37
    creating, 243–47
    expenses, 241–43
    following, 237
    organizing, 232–36

Capital gains, 325, 326–27, 332, 372
Cash flow, 231, 236–43, 259
    statement, 238–43, 259
    worksheets, 238
Certificates of deposit, 6, 87, 107,
    203, 315, 347
Change, 97–117
    acceptance of, 114
    attitude toward, 99
    avoidance of, 105–8
    awareness of, 114
    challenges of, 108–13
    conflicts in, 105–8
    creation of, 105
    enjoyment of, 104–5
    financial, 114, 115
    inevitable, 105
    in life, 103–4
    management of, 105, 114, 115
    openness to, 99–104
    opportunities for, 107
    in perspective, 113
    positive, 113–14
    problem-solving phase of, 114

Change *(cont.)*
  skills of adaptation in, 104
  women's perspectives on, 17, 20,
    27–28
Conflict
  and control, 127
  marital, 142
Consumer Price Index, 372
Control
  actual, 124–25
  dynamics of, 124–25
  financial, 119–37, 142, 143
  of future, 123
  gaining, 212
  influence of education on, 54
  loss by default, 146–49
  mindful involvement in, 124–25
  mindless responding in, 124–25
  obstacles to, 126–28, 130–37
  perceived, 124–25
  personal, 122
  sense of, 33
  theory, 124
  women's feelings on, 28–29
Credit
  buying on, 164
  cards, 128, 246, 248, 250
  of convenience, 249
  defining, 249
  establishing, 232, 247–48, 249
  histories, 248, 249
  home equity, 259
  managing, 68
  poor, 249–50
  quality, 372–73
  reports, 248
  Social Security, 293
  types of, 249
  and women, 247–50

Debt, 373
  consolidation, 246
  reducing, 246
Decision-making, 20–21, 28, 50
  ambivalence about, 121
  cognitive, 31, 176–77, 181–82,
    356
  deadlines for, 89, 92
  emotional, 31, 177, 356

  evaluation of, 182–83
  financial, 31, 175–88
  gender differences in, 178–81
  informed, 218
  investment, 67, 135, 147
  need for, 182
  positive, 182–83
  process of, 31, 178, 186–88
  procrastination and, 178, 185–86
  and research, 176
  and security, 179
  shared, 145
  styles of, 31, 176–77, 181–82
Diversification, 12, 89, 92–93, 205,
    331, 373
  dollar cost averaging, 93, 204, 318
  in investments, 27, 205, 318
  in mutual funds, 320
  role, 149, 164
Divorce, xix, 46, 47, 64, 93, 109,
    200–1
  financial effects of, xxii, 9–10
  increase in, 38
  and pensions, 8, 297
  and Social Security, 293
Dow Jones Industrial Average, 96,
    373
Dreyfus Gender Investment
    Comparison Survey, 42, 43, 59,
    178, 192, 194, 195, 196, 202,
    218–19, 254, 291, 342, 347

Education, 53–70
  continuing, 65–67, 91–92
  and experience, 64
  financial, 68–70, 214–23
  gender disadvantages in, 57–60
  gender-neutral, 55, 62–63
  importance of, 168
  importance of math/science in,
    54, 58–60, 62
  late-starting, 63–67
  parental values of, 61–63
  and risk tolerance, 79
  self-, 61, 91–92
  and self-esteem, 57, 63
Emergencies, 258, 259
Employee Stock Ownership Plans,
    302

Employment
  after retirement, 291–92
  and downsizing, 166, 168, 255
  in financial industry, 9
  gender discrimination in, xxii, 3
  intermittent, 8, 144, 253
  "job priority" in marriage, 146
  job sharing, 8
  loss of, 259
  part-time, 8, 195
  power struggles over, 145–46
  in retirement, 195
  switching, 255
  wage gap for women in, 8
ESOP. *See* Employee Stock
  Ownership Plans
Estate planning, 278–79, 363
Exercise(s)
  in calculating life insurance needs,
    265–66
  in calculating retirement income
    gap, 287–88
  in decision-making, 180
  education self-test, 56–57
  in evaluating control needs,
    128–30
  in evaluating risk-taking levels,
    77–79
  Family Self-Test, 50–52
  in identifying risk-tolerance level,
    90–92
  in net worth assessment, 381–83
  in overcoming procrastination,
    185–86
  in present/future thinking, 170–74
  in setting financial goals, 257–58
  in understanding attitudes toward
    change, 99–104, 115–17

Family
  effect on financial attitudes,
    34–47
  money discussions in, 190
  parental value on education,
    61–63
  relationships, 35–47
  support of education, 53–54
Fear
  of mistakes, 6, 178

  overcoming, 194–96
  of unknown, 6
Financial
  activities, 32
  advice, 106
  awareness, 30
  balance, 105–6
  change, 104–5, 114, 115
  checkups, 89
  concepts, 211
  confidence, 35, 36
  control, 119–37, 143
  decision-making, 31, 175–88
  dependency, 38, 46
  freedom, 73
  goals, 6, 12–13, 32, 251–62
  independence, 85, 147, 179, 210
  knowledge, 208
  misperceptions, 189–206
  myths, 189–206
  objectives, 374
  publications, 214
  research, 107
  risk, 73–96
  sacrifices, 247
  scams, 220–23
  security, 43, 54, 73–74, 109, 141,
    192
  skills, 67
  support system, 341–67
  terminology, 201
  truths, 189–206
Financial advisors, 169, 196–98,
    341–67
  accountants, 363
  barriers to using, 348–49
  Certified Financial Planner, 351,
    352
  Chartered Financial Analyst, 352
  Chartered Financial Consultant,
    352
  Chartered Life Underwriter, 352
  Chartered Mutual Fund
    Counselor, 352
  compensation for, 356
  credentials of, 351–52
  friends as, 219–20
  future-oriented, 219–20
  gender differences in using, 180

Financial advisors *(cont.)*
  gender of, 355
  interviewing, 353–55
  Personal Financial Specialist, 352
  Registered Financial Planner, 352
  risk-tolerant, 219–20
  selecting, 218, 349–50
  stockbrokers as, 350–51, 360–62
  trust in, 204
  types of, 350–51
  understanding, 359–60
  use of, 183, 184
  value of, 347–60
  for women, 357–59
Financial information, 5–7
  and networks, 11
Financial planning
  and baby boomers, 127, 159
  basics of, 66
  computerizing, 236, 256–58
  discomfort with, 53
  and feelings of control, 121–22
  future-oriented, 157–74
  and gender differences, xxi
  inadequate, xix
  insurance in, 263–79
  knowledge about, 30, 65, 207–24
  literacy in, 12
  for long-term growth, 120
  as male domain, 164
  in midlife, 281–82, 285–86
  need for, 10–11
  for old age, xix, 155–56, 271–309
  options in, 218
  present-oriented, 157–74
  publications, 215–16
  resources needed for, 202
  use of networks in, 11
  women's exposure to, 7
  women's potential for, 10–13
  for younger groups, 284–85
Financial seminars, 4, 66, 169, 214, 216, 350
  age groups for, 128
  attendance by partners, 145
  Silent Listeners in, 209–10
  women in, 12
401(k) plans, 298–301
403(b) plans, 302
Fraud, 220–23

Gender
  and advice-seeking, 180
  biases, 7, 192
  and decision-making, 178–81
  discrimination, xxii, 54, 68
  and educational differences, 53–55
  and financial control, 139–56
  and financial planning needs, xxi
  and health care costs, 10
  and pensions, 8
  and poverty, 10, 158, 200
  and risk, 81–83
  roles, 35, 37, 47, 121
  and security, 43, 54, 73–74, 83–84, 109
  and self-esteem, 54
  and Social Security, 9
  stereotypes, 37, 50, 57, 62
  strategies, 40
  upbringing differences, 34–47
  views on impoverishment, 193–94
  and wage gap, 8
  women as educationally disadvantaged, 57–60
Generation X, 128
Goals
  developing, 103
  educational, 63
  establishing, 32
  financial, 251–62
  investment, 159
  long-term, 27, 103, 204, 206, 252, 257–58, 260, 284–85
  personal, 103
  realistic, 251–62
  savings, 159, 258–59
  setting, 88–89, 251–62
  short-term, 27, 206, 252, 257, 259
  strategies for, 32
Greenspan, Alan, 205
Group Health Association of America, 273
Guardianship, 279

Health Insurance Portability and Accountability Act (1997), 269
Health maintenance organizations, 270–71, 272

Income
  budgeting, 231–32

and cash flow, 231, 236–43, 240–41, 259
current, 373
disposable, 159
fixed, 374
for investing, 159
investing for, 6
and marital status, 10
opportunity for, 8
pension, 8
retirement, 6, 287–88
Social Security, 294–96
stability of, 317
stocks, 327
taxes, 329
tracking of, 231
Individual retirement accounts, 123, 302–5
records for, 233
withdrawals from, 305
Inflation, 27, 74, 88, 278, 314
compensating for, 203
manageable, 288
risk, 87
and savings, 288
and Social Security, 294
Information
Blockbuilding Learners, 212–13
computerization of, 236, 256–58
and decision-making, 178
expectations for learning, 212
financial, 5–7, 11, 178, 209–23, 232–33
gathering of, 214–15
Keep-It-Simple Learners, 211–12
learning styles, 209–14
processing, 209–14
Ready-for-Change Learners, 210–11
repetitive, 178
Silent Listeners, 209–10
Inheritance, 125, 126
Insurance, 263–79, 363–65
agents, 363–64
calculating needs, 265–66
cash-value, 267
cost-of-living clauses, 275
costs, 267, 268, 271, 278
deductibles, 272
disability, 273–75

"gatekeeping" restrictions, 278
group, 268, 269–70
health, 269–73
health maintenance organizations, 270–71, 272
indemnity plans, 270
inflation protection, 278
life, 264–68
for long-term care, 275–78
managed care programs, 270
maximum benefits, 272
options, 271–72, 276–78
permanent life, 267
point of service plans, 271
preexisting conditions provisions, 272
preferred provider, 271
renewable term, 267
selecting, 268
straight life, 267
term, 265, 267, 268
traditional reimbursement, 270
universal life, 267–68
whole life, 267
Interest
-bearing accounts, 246
bond, 319, 332–33
compound, 260–61, 290, 307, 308
credit card, 246
deductible, 246
earnings from, 260
loan, 259
rates, 87
International Association for Financial Planning, 351
International Association of Registered Financial Planners, 352
Internet resources, 67
Intuition, 12, 60, 178, 181, 183–85, 357
Investment
accessibility, 314, 337
activities, 21
age groups and, 126–28
aggressive, 89
and attitudes toward change, 97–117
basics of, 212, 311–39
bonds, 315, 319, 322, 332–33, 371

Investment *(cont.)*
  building, 12
  buy-and-hold philosophy, 89
  cash-equivalent, 319
  clubs, 63, 67
  conservative, 27, 29, 87, 89, 161,
    315, 316
  decision-making, 67, 135, 147,
    175–88
  and decreasing risk, 87
  diversified, 27, 88, 205, 318, 331
  dollar cost averaging, 93, 204, 318
  emotional attachment to, 89
  evaluating returns on, 198
  expectations, 289
  finding funds for, 231–50
  fixed-income, 375–76
  and 401(k) plans, 299–300
  future thinkers, 161–62, 170–73
  gender difference in, 82
  goals, 159, 252, 317
  growth, 27, 307, 308, 316, 322
  guaranteed, 54, 75
  guidelines to understanding,
    227–29
  "hot tips," 92, 177, 187
  impulsive, 177
  for income, 6
  income-producing, 27, 315, 316,
    322
  intuition in, 60, 178, 181, 183–85
  knowledge, 19–20, 30–31, 207–24
  limited partnerships, 183, 315, 316
  liquidity, 259, 314, 374
  long-term, 27, 29, 290, 314, 318
  mistakes, 204–5
  monitoring, 32
  motivation for, 159
  mutual funds, 315, 319–26
  objectives, 374
  present thinkers, 161–68, 170–73,
    256
  price swings in, 75
  programs, 169, 203
  record-keeping, 329
  responsibility for, 153
  returns on, 75, 87, 218, 314, 337
  risk-free, 376
  risk pyramid, 315
  rules for, 94, 318
  safe, 75, 179
  scams, 220–23
  selecting, 204, 335–36
  short-term, 27, 87
  simple, 54, 104, 203, 342–43
  speculative, 179
  stability of, 314, 317, 337
  stocks, 315, 316, 319, 326–32
  strategies, 311–39
  time for, 159
  tracking, 198, 333–35
  Treasury bills, 87, 88, 316
  types of, 208
Investment clubs, 167, 202, 216,
    365–66
  all-female, 11–12, 169, 205
  performance of, 12

Keogh plans, 123, 306
  records, 233
Kerber, Linda, 57
Knowledge
  financial, 208
  investment, 19–20, 65
  lack of, 131–33, 207–24
  levels of, 218–19
  and power, 209

Life-Ties Study, 44
Limited partnerships, 183, 315
Living wills, 279
Loans, 232
  for establishing credit, 249
  high-interest, 246
  paying off, 246
Longevity, xix, 167, 253, 254, 286

McCall's Financial Literacy Survey,
    143
Managed care health programs, 270
Medicaid, 276
Medical savings accounts, 269
Medicare, 276
Money
  attitudes toward, 5–7, 30, 63
  borrowing, 127
  control of, 119–37, 198
  and divorce settlement, 47, 49

"duality," 43
early exposure to, 35, 36
effect of personality on dealing with, 5–7
effect of upbringing on dealing with, xxi, 4, 7, 35–50
guilt feelings about, 199–200
marital dialogues about, 150–55
and marital dynamics, 142–43
misperceptions about, 189–206
and mother/daughter relationships, 39–42
myths, 189–206
obstacles to control of, 143–45
and power, 35, 120
reality-based attitudes on, 205–6
"recycling," 247
taking charge of, 97–117
understanding of, 30–31
women's views on, xxi
Money management, 3–13
basic steps in, 88–89
change in, 97–117
diversification in, 12
effect of personality on, 5–7, 15–32
and feelings of control, 122
flexibility in, 33, 104
"learned financial helplessness" in, 289, 290–92
and marital status, 9–10, 139–56
by mothers, 43
personality traits in, 33, 162
and procrastination, 185–86
risk tolerance in, 33
skills, 128
Money market accounts, 6, 87, 94, 96, 211, 259, 315, 319, 346–47, 375
Money market funds, 321
Mutual Fund Alliance, 325
Mutual funds, 87, 203, 315, 319–26
aggressive growth, 322
annual reports, 321
"back-end load," 321
balanced, 322–23
bond, 322
costs, 320
diversification in, 320
domestic stock, 322
evaluation of, 323–24

"families," 320, 324
flexibility in, 320
growth, 94, 107, 316, 321, 322
income, 94, 107, 321, 322
international stock and bond, 323
knowledge about, 6
liquidity, 320
load, 218, 321
management of, 320, 321, 323
money market, 259, 321
and net asset value, 325
no load, 218, 321
and offer price, 325
portfolio "turn over," 323–24
prosectuses, 320–21
reporting services, 321
researching, 67
selling, 326
specialized, 323
tables, 324–25

NASDAQ. *See* National Association of Securities Dealers Automated Quotations
National Association of Investors Corporation, 329
National Association of Personal Financial Advisers, 351
National Association of Securities Dealers Automated Quotations, 327, 351
National Center for Women and Retirement Research, 4, 114, 132
Gender, Identity, and Self-Esteem Study, 34–35, 40, 63
Money Matters in the 90s Survey, 127, 128, 134, 167
Survey on Women's Financial Literacy, 9
Women Cents Study, 15–32, 50, 75, 79, 104, 106, 121, 131, 159, 166, 177, 198, 201, 204, 208, 217, 237, 253, 313, 342, 348
Networks, 132
and information overload, 178
use of, 11
women's, 11, 216
New York Stock Exchange, 327
female employment in, 9
Nursing homes, 275

Obstacles
    to control, 126–28, 130–37
    fear, 6
    to financial success, 6, 30
    lack of knowledge, 6, 30
    to money control, 143–45
    by partners, 141
Optimism, 6, 11, 29, 33, 43

Pensions, 167
    benefits, 159, 200
    company-sponsored, 114, 123, 259,
        296–304
    defined benefit plans, 296–97
    defined contribution plans,
        297–303
    and divorce, 8
    gender bias in, 8
    information, 233
    planning, 113–14
    private, 8, 10, 159, 200
    survivors' benefits, 9
Personality
    effect on money management, 5–7,
        15–32, 33
    and risk tolerance, 75–77
Pipher, Mary, 33, 43, 59
Point of service health plan, 271
Poverty
    and age, 10, 158, 200
    and gender, 10, 158, 200
Power
    of attorney, 279
    and knowledge, 209
    of money, 120
    purchasing, 88
    struggles, 145–46
Preadolescence. *See* Adolescence/
    preadolescence
Preferred provider health
    organizations, 271
PREP program, xix
Pre-Retirement Education Planning
    for Women program, xix
Probate, 279
Prudential Insurance Company, 123
Prudential Securities, 5

Records
    brokerage and other, 232–33

    locating and organizing, 232–33
    storage and safekeeping of, 233–34
*Registry of Financial Planning
    Practitioners,* 352
Relationships
    abusive, 44
    academic confidence and positive
        investment behavior, 54
    distant, 43–44
    dominant-subordinant, 38
    education/gender/self-esteem, 54
    family, 34–50
    father/daughter, 42–47
    marital, 37, 38, 139–56
    mother/daughter, 39–42
    nurturing, 43
    personal and financial traits, 104–5
    risk/reward, 27, 82–83, 206, 318
    supportive, 43
Research
    and decision-making, 176
    financial, 107
    need for, 91–92, 107
    of stock, 67
Responsibility
    financial, 113, 135
    freedom from, 127
    for future, 113
    individual, 123
    investment, 153
    personal, 122
    women and, 83–84
Retirement
    annuities, 306–7
    and baby boomers, 167–68, 290–91
    benefits, 164
    company-sponsored plans,
        296–304. *See also* Pensions
    contributions, 206
    cost-cutting measures, 286
    defined benefit plans, 296–97
    defined contribution plans,
        297–303
    Employee Stock Ownership Plans,
        302
    financial resources for, 271–309
    401(k) plans, 298–301
    403(b) plans, 302
    "gap," 287–88

goals, 271–309
housing for, 262
income for, 6
individual retirement accounts, 123, 302–5
Keogh plans, 123, 306
planning, 6
profit-sharing plans, 302
"reality," 282
redefining, 261–62, 290–92
savings, 258–59, 261, 281–309, 288
Simplified Employee Pension account, 262, 302–3
"three-legged stool" as part of planning, 123
and women, 271–72
Retirement Equity Act (1984), 9
Risk
acceptable levels of, 27
as adventure, 82
attitudes toward, 26–27
aversion to, 27, 79–81, 149–50
balancing of, 371
calculated, 88–89
currency, 323
effect of personality on, 75–77
financial, 73–96
in 401(k) plans, 299–300
gender differences in, 81–83, 94–95
holding-period, 87
inflation, 87
interest-rate, 87
liquidity, 87
management, 27, 88
market, 87
as masculine enterprise, 81–83
of not risking, 86–88
perception of, 75
personal, 75, 76
positive, 76
reinvestment, 87, 375–76
relation to reward, 27, 82–83, 206, 318
role models for, 82
-taking, 213
tolerance, 16–17, 26–27, 30–31, 33, 55, 63, 73–96, 219–20, 317
types of, 26

Safe deposit boxes, 233–34
Savings, 244
accounts, 74, 87, 93, 94, 98, 106, 203, 248, 319, 346
automatic plans, 244
of baby boomers, 160
bonds, 315, 316
budgets, 32
certificates of deposit, 6
company programs, xxii
emergency, 258
expectations, 289
goals, 159, 244–45, 258–59
in go-nowhere investments, 6
and inflation, 288
for major expenses, 258–59
money market accounts, 6
monitoring, 32
opportunity for, 8
passbook, 87, 93
personality traits in, 54, 162
programs, 121
rates, 63
retirement, 258–59, 261, 281–309
tips, 245–47
using, 252
SBA. *See* Small Business Administration
Scams, 220–23
Scudder Baby Boom Generation Retirement Preparation Survey, 11, 114, 128, 131, 134–35, 159, 203, 269, 289, 290, 298, 313, 342
Securities and Exchange Commission, 223, 351
Self-esteem, xvii, 28, 35, 38, 43, 54, 55, 57, 63, 68, 124, 131, 136, 194
Seminars. *See* Financial seminars
SEP. *See* Simplified Employee Pension plan
Simplified Employee Pension plan, 302–3
Small Business Administration, 257
Socialization, 4, 141
negative, 11
and nurturing, 12
and others' needs, 164
Social Security, 167, 253
balance needed for payout, 122–23

Social Security *(cont.)*
  benefits, 292–96
  cost of living adjustments, 294
  crisis in, 295
  disability coverage, 274
  and divorce, 293
  gender bias in, 9
  and inflation, 294
  median benefit, 10, 158, 200
  potential changes in, 123
  qualifying for, 293
  spousal benefits in, 9
  supplementing, 195
Standard & Poor's, 328, 364, 376
Stockbrokers, 347, 360–62
  discount, 361–62
Stocks, 319, 326–32
  blue chip, 87, 107, 322, 327, 328,
    329
  capital gains, 326–27, 332
  certificates, 232
  common, 315, 376
  dividend reinvestment program,
    328–29
  dividends, 326–27, 330–31
  following, 330–31
  growth, 322, 327, 374
  high-risk, 322
  income, 327, 374
  initial public offering, 316
  international, 323
  knowledge about, 6
  market crashes, 95–96
  mutual funds, 321
  options, 168
  penny, 327
  preferred, 315, 376
  price-earnings ratio, 331, 375
  purchasing, 328–30, 331–32
  researching, 67
  return on, 87, 88
  secondary issues, 327
  selling, 331–32
  small-capitalization, 316, 376
  and Social Security, 123
  speculative, 315
  as status symbol, 83
  stop order, 376
  value, 322
  yields, 330–31

Support systems, 11
Syndromes
  bag lady, 159, 190, 191–95
  "head in the sand," 207–24

Taxes, 74, 88, 314
  exemptions from, 322
  income, 132, 329
  on retirement savings, 259
Treasury bills, 316, 376
  return on, 87, 88
Trusts, 279

Unemployment, 259
United States Office of Consumer
  Affairs, 220

Value Line, 67, 321, 328, 334

Wages
  effect on pensions, 8
  gender gap in, 8
  and marital balance of power, 144
  power struggles over, 145–46
  stagnation of, 255
Wealth
  accumulation of, 3–13, 82, 126–27,
    200, 290
  and risk-taking, 82
Widowhood, xix, 111, 200–1
  financial effects of, xxii, 9–10
Wills, 279
Women
  adequacy perceptions, 59, 60
  adolescent period, 47–50
  "at risk" for impoverishment, 143,
    158, 200
  attitudes toward money, 5–7,
    18–20, 30, 43–47, 63
  attitudes toward risk, 42–43, 73, 74
  attitudes toward security, 43, 54,
    73–74, 83–84, 109
  and banking, 343–47
  chances of old-age
    impoverishment, 7–8, 158, 200
  conforming to social expectations,
    34, 39, 50

conservative nature of, 27, 29
and credit, 247–50
current collective assets of, 120
and decision-making, 20–21,
    178–81
disadvantage in education, 57–60
and education, 53–70
effect of personality on money
    management, 5–7, 15–32
feelings about control, 28–29,
    119–37
feminist movement, 126–28
as financial customer base, 9
in financial industry, 9
as financial market, 9
financial planning potential of,
    10–13
flexibility types, 108–13
and goal setting, 12
health care costs of, 10
health insurance for, 269–73
and homelessness, 193–94
identity issues of, xviii, 120
and intermittent employment, 8,
    144

and intuition, 12, 178, 181, 183–85
and investing, 19, 20, 30, 31,
    311–39
lack of exposure to personal
    finance, 7
life insurance for, 263–68
living alone, 30
longevity of, xix, 167, 253, 254, 286
long-term financial questions of, 3
multiple roles of, 12, 39, 84
networks for, 216
and pensions, 8, 10, 164, 253
perspectives on change, 17, 27–28,
    29
and power, 120–21
preadolescent period, 33–47
as present thinkers, 162–63,
    170–73, 256
and responsibility, 83–84
"rights" of, 125–26
and risk tolerance, 16–17, 26–27,
    73–96
"sandwich" generation, 127
savings orientation of, 13
stereotypical views of, xx
wage gap for, 8